Seneca Possessed

EARLY AMERICAN STUDIES

SERIES EDITORS
Daniel K. Richter, Kathleen M. Brown,
and David Waldstreicher

Exploring neglected aspects of our colonial,
revolutionary, and early national history and culture,
Early American Studies reinterprets familiar themes
and events in fresh ways. Interdisciplinary in character,
and with a special emphasis on the period from about
1600 to 1850, the series is published in partnership with
the McNeil Center for Early American Studies.

A complete list of books in the series is available from
the publisher.

Seneca Possessed

Indians, Witchcraft, and Power
in the Early American Republic

MATTHEW DENNIS

PENN

UNIVERSITY OF PENNSYLVANIA PRESS

PHILADELPHIA

Published by
University of Pennsylvania Press
Philadelphia, Pennsylvania 19104-4112

Printed in the United States of America on acid-free paper

10 9 8 7 6 5 4 3 2 1

A Cataloging-in-Publication record is available from the Library of Congress
ISBN 978-0-8122-4226-3

For Ray Birn, friend and mentor

CONTENTS

Introduction

There is no document of civilization that is not at the same time a
document of barbarism.
  —Walter Benjamin

I am going to tell a story of harrowing villainy and complicated—
but, as I trust, intensely interesting—crime. My rascals are no milk-
and-water rascals, I promise you. When we come to the proper places
we won't spare fine language—No, no! But when we are going over
the quiet country we must perforce be calm. A tempest in a slop-
basin is absurd. We will reserve that sort of thing for the mighty
ocean and the lonely midnight. The present Chapter is very mild.
Others—But we will not anticipate THOSE.
  —William Makepeace Thackeray, *Vanity Fair*

IN THE SPRING of 1821, on the outskirts of that rising metropolis of the
West, Buffalo, New York, an unfortunate Seneca Indian, as the story goes,
"fell into a state of languishment and died." In some ways his death was
unremarkable. He was not famous; indeed, we have no record of his name.
Unlike the fictional last Mohican whom the novelist James Fenimore Cooper
would bathe in pathetic glory a few years later, he was not the "last of his
race." His people, the Senecas—one of the Six Nations of the Iroquois, a
once powerful confederation of tribes, including the Mohawks, Oneidas,
Onondagas, Cayugas, Senecas, and Tuscaroras—were in the early stages of a

revival. Their resurgence would occur in response to the visions and teachings of a Native prophet, Ganiodaio, or "Handsome Lake," aided by resident agents and visitors from the Philadelphia Society of Friends, or Quakers.[1]

Two decades earlier, in June 1799, amid a lingering post-Revolutionary crisis, Handsome Lake himself had seemed to suffer an unremarkable death. He had collapsed outside the door of his daughter's cabin in a small settlement along the Allegheny River in southwestern New York. He appeared to pass away, exiting a life of dissipation and little hope. But within an hour or two, Handsome Lake awoke. Revived from his trancelike state, he announced a fabulous revelation. Authorized by subsequent visions of cosmic journeys and supernatural encounters, Handsome Lake emerged as a prophet and inaugurated a new religion. The prophet and his followers sought to revive traditional Seneca religious practice, morality, and social order by reshaping them. They focused especially on the practical problems of drunkenness, ill health, family instability, and economic distress. Blending new and old, Handsome Lake's faith sought to conserve Seneca identity, protect Seneca autonomy, and preserve the lands upon which the physical survival of the Senecas depended. The prophet's innovations were contested, both by traditionalists and those attracted to Christianity, and adherence was never universal among the Senecas. But eventually that new religion became the "Old Way of Handsome Lake," a hopeful, popular, and enduring accommodation to the Seneca's new world.[2]

By 1821, both Handsome Lake's prescriptions and the Quakers' humanitarian mission had become well established, and both enabled Seneca survival, as we will see, but neither promised earthly immortality. And in the confused cultural terrain of western New York, the undignified death of one anonymous Seneca man provoked suspicion. What had caused his demise? The answer was clear to his kin and community: witchcraft.

The nineteenth-century historian and biographer William Leete Stone reported melodramatically that blame quickly fell on "the woman who had nursed him and anxiously watched him at his bed-side," who "by aid of an evil spirit," it was alleged, "had compassed his death." Kauquatau, the accused witch, had fled across the Canadian frontier but was "artfully inveigled" back to the American side of the Niagara, tried by the local Seneca council, and promptly sentenced to death. The "sorceress," as Stone dubbed her, was killed at Buffalo Creek by a chief named Soonongise, commonly known as Tommy Jemmy. He cut her throat after the appointed executioner botched his bloody commission.[3]

What should we make of this extraordinary event? We might easily resort to a familiar plotline. Consider this scenario: the murder was a savage deed committed by a primitive people, the last brutal act of a dying race, mired in paganism, superstition, obsolete tradition, chaos, and violence. Many of the Indians' shocked and horrified white neighbors saw in this gory execution a godlessness and barbarism they believed to be ancient and hopelessly incurable. As the *Niagara Journal* reported, "The superstitious belief in sorcery, which is common to all savages, and is often confirmed by the confessions of the deluded wretches who are accused of the practice, is so strongly fixed in the minds of Indians, that no argument or reasoning seems sufficient to eradicate it."[4] That Kauquatau herself might have believed in witchcraft— and perhaps even admitted her guilt—only confirmed white Christian despair that the Senecas were a doomed people, unable to survive in the modernizing world of nineteenth-century America. As they faded from the landscape, their value to civilization was to be enshrined in white wistfulness. Romantic sentiment for the Indians' flawed nobility simply confirmed for white Americans their own refined sensibility, cultural superiority, and manifest destiny. The incident thus becomes a model for the tragic circumstances to be repeated as the United States pushed west.

In fact, however, our story is more complicated and contains a good many surprises. The witch hunt that culminated in Tommy Jemmy's act of violence was less a matter of traditional practice than it was a function of the Senecas' tacit acceptance of Euro-American misogyny. Seeing witchcraft as a female art was, ironically, a measure of "progress." Inadvertently, Christian missionaries of the previous century had helped to remake the Seneca traditions of witchcraft. Before the nineteenth century, it is unlikely that Senecas expected more women than men to practice this evil craft.

But times had changed. How much they had changed is suggested by the strangely incisive remarks attributed to Red Jacket, the famous orator and leader of the Buffalo Creek Senecas, during the inconclusive trial of Tommy Jemmy in 1821 for the "murder" of Kauquatau. As an excited editor of the *Albany Argus*, an eyewitness, reported in print, Red Jacket exclaimed,

> What! Do you denounce us as fools and bigots, because we still
> believe that which you yourselves believed two centuries ago? Your
> black-coats thundered this doctrine from the pulpit, your judges
> pronounced it from the bench, and sanctioned it with the formali-
> ties of law; and you would now punish our unfortunate brother for

adhering to the faith of *his* fathers and of yours! Go to Salem! Look at the records of your own government, and you will find that hundreds have been executed for the very crime which has called forth the sentence of condemnation against this woman, and drawn down upon her the arm of vengeance. What have our brothers done more than the rulers of your people have done? And what crime has this man committed, by executing, in a summary way, the laws of his country, and the command of the Great Spirit?[5]

Red Jacket's speech in defense of "tradition" and Seneca independence appropriated a foreign history and deployed it skillfully. If the logic of his argument seems absurd now, it was a disarming strategy then and addressed the Senecas' quest to survive as they established a space for themselves. To a considerable degree, they had little choice. They did not go out of their way to find the new historical narrative of the rising glory of America; it found them. As we will see, Red Jacket's clever words emanated from his people's colonial predicament in a "postcolonial" United States.[6]

In mobilizing comparative history to establish legal precedent, Red Jacket called the bluff of these white Americans who asserted that all Americans, including Indians, shared a legal and moral landscape, a single, historically based standard. It was not merely Seneca law and religion, but also white judicial and religious practice that had sanctioned the prosecution of witchcraft, a capital crime. The incidents at Salem, Massachusetts, in 1692 demonstrated the fact. By 1821, the republic was nearly fifty years old, and English colonization had begun over two hundred years earlier. The Revolutionary generation was passing, and white Americans sought to define themselves in terms of their collective past, extending not only to the Revolution but further back as well. They drew widely and selectively, purposefully elevating certain heroes and events from their colonial past, while rejecting or obscuring others. The year 1821 marked the two-hundred-year anniversary of the first Thanksgiving at Plymouth, Massachusetts. White Americans increasingly celebrated with pride that mythic (and actual) event, as they adopted Pilgrim forefathers as exemplars for their new nation, worthy precursors to the sainted Washington, the Revolutionary generation, and now themselves.[7]

The Salem witch trials were something else altogether. In the decade of the 1830s, Nathaniel Hawthorne would begin to confront the sordid legacy of Salem and his own culpable ancestors, in stories such as "Young Goodman Brown" (1835) and eventually *The Scarlet Letter* (1851). But in the early national present—indeed, even during the enlightened eighteenth century in colonial America—the witch-hunting represented by the Salem crisis was a profound embarrassment to white, Christian Americans, as Red Jacket surely knew. Had Red Jacket simply learned the wrong history, white auditors might have wondered, embracing an anachronism as a suitable historical model? If they were to survive at all, must Indians pass through a stage of barbarism (like that exemplified by the madness at Salem) on their way from savagery to civilization? However his speech is read, Red Jacket's reference to Salem highlighted contradictions in white Americans' assessment of Senecas and of themselves. The orator humiliated those who believed themselves better than their poor, benighted Indian brethren. His speech was not naive but purposeful. We will explore the context and meaning of such Native rhetoric below, but we should emphasize here the sophistication of the Senecas we are examining, their understanding of the available means of persuasion, and their resourcefulness in negotiating the challenges of their world.

By 1821, belief in witchcraft was common but not uncontested among the Senecas at Buffalo, some of whom had begun to embrace evangelical Protestantism. Earlier, in the context of the unsettled condition that coincided with the rise of the prophet Handsome Lake, an emergency related to witchcraft accusations *had* disrupted Seneca communities. But Kauquatau's execution in 1821 did not represent a witch-hunting crisis—it was hardly a Seneca version of the Salem outbreak of 1692. The threat at Buffalo Creek was more external than internal, as the prosecution of Tommy Jemmy by white authorities posed a significant challenge to Seneca sovereignty, which endangered all Senecas.

In the early nineteenth century, Seneca men and women found themselves in a dangerous state of dependency. How would they accommodate—how would they withstand—this new phase of an old colonialism? Could they effectively reinvent a distinct Seneca ethnic and cultural identity in the face of an intruding American society and its aggressive economy?

Consider another familiar scenario: Led by men such as Red Jacket and the Allegany chief Cornplanter, the Senecas cleaved to tradition and united in solidarity to reject white encroachment. In unity and tradition there was strength, and together, heroically committed to ancient Iroquois culture, the Senecas stood against white missionaries, settlers, and officials. Such a tale has two common endings. The Indians are ultimately vanquished and they vanish, tragically but with a nobility and integrity stemming from their unwillingness to compromise with their conquerors. Or: the Indians prevail, again nobly and single-handedly, based on their unity, which allows them to protect their land and unaltered traditions.

This alternative fantasy narrative, with either ending, is equally simplistic and misleading, in fact misrepresenting a story that is more intricate and compelling. The noble tale of uncomplicated Indian triumph is most easily told when we carefully choose to constrain the narrative or end it prematurely at the moment of a temporary but heroic victory before ultimate disaster strikes. But if we do not stop time, and the Indians suffer a romantically tragic end, we then resolve to grant them a collective martyrdom.

We know, though, that the Senecas did not die. They endured through resilience, not intransigence, and by means of resourcefulness and adaptability, not mechanistic conservatism. Their survival and rebirth was a product of women's efforts, not merely men's; it was a difficult and contested path to survival, fraught with disagreement and dissension, failure as well as success. Some embraced Christianity and white educational efforts, for example; some did not. Some would succumb to alcohol, while others avoided or overcame it. Some agreed to sell land, sometimes through selfish motives, but sometimes acting pragmatically to forestall even greater losses. Others—women in particular, attached to the soil as agriculturalists—adopted an uncompromising resistance to land sales. And Native territories did dwindle substantially, even if Senecas managed to preserve a land base and largely avoid removal— the fate of other "civilized" tribes—to lands across the Mississippi River.

Senecas survived through luck as well as skill. The Allegany Senecas, for example, were fortunate to acquire Quakers as missionaries and patrons, rather than agents of other Protestant denominations, typically much more aggressive in their proselytizing and less tolerant of those Indians who sought partial accommodations with Christianity. The Senecas were similarly the beneficiaries of other catastrophes: the War of 1812, for example. The war was an inconclusive and damaging conflict fought in part on the borderland that was Six Nations terrain. While some Native leaders counseled neutrality when it erupted, many Seneca men participated, including our defendant Tommy Jemmy. In that service to the United States they demonstrated a loyalty that helped obscure memories of the Seneca alliance with the British in the American Revolution. The failure of the United States to conquer Canada by the war's end permanently etched an international border on the North American map, which enlarged Seneca political and military significance in the early nineteenth century. More immediately, the war's outbreak short-circuited a strong push by some white officials and speculators for Seneca concentration and removal. Removal efforts would reemerge a decade later, but again they would fail.[8]

Senecas survived with outside help and despite the meddling of outsiders. Most prominently, Quakers acted as true friends to Senecas, giving them material aid and advice, offering instruction and counsels, and intervening at treaty negotiations and in the halls of government. But friendly advice is not always right. Quakers could misunderstand or provide guidance in directions Senecas chose not to go—for example, to adopt unavailing social and economic arrangements that would likely reduce, not improve, their standard of living. Much worse, of course, were those who intruded with hostile or selfish intent—for example, land company agents and public officials sometimes in their employ. Senecas suffered but survived such interference as well.

This book explores the ordeal of the Senecas in the early national period, the era of the prophet Handsome Lake (d. 1815) and extending into the 1820s. Handsome Lake played the midwife in a Seneca rebirth, but not without challenges. Through trial and error, innovation and conservatism, the Senecas reshaped their world, down to its most basic components: the nature of economic life, spiritual meaning and practice, gender organization, social arrangements and political order. If their struggle was more desperate than the ordeals of most other Americans, it was not unique. Like other Americans, the Senecas found "progress" profoundly unsettling. Choosing whether to hold to tradition or undertake the perils of transformation, they were in many ways comparable to nineteenth-century backcountry farmers, urban mechanics, or farm girls attracted by mill jobs, similarly swept up in a maelstrom of change.[9]

Seneca Possessed focuses on Seneca communities but situates Native experience more broadly in order to refine our understanding of the early American republic. We often think of Indians as casualties of the expanding republic, and they were. But non-Indians too could be overwhelmed by the avalanche of social and economic change, even if some found new opportunity in a rapidly developing America. Indians' acquisition of "civility" and (at best) interdependence would not "elevate" them so much as reduce them to the limited and dependent way of life typical of white citizens in the increasingly commercialized, and later industrialized, United States.

This was a time of transformation. America was developing new modes of agricultural and industrial production, constructing a national market economy, renegotiating issues of nationalism, identity, and roles for women, and experiencing waves of religious revivalism and reform. Examining the Senecas provides fresh perspectives on these local and national alterations. Economic growth and prosperity were tied to land and resources. Whose? In fact, Seneca homelands were among the first Native lands to be expropriated and used by white Americans to create opportunity and wealth in the early republic. Americans reshaped the landscape of central New York by imposing new forms of property ownership and by replacing the extensive and complex agricultural subsistence system of the Six Nations with one based on intensive agricultural production and extraction of commodities for nearly limitless markets. The Seneca experience illuminates a larger story, one that accounts for costs as well as benefits. The Genesee Valley became for a time America's breadbasket. By the 1830s, one of the most vibrant new industrial cities in the United States would emerge there at Rochester, connected to the world via the Erie Canal, which officially opened in 1825. Rochester was set in the heart of Seneca lands, in a place that, it is often said, had been wilderness a generation earlier. It was not.

But the Seneca story is not mere prologue. As others moved in, Senecas remained, and they continued to farm and participated in the changing economy. That involvement sometimes defied the unrealistic prescriptions of white missionaries and idealistic reformers. These white patrons might have had good intentions, but they lacked the imagination and imperatives that led Senecas themselves to develop hybrid economies of survival. Seneca persistence in subsistence farming, paired with their engagement with the expanding market economy, forces us to reevaluate the course of economic development in the era, not only for Indians but for other rural folk. We see a history here at odds with the scenarios of Frederick Jackson Turner's frontier thesis or older theories of progress from savagery through barbarism to civility. "Settlement" produced unsettlement, development created both wealth and poverty. Opportunity came with costs in the early American republic. And such costs—human and environmental—were not borne equally.[10]

Senecas were not the only Americans attempting to define their place in the United States. While few besides patriotic writers and orators worried excessively about matters of American identity—the question first posed by Crèvecoeur in 1782: "What, then, is the American, this new man?"—many faced the practical problem of how to live in the American world as women and men amid rapid change.

The Quakers faced particular challenges, which deserve some comment given how critical they are to our story. When they came from Philadelphia as missionaries to the Senecas beginning in 1798, they carried with them considerable historical baggage. The Friends' experience in Pennsylvania had been preceded by years of struggle and persecution, in the British Isles and New England, where they were banished by Puritan authorities and subjected to witchcraft accusations and even death in the seventeenth century. William Penn's Holy Experiment in Pennsylvania had gone much better, but by the mid-eighteenth century the Quakers faced a crisis of conscience in Pennsylvania as violence erupted in the colonial backcountry between Natives and white settlers. Many Quaker legislators withdrew from provincial government rather than authorize funds to prosecute frontier wars, which would compromise their commitment to pacifism and friendly relations with the Indians. If Quakers lived in a violent world, many sought to avoid complicity, to withdraw, and to seek other paths to peace. Such a path eventually led them to the Senecas in western New York at the end of the eighteenth century. By the early nineteenth century, Friends' commitment to living a principled life was challenged further, as they witnessed the persistence of slavery, the growth of a capitalist economy, and the emergence of a new evangelical Protestantism. Quakers were forced to contemplate whether they could participate in such a world, how, and on what terms. Friends would disagree, and by 1827 they experienced a schism that divided "Orthodox" and "Hicksites" along fault lines that were social and economic as well as theological. Even before 1827, the Quaker mission to the Senecas exposed some of the Friends' ambivalence and anxiety about the commercial and industrial transformation of the country. Their work with Senecas could represent both a withdrawal from the world and a means to engage and reform it.[11]

The Quaker-Seneca relationship proved important to both parties. Each learned from the other, though the lessons could be complicated. Along with the legal aid and practical skills they acquired, for example, Senecas gained insight into white American thinking about such essential matters as property, work, family, and the individual. Quakers found a nongovernmental means to fulfill their humanitarian desires. Some Quakers perhaps dreamed of reconstructing Seneca communities as models of ideal social "conversation," but mostly they focused on practical affairs—growing crops efficiently, building mills to grind corn and saw wood, reshaping Indian family life, teaching children to read and write, helping Senecas protect their land—not on utopian goals or even religious conversion.

Gender was at the center of this relationship; for each, the other's gender order was a large part of what made them strange. Gender affected how Senecas and Quakers understood each other and how they interacted. Gender was often at the heart of what Quakers hoped to change among the Senecas, and it was often at the core of Seneca resistance to Quaker prescriptions, for women as well as men. And yet each learned lessons about gender from the other, which helped both Quakers and Senecas imagine ways they might promote social change. An unintended consequence of Quaker missionary efforts, for example, appeared in the 1840s, when women's rights advocates such as the New York Quaker Lucretia Mott began to deploy Seneca gender models (at least as they imagined them) in their attempts to reform American society. Mott and others increasingly found new value in the status and power that Seneca women commanded within their communities, a status and power that had sometimes thwarted Quaker reforms. Ironically, by 1848, the rise of the Senecas could help lead to Seneca Falls.[12]

Early nineteenth-century Senecas lived at the epicenter of other critical developments in the American national experience. The act of dispossessing Senecas (and their resistance to such dispossession) forced white officials to work out the meaning of United States federalism and the relationship between state, tribal, and national jurisdictions. As the Tommy Jemmy case would reveal, the sovereignty question remained unresolved, as Senecas, New York State, and the United States made overlapping and often contradictory claims about their authority.

Federalism was a republican means of resolving the *imperium in imperio* question—dividing sovereignty and reconciling local control with a national state—but it was not always clear in practice whose order should prevail where, under what circumstances. Nor was it settled whether Indian nations themselves constituted sovereign entities—like states—within the larger federal structure. States' rights and national authority would clash throughout the nineteenth century, of course, and in 1860 the irreconcilable conflict over slavery would explode in civil war. Before this disastrous breakdown, however, in myriad ways that had less to do with the slavery question, Americans sought to work out the logic of federalism, to define the discrete realms of state and national governments. Indians found themselves in the middle of these contests, particularly because they owned considerable amounts of land. If most nineteenth-century white Americans came to believe that they collectively possessed not only sovereignty over that territory, but a property right in that land—despite the Indians' actual possession and legal claims—it remained vague who held such powers, states or the national government. The

Seneca experience in New York is part of that story, which extends through the Cherokee cases of the 1830s and the Trail of Tears. Yet Senecas, unlike most Cherokees, managed to persist in their homelands and maintain some autonomy, even as the United States and the state of New York spelled out their respective responsibilities, jurisdictions, and Indian dependence. In the spaces opened by intergovernmental rivalry, and amid white political and religious factionalism, Senecas could sometimes find refuge.[13]

Finally, that physical refuge and its environs were the setting for another critical development in the history of the early republic—the revivalism and reform that remapped America's social and religious landscape. It was not a coincidence that the newly created "Old Way" of Handsome Lake emerged out of the same Burned-Over District of the Second Great Awakening that witnessed the rise of the evangelist Charles Grandison Finney, the utopian John Humphrey Noyes, the prophet Joseph Smith, and other religious innovators. Like white newcomers in early republican western New York, the Senecas experienced a rapidly transforming and stressful world, and they acted creatively. Through the prophecies of Handsome Lake and the prescriptions of resident Quaker agents, the inventive process advanced fitfully, incorporating elements of Christianity and white society and economy, along with older Seneca ideas and practices, into a hybrid faith and new Seneca way of life. Ironically, though a revised Seneca society and religion emerged in these decades in response to the changing world around them, the Code of Handsome Lake would ultimately take its place as tradition.[14]

Issues of gender, kinship, and power were central to the Senecas' attempt to negotiate their way out of their predicament. The story that follows examines how government officials, speculators and capitalists, white settlers, Protestant missionaries and moral reformers all encroached on the Seneca people, and distinctly affected men and women. Internal debates were also gendered, particularly when they concerned overlapping kinship and community arrangements. Indeed, Seneca revitalization was the work of both sexes. Theirs is a story not of isolation and decline but of connections and persistence. Too often it has been told as a saga of declension and disappearance. It does contain its share of tragedy, and its plot is complex, but Senecas have not left the stage, and their experience is more universal than it might initially appear to be.

Seneca Possessed conjures up the title of Paul Boyer and Stephen Nissenbaum's classic social history of the Salem witchcraft crisis of 1692, *Salem Possessed*.[15]

In the spirit of Red Jacket, who pointed us toward Salem's story, *Seneca Possessed* explores how the Seneca people and their homeland were "possessed"—culturally, spiritually, materially, and legally. Like Salem, Massachusetts, Seneca territory became a site of contention as it was settled and transformed, as new forms of economic enterprise struggled to prevail, as government systems changed. Both places were colonized by outsiders and possessed in culturally specific ways. And, amid conflicts over land, modes of production, gender, and political power, both places were possessed by their indigenous devils. Both the residents of Salem and of Seneca communities struggled among themselves, as they tried to accommodate their changing times, control their destinies, find security, and define the particular natures of their social, cultural, and spiritual landscapes.

Possession is commonly defined as "property, wealth, or dominion." As legal historian Stuart Banner has demonstrated, the roughly fifty-year period following the American Revolution—the period of this book—witnessed a radical transformation of legal thought about Native land. It culminated in the 1823 landmark Supreme Court decision *Johnson v. M'Intosh* in which Chief Justice John Marshall asserted that American colonists, through discovery and conquest, had acquired the right to "ultimate dominion over the land," including the "power to grant the soil, while yet in possession of the natives." As Banner shows, Marshall was a poor (if influential) historian. In fact, throughout the colonial period Britain and its colonial governments had not claimed such rights, through discovery or conquest or any other means. They had recognized Indians as the "owners," "proprietors," or "possessors" of their land, in the same manner as Europeans. In 1823, Marshall acknowledged Indians "to be the rightful occupants of the soil, with a legal as well as just claim to retain possession of it," but he claimed they were not the land's owners. "Indian ownership," ambiguously defined by Marshall, was considered inferior to the ownership vested in European powers and was thus inferior to the claims of white speculators and settlers to whom such lands were granted. Senecas lost possession of vast tracts during the early nineteenth century, but they continued to possess other lands. *Seneca Possessed* maps the shifting meaning of Seneca property, wealth, and dominion—of what they possessed and how they possessed it.[16]

Possession can also mean "domination by an extraneous personality, demon, passion, or idea." *Seneca Possessed* traces the contests for ascendancy among extraordinary figures, both Senecas and outsiders, competing for Seneca hearts, minds, and souls. At times Senecas believed their neighbors and kinspeople to be possessed by demons, and some acted to purge such evil from among them—Tommy Jemmy, for example, in the spring of 1821. Seneca men and women were possessed by passions, the feelings natural to all people—fear, anger, love, and joy—enlarged during periods of tumult. At times such possession seemed to take on the torturous characteristics of a religious passion—the prolonged suffering of martyrs. And Senecas were possessed by new ideas, which promised revival, offered by Handsome Lake, by Quakers, and by other Christian missionaries.

Finally, *possession* can mean "control or mastery," not merely of property but of selves. To be self-possessed is to exhibit control or command over one's powers, to exhibit presence of mind or composure. *Seneca Possessed* scrutinizes this quest for mastery as well. It examines a people known historically for their self-possession, whose collective composure was severely challenged by the crises they faced in post-Revolutionary America. It analyzes that ordeal and the Senecas' successes in fending off cultural and material dispossession, as they countered white prepossessions and assaults and constructed a new way to survive as Senecas.

In 1821, an anonymous Seneca man was prematurely dead, the Seneca "witch" charged with killing him had her throat cut, and a Seneca chief, who had acted as her official executioner, found himself in a Canandaigua jail, indicted for murder. Would Tommy Jemmy join Kauquatau and her alleged victim in an unnatural death—the punishment for a capital crime? What had he done? What possessed him? Answering such questions will require us to thicken the plot and to cover several decades to explain how Tommy Jemmy came to wield that knife in the spring of 1821. *Seneca Possessed* explores the fluid meaning of Tommy Jemmy's act, its larger context, its implications and consequences. It is a complicated story—history, not murder mystery—but to simplify it would be a crime.

The nature of events dictates that *Seneca Possessed* cannot be a linear history, a one-thing-after-another, chronological retelling of a two-hundred-year-old narrative. So, a word about organization: Part I ("Dominion") examines the perils Senecas faced in the wake of the American Revolution and the colonial background that shaped them (and their post-Revolutionary tribulations); it defines a Seneca problem. Part II ("Spirit") probes the Senecas' religious response to those troubles—particularly the prophecy of Handsome Lake and the hybrid religion he founded—as well as the new dilemmas engendered by that nativist revival. It analyzes Seneca solutions and the fresh quandaries that solutions themselves can (and did) produce. Part III ("Mastery") focuses on the Quakers and their Seneca mission—their own diagnoses and prescriptions for the afflictions they saw among the Indians. In turn, it analyzes the drawbacks inherent in those Quaker reforms, and the Senecas' efforts to respond and endure in the face of such measures. Finally, it takes our story of accommodation, resistance, and persistent negotiation through the 1820s—the fiftieth anniversary of American nationhood and the decade of the Erie Canal's inauguration—by which time the Senecas had developed the religious, cultural, and political tools to survive, despite the difficult path ahead of them. These parts sometimes overlap chronologically but do not cover the same ground; they adopt different angles of vision to allow us to see the field more clearly and completely—a necessary accommodation to the distant time and place we seek to understand, an arena of astonishing volatility and variegation.

Like William Makepeace Thackeray's *Vanity Fair*, "Our history is destined . . . to go backwards and forwards in a very irresolute manner seemingly, and having conducted our story to to-morrow presently, we shall immediately again have occasion to step back to yesterday, so that the whole of the tale may get a hearing." But, Thackeray reasons, "the romancer is obliged to exercise this most partial sort of justice. Although all the little incidents must be heard, yet they must be put off when the great events make their appearance." Such events are "entitled to the pass over all minor occurrences whereof this history is composed mainly, and hence a little trifling disarrangement and disorder was excusable and becoming." And so we raise the curtain, not on Thackeray's Chiswick Mall but in western New York. To paraphrase his "History Without a Hero," this is Buffalo, "not a moral place certainly; nor a merry one, though very noisy."[17]

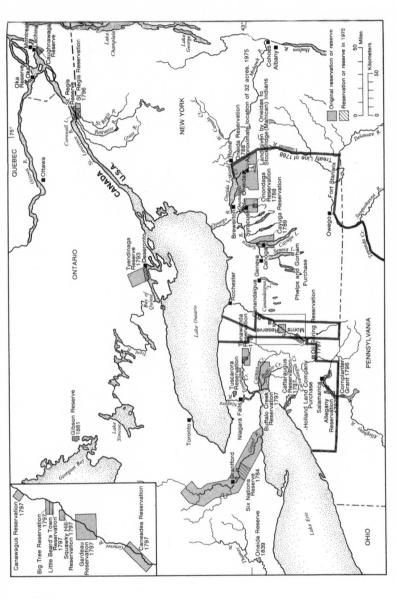

Figure 1. Iroquois reservations and reserves (dates are given for those established after the American Revolution). Cartography by Judith Crawley Wojik, reprinted from Bruce G. Trigger, ed., *Handbook of North American Indians*, vol. 15, *Northeast* (Washington, D.C.: Smithsonian Institution, 1978).

PART I

Dominion

CHAPTER I

Colonial Crucible and Post-Revolutionary Predicament

Civilization or death to all American savages!
—Fourth of July toast among American officers preparing to
invade Iroquoia (1779)

WHEN THE SENECA man Tommy Jemmy approached Kauquatau's house about three miles from the white settlement of Buffalo, New York, in early May 1821, he came as an angel of death. Did Kauquatau know her executioner, and did she apprehend the nature of his mission? Did she willingly accompany him to the nearby field where she would die? Newspapers would later report that Soonongise, commonly known as Tommy Jemmy, induced the suspected witch with an offer of whiskey. Did he? Perhaps they drank together as Tommy Jemmy sought to steel his nerve or disarm his victim. Or perhaps they lingered a while, absorbing the sun of a late spring afternoon before he took her life. Did the executioner work with dispatch or with hesitation? Was the deed done cleanly or crudely, noisily or in silence? We do not know the answers to these questions.[1]

Death has an indisputable finality. Yet the impact and implications of Kauquatau's violent end were then, and remain, highly ambiguous. If the fact of her death and the identity and method of her killer are clear, all else fades into shades of gray. Either the death was an instance of capital punishment, or it was itself a capital crime—murder. Only fifty years earlier, if the death of a Seneca woman at the hands of a Seneca man had come to the attention of white authorities, it would have been of no consequence to them. Even if the victim had been a white colonist and the alleged killer a Seneca, and especially if the murder had occurred in the backcountry of New York or Pennsylvania, it is unlikely that white courts would have become involved. In the late colonial period, intercultural crime and punishment in Indian country required diplomacy rather than conventional jurisprudence. That Tommy Jemmy now found himself subject to arrest and trial, surrendering himself willingly and seeking exoneration through the courts of New York State, suggests how much the political landscape had changed in Iroquoia and western New York. The Senecas, by 1821, had fallen within the jurisdictions of New York State and the United States. They now lacked the autonomy, independence, and sovereignty that Senecas and other Six Nations Iroquois had enjoyed throughout the colonial period.[2]

Tommy Jemmy's trial, however, would challenge all such assumptions about power and sovereignty. If the Senecas were a conquered people, as some tried to allege, the terms of their conquest were ill defined, their sovereignty, though diminished, still recognizable, their power not inconsequential. In fact, as we will see, Tommy Jemmy—and the Senecas generally— managed to prevail in court, not by denying the facts but by successfully contesting their implications. Crucially, the defendant would make the case for a sort of semi-sovereignty within the larger American federal structure.

Trials

When white authorities learned of Tommy Jemmy's execution of Kauquatau, they called a coroner's inquest, which found his act to be "wilful murder," and issued a warrant for his arrest. Accounts of subsequent events vary. According to one witness, following Tommy Jemmy's detention, a group of angry, armed Seneca men led by Red Jacket gathered in Buffalo to protest his incarceration. Though whites feared violence, crisis was averted when Captain Pollard, another Seneca chief and rival of Red Jacket, persuaded the Indians to disperse. According to another account, this confrontation never occurred.[3]

Authorities encountered trouble finding someone willing to serve the warrant on Tommy Jemmy. Eventually one Pascal Pratt, who was friendly with the Senecas and spoke their language, agreed to take on the task. Peacefully served, Tommy Jemmy, accompanied by Red Jacket and a large contingent of Seneca men and women, turned himself in the following day. Both versions of the story suggest that, despite the commitment of the white citizens of Buffalo to extend their jurisdiction to internal Seneca matters, they felt a sense of trepidation, intimidated by Seneca power and the potential (real or imagined) for Seneca violence. They were forced to accommodate, or at least to contemplate, the relationship between legal and extralegal power, the relative degrees of "right" and "might" they and their Seneca neighbors possessed in this fluid world.

Local newspapers reported that the prisoner was a well-traveled Seneca chief who possessed "more than a common share of intelligence." Yet, they noted with surprise, "He appears not to be conscious of having done any thing criminal or improper in the murder he has perpetrated."[4] Throughout the proceedings,[5] Tommy Jemmy, Red Jacket, and Tommy Jemmy's lawyer before the New York Supreme Court, Thomas J. Oakley, a former member of the U.S. House of Representatives, the New York Assembly, and recently New York State attorney general, did not dispute the fact of the execution but argued that it had been performed in Seneca jurisdiction (independent of the state of New York, as defined by treaty and federal law), according to Seneca legal codes. It was thus a legal, not an illegal, act. It did not constitute murder at all but was, rather, a legitimate use of violence, sanctioned by Seneca law. To repeat Red Jacket's questions: "What have our [Seneca] brothers done more than the rulers of your people have done? And what crime has this man committed, by executing, in a summary way, the laws of his country, and the command of the Great Spirit?" As the trial proceeded, the puzzled white jury seemed convinced that the Senecas were in fact an independent people and that their own state courts lacked jurisdiction. The judge therefore referred the case to the New York Supreme Court, where it was argued in August 1821. That trial produced a wide-ranging examination of the laws, treaties, and public history of the Indians from the time of discovery, and, after mature consideration, the court decided to offer no judgment. It preferred not to recognize the independent jurisdiction of Indians on reservation land within New York State, yet it was unable to deny the Senecas at least a qualified sovereignty. In addition, the court seemed persuaded that the case was not one of murder exactly, at least as the Indians understood it, yet it remained reluctant to sanction the execution. In the end, the justices threw up their hands and, with the consent of the attorney general, released the prisoner.[6]

Figure 2. *Sa-go-ye-wat-ha, Seneca Chief Red Jacket,* painted by R. W. Weir, engraved by M. J. Danforth, ca. 1830–80. Courtesy of the Library of Congress, Prints and Photographs Division, Washington, D.C.

In the immediate aftermath of the Revolution, Americans had construed their victory as a "conquest" of those Indians aligned with Britain. The Senecas had been on the losing side. At the Treaty of Fort Stanwix in 1784, white officials called the Senecas "a subdued people; you have been overcome in a war." This was not exactly true. And the United States was soon forced to abandon its theories of conquest. As the legal historian Stuart Banner demonstrates, nineteenth-century American law recognized that "Indian tribes were sovereign entities of a sort." He writes, "Exactly what that sovereignty entailed was in dispute, but all agreed that Indian tribes had always governed themselves internally by their own laws. The United States had always respected that sovereignty by negotiating treaties with Indian tribes rather than regulating them directly." The United States Constitution had given Congress the power to regulate commerce, which was widely understood to invest the federal government "with virtual plenary authority over Indian affairs, even as to Indian tribes located within the boundaries of existing states." But, Banner notes, "The tribes had always been allowed to govern themselves within their own unsold territories. No state government had ever thought it possessed the authority to strip an Indian tribe of this power of self-government and exert its own sovereignty over members of the tribe."[7] The Tommy Jemmy trial seemed to confirm this reality.

Governor De Witt Clinton reviewed the situation and proposed a legislative remedy. In April 1822, the New York Assembly passed a law specifically asserting state criminal jurisdiction over Indian tribes within state boundaries, while explicitly pardoning the less-than-convicted Tommy Jemmy. This solution reflected the ironies and ambiguities embedded in the case. The state of New York seemed, implicitly, to recognize Seneca sovereignty as it attempted to extinguish that sovereignty by legislation. In doing so, the state unwittingly endorsed (or at least undermined its own moral condemnation of) the Seneca act—the execution of a "witch"—which it defined as "barbaric." The proceedings seemed to acknowledge that on Seneca reservations the rule of law—a jurisprudence more ancient than that of New York State— held sway. Seneca law and order looked to many white New Yorkers like chaos and savagery, but the Tommy Jemmy trial disabled this simplistic view and challenged New York's moral and legal superiority. New York State nonetheless sought to replace Seneca jurisdiction and law with its own. And to complicate matters further, its assertions of sovereignty collided not merely with those of the Senecas but with those of the national government as well, which claimed exclusive authority to govern American Indian tribes and to extinguish their right of occupancy.[8]

Of course, to assert authority is not necessarily to possess it legally. New York's legislation posed a number of questions, many of which remained unresolved. Matters of jurisdiction continued to be muddy. Albany's claims conflicted with those more solidly asserted by the federal government and the Senecas themselves. And, as always, the law in practice could diverge considerably from the law on paper. The region encompassing Seneca lands did not immediately dissolve into a single, state-dominated social and political order. Perhaps New York State law applied to all Indians on reservations contained within New York, diminishing Seneca and other Indian sovereignty. Perhaps not. In retrospect, we might conclude that the state had overstepped its authority, as would become clearer in the landmark Cherokee cases of the 1830s.

In *Cherokee Nation v. Georgia* (1831), the United States Supreme Court rejected the claim that the Cherokees were a fully sovereign foreign state, but Chief Justice John Marshall's decision nonetheless defined the Cherokees and other tribes as "domestic dependent nations." As such, their relationship with the federal government "resembles that of a ward and a guardian." In the next year, in *Worcester v. Georgia* (1832), Marshall declared, "Our history furnishes no example, from the first settlement of our country, of any attempt on the part of the crown to interfere with the internal affairs of the Indians." He concluded, "The Cherokee nation . . . is a distinct community occupying its own territory, with boundaries accurately described, in which the laws of Georgia can have no force, and which the citizens of Georgia have no right to enter." The Marshall court thus found the Cherokees (and, by implication, other Indian nations) to possess a kind of semi-sovereignty. The Senecas, like the Cherokees, were subordinate to the federal government, but they were *not* subsidiary to state governments; they were outside of their control altogether. The *Cherokee Nation* and *Worcester* decisions implicitly rejected New York State's legislation of 1822 as unconstitutional. But that mattered as little in New York as it did in Georgia. The Empire State faced no official challenge to the jurisdictional claims it advanced in the wake of *Tommy Jemmy v. New York* until the early twentieth century.[9] But we get ahead of our story.

The Tommy Jemmy trial was an ambiguous victory for the Senecas, but a victory nonetheless. It exemplified the new threats Senecas faced in the early republic—to their sovereignty and their national endurance. And it displayed the cultural and political assets developed in the first two decades of the nineteenth century—with the assistance of the prophet Handsome Lake and Philadelphia Friends—which enabled their provisional success and long-term survival. It challenged the myth of the vanishing Indian and belied the rumors—or prophecies—of a Seneca death foretold. Like Tommy Jemmy, the Senecas would have been unable to prevail if they had been a wholly "traditional" people, unwilling to adapt. Instead they displayed resourcefulness and creativity, as they had for generations. Difficult times demanded innovation. To understand Seneca ingenuity, and to understand the Senecas' post-Revolutionary predicament, we must look to their past—to the colonial period and the desperate years during the American Revolution and its aftermath. Tommy Jemmy is really the end of our story—and so we must now leave him for an extended search into the origins of his people's predicament, the revolutionary transformations of the American republic and the landscape Senecas possessed, and the emergence of a new world shaped by Quakers and a Native prophet.

The Specter of Colonial Power

By the time of Handsome Lake, the people of the Iroquois Six Nations—Mohawks, Oneidas, Onondagas, Cayugas, Senecas, and Tuscaroras—had experienced European colonialism for two hundred years. The Senecas and other Iroquois had approached their colonial rivals and allies with considerable confidence. Their self-possession was often read as arrogance, as the Anglican missionary Henry Barclay suggested in 1741: "They seem to always have Lookd upon themselves as far Superiour to the Rest of Mankind and accordingly Call themselves *Ongwehoenwe* i.e. Men Surpassing all other men."[10] Barclay's perception notwithstanding, by the mid-eighteenth century the Iroquois had endured devastating epidemics, debilitating warfare, and unwanted incursions by Christian missionaries, merchants and traders, land-hungry speculators, settlers, and squatters. Through traditional practices of amalgamation with outsiders, adoption of captives and refugees, and resourceful diplomacy and domestic politics, the People of the Longhouse had weathered the storms of the seventeenth and early eighteenth centuries and emerged as powerful allies of Great Britain as it sought to consolidate its North American empire.[11]

Much had changed in Iroquois life. Iroquois people covered themselves in cloth as well as skins, kept orchards and European livestock to supplement their diets, lived in new places and under changed domestic arrangements, imbibed alcohol and struggled with its social effects, and used knives of steel and guns of European manufacture in their hunts and warfare. Some among them found new European religious ideas and practices meaningful. Their material lives were inextricably tied to British, Dutch, and French traders and colonists, yet the Iroquois people remained Iroquois; their confederation retained a considerable measure of territorial integrity, political autonomy, military strength, and diplomatic leverage. The borderland that simultaneously separated and joined Iroquois and European colonial societies entwined them in a relationship of mutual dependence, or interdependence, rather than resigning the Iroquois to a state of dependency. Despite some community fragmentation and migration, Iroquois society generally continued to hew to older patterns of social life, preserving localism, consensus, matrilineal kinship descent, and matrilocal residence (living with the relatives of wives and mothers, rather than husbands and fathers), which offered women considerable status and authority. On the eve of the American Revolution, the Six Nations hardly fit the stereotype of a timeless, primitive Other, but neither had they abandoned their earlier identity. Their collective adjustments to colonial intruders had been difficult but selective and largely accomplished on their own terms.

In the Six Nations' experience, the European colonial intrusion could resemble aspects of witchcraft—it was a sometimes overt, sometimes covert insinuation of power that could harm, even kill. In its material, intellectual, and spiritual manifestations, European power could be appropriated and deployed for good, but it could also prove malevolent. Not all who consulted spirits were witches. For the Iroquois, *orenda*—power—was a potent but neutral force. Witches mobilized it for evil rather than for good. Colonists and their culture embodied a similar potency, which could benefit or damage Native societies, depending on how it was used.[12]

European material goods, manufactured from exotic materials and offering radical technological innovations, transformed Native life. Books and writing generally depersonalized and archived information, allowing secret communication over vast distances of space and time. They could communicate facts, but they could also distort spoken words, broadcast rumors and lies, and inscribe swindles. Religious texts, such as the Bible, contained the Word of God for believers, but for their opponents they could be seen as manuals for a dark art. We might otherwise simply dismiss Native suspicions as superstition, if we did not possess evidence of the evil done to Indians by military orders, death warrants, deceitful treaties, and fraudulent land titles. Guns were more obvious implements of power, which destroyed life. They made hunting easier and enlarged the capacity of Indian military forces, but firearms also made intertribal warfare more deadly and Native soldiers more dependent on European manufacturers, suppliers, and blacksmiths. Dark power also appeared among Indians in the form of rum and other types of alcohol. If liquor altered mental and physical states, lubricating communication with colonial Europeans (and perhaps supernatural forces as well), Demon Rum could represent witchery, as a substance that corrupted bodies, minds, souls.[13]

Similarly, powerful colonial ideas and institutional arrangements—individual property ownership, patriarchy, or the impersonal market—increasingly insinuated themselves in Iroquois lives and, some might say, proved corrosive. Christian religious concepts and ritual practices—heaven and hell, a martyred God, baptism and Holy Communion—represented new sources of power to help colonized Indian peoples cope with dislocation; but these undermined traditions, bred discord, and destroyed communities—a characteristic effect of witchcraft to members of the Six Nations. In the wrong hands—in the hands of a witch or sorcerer, working overtly or covertly—these new powers threatened to destroy Iroquoia. In a visceral sense, a colonized people are a people bewitched. During the eighteenth century, the Six Nations struggled to turn liabilities to their advantage and to mobilize for good.

European material goods, technologies, and ideas entered Iroquoia as Iroquois people established direct contact with explorers, soldiers, traders, missionaries, diplomats, and settlers. In the seventeenth century, the League of the Iroquois sought to assimilate these new peoples into their world, on their own terms, building alliances and transforming outsiders into kin when possible, and prosecuting war with those whom they could not absorb or who insisted on separation and hostility. The century saw devastating waves of pestilence and warfare and an "invasion within," carried into Iroquois villages especially by Jesuit priests determined to convert the Native people of North America.[14]

Deadly pathogens imported inadvertently from Europe first infected Iroquoia in the shadowy period before many Iroquois people had even seen the

Dutch or French. Other epidemics followed direct contact. Jesuit observers—unaware of their likely complicity in spreading the contagion in Iroquoia—commented that such afflictions "wrought sad havoc," leaving Iroquois villages "nearly deserted, and their fields only half-tilled." The devastation continued into the eighteenth century, and Iroquois population generally descended through cycles of debilitating epidemics, marginal recovery, and renewed reductions through recurrent pestilence.[15]

When they contemplated the epidemics that raged through their population, Iroquois people reached for answers. The notion that witchcraft might be a by-product of colonization seemed to them a distinct possibility. During the seventeenth century, at least some Iroquois observers believed that the Jesuits among them "carried Demons." One Jesuit reported the Indian opinion that "we and our doctrine tended only to their ruin," and another acknowledged, "It is true that, speaking humanely, these Barbarians have apparent reasons for thus reproaching us—in as much as the scourges which humble the proud precede us or accompany us wherever we go." One missionary priest concluded, "Such an accumulation of miseries as overwhelms them would, it seems to me, strengthen them in the belief which they had at the very beginning, that prayer causes them to die; that we were sorcerers, who had conspired against their lives." It was no great leap for Iroquois people to associate Jesuits with the outbreaks of disease that afflicted Native villages wherever the missionaries went and to interpret those epidemics as the covert attacks of black-robed "witches." Not all blows to the health and vitality of Iroquois people, they believed, came from the covert assaults of sorcerers; the failure to perform necessary rites and ceremonies, or to live life properly, had its consequences. But Iroquois men and women continued to show great concern that they could be victimized by witches—by those among them who professed friendship, even kinship, and showed no outward enmity, but who could afflict them secretly with sickness and death.[16]

Warfare was another scourge. Precolonial life among the Iroquois was not Edenic; warfare was traditional and ever-present. But colonial incursions transformed it and made it more extensive, geopolitically complex, and murderous. The Five Nations often found themselves at odds with New France and its Native allies. Even when they prevailed militarily, this warfare proved costly, unsettling, and deadly. Iroquoia suffered devastating invasions in the seventeenth century, and the Five Nations felt imperiled by their entanglement in the growing imperial conflicts between England and France. By both inclination and necessity, they sought peace. In 1701, the Five Nations brokered a "Grand Settlement" with English and French authorities. The accord sought to establish Iroquois neutrality between the two imperial foes; by playing the English and French off against each other, the Five Nations maintained their own cultural, political, and territorial integrity. A "Covenant Chain" bound the parties together in a series of alliances between the Iroquois, their Indian allies, New York, other English colonies, and the French. Although violence continued to flare up occasionally between the Iroquois, New France, and Native rivals, the Six Nations maintained their neutrality and power.[17]

But with Britain's victory over France in the so-called French and Indian War, the Six Nations lost a critical link in their Covenant Chain. The Iroquois could no longer command their previously decisive mediating position—strategically or economically—following French removal from Canada. The war's end encouraged westward Anglo-colonial expansion, threatening Iroquois control over their homeland and especially those lands farther west and south where their claims were more tenuous. The Proclamation of 1763 expressed the English Crown's appreciation of the dangers related to such white expansion (costly warfare, disputed territorial claims and land titles) and prohibited colonial settlement beyond a line running, roughly, along the crest of the Appalachian Mountains. As the imperial crisis grew in the 1760s, toward the rupture of 1775, when shots were first fired at Lexington and Concord, the Six Nations remained a sovereign people but found themselves in a deteriorating position.[18]

From early in the seventeenth century, the Iroquois had faced the incursion of missionaries. The Dutch Reformed ministers of New Netherland showed relatively little inclination to proselytize even among the closest of the Five Nations, the Mohawks. But the Jesuit priests of New France proved to be more committed to religious and cultural transformation. Their approach was neither patient nor predicated—like other Christian missions—on the Indians' prior reduction to "civilization." The Iroquois contrasted French and Dutch clerical behavior; the Dutch "have preserved the Iroquois by allowing them to live in their own fashion," one Iroquois observer noted to a Jesuit chronicler, but "the black gowns [the Jesuits] have ruined the Hurons by preaching the faith to them."[19]

Jesuit missionaries achieved limited success in their various incursions into Iroquoia. Their efforts created a mixed legacy of conversion and evasion, as some embraced Christianity while others pushed it away and fashioned tools of religious resistance. Iroquois culture valued domestic tranquillity; it taught women and men to stifle explicit expressions of disagreement or criticism. Yet Jesuit missionaries played by different rules. After ingratiating themselves within Iroquois communities, the so-called Black Robes soon emerged as irritants—impertinent men who ceaselessly questioned Native people about their religion and persistently argued the error of Iroquois ways. They sparked troubling debate where there had been consensus, aggravated Native factional tendencies, and undermined the smooth functioning of households and lineages. A single convert within a longhouse could upset social arrangements and prevent others from satisfying collective ritual obligations. Iroquois villages attempted to remain calm under such pressure, but eventually patience wore thin and dangerous social fissures opened, splitting communities into pro- and anti-French, traditional and Christian, factions. In the 1670s, such fault lines shook the Mohawks and Oneidas to the extent that they produced a rupture—numerous converts followed Jesuit priests to a mission settlement on the Saint Lawrence River at La Prairie de la Madeleine, called Caughnawaga (after an old town in the Mohawk Valley, the source of many of these emigrants).[20]

By this time, there were Protestant as well as Catholic Mohawks. In 1703, the Society for the Propagation of the Gospel in Foreign Parts (SPG) had dispatched the English minister Thoroughgood Moore to New York as a missionary counterweight to the Catholic Jesuits proselytizing among the Iroquois. He made little headway among the Mohawks, who seemed satisfied with the unobtrusive Dutch Reformed clergy. But later in the eighteenth century, other Anglican, Congregationalist, and Presbyterian ministers achieved some success with the Mohawks and other Iroquois people, most notably the New Light Presbyterian minister Samuel Kirkland with the Oneidas. Christian missionaries had an impact in Iroquoia. They advanced colonial goals, offered new forms of power to some, and introduced new dissonances into Iroquois lives. Some Iroquois became converts, either as Catholics or as Protestants (and some Christian Indian converts became Iroquois), but others adopted alternate, hybrid forms of Christianity, or rejected it altogether. The strain of religious competition taxed the Six Nations' powers of adjustment, and the new religious diversity within Iroquoia sometimes precipitated fractures, as in the case of Kahnawake Mohawks. But it could also produce a countervailing cultural strength. When hordes of Christian missionaries, as well as representatives of the Society of Friends, appeared among them in the 1790s, the Senecas drew on a long history of encounters with Christianity.[21]

The experiences of the colonial period annealed the Iroquois. Disease reduced their numbers. Warfare increased, took new forms, and became more lethal. And missionaries challenged Native consensus. Through traditional mechanisms, Iroquois communities condoled the living and reconstituted themselves. They augmented their population and power through adoption, gathering refugees and integrating fragment peoples as Iroquois. Resilience was an acquired trait, one they would need in early national America. The colonial experience also required that the Senecas and other Iroquois hone their political skills, as they pursued a diplomacy of balance—playing rivals off against each other, working to maintain their place in the center. This was a dangerous but unavoidable game, which became more difficult when France succumbed in the Seven Years' War. But it would be replayed as the Senecas occupied new intermediate places between Britain and the United States during the Revolution, on the borderland between the United States and Canada, and within the uncertain American federal terrain between the national and state governments. As in the colonial period, such diplomacy would require a sophisticated understanding of their partners' interests, values, and fears. Perceptive leaders such as Red Jacket proved able to identify the divisions among their rivals and to deploy the available means of persuasion.[22]

The colonial era similarly sharpened the tools Senecas employed in their internal political affairs. Traditional Iroquois society emphasized localism and consensus. During the seventeenth and eighteenth centuries, Iroquois communities exercised autonomy while building new means of national coordination through their league. They did not always agree. Some went their own way, literally. Seneca communities remained fluid. They would maintain a national identity and act in concert in the early republic, but they would also exercise degrees of independence. Such division could weaken the Senecas, but it could also be a source of flexibility and strength. The new problems and decisions the Senecas faced in the early national period—to accept or rebuff Christian teaching, to embrace or reject secular education, to change modes of production or adhere to tradition, to sell some land or refuse any diminishment of their homeland—would strain their ability to reach consensus, not only nationally but locally. But earlier, in the colonial period, Senecas had endured predicaments that were confusing and divisive. The experience helped prepare them for an unpredictable future. Disagreement and factionalism were not unprecedented; in the face of novel dangers, Seneca factions could be drawn into new Native coalitions to complicate the efforts of opponents seeking to dispossess them.

Continuing encroachment by white armies, missionaries, settlers, and officials would threaten Seneca land and resources. And it would endanger other traditional characteristics of Seneca life—its commitment to matrilineal social organization, its gendered division of labor, and the high status it assigned to women, for example. New periods of crisis would enflame traditional fears of witchcraft, especially when Senecas groped to explain widespread ill-health and misfortune.

Throughout, however, the Senecas did not display a mechanical adherence to "tradition." As in the colonial period, they showed a willingness to adjust, to seek new forms of sacred power, and to embrace innovation. They understood change. The physical and political landscape of Iroquoia had been altered before, as they constructed their confederation and accommodated colonial newcomers. Human and natural boundaries shifted, new neighbors arrived, sometimes conflict erupted, new relationships formed. Senecas were not isolationist in their orientation; they willingly engaged outsiders, on their own terms whenever possible. They preferred peace over war, but they were not pacifists, which became brutally clear as the colonial period concluded in violence and revolution.

The Six Nations had long suspected the ambitions of white colonists and resisted their encroachment, which only intensified after the Seven Years' War. In 1763, the Seneca chief Serihowane complained to the superintendent of Indian Affairs Sir William Johnson, "Your people are ungovernable. . . . [They] entirely disregard, and despise the settlement agreed upon by their Superiors and us." He urged Johnson to "restrain your people . . . make them lay aside their ill designs, and encroachments." In another meeting, at the superintendent's estate, Johnson Hall, in March 1768, a Six Nations spokesman objected, "Your people come from the sun, rising up our rivers to the west, and now they begin to come upon us from the south, . . . but nothing is done to drive them away." He urged imperial authorities to address the problem immediately, "or they will eat us up, for your people want to chuse all the best of our lands, tho' there is enough within your part with your own marks upon it, without any inhabitants. Brother, this is very hard upon us." The Iroquois promised then to halt the advance if imperial authorities failed to do so: "we will do it for you, our legs are long, and our sight so good that we can see a great way thro' the woods, we can see the blood you have spilled and the fences you have made, and surely it is but right that we should punish those who have done all this mischief."[23]

The Senecas managed to preserve their cultural integrity and political autonomy through the era of the American Revolution, which would present the Iroquois' most difficult test. If the Revolution elevated American rebels to independence, and expanded their opportunity, it threatened to have the opposite effect on the Six Nations. Such was the colonial crucible, which forged the Seneca.

The Senecas and the American Revolution: Iroquois Independence

The American Revolution was most revolutionary, and most violent, when it faced west, where white militia and Continental soldiers confronted Native people, the largest body of "loyalists" in America. In a revolutionary act as radical as any in the French or Russian Revolutions, victorious patriots expropriated Indian land and redistributed it to white Americans pushing into the new nation's "Empire for Liberty." Sacred documents, such as the Declaration of Independence and the Constitution, had little to offer Native Americans—indeed, they seemed to curtail rather than protect rights—and most Indians sought to avoid the embracing arms of state and federal governments.[24]

There was "never a more total revolution" than in New York, a contemporary observer wrote in 1775. Like other such radical transformations, New York's revolution entailed unprecedented violence and destruction. As historian Edward Countryman has written, "No state experienced the Revolutionary War with greater ferocity or over a longer period than New York." From May of 1775, when the Green Mountain Boys took Fort Ticonderoga, to November of 1783, when British troops finally evacuated New York City, New York found itself at the heart of the complicated struggle with Great Britain and itself. The state experienced warfare—some ninety-two battles in all—not only around New York City and in its northeastern corner at Lake Champlain, but in its interior as well, at Saratoga and the Mohawk Valley, at Cobleskill, Andrustown, German Flats, Unadilla, and Cherry Valley, and in Iroquois country as far west as the Genesee River. Even after the Treaty of Paris was signed in 1783, disputes and tension simmered between British subjects, American citizens, and those Iroquois people caught in between, particularly at the far western Niagara frontier, which New York shared with

British Canada. These pressures would ultimately boil over in the War of 1812 and enmesh the state again in combat along its northern frontiers—at Lake Erie, the Niagara River, Lake Ontario, the upper Saint Lawrence Valley, and Lake Champlain.[25]

The Revolutionary War cost New York dearly in lives and property and proved profoundly unsettling. General John Sullivan's campaign of 1779 destroyed the Iroquois homeland, exposing Iroquois people to starvation and exposure, while Indian raids continued to exact a price on white settlers. In Tryon County alone, countless structures and crops were destroyed, innumerable livestock were slaughtered, 12,000 farms were abandoned, 380 women were left widows, and some 2,000 children were rendered fatherless. New York City was nearly consumed in fires early in the war, as patriots abandoned the city to loyalists and occupying troops. In the areas surrounding the city, bitter partisan intrigue, covert action, and deadly conflict riddled the landscape. Throughout the war and in its aftermath, loyalists were dispossessed and punished, causing hardship and misery among losers but creating opportunities for winners. Within the partisan culture that emerged, new men rose to influence and power, the political arena itself expanded, and New Yorkers generally scrambled to repair and remake the state's economy. An emergent republican ideology invested supreme importance in agrarian life and land ownership, which bestowed on yeomen both economic and political competency. The vast tracts of "free land" in New York, newly available after the Revolution, would help underwrite the American experiment in republicanism.[26]

Almost immediately, the Empire State began to earn its name. Liberty, for those fortunate enough to possess it, meant release from earlier political and economic restrictions. And those liberated enthusiastically embraced the pursuit of happiness—that is, economic opportunity—sometimes at the expense of unfortunate others. Among the greatest sources of such opportunity and wealth were the rich agricultural lands in central and western New York, formerly controlled by the Six Nations but now opened by British (and, by implication, Iroquois) defeat. Colonists had coveted this territory for years, but they saw it firsthand and dreamed about its agricultural potential during their invasion of Iroquoia. They marveled at the bounty the land produced, as they destroyed acres of crops and hundreds of bushels of grain, and were captivated by "beautiful" plains "covered with fine grass, such as clover, spear & fowl-meadow grass . . . 8 or 10 feet high." Camped near Tioga, on the Pennsylvania–New York boundary, John Burrowes, a soldier serving with

Sullivan in 1779, was amazed and delighted to gaze upon "a large bottom or beautiful plain, not a stump to be seen, a great burthen of wild grass. And with little industry (from appearance of the soil) would make most excellent meadows." Men such as Burrowes would return in the following decades— not merely to the upper Susquehanna but also to the Finger Lakes and Gene- see region—to take up these less-than-virgin lands. They would transform them into commercial farms, integrating the landscape into a new national market economy. Former Iroquois territory thus became the greatest source of confiscated wealth produced by the Revolution in New York. It fell to grand speculators, settlers, and squatters and fueled New York's astonishing economic development. The dispossessed Iroquois domain made life, liberty, and the pursuit of happiness possible in New York.[27]

Looking East from Iroquoia

As the imperial crisis erupted into war after 1775, the Six Nations understood that conflict to be essentially a family quarrel, and they tried to stay out of it. Initially both the Continental Congress and British officials encouraged Iro- quois neutrality. But by early June 1776 the British Indian agent Colonel John Butler began efforts to recruit Seneca warriors at Niagara. They rebuffed Butler, even though they remained suspicious of the American rebels. As Cawoncaucawheteda, or Flying Crow, a Seneca war chief, told Butler,

> You have called us here to open Our Eyes, to break the Peace we
> live in with our American Brethren and to ask our help to fight
> them. . . . We have now lived in Peace with them a long time and
> we resolve to continue to do so as long as we can—when they hurt
> us it is time enough to strike them. It is true they have encroach'd
> on our Lands, but of this we shall speak to them. If you are so strong
> [a] Brother, and they but as a weak Boy, why ask our
> assistance[?] . . . You say they are all mad, foolish, wicked, and
> deceitful—I say you are so and they are wise for you want us to
> destroy ourselves in your War and they advise us to live in Peace.
> Their advice we intend to follow.[28]

The Seneca chief Kayashuta cautioned, "We must be Fools indeed to imagine that they regard us or our Interest who want to bring us into an unnecessary

War," and at Fort Pitt in July 1776, he declared, "We will not suffer either the English or Americans to march through our country." Later that autumn, Kayashuta warned the Americans to restrict their fighting to coastal regions and "not to come into our Country to fight, lest you may stumble and fall on us so as to wrest the Chain of Friendship out of our hands."[29]

Yet the Continental Congress had already resolved—like its British adversaries—to abandon its policy of Indian neutrality, deciding on May 25, 1776, to seek direct military alliance with Native people and authorizing General George Washington to raise a force of Indian soldiers.[30]

Meanwhile, the conflict aggravated tensions within Iroquoia and eroded the Six Nations' ability to act in unison. Their deliberations were heated and ultimately inconclusive. Oneidas told the Reverend Samuel Kirkland, for example, that "they never knew a debate so warm & contention so fierce to have happened between these two Brothers, Oneidas & Cayugas, since the commencement of their union." Mounting dangers forced each nation to formulate its own strategy. The Oneidas and Tuscaroras saw greater advantage in supporting the American rebels. By the 1770s, they occupied a vulnerable position on the Indian-white frontier of settlement. Whatever the outcome of the conflict, they reasoned, New Yorkers would continue to expand; only alliance with their white colonial neighbors offered any hope of avoiding dispossession. The Mohawks, on the other hand, had already lost much of their land. They favored the British, based on their ties to Sir William Johnson and his family and the partisan guidance of their leader Thayendanegea (Joseph Brant). Onondagas tried to maintain neutrality, but they were unsettled at this critical moment by a smallpox epidemic, which killed some ninety people, including three principal sachems. In January 1777, the Six Nations' council fire at Onondaga was extinguished, "dissolving their Body-politic," according to Kirkland. Its expiration signaled political stalemate and crisis, but it also offered some advantages. It permitted the Six Nations greater flexibility, allowing them to avoid direct confrontation with each other and legitimating their individual actions.[31]

The Iroquois were dragged into the escalating conflict. Deteriorating conditions ultimately pushed Cayugas and Senecas into the loyalist camp. Senecas went to the British siege of Fort Stanwix in 1777, they believed, as neutral observers, but they found themselves engulfed in the action and forced "to fight for their lives," recalled Mary Jemison, an adopted Seneca woman. The beaten Senecas returned to their villages in shock and grief; Jemison's community alone suffered thirty-five killed, including five chiefs, and numerous wounded. Moreover, during the melee the Senecas' camp had been plundered, causing the loss of medicine bundles critical for curing wounds and reviving health. These losses were disastrous for a people who fielded only a thousand warriors and whose mode of fighting was designed to avoid casualties. "Our town exhibited a scene of real sorrow and distress," Jemison remembered. "The mourning was excessive, and was expressed by the most doleful yells, shrieks, and howlings." Worst of all, the battle at Oriskany pitted Iroquois against Iroquois—Mohawks, Cayugas, and Senecas against Oneidas and Tuscaroras. Loyalist Iroquois burned Oneida fields and houses, and Oneidas in turn attacked and destroyed Mohawk crops and dwellings. Onondagas desperately tried to remain nonaligned, but they too were swept into the conflict by 1779, as American soldiers attacked their homeland.[32]

The battle of Oriskany was the bloodiest internecine Iroquois encounter of the war. Governor Blacksnake, the Seneca leader, later remembered the slaughter as the worst he had ever seen: dead bodies littered the field and "the Blood Shed [was] a Stream Running Down." Oriskany's horror seemed to repel Iroquois combatants on both sides. Though circumstances strained the Iroquois Great Peace, during the remainder of the war the Six Nations focused their attacks on white opponents and avoided conflict with each other. Iroquois brethren found themselves on opposite sides, sincerely committed to victory, but they nonetheless shared a common motivation: Iroquois self-defense and survival.[33]

Despite their efforts to minimize the war's damage, the Six Nations suffered devastation. In 1779, General Washington commanded General John Sullivan to march on the Iroquois homeland, "cut off their settlements, destroy their next Year[']s crops, and do them every other mischief which time and circumstances will permit." "It will be essential to ruin their crops now in the ground and prevent them planting more," Washington instructed.[34]

Mary Jemison was among the Senecas residing on the Genesee River who lived through this catastrophe. Before Sullivan's troops reached them, Senecas knew of his advance, "burning and destroying the huts and cornfields; killing the cattle, hogs and horses, and cutting down the fruit trees belonging to the Indians." Suffering "every thing but death from fear," women and children evacuated their villages. After contemplating battle, Seneca men determined they lacked the forces to confront Sullivan and abandoned their homes, fields, and stores of food. Jemison and other women and children were sent to relative safety farther west toward Buffalo. Meanwhile,

Sullivan's army destroyed all before them, leaving "nothing but the bare soil and timber." The soldiers' departure eventually allowed the Senecas to return, but "what were our feelings," Jemison asked the readers of her narrative to imagine, "when we found that there was not a mouthful of any kind of sustenance left, not even enough to keep a child one day from perishing with hunger"? Their misery was compounded that winter, "the most severe that I have witnessed since my remembrance," according to Jemison. "The snow fell about five feet deep, and remained so for a long time, and the weather was extremely cold; so much indeed, that almost all the game upon which the Indians depended for subsistence, perished." Senecas were "reduced . . . almost to a state of starvation through that and three or four succeeding years." "Many of our people barely escaped with their lives," Jemison remembered, "and some actually died of hunger and freezing."[35]

In September of 1779, Washington reported to his protégé, the Marquis de Lafayette, "the entire destruction of the whole Country of the Six nations." General Sullivan had written Washington of his victory over a combined British, Tory, and Indian force from Niagara, and his destruction of "between 15 and 20 Towns" as well as "Crops and every thing that was to be found." Sullivan advanced through the interior Iroquois towns, Washington wrote, "with a view to complete the desolation of the whole Country, and [to] Remove the cruel inhabitants of it to a greater distance, who were then fleeing in the utmost confusion, consternation, and distress toward Niagara, distant 100 Miles through an uninhabited wilderness."[36]

In the end, the American forces under Sullivan managed to destroy forty-nine Indian towns, burn 160,000 bushels of corn, spoil a "vast quantity of vegetables of every kind," and cut down orchards of apple and peach trees during their devastating campaign. The waste confirmed the extent to which the Senecas and other Iroquois were a settled, agricultural people, not "wandering savages" inhabiting a wilderness. The historian Joseph R. Fischer concluded, "Sullivan's raid . . . neither brought peace to the frontier nor measurably assisted in the final outcome of the war. On a practical level the expedition turned out to be a well-executed failure." Nonetheless, Iroquoia was in ruins and its people, while not destroyed, were divided and demoralized. Among the Iroquois, these actions earned Washington the name "Town Destroyer."[37]

The Six Nations survived, though by the spring of 1780 only two of their thirty towns had escaped destruction. The rest lay in ashes or had been abandoned, with their former residents dead or dispersed into makeshift refugee camps. There they struggled against the cold, hunger, scurvy, and dysentery and contemplated their future. Yet, as the chief Kayangaraghta told Sir Guy Johnson, "we do not look upon ourselves as defeated for we have never fought." In 1780 they did fight, carrying devastation to the New York and Pennsylvania frontiers throughout the remainder of the war. The Treaty of Paris formally terminated the war in 1783. Although Iroquois loyalists had not been vanquished on the battlefield, and though they continued to assert their independence, they were ignored and subsumed in the peace negotiated between Great Britain and the United States. The treaty made no provision for protecting Iroquois property; indeed, it formally transferred all of the lands south of Canada and as far west as the Mississippi River to the new republic. Loyalist Iroquois, deserted by their European ally, faced a difficult choice: accept exile in British Canada, or negotiate an uncertain future in their remaining homelands with the expansive Americans.[38]

The Senecas chose the latter course. Like other members of the Six Nations, they faced the new republic in a weakened state. A demographic crisis that began with the Revolution would reduce the Iroquois population by about half by 1797. The systematic destruction of their homeland—their houses burned, their orchards razed, their livestock or game slaughtered, their stores of corn, squash, beans, and tobacco, and their standing fields of cereal and vegetable crops, put to the torch—proved devastating in ways that we can hardly imagine. Pestilence soon joined death, homelessness, and famine among the Iroquois. Besides dysentery, epidemics of measles and smallpox plagued them. By 1794, no more than four thousand Iroquois remained of the some eight to ten thousand People of the Longhouse alive in the 1760s, a population that had been sustained only through the adoption of other Native remnant peoples over the previous century.[39]

Following the war, the Senecas arrayed themselves in western New York. They lived in villages at Buffalo Creek, near Buffalo, at Tonawanda, just to the north, at Cattaraugus, to the south and touching Lake Erie, in small settlements along the Genesee River, and at Allegany, farther south, just north of the Pennsylvania line along the Allegheny River. The precise boundaries and dimensions of their territory would be defined at the Treaty of Big Tree in 1797, but they would remain contested, with the lands themselves subject to white dispossession efforts. By the 1830s, even these homelands would be greatly reduced with the loss of Buffalo Creek and other reserves.[40]

Throughout their residual territories, Senecas attempted to survive, employing their old ways along with any innovations that might forestall their demise. Change had always been a part of Seneca life, but now—in the immediate aftermath of the American Revolution—a particular urgency inspired their improvisation. Life must have seemed hellish at times, but in retrospect it was something more transitory if grim: a Seneca purgatory.

Seneca Purgatory: The Toil and Trouble of Mary Jemison

Christian theology and common usage define *purgatory* as a place of prolonged torture and suffering, a place to perform or endure painful penance in anticipation of eventual deliverance. Post-Revolutionary Iroquoia, for Seneca and other Iroquois people in the 1780s and 1790s, was an undeserved purgatory, an inescapable arena of trials and tribulations. Deliverance remained uncertain. Life was harsh and immediate prospects were poor, either because Seneca people lived on land that was relatively marginal and unproductive or, conversely, because they occupied landscapes so productive and valuable—for commercial agriculture, natural resource development, or transportation links—that they attracted the covetous eye of white settlers, land jobbers, and developers.[41]

What was it like to live in these Seneca communities, still reeling from the shock of war? Let's consider the situation in just one place, along the Genesee River, in the heart of the traditional Seneca homeland, reluctantly abandoned by most Seneca people during Sullivan's campaign in the Revolution. A few stalwart Senecas, such as Mary Jemison and her family, managed to hang on there through the 1820s. Jemison was a white woman naturalized by the Senecas. She had been captured in her youth and chose to remain with her adopted people for the rest of her long life. Jemison's story is unique; she and her family lived away from the larger Seneca communities farther west—Buffalo Creek, Allegany, Cattaraugus, and Tonawanda—which in varying degrees managed to construct a new Seneca order. But life along the Genesee was exemplary, suggestive of the larger travails that possessed the Senecas in these transitional, post-Revolutionary years.[42]

Like other Senecas, Mary Jemison lived among a growing number of white settlers. For Jemison, and for Senecas generally, it was sometimes difficult to judge the character and motives of these newcomers. She welcomed and embraced some; others she found troubling, intrusive, and unsavory. Some were clearly dangerous. Could they be trusted? How might she protect herself, her family, her community? The newcomers often sought what Jemi-

GARDEAU, THE FORMER HOME OF MARY JEMISON, AS IT APPEARED IN 1872.

The frame dwelling seen in the background stands very nearly on the spot where stood the cabin made of hewn logs which was occupied by Mary Jemison at the time she narrated the history of her life to James E. Seaver.

Figure 3. *Gardeau, the Former Home of Mary Jemison.* From James E. Seaver, *A Narrative of the Life of Mary Jemison, Deh-he-wä-mis,* 6th ed. (New York: G. P. Putnam, 1898). Note that this landscape, even in the early nineteenth century, appeared relatively indistinguishable from other "pioneer" settlements, suggesting the extent of Seneca transformation by this time. Courtesy of Special Collections, University of Oregon Library.

son and the Senecas possessed—land and independence. Native people, coerced to accommodate their new white neighbors, nonetheless sought to secure what they had. Sometimes they failed. In this unsettled world, marriages, families, and domestic arrangements deviated from the forms conventional within either Iroquois or white society. It was sometimes unclear which economic strategies would most likely yield subsistence or comfort. Safety and security were elusive. And it was not always certain whose law, whose customs, whose values applied.

The strange career of Ebenezer Allen, who lived for a time among Mary Jemison's Senecas on the Genesee, offers us a glimpse of that Seneca purgatory. Allen was not a government official, a speculator, or a missionary. He proved to be both friend and foe to the Senecas, an untrustworthy man who sometimes intervened to protect Seneca welfare, but one who acted more frequently and vigorously to promote his own self-interest. His actions too often tormented his Native hosts. Allen exemplified the threats Senecas faced—to their hold on land, to the maintenance of their families and social life, to their physical survival. He personally embodied the fraud, abuse, and violence common to the Seneca condition in these desperate years. Yet Jemison befriended and shielded Ebenezer Allen, even concealing him from other Iroquois who sought his capture. Her account, told in matter-of-fact terms, provides a complicated portrait of an unpleasant frontier character and the roiled Seneca world he passed through.

Allen was a Tory. He fled Pennsylvania patriots and, early in the Revolutionary War, accompanied Indian assaults on white upper Susquehanna settlements. He was an enthusiastic soldier, exceeding Native soldiers in cruelty and including women and children among his victims. He was also a bigamist and alleged murderer, Jemison tells us, going so far as to make a woman a widow in order to acquire her as his wife. Yet Jemison accepted Allen on her lands and at times in her house as a political refugee. Soon after his arrival, Allen began to cause trouble. He acted the rake in his seduction of a resident Nanticoke woman, married to another white man living on Jemison's land. In a fit of jealousy, the offended husband beat and dragged his wife to the Jemison family doorstep, only to be driven off by Jemison's husband, Hiokatoo. The troubled couple eventually moved away to Niagara, and Allen continued to live and work on Jemison's land. When the war ended, Allen embarked on a series of disreputable enterprises, diplomatic, commercial, and amorous.[43]

In Iroquoia, even after the Treaty of Paris, tensions continued to bubble on the borderlands of the new American republic and British Canada. Allen acted benevolently if fraudulently to promote peace in western New York when he obtained a wampum belt—a traditional symbol and token of peace—and presented it without authorization to American military authorities. Allen misrepresented it as a peace overture of pro-British Iroquois on the Niagara frontier, who in fact remained disgruntled. Though improperly tendered, the sacred wampum belt commanded the respect of the disaffected Iroquois. They acquiesced to the American military commander's acceptance of the belt and the peace it represented. The ruse helped to calm the borderlands of western New York, but it brought little peace to Ebenezer Allen. A party of Iroquois left Fort Niagara to apprehend him to answer for his meddling. Surprisingly, Mary Jemison helped Allen elude them. She hid the self-appointed diplomat, provided safekeeping for his valuables, and found ways to provide food and intelligence critical to his survival. She and her people considered Allen "an innocent man" and believed "the Niagara people were persecuting him without just cause." Ironically, Allen was eventually betrayed, not by Jemison and other Senecas living along the Genesee, but by fellow white settlers. In this variegated world, race, ethnicity, or nationality competed with other factors in the complicated struggle to reconstitute social order. It was not easy to know whom to trust. Friends and foes could be hard to distinguish.[44]

Allen survived his imprisonment and trial and soon returned to the Genesee via Philadelphia, bringing with him a stock of dry goods and liquor to trade for ginseng and pelts. Displaying the growing Seneca engagement with the expanding commerce of the early American republic, Jemison assisted Allen in selling his merchandise and preparing the skins and ginseng for market (she assumed in Philadelphia), perhaps hoping to share in his profits. But he took his trade to Niagara, and apparently Jemison got no portion of Allen's earnings, whatever they turned out to be.[45]

The ambitious Allen next turned from commerce to farming, working different plots, including one at Genesee Falls, later the site of Rochester, where he built a gristmill and sawmill. During this period, Allen might have had a hand in the drowning death of an old German man living with him, and Jemison relates his marriage to a young woman, Lucy, despite the fact that Allen already had a wife, an Indian woman named Sally. Sally and Lucy, vulnerable and with limited options, apparently found a way to accommodate their predicament, sharing the Allen hearth and home amicably, according to Jemison. But within a short time, Allen sought to add yet another wife to his household, luring an old man and his young bride to his property and murdering the man, pushing him deliberately into the river to cause his death. Jemison writes, this act "left his young widow to the protection of his murderer." The unfortunate widow lived with Allen for a year, "in a state of concubinage," according to Jemison, before she ultimately left him.[46]

Shifting again, Allen returned to the site of a former farmstead at Mount Morris. We can speculate whether he had antagonized his immediate neighbors, or run into some other unreported trouble, or simply sought a new opportunity. Allen married once more, taking Morilla Gregory as his third wife. Sally and Lucy objected to the arrangement and, whipping the unfortunate Morilla, forced Allen to keep her in a different residence, "a small Indian house a short distance from his own." Yet Morilla eventually bore Allen four children, and she was joined by her sister, who became, perhaps, another of Allen's "concubines." Such arrangements might have scandalized Jemison and others, both Indian and white, but there were limited means to enforce the conventional moral or legal rules of either society in this transitional world.[47]

In 1791, exploiting the fact that some of his children (Mary and Chloe) were Indian—that is, the daughters of a Seneca woman, giving them identity and standing within the matrilineal Seneca society—Allen prevailed on Seneca chiefs to grant them a tract of land four miles square, the land where he and his unconventional family resided. Jemison reports, however, that Allen "so artfully contrived the conveyance, that he could apply it to his own use, and by alienating his right, destroy the claim of his children."[48]

In land dealings as in all else, Allen personified the great contemporary fear, not only among Senecas, but throughout the protean early republic— fear of the counterfeit. Post-Revolutionary America was a time of tumult. Older social hierarchies had dissolved and new ones were in the making. A world in which one might know everyone face to face was giving way to one filled with interactions among an anonymous and changing cast of characters. People moved, lived in new places, and did new things. A more democratic and chaotic political culture was emerging, as was a volatile and impersonal commercial economy. We associate such transformations with cities, but much of the country was new; newly settled places could be unsettling, including the Genesee country. Figures such as the infamous confidence man Stephen Burroughs exploited these changing conditions, acting with insincerity, misrepresenting themselves, gaining others' confidence, and getting rich at others' expense. Burroughs counterfeited banknotes as well as his various identities. "In a society increasingly organized around the pursuit of wealth," historian Stephen Mihm writes, "Burroughs seemed both to his critics and admirers an extreme incarnation of the self-made man."[49] Ebenezer Allen never printed phony banknotes, but he counterfeited identities and cultivated the confidence of Mary Jemison and her people, playing by his own rules and taking advantage of unsettled conditions.

Allen's swindle might symbolize the larger frauds being devised for the Senecas. After "having secured the land, in that way, to himself," Jemison recounts, Allen ventured to Philadelphia and sold his children's land to the Revolutionary financier turned real-estate speculator Robert Morris. And after disposing of the property, he abandoned wife Sally and daughters Mary and Chloe and shamelessly absconded with his two white wives and their children to Upper Canada. At the Treaty of Big Tree in 1797, one of Allen's Seneca daughters pressed her claims to the land in question, but she failed to establish her right and lost the land to Morris's creditors. Allen would make one last appearance along the troubled Genesee, suspiciously in an attempt to intercede on behalf of his deserted and dispossessed daughter. He somehow convinced Mary Jemison and a "half Indian" woman to approach Robert Morris's son Thomas, to urge him to restore his daughter's property. Morris asserted the validity of his own claims and declared "he had no land to give away, and that as the title was good, he would never allow Allen, nor his heirs, one foot." Beyond the self-interestedness of Morris's reply, we detect exasperation in his tone, directed at a man who inspired little sympathy. It is hard to believe that Ebenezer Allen was remorseful and determined to make amends after abandoning his parental duties, violating his daughters' and their people's trust, and alienating their birthright. More likely, he saw the chance to enrich himself through yet another fraud by selling the land he never owned to the same buyer twice.[50]

That a scoundrel such as Ebenezer Allen could thrive along the Genesee in the years following the Revolution tells us plenty about the Seneca predicament. Although Seneca communities like Jemison's continued to occupy and farm their homeland, life was chaotic, peopled with interlopers who overstayed their welcome, violated their hosts' trust and hospitality, and could not be easily expelled. Allen was the sort of white man that high-minded officials and missionaries would complain about, as they sought to isolate, "civilize," and assimilate Senecas and other Native people in the nineteenth century. This was a violent world, one in which murder could go unpunished and the options of vulnerable denizens could be so limited that they were forced to live with their tormentors, even the murderer of one's husband. For Allen's unhappy white brides or concubines, escape, when possible, was an attractive option. But Seneca people of the Genesee were a stationary target; removal to effect greater safety held little appeal for a people so attached to their homeland. And that homeland faced grave dangers, not only from grand speculators such as Robert Morris, but from encroaching squatters, and even from those who gained Seneca trust as insiders, becoming members of Native families and households. Most troublemakers among the Senecas, unlike Allen, did not go away.

Mary Jemison was lucky in some respects; Seneca leaders granted her title to Gardeau, her lands along the Genesee, and she secured them in the Treaty of Big Tree in 1797. In later years, when she was incapable of farming, she successfully leased her property to white settlers "to till on shares," allowing her to retain her land and survive in the presence of an expanding white population. Yet Jemison was forced increasingly to depend upon—and, perilously, to place her trust in—white settlers around her.[51]

She experienced both support and betrayal, the latter most clearly in the deeds of one George Jemison, a destitute white vagabond who claimed to be her cousin, the son of a brother of Mary's father, whom she did not know he had. Mary Jemison received him "as a kinsman, and treated him with every degree of friendship which the situation demanded." She paid his debts, set him up on her flats, furnished him with a cow and other livestock, farming implements, furniture, and provisions. George repaid her with ingratitude and fraud, when he entreated her to grant him the land he farmed and, when she complied, exploited her inability to read by doctoring the deed to encompass four hundred—rather than forty—acres. With the intervention of others, including a white neighbor she trusted, Mary Jemison recovered some of this land, but other plots proved irretrievable—her "cousin" George continued to hold his tract, before selling it away to a "gentleman in the south part of Genesee county."[52]

In her final years, in a confusing set of maneuvers, Jemison consented to the transfer of most of her reserve to white purchasers, and in the end she vacated the Genesee Valley altogether, leaving for Buffalo, where she lived out her life. Though she was neither gullible nor incapable, Jemison did not ultimately fare well in the overheated contest for real estate in western New York. Nor was she able to construct a secure social order at Gardeau. Hers was a cautionary tale, exemplary of the dangers that would face the Senecas more generally.[53]

Mary Jemison's narrative was advisory in other ways as well: it suggests the hazards that internal division posed to the Senecas, who found it difficult to agree on the best path toward survival. Jemison experienced anguish over the loss of her three sons, all victims of tragic, violent deaths. Distressing sibling rivalry drove one son, in two different violent encounters, to kill his two brothers. The first murder was an act of self-defense by one sibling, John, against a drunken assault by another, Thomas. "Having passed through various scenes of trouble of the most cruel and trying kind, I had hoped to spend my few remaining days in quietude, and to die in peace, surrounded by my family," Mary Jemison wished. The devastating fratricide, however, "seemed to be a stream of woe poured into my cup of affliction, filling it to overflowing."[54]

Although he had initiated the attack and died as a result of it, Thomas Jemison's passing was particularly tragic. He was reported to have been a great man, "naturally good natured, and possessed of a friendly disposition," a skilled counselor and chief, who represented his people well in diplomatic encounters in Philadelphia and with "the people of the states." His mother believed his untimely death was the result of his intemperance—he was a victim of "ardent spirits—a poison that will soon exterminate the Indian tribes in this part of the country, and leave their names without a root or branch." John Jemison later compounded his mother's sorrow when, in another drunken brawl, he killed her youngest son, Jesse. Finally, he too lost his life violently during an alcohol-induced melee, which ended with his throat cut and his skull smashed.[55]

These heartbreaking events bespeak the distressed nature of Seneca life in this period. Before his death, Thomas Jemison persistently harangued his brother John, who in the end became his killer. Among his most common criticism, Thomas objected to John's polygamy—he had two wives—and though such practices were not uncommon in their marginal world (consider Ebenezer Allen's household), they were inconsistent with Seneca tradition and at odds with social standards among either Senecas or white Christians. Thomas considered John's situation "a violation of good and wholesome rules in society, and tending to destroy that friendly intercourse and love, that ought to be the happy result of matrimony and chastity."[56]

Thomas's constant, moralistic reprimands must have been intolerable, but he might have been able to control his hectoring had he not succumbed to alcoholism. The Senecas and other Indian people by now had extensive experience with the liquor trade and its debilitating social effects. Jemison's account, as well as the persistent complaints of Native leaders, including the prophet and reformer Handsome Lake, testify to the increased presence and more devastating impact of alcohol in their topsy-turvy world. Alcohol would become one of the most prominent demons that the Seneca prophet and the missionary Quakers would battle. For now, the inability of Thomas and others to control their addiction added another dimension to the growing dysfunction and dependency of the Senecas.

Finally, as Mary Jemison relates, Thomas Jemison perceived the presence of a more covert and insidious danger lurking within his community and family. He suspected and accused his brother John of the most serious transgression—witchcraft. It's hard to evaluate Thomas's charge from such a temporal and cultural distance, but in times of vexation and confusion, in which the causes of crisis were clouded and means to respond unclear, Seneca people suspected the evil work of witches. We may now doubt witchery as an actual source of Seneca social and physical dislocation, but such indictments reflected the toil and trouble of the Senecas' new world. And they would continue.[57]

But John Jemison's death, unlike Kauquatau's in 1821, was not a judicial execution; it was murder. Thomas Jemison was no Tommy Jemmy. These differences are critical and suggest what lay ahead. Although white observers failed to see it, Tommy Jemmy's violent act signaled a new Seneca order, and his trial represented a more capable defense of Seneca sovereignty and self-determination, despite the continuing perils they faced.

At the end of the eighteenth century, with their confederacy fractured, and driven to the brink of dependency, the Senecas and other Iroquois nonetheless sought to protect as much of their homeland as possible, to find new ways to subsist, to overcome the dangers of alcohol, to defend their sovereignty and autonomy, and to fend off cultural annihilation. In short, they struggled for their own life, liberty, and pursuit of happiness in post-Revolutionary America. This was a period of turmoil for the Senecas, who—like Mary Jemison's family—confronted inner demons as well as external threats, not only a persistent encroachment but internal division and the specter of witchcraft within their communities. From this nadir, Seneca people would revive and reinvent themselves. They would do so in the presence, and with the help, of an uncommon set of resident visitors, members of the Philadelphia Yearly Meeting of the Society of Friends, or Quakers, whom we will examine in Chapter 4. But we turn now to the visions of a Native prophet, Ganiodaio, or Handsome Lake, and the genesis of a new, revitalizing Seneca religion, witnessed at its birth by those newly arrived Friends in the summer of 1799. Was Handsome Lake the prophet who could help the Senecas escape from their purgatory?

PART II

Spirit

CHAPTER 2

Handsome Lake and the Seneca Great Awakening: Revelation and Transformation

A few years since, an Indian, at the Alleghany river, half-brother to
the noted Cornplanter, gave out that he had communications from
the Great Spirit, which he was commanded to make known to the
different tribes of Indians. . . . He inculcates on his followers, that
they sell not their lands; that they refrain from the use of ardent
spirits; that they put not away their wives; that they cultivate their
lands; live industrious lives; and maintain the religious customs of
their ancestors.

—"Religious Intelligence," *Christian Observer* (February 1808)

"THE WINTER OF 1799–1800 was in western New York long called the time
of the Great Revival."[1] So wrote the historian of American religion Whitney
R. Cross as he considered the onset of the Second Great Awakening. Cross's
landmark study of the nineteenth-century rise of enthusiastic religion, new
prophets, and new sects expanded historians' vision of the awakening, focusing attention on the Burned-Over District. As we have seen, this volatile
region was the ancient home of the Senecas and other members of the Six
Nations of the Iroquois. That Indian presence continued even after the new
United States asserted its dominion and New York extended its own claims
of jurisdiction. Yet Cross never mentioned the Senecas or any other Native
people in the pages of his book, treating the Indians as if they had vanished.

Cross's neglect was doubly unfortunate because at this pregnant historical moment an Indian revival, a new prophet, and a new religion emerged dramatically at the western margins of the district—at the Allegany reserve, among the Senecas, in the southwest corner of New York State. The Seneca leader and prophet Ganiodaio, or Handsome Lake, anticipated by a matter of months the surge of revivals that swept through early national and antebellum America when he experienced the first of a series of visions in the summer of 1799. Seneca life would never be the same. The advent of Handsome Lake's new way should be understood on its own terms, but it did not occur in splendid isolation and should be considered in the context of American revivalism. Not merely a product of white evangelism, the Seneca awakening, like other revivals, represented a creative adaptation to changed circumstances. Those adaptations varied in part because of the different religious traditions that Indians and whites possessed, the different predicaments that they faced, and the necessarily different responses such circumstances inspired. Nonetheless, the distinctive Seneca revitalization represented a variation on a larger American theme, an indigenous expression of the Second Great Awakening.[2]

Burning Over Iroquoia

Whitney Cross wrote about western New York in this era, "Upon this broad belt of land congregated a people extraordinarily given to unusual religious beliefs, peculiarly devoted to crusades aimed at the perfection of mankind and the attainment of millennial happiness. Few of the enthusiasms or eccentricities of this generation of Americans failed to find exponents here." According to Cross, some christened it the "infected district," while others "came to call it the 'Burnt' or 'Burned-over District,' adopting the prevailing western analogy between the fires of the forest and those of the spirit."[3] Pioneers often employed such burning to clear the land of trees, to make fields capable of producing marketable grain. Much of this land had been previously cleared by Indian people and produced a horticultural plenty—it was not simply forest primeval—and much of that bounty had been destroyed, as we have seen, in the conflagrations of General Sullivan's Revolutionary War campaign. As Senecas were pushed west from the Genesee River toward Lake Erie, fresh fires cleared a novel commercial agricultural landscape, resettled by white pioneers fired by a new religious enthusiasm, which helped them accommodate their rapidly changing world. They drew both on traditional Protestant religious ideas and on less orthodox innovations, participating in revivals that would culminate in the Second Great Awakening.

The growing presence of white Christian settlers intensified the impact of missionary intrusions on the Senecas, which had been occurring in Iroquoia for two centuries. The Christian message and its demand for fundamental Native reformation became more immediate and constant, at times offering an unsettled people a means to survive. But it also exacted a price, particularly on those who saw in Christianity the destruction of cultural identity and integrity. Natives and newcomers alike experienced a new world in early national western New York—one radically different from the ones they had known, with unevenly distributed opportunities and dangers. Seneca people responded, not primarily by becoming evangelical Christians, but by transforming themselves into new-model Senecas, many of them followers of Handsome Lake and his *Gaiwiio* (or Good Word).[4]

Senecas and other Iroquois found themselves the renewed objects of various missionary programs following the American Revolution. Already on the scene was the New Light Presbyterian minister Samuel Kirkland, who had failed as a missionary to the Senecas in the 1760s, but who achieved greater success among another of the Six Nations—the Oneidas. Kirkland continued to guide the Oneidas during the Revolutionary War, serving Congress as a chaplain and political agent as well as missionary. After the war, Kirkland remained among the Oneidas, supported by the Boston-based Society for Propagating the Gospel among the Indians and Others in North America, as well as by the Scots Society for Propagating Christian Knowledge. Kirkland's mission bore fruit, but his partisan presence exacerbated Oneida factionalism, and his complicity in land deals that dispossessed the Oneidas undermined his credibility. Despite his ministry, Oneida converts constructed a syncretic Christianity.[5]

Others—supported by the New York Missionary Society, the Massachusetts Missionary Society, the Shaftsbury Baptist Association, and the Indian Committee of the Philadelphia Society of Friends—soon joined Kirkland proselytizing in Iroquoia, building on the Christianizing efforts of generations of evangelists. By the early nineteenth century, New York seemed crowded with them. Following his tour of the region, in 1805 the Reverend Jacob Cram wrote that, since the turn of the century, "not far from thirty regular preachers of the word of life have come to reside in the western counties of New York." "Many churches have been gathered," he observed, "and several meeting-houses have been erected since that period." Though Cram referred here primarily to white settlers, the Iroquois people of western New York were similarly exposed to these Christianization efforts. At the end of the eighteenth century, at a time when they were most vulnerable, Senecas endured a new surge of proselytizing, both directly from diligent missionaries and indirectly through their increasingly more numerous, white Christian neighbors.[6]

Resurgent, evangelical Christianity swelled across western New York, carried by the wave of white migration. While more famous revivals stirred in Kentucky, so too did they emerge in New York in the late 1790s, spreading west with the religious enthusiasm and enthusiasts of the Yankee hill country of New England especially. Wherever New York pioneers settled, even if temporarily isolated and sometimes fallen into irreligion, other "settlers inevitably arrived, churches formed, and revivals occurred," according to Cross. Despite differences in revival practices and theology, nearly all sects and denominations embraced emotionalism and all grew dramatically during the surges of awakening. New York became the intense center of revivalism in the Northeast. The enthusiasm culminated in the year 1800, followed by new peaks of excitement from 1807 to 1808 and after the end of the War of 1812.[7]

Fervent, sometimes eccentric Christianity percolated among frontier inhabitants in western New York. Baptists, Methodists, Freewill Baptists, Unitarian Baptists (or "Christians"), Quakers, Universalists, and even less orthodox Christians, such as Jemima Wilkinson's Community of the Publick Universal Friend, coexisted with Presbyterians and Congregationalists, who themselves cooperated under the 1801 Plan of Union. An array of missionary and benevolent societies supported the work of itinerant or circuit-riding preachers. Settlers who had grown up in various belief communities found themselves liberated from older constraints, jumbled together, sharing isolated meetinghouses, and listening in common to whichever preacher was available. These unsettled circumstances seemed to dictate cordial interdenominational relations, particularly as "missionaries" (that is, those ministering to "unchurched" white settlers) shared a common purpose: to awaken and cultivate piety, not sectarian peculiarities. Yet, paradoxically, nonsectarian revivalism engendered "interdenominational strife of a bitterness scarcely to be paralleled," according to Cross. Elkanah Watson, a Baptist missionary in Ontario County, was typical. Writing in 1817, he reported, "I do not administer to a church in this Neighborhood where I live, for there is none—my congregation has . . . some nominal Baptists, presbyterians, congregationalists; and some of them have been . . . deeply tinctured with Arminianism; several Universalists; and there are a number of nothingarians, and profane vulgarists . . . that sometimes attend my preaching."[8]

Although clerics like Watson could demean their neighbors as unchurched or even vulgar, these same proselytes typically exhibited sympathy with Christian preachers, attended services, and contributed materially to local religious enterprises. But too few became actual professing members of the church proper, and it was the quest to win these souls, not merely for Jesus Christ but for particular denominations, that inspired companies of missionaries in western New York. Revivals were less a matter of converting complete outsiders than of enlisting sympathetic but uncommitted allies in full membership, and they were often unavoidably interdenominational because numerous ministers—sharing space and communities—found themselves fanning the flames of religious awakening together. Although espousing a cooperative spirit, preachers often practiced a sort of sectarian nonsectarianism—that is, they saw their own faith as authentic, legitimate Christianity, while other preachers in their view imposed peculiar, divisive doctrines. The ensuing competition was not a free-for-all, but it nonetheless helped mold a volatile, erratic, unsettled religious landscape. Even the eventual federation of various organizations into the American Home Missionary Society in 1826 only added fuel to the sectarian fires, as it encouraged the multiplication of churches, beyond what individual communities could sustain on their own, aggravating the competition among faiths. Some found this denominational competition confusing and repulsive—Joseph Smith, for example, who eventually founded his own faith, the Church of Jesus Christ of the Latter Day Saints, or Mormons. Senecas, for their own reasons, would react to denominational rivalry as well, using it to justify adherence to both their traditional faith and Handsome Lake's new religion.[9]

The early fires of the Burned-Over District not only forged a complicated religious world in the early nineteenth century; they prepared the ground for "luxuriant new growths" of religious expression within traditional Christian practice, in the unprecedented urban revivals of Lyman Beecher and Charles Grandison Finney, in the flowering of new faiths, such as Mormonism, Millerism, and Spiritualism, and in the emergence of various utopian social experiments. Western New York was a chaotic religious landscape, and Senecas were increasingly enveloped in that tumult. The cacophony and competition of Christian preachers provided Native people with opportunities as well as dangers. New creeds and practices offered Senecas new options for selective adaptation, and sectarian rivalry may have worked to undercut the power of individual churches, perhaps dampening the impact of their encroachment, lending weight to Indian critiques of particular missionaries, and making it possible for Senecas and others to play one denomination off against another.[10]

Senecas along the Genesee felt the full religious assault directly, through encircling Christian neighbors as well as missionaries. Farther west, at Tonawanda, Cattaraugus, and especially Cornplanter's community along the Allegheny River, greater isolation made these intrusions less direct, except to the extent that missionaries sought them out, which they did with increasing frequency in the first decade of the nineteenth century. On the other hand, Buffalo Creek—the place of the new Iroquois council fire, where many Senecas had relocated during the Revolution—attracted early missionary attention. Buffalo represented a strategic nexus between the United States and British Canada and the gateway to the Great Lakes country. Religious itinerants passing through preached to the resident Indians and sought a more permanent presence for their religious institutions. They often got more than they bargained for. As early as 1801, the New York Missionary Society attempted to operate a school at Buffalo Creek, but it did not survive for long. Senecas remained suspicious of white Christian motives and continued to reject missionaries. In 1811, while rebuffing the minister John Alexander, they accepted Jabez Backus Hyde as a teacher for their children at Buffalo Creek. The War of 1812 interrupted Hyde's work, which continued irregularly thereafter through the decade. The New York Missionary Society eventually designated Hyde as a catechist (religious instructor), rather than a full-fledged minister; only in 1818—and not without controversy—did the Senecas and their Iroquois kin at Buffalo Creek covenant with the society to accept a full missionary presence. Throughout, the Seneca leader Red Jacket remained a thorn in the missionaries' side.[11]

Red Jacket complained to Alexander that "Great numbers of black coats have been amongst the Indians, and with sweet voices, and smiling faces, have offered to teach them the religion of the white people." Observing that Indians farther east had converted, he asked, "What has it done for them?" Since taking up Christianity, "they are a divided people—we are united— they quarrel about religion—we live in love and friendship—they drink strong waters—have learnt to cheat—and to practice all the vices of the white men, which disgrace the Indians, without imitating the virtues of the white men." "Brother, if you are our well wisher," Red Jacket cautioned, "keep away and do not disturb us." "Brother: You wish us to change our religion for yours—we like our religion and do not wish another."[12]

In an earlier exchange with the Reverend Jacob Cram, at Buffalo Creek in November of 1805, Red Jacket had noticed and ridiculed the diversity—and sectarian conflict—among Christian denominations, which further undercut their credibility: "You say there is but one way to worship and serve the Great Spirit. If there is but one religion; why do you white people differ so much about it? Why not all agree, as you can all read the book?" "We never quarrel about religion," he countered, not altogether honestly. Red Jacket advocated religious separatism: "The Great Spirit has made us all, but he has made a great difference between his white and red children . . . ; why may we not conclude that He has given us a different religion according to our understanding?" He ultimately pleaded simply to be left alone. "We do not wish to destroy your religion or take it from you. We only want to enjoy our own."[13]

Observing Christian evangelizing around him at the western margins of the Burned-Over District, Red Jacket remained wary. He told Cram, "Brother . . . you have been preaching to white people in this place. These people are our neighbors. We are acquainted with them. We will wait a little while, and see what effect your preaching has on them. If we find it does them good, makes them honest, and less disposed to cheat Indians; we will then consider again of what you have said." Afterward, as Cram stalked off, refusing to shake hands with his Indian interlocutors, he might have seen the Senecas' future less in the fires of religious revival than in the flames of hell; in his opinion, "there was no fellowship between the religion of God and the works of the devil." Perhaps, but Cram and other Calvinists were bedeviled, not merely by Senecas, but by fellow Christians. Surprisingly, accounts of Red Jacket's victory over Cram quickly found their way into print, published by white anticlerical opponents. They aimed their attacks at Calvinist dogma and ecclesiastical authority, and they employed Indian voices rhetorically to embarrass and disarm their evangelical rivals. In the process, though, they could enable Native resistance to Christianity itself, helping the Senecas to find space to reinvent themselves and resist encroachment.[14]

At the edge of the Burned-Over District, the work of the Society of Friends among the Senecas would have a similar impact, like "backfires" set to control a forest fire. The Quakers were no less committed or diligent than other missionaries, nor were they cultural relativists eager to credit Seneca religious beliefs and social practices. Their goal was to effect the radical conversion of the Senecas through a program of "civilization" and Christianization. Yet their tactics and approach varied considerably from those of other denominations. The Quaker presence helped to check the spread of other Protestant missions into some Seneca communities, largely containing them to the small-scale educational and religious efforts of Jabez Backus Hyde and the New York Missionary Society at Buffalo Creek, and the occasional itinerant minister. Amid this space, beginning in the summer of 1798, the Senecas had awkwardly begun to collaborate with visiting and resident Quakers. Those Friends would be on hand to witness the beginning of a new religion.

Handsome Lake's revival gave anxious Seneca people new order and direction in their lives. Religious historians often argue that revivals occur at moments of great stress and function to impose new regulations to combat the perceived chaos of social life. But as historian Paul Johnson suggested, "analyses of revivals and social control must not simply repeat that 'religion' holds 'society' together. They must define the ways in which particular religious beliefs reinforce the dominance of particular ruling groups."[15] Thus, we should ask: how did the prophecy and Code of Handsome Lake help to reconstitute Seneca society, hold it together, and in the process reinforce the dominance of particular Seneca groups? And we should remain sensitive, as Johnson cautioned, to see revivals as *religious* solutions (as well as social ones) to religious problems, not mere strategies to effect order and social control. At the heart of these social and religious questions were matters of gender. The profound alteration of their world challenged Senecas to remake their roles as women and men. For Handsome Lake, as we will see, the particular strain on Seneca manhood required an extraordinary transformation of Seneca families and womanhood. The *Gaiwiio* was a radical means to serve a conservative end. Like most revivals, Handsome Lake's would not go uncontested.

The Visions of Handsome Lake: Revelation and Apocalypse

"Now it came to pass in these days that one of the Heathen (the Brother of Corn-planter the Chief[)] lay upon his bed sick and behold he was in a trance for nearly an hour, and when his Spirrits revived again he spake of the many things which he had seen and heard." With these words, the Quaker missionary Halliday Jackson narrated the genesis of a new Seneca religion. His "Short

History of My Sojourning in the Wilderness" employed an archaic, biblical language to mark the seriousness of his purpose and the larger historic moment.[16] Not just among the Senecas, but throughout the United States, Americans were beginning to undergo revivals, experiment with communitarianism, contemplate the millennium, experience visions, hail new prophets, and found new faiths. Historian Gordon Wood has called this era "the time of greatest religious chaos and originality in American history."[17]

By midsummer 1799, the young Quaker missionaries Halliday Jackson, Joel Swayne, and Henry Simmons had been living among the Allegany Senecas for barely a year. They had arrived the previous May after an arduous nineteen-day journey through what Jackson called "a waste howling Wilderness." Welcomed by Cornplanter and his people, they set themselves up in the old village of Genesinguhta, upriver from Cornplanter's town, Jenuchshadago. There, Jackson wrote, "we began to be husbandmen and Vinedressers, and laboured abundantly in the field." The young men persisted through the fall and winter. In the spring, an optimistic Jackson was inspired to quote Song of Songs (2:12): "the winter is past, the storms were over and gone, the flowers appeard on the Earth, & the time of the Singing of Birds was come." Jackson hoped for more than the annual renewal that came each spring; he dreamed of cultural revolution among the Senecas. "And the works of our hands did prosper, and brought forth fruits of increase—And the Heathen round about us began to labour in these days and enclose fields, like unto us for they desired to become husbandmen."[18]

At other moments, however, the Quaker apostle expressed a sense of foreboding and tense anticipation. During the previous fall, he learned, death had visited Philadelphia in the form of a yellow fever epidemic. "May it not be called a day of darkness and of gloominess, a day of Clouds and thick darkness," Jackson wrote (quoting Joel 2:2). He likened this latter-day plague to the pestilence of Psalm 91:6 "that walketh in obscurity & destroyeth as at noon-day." And beyond the city, he wrote, "much of what the Armies of Flies had left, hathe innumerable hosts of grasshoppers eaten, even the green pastures and herbage of the Field." Jackson thus spoke of "judgments that were spreading abroad in the land of Columbia" as "the chastiseing rod of affliction," and he quoted Job 5:6: "affliction cometh not forth of the Dust, neither doth trouble spring out of the ground." In this world of wonder and sin, humans were the cause of their own misery. Pestilence and the destruction of locusts were "Signs of the times."[19]

Other menaces appeared closer to their new home among the Indians, which Senecas and Quakers alike found unsettling. In late July or early August 1798, surveyors arrived and camped in the village. They represented Robert Morris, the superintendent of finance during the Revolution, now a major land speculator. For the Senecas, their appearance foretold another sort of doom—loss of land and the arrival of white settlers. Jackson lamented that the surveying party sowed discord when they "did speak evil in the ears of the Heathen concerning us."[20]

Then, soon after their departure, a desperate young man stumbled into Genesinguhta, faint and starving and happy to be alive. Benjamin Shaw had lost his way and become bewildered, wandering for six days and six nights, Jackson wrote, in the "waste howling Wilderness." Shaw lived some sixty miles east and had been on his way to Jerusalem—not the ancient holy city but a New Jerusalem, a white settlement founded in 1790 on the west shore of Seneca Lake, in the heart of the ancient Seneca homeland. Shaw spoke of what he had seen there, and what he had seen was disturbing.[21]

New Jerusalem was the home of Jemima Wilkinson, the self-proclaimed "Spirit of Life from God," and her followers. Some twenty years earlier, in 1776, Wilkinson had taken to bed in a small town in Rhode Island and "died." But within a few hours, she was resurrected as the Second Coming of Christ. As messiah and prophet, Wilkinson thereafter made herself known as the "Publick Universal Friend." She took her millennial message of apocalyptic destruction on the road, preaching in towns and cities throughout New England and the Middle Atlantic states, provoking hostility and violence wherever she went. Finally, she and her followers took refuge in their New Jerusalem, a remote place, marginal in the early republic but proximate to the Senecas. "She" is perhaps not the proper pronoun to use in referring to the Publick Universal Friend; in the course of her resurrection, Wilkinson lost not only her mortal status but also her gender as a woman—she adopted masculine dress but became a Christ that was neither female nor male. Jackson wrote of her, "she did much mischief among the people, feigning herself to be a Goddess and a prophetess, and in the pride and vanity of her heart, said she could raise the Dead, & walk upon the waters, and do many mighty miracles." In that sentence Jackson had crossed out the word "wickedness" (to go along with "pride and vanity"), but his second judgment in word choice did not alter his assessment of Wilkinson's depravity. She deceived, he wrote, with "enticing words" and "was eloquent & mighty in reasoning after the carnal will of Man." The swirling competition to explain these tumultuous times became more diverse and intense with the likes of Wilkinson near at hand. And it would encompass everything from the destruction of the world to the reconstruction of gender.[22]

Henry Simmons missed the excitement of Benjamin Shaw's visit. Since the previous November, he had been living apart from the others, downriver in Jenuchshadago, as a resident schoolteacher. Simmons was thus in Cornplanter's village in late spring 1799, when it experienced its own, indigenous clouds of thick darkness and doom. "And it came to pass in those days," Jackson wrote, "that a certain woman of the Heathen dwelt in the Village of Corn planter whom they suspected to have a familiar Spirit, because they say she had done much mischief with Pison [poison] and Witchcraft." Cornplanter suspected the "witch" of murder and accused her of threatening others, including a young child, a family member. In a manner that would be repeated twenty years later when Tommy Jemmy executed Kauquatau, Cornplanter's sons found the accused woman as she worked in the fields and, in Jackson's pseudo-biblical idiom, "smote her that she died."[23]

The verb "to smite" (rather than "to kill") gave Jackson's account a scriptural quality that lent gravity to his contemporary gospel. It suggested more graphically the act's violence—a mortal blow delivered with a striking or hammering motion. The use of "smote" also lent this bloody work a certain legitimacy, perhaps even sanctity, subtly transforming the killing from an act of murder into one of justice. God and his agents most frequently smote. And a likely victim of such smiting would be a witch, following the biblical injunction: "Thou shalt not suffer a witch to live" (Exodus 22:18). "Justice was done to the Woman because she was found worthy of Death," Jackson wrote, "and in order to do away evil from among the people and put away those of Familiar Spirrits out of the land." Jackson was clearly disturbed: "my spirit was troubled because of the wickedness of the heathen, until I made further inquiry concerning the matter." But his narrative is ambiguous. He does not specify whether the Indians' wickedness resided in the "witch," the witch-hunters, or both, and Jackson leaves open the possibility that his further investigation of the matter actually addressed his concerns—that is, calmed his "spirrit."[24]

Witchcraft was controversial among white Americans, but large numbers of them continued to believe in its existence in the early republic. At this historical moment, Gordon Wood has noted, the "borders between science and superstition, naturalism and supernaturalism . . . were blurred." "The result was an odd mixture of credulity and skepticism." To rationalists, witchcraft was superstition, but for many, the presence of witches and the efficacy

THE MURDERER
DISCOVERED

Figure 4. *The Murder Is Discovered*, drawing by Seneca artist Jesse Cornplanter, n.d., ca. 1900–1909. Courtesy of the New York State Library, Manuscripts and Special Collections.

of supernatural practice remained credible. In the Allegany Seneca villages, witchcraft was frightening and uncontroversial. Its reality, essential wickedness, and grave threat were undisputed, and these events caused "no small stir amongst the People," Jackson reported. The Seneca villagers endorsed Cornplanter's mortal judgment; they could not tolerate such evil or allow their community to become a place possessed. As spring gave way to summer, suspicions lingered that malevolence remained among them, secreted in Jenuchshadago.[25]

Nonetheless, there was work to be done. On June 15, 1799, Henry Simmons was laboring just outside the village, building a schoolhouse, and Cornplanter was nearby supervising construction of a new house, when the chief received an urgent message. His brother was dying. The news was dire, though not surprising; Handsome Lake was a heavy drinker and had been in declining health for several years. Cornplanter rushed home to his stricken half brother, now surrounded by concerned family. He learned that Handsome Lake had been sitting in his daughter's house, when he suddenly arose to go outside. His daughter, knowing that her father was ill, was surprised, and she asked him where he was going. But Handsome Lake simply replied that he would return soon. At the side of the house he collapsed, "laying breathless" for a half hour by the time that Cornplanter arrived. The old man continued in his trance for another two hours. Though he appeared to die, Handsome Lake awoke to become a Seneca prophet.[26]

Simmons had stood among anxious family members who watched helplessly as life seemed to drain out of Handsome Lake. The old man lay still, and his arms and legs grew increasingly cold to the touch. Viewing Handsome Lake's comatose body, Simmons must have concluded that he would soon pass away, a victim of age, personal dissipation, and national trauma. Handsome Lake had once been a man of some status—half brother of the prominent Seneca leader Cornplanter and one of the Six Nations' fifty league chiefs. He was now sixty-four, and his health and fortune had declined as precipitously as those of the Senecas generally. On that midsummer afternoon it would have been hard to find the confidence to predict that Handsome Lake would ever revive. If he had not, few beyond his own family would have remembered him.[27]

Yet to Henry Simmons's surprise, Handsome Lake awoke, or "came to himself again," as the Quaker chronicler wrote. He did much more than that. The restored Handsome Lake talked with his brother and told him he was well. As he regained strength, he related to Cornplanter and those around

THE
SICK MAN

Figure 5. *The Sick Man*, by Jesse Cornplanter, n.d., ca. 1900–1909. The drawing perhaps depicts Handsome Lake before his first prophetic vision in 1799. Courtesy of the New York State Library, Manuscripts and Special Collections.

him a remarkable vision. Handsome Lake asked his brother to call his people together, and in a great council Cornplanter passed on his prophecy. Simmons and his Quaker missionary compatriot Joel Swayne attended the extraordinary meeting at the request of Cornplanter. The chief had Simmons inscribe a translation of Handsome Lake's prophecy for him—an acknowledgment of the growing importance of text in his changing world. Simmons recounted that the Senecas congregated in large numbers—men, women, and children—"with shorter notice than ever I had seen them before." They appeared "Solid and weighty"—that is, serious and moved by the moment. Simmons himself "felt the love of God flowing powerfully amongst us." This was the beginning of the Seneca revival, a Native fire that blazed within the Burned-Over District.[28]

Other visions followed. Handsome Lake again fell into a trance on August 8, 1799, and another on February 5, 1800. These revelations would continue until the prophet's death in 1815. In Handsome Lake's initial vision, three middle-aged, male messengers, or angels, approached him as emissaries of the Creator (another would subsequently appear and Handsome Lake himself would later become a "fifth angel"). These holy beings gave him four "words," describing the evil practices that saddened and angered the Seneca Great Spirit: whiskey (*One-ga*), witchcraft (*Got-gon*), compelling charms (*Gawenodus-ha*), and abortion or sterility magic (*Yondwi-nais-swa-yas*, literally, "she cuts it off by abortion"). The angels admonished the people to confess, repent, and avoid sin. During his second vision, they conducted Handsome Lake on a cosmic tour of the horrors into which the Senecas had descended, and he was shown the way to a righteous future.[29]

In the course of his journey, surprisingly, the prophet met George Washington and Jesus Christ. The latter criticized the behavior of whites who claimed to be Christians and endorsed the message of revitalization particular to the Senecas: "You are more successful than I for some believe in you but none in me. . . . Now tell your people that they will become lost when they follow the ways of the white man." Handsome Lake's encounter with the recently deceased George Washington revealed the national hero as a demigod, not only among white Americans but among Senecas as well, despite his reputation as "the Destroyer." The prophet's divine conversations and communion with the dead—departed family members as well as more famous and remote figures—sanctified his mission.[30]

At each stage of Handsome Lake's supernatural wandering, he—and his followers—learned lessons for proper social as well as religious behavior. They were to avoid drunkenness, stinginess, materialism. They were instructed to honor their fathers, as Cornplanter's recently deceased daughter, whom the prophet encountered in his dream, emphasized in a lament recalled by Handsome Lake. She complained to him, "her Brother thought he knew more than his Father and would not take his advice but would have his own way which was very wrong." This was a surprising directive in a matrilineal society given its failure also to recommend deference to mothers. But times were changing. And, finally, the prophet urged his people to be on guard against witches and the devil and "quit all kinds of frolicking and danceing except the worship dance."[31]

Toward the end of his celestial sojourn, Handsome Lake entered the domain of the Punisher, a horrific Seneca inferno, where he saw the tortures that unrepentant Indian women and men would endure forever. The apocalyptic threat of destruction by fire hung over them, Handsome Lake warned—the price Senecas would pay for their failure to reform. Forecasts of cosmic catastrophe proliferated in early nineteenth-century America, culminating in the predictions of a Low Hampton, New York, farmer, William Miller, that the world would end on October 22, 1844, with the Second Coming of Christ. When life went on as usual, scoffers scoffed and believers continued to believe. Handsome Lake's warnings were similarly dire if less temporally specific, but they should not be too quickly dismissed. Wilkinson, Miller, and other millennialists have often been considered crackpots, their visions outlandish. Their portrayal as irrational is based especially on the inaccuracy of their predictions about the world's end. But how absurd was Handsome Lake's millennialism, given the extreme threat his people faced, both externally and internally? White encroachment, the loss of land and resources, the assault on Native economy and culture, as well as the specter of evil that many believed haunted Seneca communities, might reasonably breed a sense of impending doom. The Seneca crisis might well have led to physical or cultural annihilation.[32]

In the hellish place that Handsome Lake visited, miscreants suffered punishments appropriate to their crimes. Drunkards ceaselessly poured molten metal down their throats, and gamblers shuffled and dealt red hot iron cards. Wicked musicians repeatedly hacked their own arms with hot iron bars as if they were playing the fiddle. These offenses violated both Seneca tradition and many Christian proscriptions. Quaker Indian Committee visitors in 1806 echoed previous missionaries when they told a Seneca assembly, "playing Cards Gameing and other idle practices" do "much harm"; "We hope you will keep out of these things as the[y] hinder the good work we desire to promote among you." Handsome Lake agreed.[33]

The Punisher reserved some tortures especially for female offenders. The sin of witchcraft was personified by a woman who was alternately thrust into a cauldron of boiling liquid and then jerked out to freeze in the cold. The angels told Handsome Lake, "The woman whom you saw will suffer two deaths in this place and when her body is reduced to dust the punisher will gather them up again and conjure the dust back into a living body and continue his sport until finally he has become weary when he will blow her ashes to destruction. Such things happen to those who will not believe in *Gaiwiio*." Given the circumstances of Handsome Lake's early visions, surrounded by suspicious deaths and an ongoing fear of covert sorcery, the prophet's condemnation of witchcraft is unsurprising. Witchcraft and witch-hunting among the Senecas was not new. Nor was belief in witchcraft exclusive to Native people in this era. Even John Wesley, the eighteenth-century founder of Methodism, had believed strongly in witchcraft and attributed disease to the work of demons. His early nineteenth-century followers would do the same. Christian beliefs influenced Seneca understanding of witchcraft, inflecting an ancient and well-established practice. The prophet's denunciation of sorcery represented no departure from tradition, but his definition and energetic prosecution of the dark art did. In the Seneca underworld that Handsome Lake visited, significantly, the witch assumed the shape of a woman, and she was not merely punished, not merely executed, but completely obliterated.[34]

As the prophet continued his journey through hell, the angels showed him a temptress who had used love magic to attract men. Formerly beautiful, she was now "parched to the bone," with exfoliating flesh and writhing serpents in all the hair of her body, exposed as naked and hideous. Soon Handsome Lake encountered a woman whose delight on earth, he was informed, had been *gaknowe-haat* (to copulate). The Punisher "lifted up an object from a pile and thrust it within her. Now the object was like *ha'ji-no ganaa* [that is, a penis], and it was red hot." "You have seen the punishment of the immoral woman," the angels told Handsome Lake.[35]

Men did not escape torture. Sanctions against male offenders seem designed (through deterrence) to create and maintain peaceful, patriarchal households, in which men enjoyed privilege but also contracted certain obligations. Wife beaters, for example, were disciplined. In the Seneca inferno, the Punisher forced an abusive husband to endure endless, agonizing burns, compelling him repeatedly to strike an image of a woman "heated hot with fire." Such men undermined the households that the Creator and Handsome Lake sought to form and nurture. Husbands and wives both were disciplined for quarreling. Yet women, unlike men, were demonized for sexual transgression, now defined in ways more congruent with white prescriptions.[36]

It is difficult to see the Punisher's brutal treatment of "immoral" women—like rape in general—as anything but the deployment of violence to demean and disempower women. These gendered and sexualized tortures surprise us, both by their severity and their focus. They represent a historical departure in Iroquois culture, and in fact they seem specific to this historical moment, unlike that which preceded or followed. They look like cultural imports from the patriarchal and misogynous society that surrounded the Senecas, at odds with Iroquois tradition. But they suggest a profound anxiety about the post-Revolutionary Seneca domestic world, its perceived social disorganization, and the gender relations at its heart. Like Jemima Wilkinson, to paraphrase the historian Susan Juster, the prophet Handsome Lake appeared at "a particularly anxious moment in the history of American [and Seneca] gender politics." The Publick Universal Friend's innovation was to challenge traditional patriarchal authority; Handsome Lake's was to attempt to establish it. Wilkinson's odd costume and demeanor "performed" a new and ambiguous gender identity in alarming fashion. The Seneca Punisher performed new tortures on the bodies of women. In the prophet's inferno, he policed the reformed gender identities of Handsome Lake's vision, as sexual violence symbolized a novel masculine control and a brutal "feminization" of those who defied the prescribed Seneca patriarchy.[37]

A revised Native theology and reformed means of living in the world would emerge from Handsome Lake's prophetic visions. His hybrid teachings and developing code reflected the prolonged intercultural conversation between Seneca religious traditions and various representatives of Christianity, which had begun in the seventeenth century and would continue into the nineteenth century and beyond. Yet, amid adjustments and innovation, Handsome Lake's prophecies largely represented continuity—not rupture—with Iroquois religious traditions.

The Theology and Social Reform of Handsome Lake

Handsome Lake's theology revised but did not displace older Iroquois knowledge and belief about God and the "supernatural." The prophet's *Gaiwiio*

Figure 6. *Handsome Lake Preaching*, by Jesse Cornplanter, n.d., ca. 1900–1909. The drawing is based on tradition and the artist's own experience in the Longhouse faith. Courtesy of the New York State Library, Manuscripts and Special Collections.

seemed to offer a new god, or at least one no longer called by the traditional name, Tharonhiawagon, the Holder of the Heavens. But this Great Spirit behaved not unlike the older one, and it is unclear whether the new deity joined or simply renamed the Tharonhiawagon of old. From the seventeenth century, some Christian missionaries had been impressed by Iroquois belief in a higher being, which encouraged Jesuits and subsequent proselytizers to hope they might be predisposed to worship their own one true God, Jesus Christ. Quakers no doubt noticed the potential for the Senecas to embrace their monotheism as well, even if they did not actively pursue Native conversion. Handsome Lake's nephew and chief disciple, Governor Blacksnake, endorsed the presence of the Friends in 1806 in this fashion: "we all know there is but one God that made and Directs us all to Do alike but we cannot all Do alike for there is so many sinners. . . . [The] Great Spirit is not Blind But can see Every thing and he is pleased with your Living amongst us."[38]

But if Quakers and other Christians approved of Seneca faith in a Supreme Being, they could not take credit for the Senecas' belief, nor could they be confident that other, lesser gods no longer inhabited the Native pantheon. If the workings of the Great Spirit might resemble the Quakers' Inner Light, the Seneca Creator was not the Christian God Almighty or His Son Jesus Christ—certainly not in the view of other, more evangelical Christian missionaries. And what did it say about Handsome Lake's new theology that he could equate himself as a prophet with Jesus Christ, whom he met in his visions and treated as a colleague, not as a savior? The Congregational minister and missionary to the Oneidas Samuel Kirkland confided about Handsome Lake in his journal, "I have never condemned him in public. On the contrary, I have expressed my approbation of many things he enjoins, which tend to the reformation of the Indians. But I have never expressed my belief that he was inspired by the Spirit of God, or that he ever had any interview with the Great God." Indeed, Kirkland saw Handsome Lake as "an impostor." And he sharply rejected the claims of the Oneida "pagan" leader, Doctor Peter, who elevated the Seneca prophet, "or *man of God*, as they stile him," above Protestant ministers who must rely on a holy book for their knowledge, while Handsome Lake "receives his directly from the same source from whence that [Bible] originated." Such a view might make the prophet less a pagan than a heretic.[39]

Handsome Lake sought to revive and maintain the traditional Iroquois ritual calendar, not to substitute a Christian one, even in modified form. Senecas did not imitate the Mi'kmaqs of the Canadian Maritime Provinces, for example, who transformed the Catholicism they learned from the French into a Native religion, to augment or replace what they had lost and to resist eighteenth-century British colonialism. The feast day of St. Anne, the Mi'kmaqs' patron saint, became an annual, "traditional" national festival, an act of self-definition and defiance. Handsome Lake instead sought to restore an ancient religious calendar. If his teachings also represented resistance and revolution, in this regard he led Senecas back to the future, taking them full circle in his prescribed observance of traditional rites and ceremonies, appropriate to the cycles of the year. In some cases, these rituals took on new dimensions—with additions to the Midwinter Festival, for example, or inclusion of the Four Beings (the four messengers to Handsome Lake) in the Thanksgiving Address—but the prophet acted conservatively.[40]

Moreover, Handsome Lake affirmed other, traditional rites, such as those surrounding dreams, their interpretation and ritual fulfillment, though with important shifts in emphasis. His own visions powerfully embodied the notion that dreams could express both wishes of the soul and extraordinary revelation. Here the prophet and his people required no Christian example or precedent, though Quakers—with their rich, complicated understanding of dreams—could see similarities with their own practices or more readily accept the idea that Indian dreams might provide insight and power.[41]

As historian Carla Gerona has demonstrated, late eighteenth- and early nineteenth-century America was "a dream-infused culture," and Quakers, like other religious groups, found in their dreams a means of dealing with modernity, helping them to revise their sense of their world and themselves. Friends in particular "used dreams to think more deeply about themselves," Gerona writes. "The Quaker ability to fantasize collectively . . . enabled them to envision a better future for and in an increasingly plural society. Both individually and collectively, Quakers transformed their dreams into creative stories that allowed Friends to define and redefine themselves, as well as their relationship to each other, to their nation, and to non-Quaker others." As Gerona notes, Seneca and white Christian attitudes toward their "night journeys" had much in common. Quaker dreams, like those of Handsome Lake, often entailed a journey, sometimes a tour of heaven or hell. Interpretation of dreams helped Quakers, like Senecas, plot courses for their everyday lives on earth, "to construct maps of the future." Both peoples created foundational myths in their dream narratives; both listened to specialists adept at interpretation; both employed formal rules and rituals in dream analysis. In both social worlds, the interpretation of dreams could prove contentious; and after the advent of the Quaker mission among the Allegany Senecas, explicating dreams at times became a cross-cultural (and sometimes controversial) enterprise, as Friends and Native leaders both sought to interpret the meaning of particular Seneca dreams and visions.[42]

Although Quakers generally downplayed catastrophic visions and constrained the effects of dreamwork in the interests of conformity, radical dreams could emerge that challenged social or religious orthodoxy. Jemima Wilkinson and Ann Lee were both former Quakers who experienced visions, which pushed them well beyond the Quaker (and Christian) mainstream. Their extraordinary dreaming helped transform them into prophets, leading them to found new religious sects and communities—the Society of the Universal Friend and the Shakers. Wilkinson and Lee were unusual, but in post-Revolutionary revivalism, dreams, visions, apparitions, and divine intervention were commonplace. Methodist itinerants enthusiastically shared their dreams with audiences. Such visions predicted salvation, foretold death, and described the realities of hell. One Methodist itinerant preacher, Freeborn Garrettson, visited heaven in a dream; another, George Peck, journeyed to hell in a vision, seeing there "nothing but devils and evils spirits, which tormented me in such a manner, that my tongue or pen cannot express." Other Methodists' dreams predicted the demise of an itinerant, who succumbed to the temptations of cards and drink, and foretold the preacher Benjamin Abbot's entry into the ministry. Abbot's autobiography featured his dreams extensively and unabashedly. Joseph Smith's revelations similarly emanated from sacred dreams. It was in a vision that the angel Moroni visited Smith and revealed the location of the "Golden Bible," later translated into the Book of Mormon in the 1820s. Such dreaming, much of it within the Burned-Over District of upstate New York, suggests that Handsome Lake's visions were not wholly unique; they were distinctive manifestations of a larger American dream.[43]

Dreams could offer power and authorize both radical and conservative teachings. In some ways, Handsome Lake's visions did both, and the Quakers at Allegany seemed to validate his prophecies, even when they sought to temper his more radical claims. Henry Simmons, the Quaker schoolteacher at Cornplanter's village in 1799, acknowledged to his hosts that Friends too fell into trances, and in the process they viewed both the "good place and the bad place" and saw "many wonderful sights." He linked the two peoples explicitly by declaring they were "all of one flesh and blood made by the Great Spirit." Simmons hardly undermined his larger endorsement of Handsome Lake's dream and prophecy when he skeptically (and privately) wrote in his journal, "perhaps as there was so much of it [the dream], the man [Handsome Lake] might not have recollected so as to tell exact as he seen or heard it."[44]

Senecas might have been influenced by the new prophetic practices they encountered among white Christians, and surely they were buoyed by the Friendly (if inadvertent) support they received, but they could find substantial prophetic precedent in their own traditions and beliefs. Prior to Handsome Lake's revelation, in 1791, an Oneida experienced a vision, which prescribed the restoration of "ancient feasts, religious dances & ball-play . . . , or no good should come to the Six nations." No Oneida prophet rose to prominence on that occasion, but the vision did galvanize opposition to Samuel Kirkland's Christian mission. Later, around the time of Handsome Lake's first visions, a prophet allegedly emerged from the Six Nations Reserve in Canada. His influence spread as far as Oneida and contributed to the revival of the white dog ceremony, abandoned a generation earlier. The Seneca prophet's cataclysmic vision—which presented a terrifying Native Hades and warned of a fiery end of the world—perhaps seems unconventional by Iroquois standards and might have been affected by Christian apocalypticism. Yet even here Senecas could recall the ancient origins of their League of Peace, ensconced in sacred myth and vitalized by ritual. The Iroquois believed that the visionary Hiawatha and a great prophet—the Peacemaker—intervened in the chaos of a distant time filled with deadly feuds to pacify combatants and create the institutions and rites of peace. We do not know whether early nineteenth-century Senecas saw their crisis as one comparable to the bloody circumstances of ancient times. But we do know that many affirmed a new prophet and his teachings, revealed in a series of dreams, as they sought a means to deal with their own grim predicament.[45]

Handsome Lake's moral reforms were his greatest innovations, and perhaps the part of his ministry most indebted to Christianity. According to the anthropologist Elisabeth Tooker, among the Iroquois and other northeastern Native people morality was not equated with religiosity, as it was among Christians. Moral transgressions were not typically punished by supernatural beings, they believed, nor would the Great Spirit reward them for good, moral behavior. "Admonitions are apt to be justified not by reference to what the supernatural will do or think, but by reference to what people will say," Tooker wrote. "The most explicit statements of Indian moral standards are to be found in the admonition of the people to one another, particularly parents to children." Handsome Lake's teachings, on the other hand, mobilized divine sanctions against certain behaviors formerly policed by mortals—worldly Seneca women and men, parents and families, clans and communities. And the prophet urged his followers to confess, repent, and avoid sin—an admonition more common among evangelical Christians than among traditional Senecas. Extraordinary circumstances required extraordinary responses. The anthropologist Anthony F. C. Wallace, for example, has described the late eighteenth-century Seneca reservations as "slums in the wilderness" and concluded that they were "not healthy communities by either white or Indian standards," with deteriorating material welfare and morale, with rampant drunkenness, violence (including the covert violence of witchcraft), and unstable households. In such an environment, confession and repression—not indulgence—of illicit or antisocial desires (as defined by the prophet) promoted health and order. Though some resisted Handsome Lake, many Senecas recognized their unprecedented predicament and abided by the new moral strictures. This code was now enforced, not merely by traditional community means (ridicule, gossip, shunning), but also by a new divine sanction.[46]

Temperance (the attempt to banish alcohol) played a crucial role in Handsome Lake's program of moral reform. This too was hardly novel, among the Senecas or throughout the early American republic. Seneca and other Iroquois leaders had complained about liquor and its effects, and had worked to keep it out of their villages for generations, though with mixed success. In the crisis of the late eighteenth century, demoralized Seneca men had more reason to indulge and increased access to drink. Alcoholic spirits often possessed them. The Code of Handsome Lake begins with "A Time of Trouble," when a party of Native men descends the Allegheny River and returns with a barrel of strong drink. They transform their village into a hell on earth—they are drunken, quarrelsome, and "beastlike," tearing the doors off their houses and rolling in their extinguished fireplaces. Women and children abandon the scene, and "dogs yelp and cry in all the houses for they are hungry." An old man becomes sick: "Some strong power holds him." He recognizes that "evil has arisen because of strong drink and he resolves to use it nevermore." The invalid, of course, is revealed to be Handsome Lake, who soon after his resolution to reform dies and is resurrected, newly empowered by his revelation.[47]

His story was to be exemplary. The prophet's battle against possession

Figure 7. *Drunken Men at Cornplanter Village*, by Jesse Cornplanter, n.d., ca. 1900–1909. Courtesy of the New York State Library, Manuscripts and Special Collections.

by demon rum or whiskey was both individual and national, fought personally and on behalf of his people. Handsome Lake's prophecy offered new
tools to combat this enemy—divine authority, based on revelation, not mere
reason. The Great Spirit told the prophet, according to Halliday Jackson's
account, that if the Indians "continued to get drunk, hurt themselves and
abuse others the[y] need not expect to come to that happy place." Like white
reformers, Handsome Lake associated abuse of alcohol with a host of other
social and economic problems—destruction of physical health, families, and
material subsistence. Among the Senecas, alcohol was also heavily implicated
in their loss of land. In the unsettled conditions of the early republic, white
Americans as well as Native people consumed liquor in surprising quantities.
By 1830, the yearly consumption of white Americans reached nearly four
gallons per capita. The Great Spirit had told Handsome Lake that "Whisky
. . . belonged to White people and was not made for Indians," but increasingly white reformers also rejected its place in their world. Nearly all revivalists condemned imbibing, and temperance societies grew, as new middle-
class values came to predominate in the antebellum United States. Handsome
Lake's prohibition might have been influenced by Christian moral preaching,
but they also drew on a long history of nativist rejection of alcohol, appealed
to Native experience and religion, and sought to solve a pressing indigenous
crisis. As Seneca chiefs explained in a petition to ban liquor on their reservations in this era: the "great Good Spirit will send all drunkards to everlasting
fire after death."[48]

The prophet's condemnation of gambling and dancing appeared to rehearse Christian revivalists' denunciations, and they seemed to forbid activities that Senecas and other Iroquois people had traditionally relished.
Handsome Lake's new proscriptions were designed to address not traditional
Indian games but a new, destructive form of gambling: card play. The visiting
Friends in 1806 who cautioned Senecas against "Cards Gameing and other
idle practices" simply reinforced the prophet's own warnings against fresh
forms of dissipation. Handsome Lake's rejection of "dancing" likewise represented an aversion to a novel behavior learned from white neighbors—one
that the prophet perceived, like Protestant missionaries, as lascivious and
corrosive to stable marriages and pure social life. Meanwhile, he endorsed
and encouraged customary religious and social dancing in conjunction with
traditional Seneca festivals. Handsome Lake's early visions occurred proximate to important religious events—the strawberry festival and the green
corn ceremony. The Great Spirit mandated renewed and continued celebra-

tion of these sacred festivals. "The Creator has sanctioned four dances for producing a joyful spirit and he has . . . ordered that on certain times and occasions there should be thanksgiving ceremonies." Quaker missionaries Henry Simmons and Joel Swayne saw these firsthand and reported much divinely approved "Singing Shouting & dancing" in the wake of the prophet's revelation. Their colleague Halliday Jackson had written earlier in his own prophetic idiom: "surely it availeth nothing your dancing and Musick and Burnt offerings—your appointed Feasts and your sacrifices." But Handsome Lake and his followers disagreed. They revived and maintained (and updated) an ancient Seneca religious cycle, marked by sacred singing, dancing, and divinely approved games.[49]

The prophet's hybrid teachings mixed old and new in the interest of tradition to promote social as well as religious revival. They sometimes mirrored Christian moral pronouncements, but in doing so they sought to eliminate some innovations (whiskey, cards, and fiddles) introduced by white neighbors and associated with destructive behavior. As the "old Chief" told the Quaker schoolteacher Henry Simmons, called to record the prophet's vision, "he liked some ways of the white people very well, and some ways of the Indians also." He was realistic about the difficulty of leading his people "out of all their own Customs," which he was reluctant to do. "As to the Worship Dance," he told Simmons, his people "intended to keep it up, as they . . . knew of no other way of Worshiping the great Spirit, [and] if they declined that they would have no manner of Worship at all." Handsome Lake's new methods and message—emphasizing divine sanctions, a potential apocalypse, and a new moral code—served a conservative purpose: to revive Seneca spiritual and material life and preserve Seneca identity and relative autonomy.[50]

The historian of New York's Burned-Over District, Whitney Cross, was more right than he knew when he wrote, "Upon this broad belt of land congregated a people extraordinarily given to unusual religious beliefs, peculiarly devoted to crusades aimed at the perfection of mankind and the attainment of millennial happiness. Few of the enthusiasms or eccentricities of this generation of Americans failed to find exponents here."[51] The Senecas were such a people. Their new religious beliefs, developed in the wake of Handsome Lake's 1799 revelations, might be considered "unusual" because they departed both from mainstream Protestant Christianity and from their own traditions in some important ways. But the prophecy of Handsome Lake was not so different from the sometimes eccentric revivalists and millennialists of the Second Great Awakening. Handsome Lake's emphasis on visions, otherworldly journeys, angelic visitations, temperance, patriarchy, even witchcraft, did not set him completely apart.

As a prophet, Handsome Lake was no odder than the remarkable Jemima Wilkinson, who now resided in her New Jerusalem, on Seneca Lake, sixty miles east of Allegany, close to the place where the Seneca prophet had been born in 1735. But unlike the Publick Universal Friend, Handsome Lake had not transcended sex. He remained a man, and his teachings promoted a new Seneca patriarchy.

Handsome Lake did not invent patriarchy, nor was he the first to introduce misogynous witch-hunting to Iroquoia. But the prophet encouraged these trends and gave them new momentum. We cannot now say whether the patriarchal dimensions of his program were unselfconsciously acquired from white brethren, or if they were deployed opportunistically to acquire white support and to constrain some of the forces of traditional power, especially represented by senior women. It is clear, however, that attacks on women would play a central role in the prophet's program, which transformed Iroquois demonology, demonized some Seneca women, and challenged women's social and religious authority.

CHAPTER 3

Patriarchy and the Witch-Hunting of Handsome Lake

> Those persons accused of Witchcraft should be threatened with
> Death, in case they persisted in bewitching the People.
> —Seneca Council at Buffalo Creek (1801)

> Some extraordinary ideas respecting witchcraft had prevailed among
> the natives for some time, which was principally insinuated among
> them by an infirm old man named Cannedin [that is, Ganiodaio,
> Handsome Lake], a half brother to Cornplanter.
> —Quaker missionary Halliday Jackson (1830)

> A belief in witches is to this day, and always has been, one of the
> most deeply-seated notions in the mind of the Iroquois.
> —Lewis Henry Morgan, *The League of the Ho-de-no-sau-nee, or
> Iroquois* (1851)

THE NOVELTIES OF Seneca witchcraft were largely invisible to white observers. They paid little heed when witchcraft accusations flew about the Genesee River frontier of Mary Jemison following the American Revolution, or even when Cornplanter ordered the execution of a witch in the summer of 1799. But by the time that Tommy Jemmy slew Kauquatau in 1821, the white public noticed. It was appalled. A Buffalo newspaper reporting the case offered a simple, unambiguous headline: "Murder." Another Buffalo newspaper, the *Erie Gazette*, later commented on the affair with the sarcastic banner "Indian Justice." The article mocked Seneca belief as absurd and reported that the Seneca defense elicited ridicule within the white courtroom. White readers throughout the early republic followed the developing story in western New York, as newspapers widely reprinted accounts. They learned that witchcraft was "a practice by no means uncommon, even among the Indians residing in the neighborhood of white settlements." The *Niagara Journal* noted with a bit of exasperation, "The superstitious belief in sorcery" remained "common to all savages." Some "deluded wretches" even confessed to the crime. Credence in witchcraft was so deep-seated among Indians "that no argument or reasoning seems sufficient to eradicate it." "Efforts to prevent it have been ineffectual." But now, finally, "civil authorities have interposed for the punishment of the offender."[1]

Lost in this self-satisfied newspaper discourse—celebrating American progress by emphasizing Indian barbarism—was any sense that Seneca witchcraft itself might be new. Belief in witchcraft and pursuit of "witches" predated the era of Handsome Lake, of course. But in his lifetime, the Seneca understanding of who was most likely to practice this dark art had changed—increasingly the "witch" appeared in the shape of a woman. The troubled post-Revolutionary years were marked by an outbreak of Seneca witch-hunting that particularly targeted women. White observers did not seem to notice. Though belief in witchcraft lingered generally in the early republic, as we have seen, many enlightened Americans considered such credence superstition and wished to ignore their own society's witch troubles in the not-so-distant past. Meanwhile, Red Jacket's citation of Salem during Tommy Jemmy's trial linked Seneca fathers with Puritan forefathers. The awkward reference was discomfiting, but the entire affair confirmed white notions about the backwardness of Indians and obscured the innovations of Handsome Lake and his followers.[2]

Witchcraft belief and prosecution came to be an embarrassment among both the Senecas and the white citizens of the United States, though for different reasons. For Senecas, witchery erupted during times of turmoil, when they suffered unusual and inexplicable calamity, and when they were divided. Material stress experienced without obvious causes or cures might increase suspicions that it stemmed from internal, covert sources. Tension over how to respond, in turn, could aggravate distrust and breed recrimination. The Senecas' greatest fear might have been fear of witches itself. Since the distant time of their mythic Peacemaker, unity and internal peace had been essential to Iroquois success. Now, in the early nineteenth century, the Senecas faced new chaos and disarray—perilous at a moment that demanded a united front to contest unprecedented encroachment. Disparagement by the white public was hardly the worst danger that Senecas would confront, though it was important to retain the goodwill of their Quaker advocates. The witch-hunting crisis that emerged with the rise of Handsome Lake would ultimately require an indigenous Seneca response. The resolution, per-haps surprisingly, would not be an abandonment of belief in witchcraft itself but, rather, the achievement of greater cultural confidence and calm, which made the eruption of a major "witch" outbreak unlikely.

Witchcraft proved embarrassing for white Americans as well because, while it lingered, it challenged the new country's progressive self-image. Not merely Indians—easily portrayed as backward—but numerous white citizens continued to believe. Since the late seventeenth century, particularly in the wake of the crisis at Salem, Massachusetts, in 1692, witchcraft belief had come under increasing attack. In the early eighteenth century, Quakers officially condemned the dark art and its trappings—sorcery, occultism, and astrology. Academic debates either rejected witchcraft completely or consigned the phe-nomenon to biblical times. Yet belief in the active agency of the devil and his minions had yet to be discarded by common folk throughout the early repub-lic, leaving behind a rich folklore of witches and demons that survived be-cause it was so integrated into everyday life. Thus Red Jacket's defense of Tommy Jemmy, which invoked the Salem debacle, stung. And Red Jacket knew it.[3]

Though the specter of witchcraft loomed in the Tommy Jemmy affair, for the Senecas the "crisis" in 1821 was actually less about witch-hunting—a symptom and a cause of social dislocation and internal division—than it was about the new attack on Seneca sovereignty—represented by New York's arrest of Tommy Jemmy and its subsequent judicial, executive, and legislative initiatives. The witch-hunting made prominent and scandalous in 1821 was a transformed version of earlier Iroquois practice. It could still be destructive, and it was certainly tragic for the victim Kauquatau. Yet in 1821 it became the occasion not for social breakdown but for a unified defense of Seneca cultural integrity and sovereignty, set within the ambiguous political land-scape of western New York and United States federalism. This successful defense was all the more surprising and significant, given the embarrassing nature of the crime—a "murder" by a self-confessed witch-hunter. Red Jacket's reference to Salem was a red herring, but it worked. One of the most potent spells cast by the Tommy Jemmy affair was how its fixation on witch-craft—an emblem of barbaric tradition—could obscure how much had changed in the Senecas' world in the wake of Handsome Lake.

Earlier in the century, witch-hunting *had* played a central role in an internal crisis among the Senecas—as a by-product of the tumultuous proph-ecies and programs of Handsome Lake. In the immediate aftermath of his revelations, the prophet had become obsessed with the dangers posed by witches, and he embarked on a campaign to purge those who menaced the Senecas through the dark arts. How Handsome Lake perceived that threat—and where he located it—stemmed in part from his understanding of how Seneca gender organization should be realigned. His witch-hunting was as new as his *Gaiwiio*—that is, it blended innovation with tradition. To distin-guish the new from the old—and to understand why such distinctions came to matter—requires some attention to the patriarchal revisions Handsome Lake prescribed for Seneca life, as well as a brief look at Seneca witchcraft in Iroquois historical and cultural perspective. Why, we might wonder, did Sen-eca witches increasingly appear in the shapes of women?

The Gender Trouble of Handsome Lake

Handsome Lake's teachings were most radical in their attempt to transform the relationships of mothers and daughters, and wives and husbands, and to erect nuclear families among the Senecas. His revelations reshaped Iroquois gender arrangements, particularly as they attempted to remake Seneca fami-lies into patriarchal units, and as they reimagined—feminized—Seneca de-monology. The evils most reviled by the prophet—and most brutally punished in the Seneca netherworld he visited—were female transgressions, revised and elaborated in the emerging *Gaiwiio*. The specter of whiskey af-flicted men and women alike, but witchcraft (increasingly feminized), use of charms, and abortion were *women's* offenses. Such female personification in Handsome Lake's grim visions heaped inordinate blame on women for the Senecas' fate, and the prophet's witch hunts seemed to focus Seneca fear on an internal and female enemy. Handsome Lake's message functioned both to elevate the social position of middle-aged men—patriarchs—and to allocate the cost of revitalization largely to women.[4]

Witch-hunting most dramatically displayed the prophet's antipathy toward unreformed Seneca womanhood and its vested interests. Its intimidating force also helped to impose the more mundane prescriptions of Handsome Lake's social reforms, which constrained women and redefined their roles and spheres. Handsome Lake's cult of true Seneca womanhood idealized those women who embodied, in a particular, revised Seneca fashion, the cardinal virtues of piety, purity, submissiveness, and domesticity.[5]

Women (and men) were expected to show their piety to the Creator by faithfully performing his ceremonies and celebrating the important cycle of festivals, as mandated in the prophet's revelation.[6] Women's purity would be protected by avoiding drink, adultery, witchcraft or other forms of magic, and abortion. Whiskey, the prophet warned, led to all sorts of evil, especially witchcraft. But the prophet focused more mundanely on matters of sexual purity as well, in a way congruent with the morality and gender arrangements of the Senecas' missionary Friends and the emerging middle class of the early American republic. Informal divorce, which traditionally allowed Iroquois women great flexibility in ending relationships and initiating new ones, simply by excluding old or inviting new partners into their houses, was rejected and defined essentially as infidelity or adultery. A woman who took up with another man while her husband was away "makes great mischief . . . and does a great wrong before the Creator." And, as in white society, a double standard favoring husbands over wives seemed to emerge in the prophet's teachings. Such "infidelity" was to be tolerated and ignored by a woman similarly wronged by her spouse. The Code of Handsome Lake dictated that a woman should welcome her philandering husband home, treating him "cordially as if no trouble had occurred. Now we, the messengers, say that the woman is good in the eyes of her Creator and has a place reserved for her in the heaven-world." Knowing all that her husband had done, she was nonetheless "to be peaceful and remain silent."[7]

Of course Seneca men were not exempt from moral prescriptions, just as middle-class white reformers were hardly willing to condone moral transgressions among males. In the new order, men should not philander, and, guided by their Friends and their prophet, Handsome Lake's followers publicly expressed a wish to reform. In the words of the Seneca spokesman John Pierce, "we will try more and more to do better for we know we dont all do right about our Wives but we mean to try to do better." Even the chiefs were expected to conform, and a male fraternity would help to enforce this aspect of the new Seneca patriarchy: "if the Chiefs dont do right we will try to help them & if one falls another will help him up." The new ideal for Seneca marriage was male-centered and emphasized peace and perpetuity. Quakers told Seneca men (with Handsome Lake's blessing) "to live in peace and harmony with their wives & not to let trifling matters part them but consider them companions for life for it was pleasing to the Great Spirit for man and woman to live together in harmony." Such expectations or apparent constraints on men seem designed to ensure stable households. They controlled male behavior, but primarily as a means to cultivate patriarchy, for they shifted the predominant authority to maintain unions from women to men. Seneca men acquired new obligations to accompany their new power, but women's status and power diminished. As Handsome Lake's visions showed, women posed the greater threat to purity—to morality, order, and peace. They were alluring seductresses, aggressive lovers, and artificers of illicit love magic and witchcraft, which could waylay or manipulate vulnerable men.[8]

Purity among Seneca women, and in their households, took on an even more literal, concrete form in the era of Handsome Lake, especially with the advent of Quaker women among the missionaries at Tunesassa beginning in 1805. We do not know if the prophet linked cleanliness with godliness and moral purity, but the missionary Friends certainly did, encouraging, for example, the production of soap as part of women's and girls' new home manufacturing responsibilities. The Quaker visitor Halliday Jackson reported, following the arrival of female Friends, that Seneca women's "persons and apparel, as well as their houses, appeared in more neat and cleanly order. And as Friends approached Some of their habitations, a pleasing mark of neatness discovered itself among some of their women, who would immediately begin to sweep their houses, and appeared somewhat disconcerted, if Friends entered their doors before they got their apartments in good order."[9]

Seneca women were to learn and practice submissiveness within their households, which became increasingly limited, nuclear, and patriarchal under Handsome Lake's guidance. The prophet had been given this message: "Tell your people that the Creator has ordered regular marriage customs." But this "regular" label naturalized a new and improved form of matrimony. The Creator preferred that "the married should live together," that is, in their own separate house, not in a larger, traditional, matrilineal household, as "man and wife." Here the prophet endorsed a trend already in progress— toward smaller, more dispersed lodges containing fewer kinspeople, related to each other not merely through a mother's, but also through a father's, line. Handsome Lake seemed to encourage a further shift, toward full nuclear, patrilineal family residence. Striking more directly at maternal authority and control, the "good message" anticipated (or described) resentment by women against men who increasingly asserted their control over the family's children; it imagined (and warned against) "the woman [who] discovers that the man, her husband, loves his child and she is very jealous and spreads evil reports of him." Ironically, as white sentimental culture was transferring responsibility for children from fathers to mothers, the prophet's syncretic prescriptions seemed to promote an older form of white patriarchy.[10]

The *Gaiwiio's* teachings sawed at the bonds that joined daughters and mothers, formerly members of the same households, with the latter representing the strongest conservative force supporting matrilinity. Mothers were suspected of intervening in their daughters' lives "to prevent further suffering" through frequent childbirth and of encouraging daughters to induce abortions through malignant magic and charms. Allegedly jealous of their daughters' happiness under new patriarchal regimes, mothers supposedly offered their daughters evil advice to turn them against their husbands. "Says the old woman," according to the Code of Handsome Lake, "My daughter, your spirits are dull, you are not bright. When I was young I was not so agreeable. I was harsh with my husband." Transforming conventional female assertiveness into shrillness, and legitimate female authority into meddlesomeness, the prophet lamented "the tendency of old women to breed mischief. Such work must stop."[11]

Along with piety, purity, and submissiveness, the nature of domesticity was being renegotiated in Seneca society. Seneca women's place had always been simultaneously in the home and beyond it, as horticulturalists and gatherers, and as participants in community politics. Though Handsome Lake monopolized great amounts of power and sometimes used it to silence or defeat his political enemies locally, women remained active in public affairs, even if such activity was not always obvious to outsiders. The Quakers would initiate a program in female domestic manufacturing among the Senecas, for example, and the prophet would endorse it. But Handsome Lake permitted women and families a choice in the matter, and he never encouraged women to abandon their farming, a social and religious, not merely an economic, activity. The Seneca experiment would yield mixed results. The relative failure of missionary attempts to impose exclusively male agriculture, individual (male) ownership of land, and noncommunal work patterns stemmed from both male and female resistance. Women retained significant reserves of power, even if it was somewhat diminished, and they continued to be more than domestic beings.[12]

Women would not shrink in the face of the "civilization" efforts of Friends, other white missionaries, or the nativist reforms of Handsome Lake and his followers. Indeed some—like Gayantgogwus, the sister of both Cornplanter and Handsome Lake, for example—continued to exercise considerable power. Gayantgogwus was described by visiting Friends as "a principal woman" in 1806 and was present (as were other women) at the council held that year between the Friendly delegation and the Allegany Senecas. She felt empowered enough to seek a separate meeting with the visitors, where she countered the speech of a Seneca man delivered the previous day. Gayantgogwus was reputed to be a forceful character with real influence over her two brothers. Handsome Lake appointed Gayantgogwus and her husband to make official "medicine," based on the instructions of an angelic messenger encountered during one of his visions. As the experience of Gayantgogwus suggests, Seneca revitalization would be negotiated, indeed even feminized in its later codification.[13]

Was there a conscious misogyny in Handsome Lake's teachings, reforms, and witch hunts? We need not reach such a conclusion, even if the emerging code and the prophet's behavior displayed clear antipathy toward certain groups of women. By the time that Handsome Lake woke up to confront his people's crisis in 1799, the ideals and practices of patriarchy had been prescribed for Iroquois society for generations. Quaker missionaries were only the most recent advocates. Times had changed. Seneca dependency now rendered the Friends' message and program more attractive and necessary as a means of survival, at least to men like Handsome Lake. Whether consciously or without calculation, the prophet imbibed aspects of white patriarchy and reworked it to fit his purposes.

Anthony F. C. Wallace has argued that Handsome Lake's reforms were designed to address the corruption, factionalism, and breakdown of family and social life among the Senecas, particularly the cultural displacement of men, ill-adapted to a new world in which their roles as warriors, diplomats, and hunters were lost or greatly reduced.[14] New responsibilities could elevate men's morale, reduce their alleged idleness, redirect their energies away from vice, and allow them to promote Seneca survival. But others might question the cost to women's place and status and to Seneca social integrity. As a reformer, Handsome Lake no doubt anticipated, and indeed soon discovered, that his programs would be contested. Resistance might be expected from those who possessed the most authority within Seneca society. Women, as owners of land and its produce, as leaders of lineages, households, and clans, and as significant if silent partners in political deliberations, were thus critical to the prophet's plans for revitalization. Yet women seemed to have the most to lose in Handsome Lake's new world, and they could represent the most serious obstacles to reform and to the prophet's authority.

Women thus made likely targets, not because they were women, but because they occupied a critical center of power within Seneca society that potentially stood athwart Handsome Lake's program. And as vital members of rival lineages and communities, women were implicated in the factionalism and power struggles that coincided with the rise of Handsome Lake and his hybrid solutions to Seneca demoralization and dependency. The complexity of this internal Seneca contest for power, reform, and survival suggests the embedded nature of gender as a vector of identity and interest, for powerful women were simultaneously women, members of families and clans, and residents of particular towns and villages. The Senecas lived in a complicated social world, and they faced real distress and confusion. The prophet's message brought empowerment and hope, but it also inspired opposition. In the early stages of his prophetic career, Handsome Lake often saw that opposition as covert and diabolical—the work of witchcraft. In defense of his prophecy, therefore, he went on the offensive against witches, whom he largely identified as women.[15]

Iroquois Witchcraft

Witches inspired near universal fear among the Senecas and other Iroquoians, and those suspected of such maleficence were hated and avoided. According to the seventeenth-century Jesuit missionary and ethnographer Father Joseph-François Lafitau, who lived among the Iroquois early in the eighteenth century, "the men and women who cast spells [sorcerers] are regarded . . . as *agotkon* or spirits because of the traffic which people think that they have with the spirits or tutelary geniuses. . . . [T]hose who cast spells have no other aim than to harm and work harm." These "evil ones" are "the authors of their curses and witchcraft." *Agotkon, utgon,* or *otkon,* for the Iroquois, was the evil force that witches personified, as they mobilized *orenda,* or power, for evil rather than benevolent purposes to injure others, even their own kin. Even Lafitau, who decried Native shamans as *jongleurs* ("jugglers"), tricksters, and charlatans, nonetheless distinguished their efforts from those of witches, who inspired considerable antipathy among the Iroquois.[16]

Witches' afflictions threatened the physical, mental, and social health of individuals and entire communities. Iroquois men and women struggled to discern whether the suffering that periodically beset them was the result of natural processes or sinister magic. When natural remedies failed to produce results, and when "dream-guessing" rituals failed to have their therapeutic effect, it became clear that witchcraft lurked nearby. In a society based on consensus and the avoidance of outward expressions of conflict, Iroquois men and women repressed their aggression, but it could simmer and bubble below the surface, searching for social and psychological fissures from which it might spew forth. Witchcraft offered a wicked person the covert means to assault antagonists within Iroquois communities, to indulge hatred, rivalry, and jealousy in a secret way. Behind affectations of serenity or stoicism could lie intense feelings and emotions; insulted or disgruntled persons could silently cultivate grudges for years and might be driven, ultimately, to seek the help of witches to punish their enemies.[17]

Fear of witches certainly encouraged circumspection and repression of aggressive acts among the Iroquois; but it also bred endemic suspicion. The Jesuit missionary Francesco Gioseppe Bressani reported in the mid-seventeenth century, "The confidence of the Savages in the multiplicity of spells and witchcraft went so far, that upon mere suspicion they often killed and burned even their fellow-countrymen, without any other accuser or judge than a dying man, who said that he had been bewitched by such a one, who was killing him." Such was the danger of witchcraft that the Iroquois, like the Puritans of seventeenth-century New England, could "not suffer a witch to live." They sanctioned the execution of witches, as quickly as the act could be carried out, and they exempted witch-killing from the rules of kin-based revenge and atonement.[18]

Witchcraft was a domestic problem. A witch discovered in one's village, even with one's own lineage or clan, was more dangerous than a witch operating from afar. He or she could tear the heart out of a family and community. "Witches," the nineteenth-century Seneca leader Ely S. Parker wrote, "are leagued with the ruling Evil Spirit." Parker had been the chief informant for Lewis H. Morgan, the pioneer American ethnologist who published *The League of the Ho-de-no-sau-nee, or Iroquois* in 1851. Parker served as an adjutant to Ulysses S. Grant during the Civil War, rising to the rank of general, and he later became the first Native director of the Bureau of Indian Affairs. Much had changed in New York, in the United States, and on Seneca reservations by 1890 when he wrote, but Parker's discussion of witchcraft in his ethnographic notes was not merely historical; he saw continued belief in witchcraft all around him. Witches "banded together wholly and solely for evil purposes," performing their malignant magic "under the cover of darkness" or when hidden in "the heart of some dense woods or boggy swamp." They struck close to home: "No one could join this wicked organization, unless they consented to torture as their victim one of their nearest and dearest blood relative or a friend whom they most loved," he wrote. "To be as a witch, was death." The danger of witchcraft was thus magnified by its subversive secrecy and proximity; and the horror of witch-hunting was its inward focus—its self-destructiveness—making the cure as devastating as the diabolical disease.[19]

Faith in witchcraft and diabolical sorcery was continuous through Seneca cultural history, but such belief and practice were inflected by gender and changing circumstances. Ethnographic data gathered in the nineteenth and twentieth centuries suggests that frustrated Iroquois men, in the face of deteriorating conditions, sometimes sought supernatural aid in hunting, fishing, or trading activities. The encroachment of white settlers, and a corresponding decline in game and fish resources, burdened these male enterprises. Meanwhile, as trade assumed greater importance, much depended on the uncertain outcome of mysterious, invisible market forces. To prevent or counteract bad luck, men were tempted to employ the services of sorcerers or witches. Some procured magical charms—considered living, nonhuman persons of great power—which required careful handling. Those who failed to propitiate them, by feeding, talking, singing, or listening to them, could endanger themselves and their families, as dishonored charms could "turn on" and "eat" their holders.[20]

Women (and sometimes men) resorted to witchcraft as well as legitimate magic in the interest of love, which could entice them to cross the line separating the benign from the malignant. The place of that line seems to have shifted with Handsome Lake. The prophet's revelation, as we have seen, prohibited compelling charms (*Gawenodus-ha*), sometimes administered in the form of a "witch powder" that could drive men insane. A certain rivalry, sometimes even hostility, lay embedded in Iroquois matrilineal social organization, particularly between older and younger men (uncles and nephews), and between married men and their mothers-in-law, who all lived in the same lodges. Domestic life can be rocky among any people, in any time and place, and the Senecas were no exception. By the nineteenth century, marriage and domestic residence patterns had shifted away from longhouses to smaller family dwellings, from older matrilineal, matrilocal models to more diverse households. In turn, different kinds of family tensions could appear. We see these expressed in Iroquois folklore collected in the late nineteenth and early twentieth centuries. These tales—of deception, seduction, possession, sorcery, and bewitchment—reflect older, gendered prescriptions and struggles, but they also reveal the newer strains, fears, and fantasies of "modernizing" Iroquois life. Wherever antagonisms surfaced in Seneca culture, witchcraft might be implicated. And as that culture evolved, so did Seneca witchcraft.[21]

Perhaps the most venerable witch among the Iroquois was Atotarho, the powerful male shaman and sorcerer of the Iroquois political creation myth. A hideous figure, twisted in mind and body, with writhing snakes for hair, Atotarho had nearly destroyed the culture hero Hiawatha with his nefarious magic before the great Iroquois Peacemaker redeemed and transformed him into a benevolent leader. Witchcraft also appears in the colonial records of New Netherland, as in the account of Harmen Meyndertsz van den Bogaert, who undertook a diplomatic and commercial mission among the Mohawks in the winter of 1634–35. Van den Bogaert observed the ostracism of Adriochten, "the most principal" chief of the Mohawks, forced to live outside his village following an outbreak of smallpox. The Mohawks attributed their affliction to their leader's witchcraft and memorialized his alleged misdeed in the name they gave him, Adriochten, meaning "he has caused others to die." Likewise, Iroquois communities repeatedly accused Jesuit missionaries of committing acts of malevolence, often attributing to them the contagions that swept through Iroquoia in the seventeenth century. These and other accounts in the documentary record of colonial America suggest that Iroquois men and women maintained a longstanding belief in witchcraft and that both sexes practiced and suffered the dark art.[22]

But the "traditional" witchcraft of the Iroquois in the seventeenth and early eighteenth centuries was remade into a hybrid practice during the crisis conditions that emerged in the time of Handsome Lake. The eruption of witchery and its feminization are understandable in this context. The Seneca landscape was roiled by violence and warfare; Seneca territory was besieged by settlers and speculators; their society and economy were unsettled; ardent spirits—liquor—possessed them; their religious beliefs were challenged; new social and religious ideas were spreading infectiously. Such times produced confusion, division, and unaccountable hurt. It was a recipe for trouble.

Domestic violence lay at the heart of the crisis—a crisis that Handsome

Figure 8. *The Pacification of Atotarho,* by Jesse Cornplanter, ca. 1906. The mythic sorcerer Atotarho is being pacified and transformed by Hiawatha, who combs the snakes from his hair. Courtesy of the New York State Library, Manuscripts and Special Collections.

Lake's revelations revealed as potentially apocalyptic. While fending off threats from abroad, Senecas apparently faced a graver menace, which resided within their households and communities. That danger was gendered. Drunkenness ruined men's bodies and destroyed their families. It turned them into madmen and made villages into hellish places. The prophet's teachings revealed the force behind all this as demonic. Just before Handsome Lake visited hell, he had a vision. Angelic visitors showed him a scene near Cornplanter's village, where numerous canoes and people gathered with "barrels of strong drink." Among them was a sinister man, hopping about, singing "the song of evil-minded spirit." The holy messengers identified the imp as "the punisher," whose "delight is to see people filled with strong drink." In later recitations of the Code of Handsome Lake, the Punisher took on some of the classic features of the devil found in Christian, European folklore—a distorted and changeable body, horns sometimes protruding from his forehead, a serpentine tail and cloven feet. His torture of a drinker, forced to imbibe molten liquid, became a warning and lesson to men, conveyed by the prophet to his people. Those who failed to reform would be destroyed in an apocalypse, alternately described as a flood or fire.[23]

At the base of Handsome Lake's prophecy and program was a gendered diagnosis of the Senecas' domestic crisis. Fermentation of alcoholic spirits symbolized the destruction of Seneca life. "Good food is turned into evil drink," the prophet warned. Lust for drink tempted men to abandon work or to trade goods (or even land) for poisonous liquor. Whiskey changed men into beasts, made them vulnerable to drowning or exposure, turned them to violence against their families, and sometimes transformed them into murderers.[24]

But if Seneca women suffered at the hands of drunken men, women themselves were among the most dangerous perpetrators of domestic violence. They were witches. The harm they inflicted was willful; it was not the result of weakness or temporary insanity, but of a sinister calculation. The aggression of witchcraft was secret and thus more difficult to notice, anticipate, and prevent. And it was directed at a woman's own kin, betraying the sacred bonds of family and community. According to the Seneca ethnologist Arthur C. Parker, "Witches do not always injure people who have offended them but more often their children or other near relatives. This is done that the person they desire to punish may see an innocent person suffer for their offenses and so be tortured the more."[25]

The offense of witchcraft was unique; so were the sanctions directed at witches. As we have seen, witchcraft was punishable by death. And the crime was so heinous that the execution of a witch was exempted from the normal rules of retributive justice—kinspeople could not legitimately seek revenge. Nor would they be motivated to avenge such killing because, as family members, they incurred the greatest danger. The violence imposed on the body of the witch marked her as beyond the pale, no longer part of a common humanity. In the domain of the Punisher, the drunkard was compelled to administer his own sanction; he drank the fiery liquor, screamed and collapsed, with "vapor steaming from his throat." The woman identified as a "witch"—more powerful and less complicit—was seized bodily by the Punisher and forced into a great cauldron of boiling liquid. She did not quickly succumb, according to the prophet's revelation, but struggled and fought the Punisher. Ultimately, the witch's body was not merely marked or punished but annihilated, her bones reduced to dust, that dust blown into oblivion. Such total obliteration radically purged the community of evil and prevented any return of the cancerous witchcraft. Drunks were reformed; witches were destroyed. And the Seneca domestic world would be restored.[26]

Almost exactly a year before Handsome Lake's first vision, and in an unrelated context, Thomas Jefferson wrote to John Taylor from Philadelphia, "A little patience, and we shall see the reign of witches pass over, their spells dissolve, and the people, recovering their true sight, restore their government to it's [*sic*] true principles." Jefferson here called for endurance, reason, and unity as he waited out the presidential term of John Adams. Handsome Lake might have had similar thoughts, given his own trouble, but he was more revolutionary and less patient. And he actually believed in witches. Handsome Lake sought to revive and transform the Senecas, unify them through his prophecy, and enhance their security. Unlike Jefferson, Handsome Lake fought fire with fire: he inaugurated a witch hunt.[27]

The Witch-Hunting of Handsome Lake

With the meteoric rise of Handsome Lake to prominence among the Allegany Senecas, witch-hunting flourished. As the Quaker missionary Halliday Jackson later wrote, the prophet, authorized by "frequent interviews" with "heavenly messengers," "succeeded in propagating a belief among the natives, that most of their bodily afflictions and disorders arose from witchcraft, and undertook to point out the individuals who had the power of inflicting these evils."[28]

Handsome Lake's prophetic career had begun in an atmosphere of dread and foreboding over witchery, which gripped Cornplanter's town in June 1799. A female witch had killed Cornplanter's daughter, many believed, and she now threatened a baby in Cornplanter's household; Cornplanter suspected an old woman with a reputation for poisoning the families of enemies, and he ordered three of his sons to kill her, which they accomplished—slashing her throat as she worked in her fields—on June 13. Such was the setting for Handsome Lake's first vision, which occurred just two days later. How heavily the matter weighed on the prophet's mind we cannot know. A council soon endorsed the execution, and even the Quaker missionary and schoolteacher Henry Simmons observed, for reasons unknown, that the suspect or victim was a "bad Woman." Handsome Lake's discourse with the fourth angel in August further legitimated the witch-slaying, and he offered new warnings when the messenger mentioned two witches in the village, one "lately killed" but another "still liveing."[29] The accounts of Simmons, Jackson, and other Friends offer few specifics, but Seneca legend recounts that Handsome Lake about this time accused an old reclusive woman of afflicting another woman with illness. The prophet and some followers confronted the woman, identified her as witch by a mark on her hand, and sentenced her to death. After a fierce struggle, she was killed.[30]

So began Handsome Lake's campaign for reform and against "witches" who threatened his community and his new way. The prophet's purges during these dark days are inscribed in the surviving documentary record elliptically, appearing in the writings of Quakers and other literate white settlers and officials when they happened to be around, or when accusations caused especially prominent crises; they emerge more clearly in the oral traditions and the religious narratives and codes that linked later Seneca believers to the early nineteenth-century time of turmoil.[31]

The naturalized Seneca woman Mary Jemison claimed in her memoir that "witches" "had been executed in almost every year since she has lived on the Genesee"—that is, from the late 1750s. She surely exaggerated when she said, "from such trifling causes thousands have lost their lives." But if the number of executions is overstated, her remark does suggest that witchery swelled in the tumult of imperial wars, the Revolution, and its aftermath in Iroquoia. Those challenging community orthodoxy in these uncertain times ran the greatest risk of witchcraft accusation, both in the Seneca Genesee

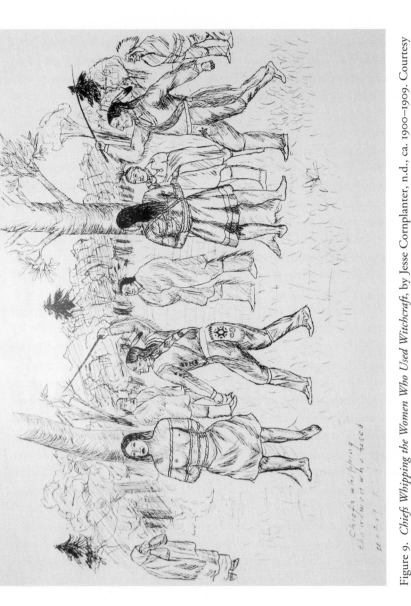

Figure 9. *Chiefs Whipping the Women Who Used Witchcraft*, by Jesse Cornplanter, n.d., ca. 1900–1909. Courtesy of the New York State Library, Manuscripts and Special Collections.

communities and those farther west at Allegany, Cattaraugus, Tonawanda, and Buffalo Creek. And increasingly in the late eighteenth and early nineteenth centuries, in the fragmentary records that remain, women predominated among those suspected and accused of witchcraft. Jemison herself faced an allegation. Among the cases her memoirs recount is the execution of an Indian "squaw" suspected of the dark art. Not only was she observed with "fire in her mouth," but she was rendered suspect as a cousin of the chief Big Tree, a leader publicly dishonored for his pro-American position in the Revolution and for his later complicity in Seneca land concessions, which seemed to profit him personally.[32]

Among the most prominent and best documented events in Handsome Lake's witch-hunting campaign was the crisis initiated by witchcraft accusations in 1801. It threatened to embroil the Senecas and local Munsee Delawares, as well as their white neighbors, in war. When the prophet's niece and Cornplanter's daughter, Jiiwi, took ill and failed to respond to treatment, Handsome Lake focused his suspicions on "sundry old women & men of the Delaware Nation" living near Cattaraugus. He included among his suspects a Munsee woman, allegedly jealous of Jiiwi for having conceived a child with Silver Heels, a young Seneca chief residing at the Delaware Indian settlement. As tensions and fears escalated, a council at Buffalo Creek supported Handsome Lake's diagnosis. It ruled "that those persons accused of Witchcraft should be threatened with Death, in case they persisted in bewitching the People." A Native Munsee doctor attempted to aid in the young woman's cure, and Seneca authorities seized a Munsee chief as a hostage. The woman's death would likely trigger the execution of the chief and other hostages, and this violence, it was feared, would escalate the conflict, with disastrous results. Seeking vengeance, the Delawares' kinspeople living to the west would likely intervene. Meanwhile, local white settlers, Quaker missionaries, the Indian Committee in Philadelphia, the governor of Pennsylvania, and the United States War Department all reluctantly became involved. The Quakers attempted to assure the Senecas at Allegany that the Munsees "have no such power [of witchcraft], and we are sure it is the bad Spirit which puts such suspicions about Witchcraft into your Hearts, in order to make discord and raise War among you." Fortunately, the afflicted young woman recovered, the "witches" apparently desisted, and major crisis was averted.[33]

According to Quaker reports, among the Munsees living at Cattaraugus "very little if any improvement either in sobriety or industry is discoverable." It may be that the apparent resistance of the Munsee Delaware community to embrace reform, whether nativist or Quaker, helped fuel the prophet's suspicions, especially given Handsome Lake's equation of whiskey and witchcraft. Moreover, Senecas had long suspected the Delawares generally, and Munsees in particular, of an attachment to witchcraft and sorcery. Intriguing as well, though frankly speculative, is the possibility that these Munsee Delawares were more readily seen as "witches" because they had been represented collectively within the Iroquois League as "women" since the mid-eighteenth century. As Seneca gender order changed in the early republic, one might wonder, did the meanings or implications of gendered metaphors and symbolic language shift as well? The "feminized" Delawares' vulnerability to suspicion, however, began in the eighteenth century, when Iroquois gender arrangements were more stable, secure, and favorable to women.[34]

Earlier in the colonial period, the Six Nations and Delawares had settled their long-standing differences and agreed to a peaceful association in which the Delawares would be "the woman"—that is, as "women," Delawares received Iroquois protection and would abandon independent warfare, focusing instead on the cultivation of peace (especially women's responsibility among the Iroquois). Though the arrangement was often misunderstood by colonial officials, operating in a differently gendered social world, the Iroquois and other Native people did not necessarily consider the symbolic relationship demeaning to the Delawares. At least not in the beginning. But the Delawares came to see things differently, as it became increasingly clear that the Six Nations exploited the relationship in their diplomacy with Pennsylvania and other colonial powers. The Delawares were infuriated when the Six Nations failed to include them or consider their interests in negotiations, and they were outraged when Six Nations diplomats conveyed land they did not own—Delaware land—to Pennsylvania authorities without consultation or consent. In the context of the imperial war and Native rebellions of the 1750s, the Iroquois-Delaware relationship broke down, and the Indian-white frontiers of Pennsylvania and New York became enflamed. Like white settlers and authorities, the Six Nations blamed the Delawares. They found it politically useful, as historian Jane Merritt has written, "to manipulate an image of Delaware enemies to degrade and punish subordinates who refused to be submissive and to maintain their own status as political partners to Pennsylvania." They implied that Delawares were supernaturally dangerous.[35]

Iroquois accusations were sincere—they believed in the lurking dangers of witchcraft—but they were also useful in controlling their defiant allies. Here the Iroquois built on a tradition of suspicion and demonization of

Delawares. In the winter of 1748, Iroquois residents of the mixed, multitribe town of Shamokin had accused a Delaware man of sorcery, beat him to death, and dismembered his body. In 1756, a Seneca diplomat complained to the Pennsylvania governor at Easton, Pennsylvania, that a Delaware "had bewitched him and that he should soon dye." The following day he suffered "a violent Pleurisy and [was] thought to be in great danger." He survived, but such events cultivated fear and distrust and prepared the ground for the crisis of 1801. Witchcraft accusations signaled a violent breach of family ties and obligations—actually, in the fragile communal order of Shamokin, or, metaphorically, in the breakdown of the Six Nations–Delaware alliance based on a family model. Witchcraft represented the violent subversion of "family."[36]

By 1810, the Munsee community resolved to leave and move west. Seneca tradition relates, however, that the great witch hunt continued. Witch fear, and no doubt fear of witch-hunters, persisted. Coupling the possibility of forgiveness, redemption, and reintegration into the community with the terrors of the witch hunt made Handsome Lake's campaign all the more effective. The Code of Handsome Lake institutionalized confession and repentance, exemplified in a parable of a formerly wicked Seneca woman who was admitted to the narrow road to heaven because she "has done her whole duty. She has truly repented." Such a mechanism for rehabilitation might have encouraged women terrified of being accused to own malefic acts or intentions falsely, as a means of preserving their lives. Confession—whether false or sincere—would have reduced the number of executions for witchcraft in Seneca communities, but it may well have had the additional effect of confirming the connection between womanhood and witchery.[37]

Seneca oral tradition preserved in the Code of Handsome Lake suggests that women predominated among the suspected and accused. The code relates, for example, an incident at Cold Spring in which a man, unsympathetic to the prophet, acted rudely by standing at the door during a council (rather than sitting) and signaling his disgust at Handsome Lake's speech by *dainidadi*—that is, through an audible expression of flatulence. The man failed to return to his dwelling that evening and was found days later sitting on a nest of branches in a swamp across the river devouring snakes. His earlier indiscretion, and his bizarre behavior, was understood to be the result of insanity, an insanity induced by the witchcraft of a woman and her daughter at Cold Spring.[38]

These and other cases display the feminization of Seneca witchcraft, an innovation of Handsome Lake and, more broadly, of his times. Generalizing from the case of these two witches at Cold Spring, who were publicly and fatally whipped, Handsome Lake himself is said to have remarked, "It was natural that foolish women should have done what these did." And it was unfortunate and dangerous that such women could covertly manipulate men, causing them to mock and resist the prophet's *Gaiwiio*. Handsome Lake's vision of the apocalypse, should the Senecas fail to redeem themselves, associated evil with women's practice of witchcraft, predicting that "a time will come when a woman will be seen performing her witch spells in the daylight. Then will you know that the end is near. She will run through the neighborhood boasting how many she has slain by her sorcery."[39]

By the time that the Seneca ethnologist Arthur C. Parker published his edition of "The Code of Handsome Lake, the Seneca Prophet" (1913), his accompanying, clarifying footnotes had effortlessly universalized the evil practice as feminine. Though employing masculine pronouns generally to refer to both males and females, Parker adopted greater gender precision when he discussed witchcraft: "A witch can work fearlessly and successfully as long as *she* remains unknown to the victim and under some circumstances even when known. A 'witched' person is often able to see as in a vision the witch wherever *she* goes and is likewise able to tell when *she* is about to approach the house." Parker's language, ethnographic study, and linguistic analysis suggest the feminization of Seneca witchcraft. Men as well as women could practice sorcery, but witchcraft had become firmly associated with women. *Witch* had become an exclusively feminine noun. "The modern Iroquois call all sorcerers and conjurers, regardless of sex, 'witches,'" he wrote. "They never use the masculine form." Witchcraft was naturalized as a particularly female dark art, and shifts in language and usage mystified earlier understandings of Seneca witchery as a gender-neutral practice. In the era of Handsome Lake, witchcraft became more like the sort on trial at Salem, Massachusetts, in 1692 and less like the witchcraft that troubled Senecas in their own distant past.[40]

The less frequent witchcraft accusation leveled against a man—as against the famous Red Jacket himself, who was Handsome Lake's Seneca rival (and nephew) at Buffalo Creek—did not necessarily contradict the general tendency toward female witchery. But it does prod us to see Seneca witch-hunting as a complex phenomenon, gendered but also affected by matters of kinship, localism, and political rivalry. If the cast of characters is often murky in nineteenth-century Seneca witch-hunting dramas, here the opposing actors were clear. Red Jacket was often described as the most prominent "conservative" leader among the early nineteenth-century Senecas, in contrast to Cornplanter, Handsome Lake's half brother, representative of Seneca "progressivism." Such labels can be more misleading than illuminating, given the volatile meanings of "conservative" and "progressive," the contest to define what was "traditional," and the ironies inherent in labeling the Old Ways of Handsome Lake "progressive." Each of these leaders, in his own way, was both conservative and innovative. Nonetheless, Cornplanter and Handsome Lake, on the one hand, and Red Jacket, on the other, at times advocated different courses of accommodation to the Senecas' common predicament. As a rival source of power, Red Jacket was sometimes an adversary of Cornplanter and Handsome Lake (whom he characterized as Cornplanter's pawn), and he could be an obstacle to the prophet's reforms. Red Jacket's oppositional position courted the prophet's ire, and in 1801 it allegedly occasioned a witchcraft accusation.[41]

The precipitating cause of their clash seems to have been disagreement over the sale of land—the so-called Black Rock corridor that ran along the Niagara River—which arose during a contentious council at Buffalo Creek in June of 1801. Handsome Lake had placed himself staunchly against any additional land sales. He represented a strong base of opposition to this particular concession, including many who felt abused by the present situation in the area, where whites had erected a fort and maintained a road that intruded on Seneca fishing grounds. The prophet sanctified his opposition by claiming to be guided not merely by living followers but by a revelation from the four angels. Red Jacket, on the other hand, perhaps representing the council, favored selling the strip of land. In the following summer, New York State would purchase this one-mile-wide shoreline parcel, with Red Jacket's pragmatic cooperation. Red Jacket insisted on reserving the Niagara River islands, which white authorities also hoped to acquire, and he sought to guarantee the continued Indian use of the beach, gathering and fishing privileges, navigation of the river, toll-free passage on any bridges or turnpikes, and the right to operate a ferry. The wisdom of the transaction is open to debate, but Red Jacket's actions were hardly unconsidered or corrupt. For Handsome Lake, however, such behavior was unforgivable, both for its alienation of Seneca land and for its defiance of the prophet's wishes.[42]

Handsome Lake's code would later immortalize (and exaggerate) Red Jacket's alleged perfidy in section 95 of "The Great Message," which narrated

Figure 10. *The Trial of Red Jacket*, by John Mix Stanley, 1869. Courtesy of the Smithsonian American Art Museum, gift of George M. Stanley (grandson of the artist) and family and museum purchase. Red Jacket, standing, points toward Handsome Lake (leaning forward) and cornplanter (to his left).

the prophet's journey, guided by the four angels, through an otherworldly netherland:

> Then the messengers pointed out a certain spot and said, "Watch attentively," and beheld a man carrying loads of dirt and depositing them in a certain spot. He carried the earth in a wheelbarrow and his task is a hard one. Then he knew that the name of the man was Sagoyewat'ha [Red Jacket], a chief. . . .
>
> It is true that his work is laborious and this is for a punishment for he was the one who first gave his consent to the sale of Indian reservations. It is said that there is hardship for those who part with their lands for money or trade. So now you have seen the doom of those who repent not. Their eternity will be one of punishment.[43]

But before the sale was made, and before Handsome Lake's followers had transformed Red Jacket into a Seneca Sisyphus, in the midst of this controversy and a broader factional rivalry, the prophet accused Red Jacket of witchcraft. Or at least that was the claim De Witt Clinton made in an address to the New-York Historical Society in 1811. Clinton lionized Red Jacket but viewed Handsome Lake as an "impostor" and tool of Cornplanter. Most nefarious for Clinton was Handsome Lake's alleged manipulation of witchcraft accusations. "The Indians universally believe in witchcraft; the prophet inculcated this superstition, and proceeded, through the instrumentality of conjurers selected by himself, to designate the offenders, who were accordingly sentenced to death," Clinton wrote. "This was considered an artful expedient to render his enemies the objects of general abhorrence, if not the victims of an ignominious death." According to Clinton, such diabolical action culminated in Handsome Lake's public denouncement of Red Jacket for witchcraft at the Buffalo Creek council in 1801. Marshaling all of his considerable oratorical powers, Clinton claimed, Red Jacket succeeded in defending himself against the charge. "The iron brow of superstition relented under the magic of his eloquence; he declared the prophet an imposter and a cheat. He prevailed: the Indians divided, and a small majority appeared in his favor." Whether these dramatic events actually occurred is not clear. But such a denunciation and public confrontation are plausible, as are the larger division among Senecas, the escalation of witchcraft charges, and the lingering rivalry between Handsome Lake and Red Jacket. As a "Religious Intelligence" report noted in 1808, the prophet functioned "as the principal chief of the [Seneca] nation; but Red Jacket, a cunning and subtile chief at Buffaloe Creek, does not believe in him; but in his public transactions he pays him respect, as he is popular with the nation."[44]

Factionalism, localism, and political rivalry are crucial in explaining Handsome Lake's censure of, and ongoing contention with, Red Jacket, but the contest should be considered in a broader, gendered context. The Buffalo Creek chief and orator often acted as Seneca women's speaker, advocating women's interests, particularly their control and ownership of Seneca land. In this role, Red Jacket associated himself with other forces of opposition and may well have represented for Handsome Lake a feminized challenger. Red Jacket managed to clear his name, as we have seen; the overreaching Handsome Lake could not make the witchcraft charge stick. Perhaps the indictment (of a prominent Seneca man) lacked credibility in the increasingly patriarchal climate the prophet had helped to create.[45]

Though available sources hardly permit the sort of statistical analysis applied to seventeenth-century New England, it does seem that among the early nineteenth-century Senecas women were more often accused than men, that accusations against women were more likely to be believed, and that women "witches" were more likely to suffer execution. In a peculiarly circular manner, increasing implication of women as witches by Handsome Lake and others may have predisposed Senecas to believe charges against women and, in a related fashion, to reject more readily those leveled against men, especially men of prominence. Even if Handsome Lake's demonization of women in witch hunts had more to do with their power than their gender, matters of gender and power are not easily distinguished, and the practical consequences of the prophet's purges were significant—accusing women predominantly tended to suggest that women more than men performed witchcraft.[46]

Handsome Lake, who, some believe, died at the hands of a witch in 1815, persisted in his pursuit of "witches" throughout the rest of his days. All hostility or opposition to his prescriptions could be explained literally as malevolence. But he did not sustain the witch-hunting pace of his early prophetic years. And the promiscuity of his accusations clearly troubled other members of the Seneca communities, both Native and white. Though direct, detailed accounts of witch hunts in these years often elude us, the reaction of Quaker missionaries and Seneca chiefs in 1809 to such violence suggests their impact. In about 1808, a "witch" was killed in front of the Cold Spring longhouse, where Handsome Lake lived. A council between Seneca leaders and visiting delegates of the Friends' Indian Committee, who convened at least in part to deal with a witch-hunting crisis among the Allegany Senecas, suggests it was not an isolated incident. At the meeting, Cornplanter expressed his hope that "we shall be careful in the future how we take the lives of any for witchcraft without being sure that they are Guilty, and he thought it very difficult to prove it." In a follow-up letter the next year, the Quakers residing nearby at Tunesassa remarked with relief, "Since the subject of witchcraft was treated by the Committee who was here last fall, the Indians have concluded in council to take no more lives on that account." By then, Handsome Lake, having lost some of his influence, had removed to Tonawanda.[47]

But, ironically, while Quakers sought to persuade Senecas that witchcraft was mere superstition and delusion, their references to "Good" and "Bad Spirits" may well have confirmed Seneca beliefs in the reality of witches, even if particular accusations lacked merit. In advocating temperance, for example, a Friend in 1802 had written, "Cornplanter and his brother [that is, Handsome Lake] has [*sic*] endeavored to suppress the use of strong drink by propagating a belief amongst the Natives that whiskey is the Great Engine which the bad spirit uses to introduce Witchcraft and many other evils amongst the Indians. This *together with the advice of the Friends* has for the present had a favorable effect." The Quakers' use of language similar to Handsome Lake's in their own prescriptions, and their cooperation in Native reform, seemed to signal an endorsement of sorts. Friends told their Seneca brethren in 1815, for example, "Brothers, we are sensible that there are two spirits at work in the minds of men. The one produces in us a disposition of love and good will toward all men, and is a comforter for all good actions. The other excites the evil thoughts and desires, and influences to bad action. . . . So we believe it is in our power to resist the evil spirit and conquer all the evil propensities of our nature, by obeying the Good Spirit, and by daily watching, and prayer to him."[48]

Was not Handsome Lake trying to obey the Great Spirit and resist evil? Witches opposed him, embraced evil, and threatened his people. We must imagine how Senecas would have interpreted the unusual and disturbing warning Quakers had given their Allegany Seneca hosts in 1807: "such of your people who try to oppose this good work will feel trouble in their minds because, it is like injuring their own flesh, and, putting out the eyes of the Children. . . . If you turn your back on, and despise this good work, . . . you will displease the good spirit and certainly bring back trouble on your own minds." Such remarks would have been easy for Seneca listeners to assimilate into a worldview that stressed the potential in humans to deploy *orenda*, or power, for good or for evil, through righteous acts or through witchcraft. Would the consequence of resistance to the Quaker mission be covert aggression, the mobilization of destructive power through witchcraft? Such remarks could have confirmed a consensus of opinion among Quakers and Senecas regarding the existence and grave dangers of the dark arts.[49]

As in the Salem witchcraft crisis of 1692, when the trials at Allegany ended, fear of witchcraft did not. Massachusetts clerical leaders such as Increase Mather criticized the use of spectral evidence (convicting the accused based on the appearance of "specters," or ghosts, unseen by all but some accusers), but they did not challenge belief in the manipulations of Satan himself. Indeed, Puritan ministers momentarily inflated conceptions of Satan's power by arguing he could possess souls without the permission of his victims. Likewise, while the numbers accused and the procedures used to prosecute "witches" in early nineteenth-century Seneca communities drew criticism, the very existence of witches, and their malefic power, was not rejected.[50]

The Quakers' unintended encouragement of belief in evil spirits, even witches, was doubly ironic. Friends themselves had endured a history of persecution, having been banished, accused of witchcraft, and sometimes executed in seventeenth-century Massachusetts Bay for defying Puritan orthodoxy, and in Salem in 1692 Quakers had proven vulnerable and suffered indictment.[51] A collective memory of persecution might have weighed on the minds of the Philadelphia Friends who journeyed to Allegany and Cattaraugus in 1809. In the context of their carefully worded message to the Senecas, urging Senecas "to think very seriously indeed before you condemn and kill any for supposing them guilty of witchcraft," the Quaker delegates referred specifically to the Salem crisis: "above an hundred years since such a practice prevailed in our neighborhood among white people, and before it was put a stop to, some of those who had been Judges of others were themselves charged with the same offences and executed." How their Seneca interlocutors absorbed such information remains unclear, though in their selective adaptation Seneca leaders like Red Jacket (as we have seen in the Tommy Jemmy trial) apparently considered such a memory available for appropriation.[52]

Handsome Lake's followers, if not Handsome Lake himself, came to reject the execution of witches. Opposition to apparent excesses (especially when prominent men were accused) forced the prophet to moderate his indictments, and even to leave the Allegany settlement of Cold Spring for

Tonawanda. But outlawing witchcraft was not the same as denying its presence. Declaring the illegitimacy of witchery in fact was nothing new; it had never been socially sanctioned. And Handsome Lake's witch hunts themselves seemed to confirm that witchcraft—the evil, covert resistance to his nativist reform—remained a threat. In a self-fulfilling fashion, then, the prophet's assault on witchcraft itself helped to keep witchcraft alive.

After Handsome Lake's death, another incident involving witchcraft erupted at Allegany, which again prompted Quaker intervention. A delegation of Friends visiting from Philadelphia in October of 1817 was beckoned to Cold Spring, where they found the chiefs in council and in "great distress." A local man had just been buried, but in his lingering sickness he had claimed to be bewitched. Worse yet, he had "charged one of their Chiefs with having some agency in it," and the deceased man's brother now threatened to take revenge. According to the Quaker chronicle of these events, the Seneca chiefs "wish'd our interference." Obligingly, the Quakers assured them that the victim's death had not been the result of witchcraft and that "it is quite time you took measures to do away [with] such notions among your people." "Brothers—you must by all means prevent one killing another for such supposed, or even real injuries," they urged. Curiously, their remarks expressed more disdain for taking justice into one's own hands than for the delusion of witchcraft that threatened to call forth the vengeance of the bereaved. Again, the Quakers seemed to emphasize that the particular case lacked merit, not that the "supposed, or even real injuries" of witchcraft did not exist. The chiefs visited the accusing man and were able to restore him to reason, thus ending the crisis, to the great relief of the Seneca leaders. We can only speculate whether such community pressure would have been mobilized to dissuade the accuser if the object of his charges had been a woman. In these unsettled circumstances, it was not always certain if such charges would be read as the irrational expressions of feverish delirium and deep grief, or as the legitimate diagnosis of a witch's malignancy. In this case, perhaps, the perceived excesses of earlier witch hunts had produced a post-Salem-like recoil from the promiscuous accusation and prosecution of a "witch."[53]

Seneca women were not mere victims of Handsome Lake's reforms, any more than the Iroquois generally were, simply, passive victims of United States colonialism, Christianization, or the market revolution. The power of the prophet's message made it compelling, and the new religion's teachings offered a means of accommodating change while maintaining Iroquois ethnic identity and protecting some measure of Seneca autonomy. People and communities in stress often reinvent themselves in order to survive, but the new identities available to such groups are limited by imagination and constraining circumstances. Women as well as men somehow found in the new way of Handsome Lake a prospect they could imagine, and as they followed the prophet—either as devotees or, more distantly, as fellow travelers or reluctant political allies—they negotiated and renegotiated the terms of his charter and their own future.

Handsome Lake advocated collective ownership of agricultural production, supported Seneca traditions of reciprocity and sharing, and opposed simple integration into the new republic's commercial economy or a mechanical acceptance of Quaker economic programs. In addition, the prophet's religious reforms were as challenging to Christianity as they were to capitalism, as he vigorously promoted the revival of ancient ceremonies and distinguished the *Gaiwiio* from the Gospel. Handsome Lake's teachings sought to transform family structure and relationships, particularly between mothers and daughters and husbands and wives. Yet in other respects he promoted traditional Seneca roles for women—which could help conserve women's social and economic identity and power—and he found allies and partners among some powerful Seneca matrons. The world is a place of compromises, and an atmosphere of crisis and fear (and witchery) might have encouraged Senecas to support Handsome Lake, despite skepticism about some of his program. The prophet's *Gaiwiio* and a unified front could promote Seneca safety, social harmony, and economic competence.[54]

Seneca women in particular may have found their adjustments painful—the new Seneca "traditional" world strikes us, perhaps, as much harsher and less respectful of women than the older Seneca traditional world. But the evolving predicament of the Senecas inflicted pain on men as well as women. Ironically, as the new religion became the "Old Way of Handsome Lake," it was increasingly "feminized." Post-Revolutionary developments in the United States (destruction and alienation of Native hunting grounds, U.S. monopolization of military activity, and reduction of Native peoples to diplomatic insignificance) undermined traditional male activities—that is, hunting, warfare, and diplomacy. At the same time, despite Christianization and "civilization" programs, women's traditional activities among the Senecas—particularly farming—flourished. And as a result, the rituals associated with women's social and economic contributions persisted. In a sense, the patriarchal nature of Handsome Lake's Good Message might be read as a male attempt to restore a gender balance in Iroquois traditional life.[55]

When Handsome Lake died in 1815, he left no formal gospel. His influence continued but waxed and waned in the absence of the charismatic prophet himself. His nativism revived to combat new threats of dispossession and removal late in the decade, but his followers also feared that Senecas might lapse into the behaviors that had produced decline and social crisis. Significantly, the codification of Handsome Lake's *Gaiwiio* was initiated by women—faithkeepers at Tonawanda. Concerned about backsliding, they met, decided to enlist the Tonawanda chief Jimmy Johnson, who was Handsome Lake's grandson, and implored him to recall and revive the teachings of the prophet. After an initial reluctance, Johnson agreed. He summoned up his grandfather's revelations and lessons and preached them publicly. That successful recitation of the Good Message was repeated annually at Tonawanda. From there, it spread to other Iroquois communities and was ultimately recorded as the Code of Handsome Lake in the 1840s. Women such as those at Tonawanda worked with other believers—male and female—over generations to institutionalize the Longhouse religion. In the process, they created a faith that accorded women status and conserved women's religious roles.[56]

As the *Gaiwiio* matured, women occupied a prominent position in the Longhouse religion, as ritualists, as deaconlike "faithkeepers," and as "fortunetellers," interpreters of signs, diagnosticians, and prescribers of remedies. Seneca mothers remained primarily responsible for rearing children, in part because Seneca fathers continued to spend extended periods away from home, engaged in new economic activities—natural resource extraction, processing, and trade—congruent with older cultural patterns. Mothers thus assumed considerable responsibility for religious instruction and acquired significant roles within the new religion, even under diasporic conditions off of reservations. As a modern student of Iroquois culture has observed, "Especially in the cities women are the communicators and facilitators, and they allocate to themselves leadership roles. Men do not seem to object, perhaps because heeding a woman in the role of matron or faithkeeper has long been a cultural trait. Thus religion and social change is effected through many small increments by both women and men." The theology and practice of the *Gaiwiio* evolved into a lived religion that proved supportive and meaningful to women as well as men.[57]

If Senecas were unnerved by the witchcraft crisis of the early nineteenth century, and for a time reeled under the prophet's witch-hunting, they recovered their self-possession, codified and assimilated Handsome Lake's *Gaiwiio*,

WOMEN'S DANCE

Figure 11. *Women's Dance*, Jesse Cornplanter, n.d., ca. 1900–1909. Courtesy of the New York State Library, Manuscripts and Special Collections.

and blunted the misogynous effects of the prophet's reforms. The events surrounding the Tommy Jemmy trial of 1821 are significant for what they did not do—they did not represent or ignite a new, internally divisive, and destructive witch-hunting crisis. By then, Senecas had come a long way in reviving themselves, preserving their identity and culture, and forging tools to defend their sovereignty. Still, the Tommy Jemmy incident demonstrated that belief in witchcraft itself persisted, and witch trials—even executions— would continue.

In the 1930s, the young anthropologist William N. Fenton gained the trust of Seneca men and women at Allegany, while he researched his doctoral dissertation. He would continue to work with—and learn from—Iroquois people for the remainder of his distinguished career. In the summer of 1933, he first encountered an elderly man, Wood-eater, who became one of his chief informants. Wood-eater was the bane of the local white missionary because he was "among those who caused the most consternation in the work of Christian uplift." Wood-eater, seventy years old when Fenton met him, was a principal speaker for the Longhouse faith and a brave, hardworking man; he had been a seasonal farmhand, a railroad worker, a carpenter, a timber rafter, and once a talented runner, lacrosse player, and baseball player. But to the end, Fenton noted, Wood-eater disliked and feared those of another Longhouse faction. He wrote, "I have observed him taking a potion to ward away witchcraft, which he thought his rivals were attempting, before going up to the longhouse to speak." Even amid the greater safety and self-possession of Senecas in the twentieth century, the Seneca landscape remained a place possessed.[58]

A specter haunted western New York in the early nineteenth century—indeed, it continued to do so one hundred years later—and that specter was witchcraft. Witches remained a credible threat for many Seneca women and men. Witchery and witch-hunting expressed the tensions and conflicts over domesticity, gender, and power that beset the Senecas in their new—and renewing—world. The revival of Handsome Lake offered a nativist solution to the crisis Seneca people faced. It promised domestic reconstruction and peace, national unity and integrity, survival and a Seneca millennium. Among the chief sources of problems are solutions, however, and Handsome Lake's prophetic leadership was no exception. The prophet saw witch-hunting as a necessary response to degeneration and chaos, but his campaign exacerbated fear and dangerous division.[59] Senecas sought a native solution to this nativist problem. Sometimes to the frustration of Handsome Lake, they moderated their witch-hunting, constraining its reach and raising the threshold for accusation and conviction. Simultaneously, they defended their belief in witchcraft itself and their right to prosecute it.

As the Tommy Jemmy case showed dramatically in 1821, that Seneca defense became its best offense, despite white public outrage over Native "superstition" and violence, supposedly a relic of their unredeemed savagery. Senecas such as Red Jacket managed to exploit white American anticlericalism, denominational rivalry, continued white belief in supernaturalism, and perhaps the growing values of religious toleration and freedom to challenge condemnation of Seneca beliefs. And, as the Tommy Jemmy case also demonstrated, Senecas defended their witch-hunting on legal, jurisdictional grounds, turning their embarrassment of witches into a point of pride—a means to unify and promote Seneca self-determination and autonomy.[60]

Throughout our story, Quakers have been present—assisting, encouraging, sometimes contesting the Senecas as they remade themselves in the early nineteenth century. They were on hand in June 1799 when Handsome Lake died and was resurrected as a Seneca prophet. Their diligent efforts in documenting this and other events critical to Seneca history were incalculably important. And their Friendly work would continue among the Senecas for decades. They have until now lurked in the background, not because they were unimportant, but because the Senecas themselves were the primary architects and builders of their own revival and survival. But the Senecas' struggle occurred in association with a Quaker mission that fundamentally affected its nature and course. And the Senecas operated in a larger context of social, economic, and legal transformations they were forced to accommodate. Native people in the early American republic—as in other times and places—did not exist in isolation; even when self-possessed, Seneca lives and culture were contingent.

The solutions that Handsome Lake prescribed for his people were, by necessity, designed to solve problems that Seneca people did not necessarily create themselves, and they drew not only on Seneca tradition but on external sources—particularly the advice of Philadelphia Friends. We now turn to the Quakers, thickening our story's plot and shifting our perspective, to examine these Friends and their mission more systematically—to analyze the religious, social, and economic solutions they proposed and imposed to address the Senecas' post-Revolutionary predicament. The Quakers played a critical part in helping Senecas revive, restore their cultural integrity, defend their sovereignty, and preserve a portion of their ancestral lands. They assisted—

sometimes inadvertently, and sometimes in ways that complicated—the basic nationalist goals of Handsome Lake, Cornplanter, Red Jacket, and the Seneca people generally. Although their help would prove essential to Seneca survival, the Senecas found it imprudent to embrace Quaker prescriptions wholesale. The recommended solutions of the Friends, as we will see, were sometimes the cause of new Seneca problems.

PART III

Mastery

CHAPTER 4

Friendly Mission: The Holy Conversation
of Quakers and Senecas

> We desire not to fill your ears with words, but rather to recommend
> you to retire and gather your minds into Quiet and Settlement. . . .
> You will be in the way of receiving light knowledge and Counsel
> superior to any we can impart for there is a divine principal of light
> and grace in every heart.
>   —Quaker missionary Halliday Jackson to the Senecas (1806)

> We find that Friends are different from other people[;] they do not
> speak roughly to us, and what they say is like our friends and in-
> tended for our good.
>   —Cornplanter (1809)

IN THE SUMMER of 1798 Quaker missionaries first arrived among the Senecas. They looked forward, hopeful about the future, but that beginning had
a significant past. The Quakers knew that Senecas had been possessed by
unprecedented dangers in the post-Revolutionary years. And they were on
hand when Handsome Lake, through his prophecies and programs, developed a hybrid religious and social solution to Seneca perils. As Handsome
Lake's teachings took shape, Quaker missionaries offered their own assessment of the Senecas' travails, and they too prescribed solutions.

The Friends' and Handsome Lake's religious programs were clearly at odds. Yet, surprisingly, Handsome Lake's ministry did not threaten the Friends' mission, nor did the Quakers' holy undertaking fundamentally challenge the *Gaiwiio*. The presence of Quakers meant the relative absence of other, more meddlesome Christian missionaries. And the prophet proved able to cultivate his new way within a space inadvertently opened and defended by Quakers. None of this was a conscious strategy. But the Friends in turn benefited from Handsome Lake's measured support of their social program. Quakers were unusual missionaries. And their cooperative approach made for a strange, unplanned, but vital partnership with the Senecas, characterized by disagreement as well as agreement, but consistently supported by mutual respect and toleration.

In 1811, the Philadelphia magazine *Port Folio* would publish a diatribe it attributed to "the Prophet of Alleghany." Allegedly, he was addressing his people on the Genesee River in June 1802, seeking to counter the appeals of a "missionary" whose work represented the culmination of colonial ruin: He began with a catalog of indictments: "They have driven your fathers from their ancient inheritance—they have destroyed them with the sword and poisonous liquors—they have dug up their bones, and left them to bleach in the wind." Now, the Handsome Lake figure railed, missionaries aimed "at completing your wrongs, and insuring your destruction by cheating you into the belief of that divinity, whose very precepts they plead in justification of all the miseries they have heaped on your race."[1]

The Quakers were decidedly *not* the missionaries the Seneca prophet supposedly excoriated here. Handsome Lake saw them as partners, not opponents, a potential antidote to the poison of white encroachment. His chief disciple, Governor Blacksnake, would tell the Friends in 1806, "all the Indians and the white People know that the Great Spirit talks with our Prophet. . . . Your young men [resident missionaries] and us are like one[.]when we want anything done we consult them and they assist us, and our Prophet tells us what to do and so we get instruction from both." The Quakers, for their part, resisted any urge to dispute Handsome Lake's prophetic status publicly, and they were eager to advance their mission through collaboration and without aggressive proselytizing. They practiced restraint, refused to assert their doctrines, and counseled quiet reflection among the Senecas, as capable as any people to receive the Inner Light.[2]

The Friends' charity and forbearance would help enable Seneca revitalization in ways they could hardly imagine. They engaged the Senecas in a long-term conversation of words and deeds and aspired to transform them, but the Quakers' greatest contribution to Native survival might have been their willingness to take "no" for an answer.

Holy Inoculation: Quakers among the Senecas

As the evangelical fervor of the Second Great Awakening began to blaze though the Burned-Over District of New York and beyond, the arrival of the Society of Friends among the Senecas produced a firebreak of sorts. The Quakers were just as steadfast as other missionaries, and just as devoted to Native cultural and religious transformation. Like others, they sought a fundamental alteration of the Senecas through a program of "civilization" and Christianization. But the Friends' attitudes and methods varied considerably from those of other denominations. And the Quaker presence buffeted the Senecas from other diligent Protestant missionaries, limiting their exposure to the modest educational efforts of the Baptist teacher Jabez Backus Hyde at Buffalo Creek and to the sporadic appearance of itinerant preachers. In the summer of 1798, within this fertile space, the Senecas and Quakers tentatively began their collaboration.

The Friends pursued a course markedly different from the mission of other, occasional evangelists who passed through. Forgoing preaching, resident Quakers acted as friends and technical advisers. The Senecas at Allegany welcomed them and appeared open to their program of technological acculturation, which the Quakers saw simply as "civilization." Unlike other denominations pursuing an aggressively Christian assimilationist program, the Society of Friends could make a convincing case that it had no ulterior motives, would not proselytize or teach "peculiar doctrines," and did not seek economic gain, particularly through the alienation of Indian land. Their purpose, articulated generally through the newly established "Indian Committee" of the Philadelphia Yearly Meeting, was simply to introduce among the Indians "the most necessary arts of civil life" and "useful practices: to instruct the Indians in husbandry & the plain mechanical arts & manufactures directly connected with it."[3]

The Congregational minister Jacob Cram witnessed the Quaker operation at Allegany firsthand when he visited in September 1805. He was perturbed. "The Senecas call the Clergy Logeteshtosh, i.e. expounders of writings," he wrote. "The Quakers they call Deweista, i.e. people for peace; people who will not deceive or wrong them." For the Allegany Seneca leader

Cornplanter, that distinguished the Friends from other missionaries, whom he rejected along with their Good Book. According to Cram, "He [that is, Cornplanter] has observed that ministers of the gospel attend treaties when the Indians sell their lands. That they do not labour to prevent the sale of them." Cornplanter was particularly embittered by one such minister who "was the means of his being defrauded out of a reserve of twelve miles square, by giving him a paper, which was supposed to be a security for the land, but which proved to be of *no use*." If Cram was noncommittal on the matter of ministerial advocacy or complicity in fraud, he disapproved of the Friends' toleration of Native religious practice, such as the white dog ceremony, in which a dog was ritually killed and consumed. That traditional religious rite had been famously revived by Handsome Lake, not merely among the Senecas, but also among other Iroquois people, including the more heavily Christianized Oneidas. With a certain condescension Cram wrote, "The Quakers seemed to suppose there was no great hurt in these ancient religious usages of the Indians. That they were sincere in them, and went according to the light they had." Listening to the Quakers address the Senecas—urging them merely (and inadequately, in Cram's view) to attend to "the light within"—the Congregational minister waited in vain to hear words that "brought any thing of the gospel to view."[4]

All Christian missionaries sought to bring the Gospel to the Indians, and uniformly across denominations they believed such a mission to be inextricably linked with another, to "civilize" the Indian—the often benevolent but nonetheless ethnocentric project of transforming Native people into passable versions of themselves. For early national white Americans, civilization was the achievement they uniquely embodied, at least ideally. It entailed economic individualism—particularly grounded in an agricultural life of toil tied to the land—and the male political liberty that even modest economic success enabled. The "pursuit of happiness"—as an inalienable right inscribed in the Declaration of Independence—seemed to express this equation well. "Happiness" (economic competence) was a goal universally available if pursued diligently through individual initiative and hard work. At least, that was the promise, expressed in universal language but extended exclusively to white men. Virtue—not merely political but moral—in one's pursuit would promote success and suggest (if not guarantee) spiritual as well as earthly happiness. Civilization in this culturally and historically specific sense upheld a particular moral code and set of social customs, regulating everything from gender and sexuality, to marriage and family, to dress and adornment, to food and drink, to health and hygiene. In the early nineteenth century that code was being defined and refined by an emerging middle class, with its particular Christian sensibilities, in ways that would ultimately characterize Victorian America. And Indian missions could operate as laboratories for reformers cultivating these new Christian virtues.[5]

But if there was wide agreement among most non-Indians that Native people required both the Gospel and white Americans' peculiar cultural apparatus, approaches toward achieving such a goal varied and diverged among missionaries, despite the often-voiced notion that all Christians were engaged in a common evangelical and benevolent enterprise. If some Baptists and Methodists had faith in the miracle of the Word itself to transform Indians, Congregationalists, Presbyterians, and particularly Quakers generally believed "civilization" had to precede Christianity. As one Christian commentator put it, "the Gospel . . . requires an intellect above that of a savage to comprehend. Nor is it at all the dishonor of our holy faith that such men be taught a previous lesson, and first of all be instructed in the emollient arts of life." In practice, most missionaries pursued both social and religious transformations simultaneously, but none seemed as patient—or even reticent—in sharing their particular creeds and rituals, or their criticism of Indian religious practice, as the Quakers.[6]

Quakers sometimes referred to themselves as "Friends of Truth" (drawing from John 15:15), and from the beginning they sought to spread that gospel. As their founder George Fox had urged, "Be obedient to the Truth, and spread it abroad, which must go over all the world, to professors, Jews, Christians, and heathen, to the answering witness of God in them all." Friends believed that all were born with both Adam's sin and Christ's redeeming seed. Which one festered or germinated depended fundamentally on the environment in which such persons were nurtured. Renovation of the Indians' corrupt world, then, required immediate attention in order to prepare the ground for Native conversion and redemption. The Indian Committee's letter introducing its missionaries to Cornplanter's people in April 1798 assured the Senecas that the "Voice of the Good Spirit" is "within you" and "all other People in the World." But it went no further in its theological instruction or prescription, and the resident Quakers persistently steered clear of preaching and catechizing.[7]

Even after more than twenty years among the Senecas, the Philadelphia Friends' mission remained religiously circumspect. When controversy erupted and factional cleavages gaped at Allegany, Cattaraugus, and Buffalo over the matter of Christianity in the summer of 1820—should Senecas adopt Christianity or remain "pagan," and if the former which sect should they embrace?—the Quakers would refuse to take a position. Their Seneca hosts implored them: "and now we want you to tell us which is the best plan for us to pursue—whether white people's [religious] customs, or our old ones." A Seneca council pleaded, "Put us right about it, and give us your advice on the subject, whether we shall keep the sabbath, or continue to adhere to our former practice of worshipping the Great Spirit." Equating the Native "Great Spirit" with the Christian God, the Quaker interlocutor steadfastly replied: "we do not wish to force upon you any of our performances in religion. We think it right that every man should follow the teachings of the Good Spirit, in his own heart, which, if attended to, would always lead him in the right path." Again, the Seneca council pressed the Quaker for "a more decided reply," but none was forthcoming.[8]

Such catechistical reticence raises the question: What brought Philadelphia Friends to Allegany in 1798, in time to witness the birth of a new Seneca religion and help advance Seneca revitalization? The answer was political and social as well as theological.

Peaceable Kingdom, Peaceable Republic?

The Quaker commitment to Indian reform and benevolence was as deeply ingrained in the Friends' own identity, history, and mythology as it was in their contemporary religious ideas, their social and political analysis, and their humanitarian impulses. Philadelphia Quaker leaders had explained to Secretary of War Henry Dearborn in 1801 that they remembered "with gratitude" the Indians' "kindness to our forefathers": "They were received & assisted in the most friendly manner on their *landing* in this country, then an uncultivated wilderness." Since then, they wrote, "Great harmony was maintained with the Natives & has continued down to the present day, it having been our constant care to discourage encroaching on their Lands, to deal justly with them & to warn & guard our members from introducing among them distill'd spirits. These people have handed down from Father to Son their high esteem for their brother Onas." Later, a Baltimore Quaker similarly explained, "When our ancestors sought a refuge from persecution in the old world, and landed in this country with William Penn, the natives received them with hospitality—we were then poor and helpless—they kindly administered to our necessities; and being in return treated with justice, a reciprocal feeling of mutual good will was established, which has never for a moment been clouded or interrupted, and they have on many occasions, as on the present one, when in distress, thrown themselves upon our sympathy and friendship."[9]

The Quaker ideal of a Peaceable Kingdom—later graphically displayed in the paintings of the self-taught Quaker artist and preacher Edward Hicks—had become tarnished by the middle of the eighteenth century.[10] William Penn had died in 1718. His three sons—two of whom converted to the Anglican Church—proved less committed to Quakerism, less capable as proprietors, and less concerned about the just treatment of Pennsylvania's Native inhabitants. Particularly damning was the infamous Walking Purchase of 1737, which defrauded Delaware Indians of thousands of acres of land and helped precipitate warfare along the borderlands of Anglo North America. In the 1750s, such conflict engulfed Penn's Woods, creating an unprecedented crisis and posing a dilemma for the Quaker-dominated Pennsylvania Assembly: should money and troops be appropriated for defense—that is, for warfare? Such actions struck many as inconsistent with Quaker beliefs. For Quaker legislators, approving military action might violate fundamental pacific principles; yet under the circumstances failing to do so might abandon the province's frontiers to death and destruction.[11]

Quakers themselves were divided. Some found a way to classify military action as "defense" and thus justify their own participation in a government that sponsored it. But ultimately the Society of Friends withdrew from government, unable to reconcile its beliefs and the demands—especially the escalating military demands—of governing. Some Friends acknowledged their own culpability, arguing that better stewardship of Indian affairs, in the benevolent spirit of William Penn, would have prevented the circumstances that now embroiled the borderlands and necessitated their own political withdrawal. Estranged from government and the course of political affairs, sensitive to their historical and religious responsibilities, and moved by the real grievances of Indians, such Friends sought an alternative, private means to ameliorate the causes of war, thereby making it unnecessary.[12]

In this context, and amid efforts to revive Quakerism itself at midcentury—to promote higher ethical standards, greater discipline, and renewed commitment to the principles of order, integrity, humility, and simplicity—Pennsylvania Friends took new interest in the plight of Native people in their province and on its frontiers. In 1756, Israel Pemberton Jr. and other Quakers

Figure 12. *Peaceable Kingdom*, by Edward Hicks, ca. 1834, oil on canvas. Courtesy of the Board of Trustees, National Gallery of Art, Washington, D.C., gift of Edgar William and Bernice Chrysler Garbisch.

organized the Friendly Association for Regaining and Preserving Peace with the Indians by Pacific Measures to investigate Native grievances and to address their legitimate complaints. While the organization never gained official recognition and achieved only limited success, its work continued through the efforts of committed Friends and was reenergized in the post-Revolutionary War period. In the late 1780s and 1790s, Philadelphia Quakers embraced the Allegany Seneca chief Cornplanter and other Iroquois delegates during their visits to the City of Brotherly Love (the nation's capital). And they attended treaty negotiations—at Newtown in 1791, Sandusky in 1793, and Canandaigua in 1794—as invited observers and Indian advocates.[13]

In 1795, the Philadelphia Yearly Meeting formed a committee "for the civilization & real welfare of the Indian natives" and developed plans to aid the Six Nations and other Native groups systematically through a "civilization" program. With the help and endorsement of U.S. Secretary of State Timothy Pickering, who vouched for their benevolent motives, the Quakers quickly initiated efforts to assist Indians throughout the United States by supplying technical aid and equipment; they invested more directly and personally by founding missions first at Stockbridge and Oneida and then at Onondaga and Cayuga in 1796. In 1797, they pledged their support to the Senecas, and by May 1798 three Quakers (accompanied by two senior representatives of the Yearly Meeting) arrived at Allegany, the settlements of Cornplanter's people along the Allegheny River, to found a Seneca mission.[14]

Without questioning the humanitarian motivation and impact of these efforts, it is nonetheless worth acknowledging that Quaker Indian advocacy burnished the Friends' self-image and helped rehabilitate their reputation and enhance their public role in the early republic. Their quasi-official function in Indian affairs constituted a form of public service. It lent the Society of Friends honor, legitimacy, and renewed influence, which had been compromised, not merely in colonial Pennsylvania politics, but during the American Revolution, when patriots reacted to Quaker pacifism (and sometimes loyalism) with suspicion and persecution. Activism on behalf of Indians allowed Friends to affect public policy in an area of great importance—critical to the social, political, and economic development of the country—and to do so in a way that dovetailed with federal Indian policy. As Secretary of War Henry Knox articulated it in 1789, the United States reserved a "right of conquest" through "just war," but it expressed a preference for negotiation, land purchase, "distributive justice," and peace.[15]

Missionary work provided a means to demonstrate the Quakers' own, divinely approved vision for a civilized, just, and holy world. The nature of that work, as it emerged among the Senecas, would be unique, at odds with the evangelism of other Protestant denominations. It would be influenced by their distinctive theology, by the particular circumstances of individual Quaker agents, by the interests and rational calculations of Seneca men and women they encountered, and by the ever-shifting conditions in western New York. And it was conditioned, not only by the Quakers' recent political travails, but by their own longer historical experience of persecution and transcendence.[16]

Quakers believed Indians no less than others could embody the Inner Light. Other Protestants similarly regarded Indians as capable of conversion, but few of them could approach their potential converts with the simplicity, humility, and confidence of Friends. Because Quakers held that all divine inspiration came from the same source—the indwelling Spirit of God—it was irrelevant who actually preached, women or men, or even Indians eventually. No Christian denomination seemed more willing to equate its God with the Indians' Great Spirit. Quakers sought an authentic, primitive religious practice, divested of external forms (such as baptism or communion), and this minimalism relieved Quaker missionaries from the obligation to teach and impose complicated doctrines and rites, which often antagonized Native proselytes. Moreover, Quakers felt less urge to catechize their hosts on Protestant Christianity's basic "truths"—man's fall, his essential depravity, his redemption through Christ's atonement—and thus avoided the alienating and often counterproductive act of informing prospective Indian converts of their sinfulness and utter reprobation. The Quakers, a denomination that permitted female preaching and offered women important roles within the church, may have been better suited to a mission among the Senecas than other Protestant sects, which were more clearly patriarchal. And Quaker pacifism may have resonated uniquely with Senecas, for whom peace (though not pacifism itself) was a deep cultural value. For Quakers as well as other Protestants, their missionary work sought to cultivate piety, morality, order, and industry, but holiness expressed itself in different ways and for Friends was subsumed more fully in the work and regulation they promoted among the Senecas.[17]

Although comparatively benign in its soft-peddling of Christianity, and although relatively effective in promoting the prosperity and survival of its Indian subjects, the Quaker mission's ultimate goal was nonetheless ethnocentric. It sought the fundamental transformation of Seneca society, to be remade in the idealized image of the American yeoman and his wife. The Friends' civilizing program was deceptively simple, as it stressed order and industry. But what did that really mean? Order meant patriarchal, nuclear households. It meant monogamy and fidelity in marriage, not frequent or haphazard divorce. It meant a landscape of discrete, individually owned farmsteads, owned and worked by men. It meant plowed furrows, not corn mounds and tangled vines. It meant female domesticity, women-centered homes, where women focused their labor exclusively. It meant wheat not corn, cattle and hogs, not horses. It meant flax, not furs. It meant sobriety, modest clothing, and short hair for men. It meant soap, not bear grease. It meant water, not alcoholic spirits.

Industry meant hard, diligent toil in agricultural ground for men. It meant clearing forests for fences and fields, for houses and barns, not to sell as timber. It meant spinning and sewing, not sowing and reaping for women. It meant cleaning, not gleaning. It meant filling the days with manual labor, banishing idleness and the frivolous or dangerous activities that wasted time and bred sinfulness—"frolicking," dancing, drinking, gaming, gossiping. It meant school, not unstructured recreation, reading and writing, not running and romping. Such prescriptions were simple common sense to Quaker philanthropists and agents among the Senecas—they were essential to Indian survival under the circumstances. Adopting them, Quakers supposed, was a matter of Seneca self-interest. But one must not underestimate the enormous transformation this program required, even when Seneca calculations determined that some of this medicine was necessary.[18]

Property, work, marriage, and alcohol—not necessarily in that order—attracted the most attention among Quaker reformers engaged in the task of helping the Senecas to help themselves. Critical to their project was the demolition of communal ownership of property and collective patterns of work, as well as the reformation of Seneca morality, especially the debilitating drinking habits of some and Native marriage customs and sexuality. From the beginning of colonization, the gender arrangements of Native societies had intrigued and disturbed European newcomers. As much as any other customs or characteristics, Native "marriage" and work patterns marked the Indians as "savage." This was particularly the case among peoples such as the Senecas, with a tradition of matrilineal order—which reckoned identity and family descent through mothers rather than fathers—and with a subsistence based on women's horticulture (and land ownership). Quakers, like other white, middle-class reformers emerging in the late eighteenth and early nineteenth centuries, focused particular attention on realigning Seneca gender roles to conform to their own expectations and hoped to remake Seneca extended, maternal families into more discrete, nuclear units. Such families, then, would become independent, patriarchal economic and affective bodies, which would provide competency and comfort and promote social and political order.[19]

The Quaker Mission at Allegany

After an arduous journey of nearly three weeks, five Quaker men—two elders and three young missionaries—arrived from Philadelphia at Jenuchshadago, or Burnt House, Cornplanter's village on the Allegheny River. It was May 17, 1798, a Thursday; but that meant almost as little to the Friends as it did to the Indians, if for different reasons. Quakers had banished the pagan-derived names for the days of the week from their calendar (Thursday was simply the fifth day), while the "pagan" Senecas used their own nomenclature and calendar, which lacked not only a day named for the god Thor but the Christian Sabbath as well. The visitors had been invited and were expected. Cornplanter told them, "I have heard of your comeing for many days." But the Quakers knew this only because Cornplanter's son Henry, who had been educated in Philadelphia, could translate for them. It must have been a bewildering experience for Halliday Jackson, Joel Swayne, and Henry Simmons, and their senior colleagues, John Pierce and Joshua Sharpless. As Halliday Jackson later wrote, in the scriptural style he affected, "the people spake unto us in a strange Language and we understood them not." But the Senecas welcomed them. In the translated words of Cornplanter, "I . . . rejoice in my heart to see you this day, and am thankful to the Great Spirit for your safe arrival and preservation on the way."[20]

The Quaker sojourners found the Seneca women unavailable, detained by their spring planting. They had been greeted instead by Seneca men "standing in companies sporting themselves with their bows and arrows and other trifling amusements"—confirmation, perhaps, of the conventional if prejudicial white images of Indian male idleness and female drudgery. The Friends commenced immediately to construct a "comfortable two story Log House" and demonstration farm at Genesinguhta, above Cornplanter's village on the Allegany reservation, to provide their Native clients with exemplary experience in "advanced" rural life. And in little more than a week, they outlined an incentive plan to encourage full Seneca participation in their program. By now, Seneca women were on hand to evaluate the newcomers. Their assessment, as collective owners of the land, heads of families, and primary "bread winners," would be crucial, though the Quakers' gendered language expressing gratification for early cooperation—that they and the Indians "seem to agree like *Brothers*, having but one mind in everything we do"—belied a certain innocence of Seneca social and political order.[21]

The Friends' incentive program, offering bonuses for Seneca production of prescribed commodities, displayed Quaker hopes for a Seneca metamorphosis. Proper men's and women's activities were distinguished from each other and encouraged. "Brothers," they declared, "We will give to every Indian man living on this river, who shall raise 25 Bushels of Wheat or Rye, in one year, on his own land, not worked by white people, the sum of two dollars." Similarly rewarded was the production of Indian corn, potatoes, and hay, "put into a Stack or barn, not being mowed, or drawn in by white people." Women, on the other hand—offered no incentive for their customary horticultural work—were encouraged to pursue domestic occupations. The Friends promised, "For every 12 yards of linnen cloth, made by any Indian woman, out of flax raised on her own or her husband's land, and spun in her own house, the sum of two dollars to be paid to the woman." Woolen cloth and linsey (or linsey-woolsey—that is, a combination of linen and wool), from the wool of her own or her husband's sheep, and "spun in her own house," garnered the same reward. And to facilitate industry and maintain sobriety, such dividends were collectible only by those not "intoxicated with strong drink, at least, for the term of six months before such application." This incentive plan, with its implied prescriptions about proper modes and goals of production, and its specific spatial arrangement of the Native landscape—placing the Seneca woman, for example, on "her husbands land" and "in her own house" (that is, *not* in a larger communal, matrilineal dwelling or female agricultural space)—can stand in large part for the entire Friendly program.[22]

It stressed individual male ownership of property and agricultural toil, to promote the Jeffersonian goals of yeoman virtue and economic independence. It rejected the Senecas' corporate ownership and female control of farmlands, implicitly suggesting that this traditional arrangement would disincline Native men to perform work (that is, as work was defined by white reformers) or to assume the responsibilities of manhood. Such reforms specifically precluded the possibility that others—white tenants perhaps—might work Seneca lands. They reflected a class and ethnic bias that prevented Quakers or other white Americans from imagining that Senecas might emulate those white landlords—such as Jefferson himself or the great New York proprietor William Cooper—who did not themselves toil but directed others (renters or even slaves) to work for them. Nor could they imagine or condone a future Seneca collectivist world akin to later utopian experiments that emerged in various parts of New England, the Burned-Over District, or farther west.[23]

Despite the dissonance, many Quaker goals meshed with Seneca ones. The Indians were not averse to technological innovation and proved creative in their integration of new ideas and technologies into older patterns of life. Some were enthusiastic about acquiring facility in spoken English and the ability to read and write. And many were pleased to benefit from Quaker technical assistance and their infusion of capital for equipment and improvements, such as roads, sawmills, gristmills, and blacksmith shops. And, as we have seen, some Native leaders, such as Handsome Lake, preached moral reform—especially temperance—as loudly as Quaker or competing Protestant missionaries. Bitter differences could arise among the Senecas about the proper course for accommodation with the ever-encroaching white world, but few indulged in the illusion that no accommodation was necessary. As some Senecas confided to the resident Friends, "they saw that the white people would settle all round them; that they could not live unless they learned to farm & follow the white peoples ways."[24]

That accommodation was gendered, with, for example, some men perhaps more likely than women to abandon the traditional sexual division of labor and cooperative work patterns or to establish new household arrangements. On the other hand, some disputes over the proper response to changing times cut across gender lines, with factions cleaving along contours of kinship or local residence, for example, dividing Seneca men and women into camps according to their relative positions on religious changes or on land controversies. But often, Quaker and Seneca reformation plans meshed, and when they did not Quakers generally moderated their rebukes and refused to coerce their hosts.[25]

The Quakers settled at Genesinguhta (Old Town), about nine miles above Jenuchshadago, Cornplanter's town, because it was within the forty-two-square-mile Allegany reservation guaranteed to the Senecas in the Treaty of Big Tree in 1797, not located on Cornplanter's private property. Improvements made there by Quaker agents would therefore accrue to the benefit of the Senecas generally, not simply to their leader. The site had been largely abandoned, except for three or four Seneca families who had not been driven out by previous flooding, but it encompassed some 150 acres of good land partially cleared. Swayne and Jackson were hard at work at Genesinguhta, building their new house and barn, laying out and fencing fields, and transforming the landscape according to their standards, and Simmons was busy organizing a school for Native children at Jenuchshadago, where most Senecas lived, when the senior Quaker men Pierce and Sharpless departed on June 7, 1798. Progress was slow, both in convincing pioneer Senecas to develop their own farms in yeoman fashion and in persuading young Seneca scholars to persist in their studies, particularly during pleasant weather.[26]

But by the next summer, the Quakers wrote that "divers of they [sic] men have assisted in the labour of the field—one Indian has fenced a farm near ours, and more are about doing it." In the fall, Indian Committee visitors reported promisingly that "some Indian men are beginning to help their women to work, and raise corn, and make fences." The visitors told Cornplanter, "It has been some satisfaction to us riding through your Town, to see marks of industry taking place." They detailed the improvements— better, warmer houses, cleared land planted with corn, potatoes, beans, squashes, and cucumbers (if not yet wheat or rye)—and they urged the Seneca men to clear more land "and make it fit for Ploughing." They hoped to see the Indians "Fencing it; Planting it with Corn, and Sowing it with Wheat; you will then have a supply of Provision more certain to depend upon than hunting." Noting the increase of the Senecas' stock of cattle, the Quaker observers expressed pleasure at the Indians' success in animal husbandry, which they adopted more quickly and enthusiastically than the plow. Amid some setbacks, particularly in the face of opposition to male agricultural work, which (unlike animal husbandry) transgressed gender roles, the Quaker cultural experiment continued to progress. Soon a few Seneca men proved willing to try their hand at plowing. By the autumn of 1800, the Friends reported, "Divers of the Natives continue to incline to build themselves better Houses, and some at times assist the women in the labor of the fields, so that we are indeed to believe that gradual improvement prevails amongst them in the habits of civilized life."[27]

Quaker faith in the progress of their Seneca brethren was justified by their continuing adaptation and success in establishing more secure and prosperous agricultural and domestic lives. In the spring of 1802, and in a follow-up letter in November, which became a treasured document among the Senecas, President Thomas Jefferson lent his support to the Seneca reformation program and to its key supporter, the Seneca prophet Handsome Lake, who had endorsed much of the Quaker secular agenda. "Go on then, brother, in the great reformation you have undertaken," Jefferson wrote to Handsome Lake. "Persuade our red brethren then to be sober, and to cultivate their lands; and their women to spin and weave for their families. You will soon see your women and children well fed and clothed, your men living happily in peace and plenty, and your numbers increasing from year to year." Jefferson addressed his congratulation and encouragement to Handsome Lake for his renovations, yet he actually described the Quakers' program. In fact, the efforts of the prophet and the Friends overlapped, though they were not identical. But under the dual influences of the Quakers and Handsome Lake, the Senecas did seem to prosper, or at least they had begun to pull themselves out of the desperate conditions they had recently faced.[28]

The reported progress, and the apparent consensus on how to achieve it, masked some substantial differences between Quakers and Senecas, however—differences that would linger. Farming itself was hardly an innovation among the Senecas, of course, and despite Quaker optimism, Senecas had not substantially remade their gendered division of labor. Quakers were impressed by the work they saw some Seneca men perform, but Iroquois men had traditionally assisted women in the hard physical work of preparing fields and building houses. Clearing fields or building fences or even plowing did not make Seneca men, in their own view, cultivators of the soil. The fences they constructed kept out foraging animals and protected crops, but the fields they enclosed were not necessarily individually owned—and certainly not by men. Fenced plots could continue to be worked communally by women, who retained their control of the primary means of subsistence. And new tasks assumed by Seneca men and women—whether plowing or spinning— would not necessarily replace the work they traditionally performed. More likely they would add to their toil or would be integrated only as time and circumstance allowed.

As the Quaker demonstration farm flourished at Genesinguhta, and as more Senecas moved into the vicinity, leaving Cornplanter's private holdings and taking up land on the Allegany reserve, the Friends began to hear some rumblings of criticism. Some skeptical Senecas questioned Quaker motives: Did the Friends "enjoy such and such benefits from their land"? In order to establish their independence, demonstrate their disinterestedness, and maintain their credibility, the Quakers determined to move their farm to proximate nonreservation land. They identified and purchased such a site in the fall of 1803 at Tunesassa, on Tuknessasah Creek, about two miles above Genesinguhta and a half mile from the reserve. The move inspired some concern among the Senecas, prodding Handsome Lake to assure the Friends, "we wish to make your minds perfectly easy, we are all pleased with your living amongst us, and not one of us wants you to leave our Country." Handsome Lake did not thwart the relocation but did express his hope "that you settle near us." "We want you to be near us," he said, "that you may extend further assistance & instruction, for altho' we have experienced much benefit from you, and some of our people have made considerable advancement in the knowledge of usefull labour, yet we remain very deficient in many things, and numbers of us are yet poor."[29]

Cornplanter similarly urged the Quakers to continue to live nearby, while he publicly acknowledged the Friends' integrity and assistance: "we now want you to stay with us, and stand between us and the white people, and if you see any of them trying to cheat us, we wish you to let us know of it, or if you see any of our people trying to cheat the white People, we wish you to let it be known also, as we confide in you that you will not cheat us." Such comments expressed a genuine commitment to the Quakers' ongoing presence, and yet Cornplanter's endorsement is significant for what it did not say. Its stress on education, material assistance, and the protection Quaker advocacy might offer against white infringements or fraud fell short of an explicit support of the Friends' full program of radical change, including male agricultural work, male ownership of property in severalty, or female domesticity.[30]

For their part, the Quakers continued to find the sobriety and industry of the Senecas encouraging. Visiting Indian Committee representatives were particularly impressed to see the new twenty-two-mile road constructed by the Senecas, which opened communication between the upper and lower Allegany settlements. The Friends began to formulate plans to expand their instruction and aid to Indian women more directly, and they recommended that Quaker women join the mission at Tunesassa. Meanwhile, the progress among the Senecas, and their openness to Quaker effort, seemed to be general, extending to other communities at Cattaraugus and Buffalo. At a council on October 2, 1803, the Buffalo Creek Seneca leader Red Jacket recounted approvingly, "that about two years since some of their people began to help their Women [that is, in farming] and to leave off drinking Whiskey[,] that such as had done so lived more comfortably than they used to do." Red

Jacket invited the Friends to return in two more years, assuring them they would "find them better Farmers and not in practice of using strong drink &c." Passing through Buffalo Creek a year later, some Baltimore Friends witnessed "several of their principal chiefs and young men engaged in ploughing—to one of their ploghs we saw 6 oxen—others were engaged in clearing and preparing their lands for cultivation."[31]

The Seneca mission continued to advance with the construction of new farms and houses. By 1805, Seneca families—followers of the prophet in particular—had established a new settlement at Cold Spring, about three miles above Tunesassa. Meanwhile, Handsome Lake continued to advance his nativist reformation—sometimes through witch hunts that further unsettled Seneca life. The resulting disruptions and difficulties endured by Seneca people were sometimes noticed, but they received less attention among the Friends, who were encouraged by the prophet's apparent cooperation and focused diligently on making their own enterprise a success. By this time, they had completed the Tunesassa mission and had begun to operate a new gristmill and sawmill. The year 1805 also marked the arrival of additional missionaries, Benjamin Cope and his wife Rachel, as well as another woman, Hannah Jackson.[32]

Transforming Seneca Womanhood

Seneca women had figured in Quaker plans from the start, and as they worked to transform gender roles and prescriptions for men, so the Friends sought to remake the gender arrangements for Seneca women. If the Quakers' initial incentive program offered premiums for women who successfully managed to perform the conventional domestic tasks of white farm women—spinning, weaving, sewing, and the like—no female Quaker missionaries were immediately available to facilitate the project. The Friends realized that any fundamental change in Seneca society would require women's approval, and they began to cultivate it, at least indirectly, surmising, for example, that suppression of drunkenness would benefit women, who less often imbibed and more often fell victim to whiskey-induced violence or dissipation of scarce funds. Moreover, their arguments for male agriculture were designed to appeal to both men and women. The former, Quakers hoped, would feel a greater, manly responsibility in providing family subsistence and in reducing their women's physical labor—toil inappropriate to the weaker sex. The

latter, the Friends believed, could recognize the advantages in reduced horticultural labor, which liberated time to spend in proper domestic pursuits that
would enhance domestic life. Gristmills were celebrated for "lessening the
labor of women" (who traditionally ground corn) as well as encouraging the
use of alternative, more noble grains, wheat or rye. An 1803 report had reasoned, "As the men accustom themselves to labour the Women have less
drudgery to perform, we therefore believe their situation should claim our
serious attention, many we doubt not would gladly receive instruction." Various Quaker speakers emphasized, as had Jefferson in his letter, that men's
new work regimen materially benefited women and children. The Friends
must have been gratified to hear these words echoed in Red Jacket's council
remarks in October of 1803, recognizing the achievements of Seneca agricultural pioneers: "the women and children of such men [were] now comfortably fed & clad—formerly they were almost naked and often hungry."[33]

Women's instruction was initially hampered by the lack of tools and
supplies, but Seneca women were apparently willing students of the domestic
arts. Hannah Jackson reported in February of 1806 that several women and
girls attended their lessons, learned to make soap and to "Spin and Knit a
little, and appear Desirous to improve." By the next year, the mission boasted
a comfortable schoolhouse and dormitory for women who sought Friendly
instruction in spinning; "a few have made a considerable progress, and have
now got a small Piece ready for the loom." The women were now encouraged
not merely by Quakers but by some of their own leaders, women as well as
men.[34]

There were occasional roadblocks, as there were in the Quaker effort to
remake Seneca men. Some, such as Johnson Silverheels, attempted "to dissuade and discourage the Indian Women from learning to spin &c." These
obstructions, "artfully calculated to cooperate with their ignorance and create
an aversion to such employments," were surmounted by others, including
Handsome Lake, who saw value in the new Quaker ways. Particularly important was the endorsement by "a few of the Chief Women (who Continue to
encourage a perseverance in learning)." Their number included the influential sister of both Cornplanter and Handsome Lake, Gayantgogwus, who
contradicted Silverheels and encouraged the Quakers. "[T]he Women wished
the Girls to learn & many of the Girls also wish'd to be instructed," Gayantgogwus told the former resident missionary Halliday Jackson, visiting in
1806, and she expressed confidence in the female Quaker missionaries, who
"were fully capable of instructing them." The Seneca matron treated Jackson

and his colleague John Philips to a demonstration of the developing Seneca skills in the household arts—"Several Girls came in this afternoon and spun and knit a little," including Gayantgogwus's granddaughter and another of her young relatives.[35]

At a council to address the matter in January of 1807, the Friends made their case: "We think it is now time for you to begin to take more of the Burthen off your poor Women, and give them time and liberty to learn such things as will be of use to them. you well know that a few years ago many of your Warriors despised work. and was ashamed to be seen in the field with a Hoe. you then thought it was very disgraceful to be employed in such things. but Brothers, you now begin to see the great advantage it has been to your men to learn habits of industry. Just so will be with your Women." Although the meeting was hardly an exclusively male event—the Quaker account noted specifically the inclusion of "principal women"—the Friends approached the assembly as if it was, addressing the Seneca council as "Brothers." The Quakers displayed in the process the patriarchal assumptions deeply embedded in their project. They also betrayed a peculiar, gendered understanding of "work." While they implied that all male economic activity outside of agricultural toil amounted to idleness, they suggested that farming was a burden for women—that it was inappropriately taxing for their sex. Yet they seemed to imply that women had not yet learned "the habits of industry," which for women properly centered on the home and domestic production. Further, in relieving women of agricultural responsibilities as a means to ease their "burthens," the Quakers failed to notice the irony that they were about to impose even more burdensome (and less rewarding) tasks on Seneca women. The Friends' clients may well have been struck by the illogic in the message, but they were too polite to mention it, and some Senecas continued to hold back. The Quakers earnestly reported that their appeal "appeared to have a good effect." A yearly summary report in 1807 concluded, "some of the indian women and girls appear much disposed to be instructed by our women friends, many of them have already learned to make soap, and some can spin and knit a little, and are much more clean in their persons and clothes than before our women came."[36]

Halliday Jackson, who had been among the founders of the Quakers' Seneca mission in 1798, was astonished by the transformation in Indian life he witnessed upon his return visit in 1806. "Their improvement in divers respects since I left them has rather exceeded my expectations & quite equal to any improvement I have observ'd in any of the new settlements made by

Whites in the same length of time & their houses better put up & fences in a general way far superior to those made by White Settlers in the Back parts of Pensylvania & York State." Jackson calculated that some one hundred new houses had been built since the Indian Committee last visited three years earlier. Most were constructed of hewn logs, and many were covered with shingles and graced with panel doors and glass windows; some were two-story dwellings. Significantly, such farmsteads were "more detatchd from each other than formerly"—signaling, the Quakers hoped, a growing commitment to landholding in severalty (that is, individual rather than collective ownership) and individual family farm production.[37]

One of the most striking features of reformed Seneca life for Jackson was the Indians' cleanliness, which bespoke order, industry, and godliness, and which was attributable to the influence of women. The Senecas "appeard more steady in their Conduct & more Clean and decent in their dress than I had ever saw them before—Their houses are also kept much cleaner than formerly, and one thing I several times observed which I thought something of a novelty among Indians [gap in manuscript] indication that they were beginning to be asham'd of their dirty way of living that when the women saw us approaching their Doors they immediately began to sweep their houses."[38]

Instruction in "the useful arts of house-wifery" had only just begun, but the new Seneca commitment to cleanliness was emblematic of the progress and good prospects of the gendered "civilization" program. Not only did clean houses, unsoiled clothes, and scrubbed faces signify purity and order; they were the product of hard female work (sweeping, soap-making, washing—women's industry). Cleanliness implied that women had begun to embrace not merely the tasks of white domesticity but some of its values as well. But how deeply Seneca women had invested in such domesticity—particularly its economic and political subordination of women, which some white women increasingly found problematic—remained unclear to Friendly observers such as Halliday Jackson and the less experienced and less tolerant John Philips.[39]

Marriage: Holy Conversation or Carnal Talk?

At the core of domesticity—and of the entire gender assemblage—was marriage, an institution that commanded Quaker attention and that, in their view, required reform among the Senecas. From the beginnings of American colonization, marriage had loomed large in European assessments of the Native people. As the historian Ann Marie Plane has argued, marriage, though among the most intimate of social relationships, nonetheless stood at the center of "some of the most public struggles of colonial states and societies: struggles between European and indigenous understandings of right and wrong." Marriage lay at the heart of the European and colonial social order—it not only structured social and sexual intimacy, but it defined individual identity and gender relations, legitimated and socialized children, ordered the distribution of property across generations, and provided the ability to subsist—life itself. Marriage functioned as a model for order in the larger society—the family it created was a "little commonwealth." The institution, though it would change over time, remained so basic to white American life that alternative social arrangements—like those of Native people—were hard to imagine as legitimate; indeed, they could be frightening. The colonial project to "reduce" Indians to civility—which endured into the early national era—was in large part an effort to transform Native sexual and domestic life, to remake their gender order, by creating and imposing new forms of marriage.[40]

The Senecas had traditionally lived in matrilineal and matrilocal arrangements—in multifamily longhouses—in which one's identity, social place, and subsistence were determined not so much by "families" as by lineages, clans, and villages. Personal and group identity was defined particularly by mothers, and traditionally men had joined wives in maternal residences rather than the reverse. In practice Seneca social and domestic arrangements could be more diverse and complex; and by the early nineteenth century, Seneca households had shrunk in size and varied across a range of matrilocal and "virilocal" residence patterns—that is, wives sometimes lived in husbands' houses and sometimes husbands lived surrounded by their wives' kin. In this dynamic social world, Senecas continued to emphasize localism and cultivated communities constructed of kinspeople.[41]

Although they could not have been ignorant of conventional Iroquoian kinship and domestic practices, at least in modified form, the Friends seemed to disregard such arrangements, implicitly treating them as outdated and in need of transformation. Accepting the persistence of women's collective, autonomous domestic lives ran against the grain of the larger Quaker program, potentially frustrating the transition to individual, male property ownership, intensive plow agriculture, and female domesticity. The Friends may have been less overtly patriarchal in their outlook than other denominations and had no misogynous intentions, but the idea of extended families of women clustered in adjacent houses, if not in multifamily longhouses, did not square with their vision of discrete, nuclear (male-headed) families spread across a segmented agrarian landscape. Their models were the industrious Quaker families of Pennsylvania's Delaware Valley, who succeeded through hard work, "holy conversation," and carefully orchestrated generational transitions, which guided children through adolescence to marriage and adulthood.[42]

Like other early nineteenth-century humanitarians, the Quakers regarded the Indians, at least metaphorically, as children. To deride such an attitude simply as condescending (which, of course, it was) is to leave critical analysis of their Seneca mission incomplete. How did Quakers regard and treat their own offspring? And how might such an approach, when applied in their Native missions, have affected the Senecas, who were themselves capable of manipulating the Friends? Quakers regarded their children not as sinners in need of conversion (in Calvinist fashion) but as innocents to be nurtured and preserved from corruption. Ideally, they treated their children with considerable affection (based on religious beliefs rather than sentimentality), felt compelled to provide them with the training and material means (primarily land) to live prosperous lives, and granted them greater autonomy in life decisions, such as marriage. Quakers believed humans discoursed in two "languages"—"holy conversation" and "carnal talk." Friends sought to promote the former, which they understood as much more than mere speech—"conversation" meant deeds as well as words, not mere professions but actions. Quakers attempted to live their faith, so that they became embodiments of the Word, not simply preachers or professors. Friends therefore worked to cultivate ideal social, economic, and religious communities in which holy conversation could thrive—not only to serve God and promote their own salvation but also to nurture future generations who too might discover the Inner Light, be guided by it, achieve material comfort, and realize their spiritual promise.[43]

Critical to the Quakers' objective of creating and nurturing ideal communities based on holy conversation were their marriage disciplinary procedures. Friends carefully examined prospective brides and grooms to ensure the appropriateness and likely success of their matrimony, and they considered infractions that might occur after nuptials. Marriages took up more time at women's and men's meetings than any other business and involved the community intrusively in family matters. Nonetheless, although parental and community approval was essential, a successful marriage stemmed from love and the willing consent of those involved, woman as well as man. From the beginning, George Fox and other Quakers had reconceived conventional marriage and family, recognizing women as spiritually equal and essential to the encouragement of the Spirit. They promoted wives as full marriage partners, who merited authority within families and communities, especially in areas in which they were regarded as experts—sex, childbirth, and child-rearing. The Quaker marriage discipline, when it succeeded, may not have produced modern, egalitarian marriages, but it did offer Quaker women more authority and involved them more fully in the regulation of their households and communities than was the case among other denominations, making Quaker women more equal not only before God but in their earthly lives. This Friendly interference was carefully calibrated to constitute guidance rather than coercion and designed to promote, ultimately, strong, sustaining, independent (but not isolated) nuclear families. Ironically, religious historians sometimes call these arrangements "tribal." But the Quakers were a different tribe from the Senecas.[44]

With marriage discipline central to the Friends' design of their own families and communities, it is not surprising that they would address Seneca marriage with great interest and concern. What seemed to trouble Quaker observers—and other Christian missionaries—was the apparently easy, ill-considered, or hasty contraction of Indian marriages. In fact, such espousals were often governed by careful planning and deliberation, which involved considerable involvement of families—in short, Senecas were governed by a Native domestic, kinship discipline, though one largely opaque or that seemed improper to white observers. Quakers may have been less troubled than others by the significant role that Seneca women had in selecting partners, but they shared the general Christian disapproval of the limited duration or too easy termination of Native marriages.[45]

John Philips's journal of his visit to Allegany in 1806, for example, recounted the additional instruction offered by a colleague during their council with the Senecas: "I B [Isaac Bonsal] address^d them upon the improproty of putting away their wifes and marrying others &c. and Queryed whether they had felt something in their mind which Convicted them of doing Evill in such Conduct &c." Halliday Jackson's journal entry chronicling the same event reported the Quakers visitors "encourageing them to live in peace and harmony with their wives & not to let trifling matters part them but consider them companions for life for it is pleasing to the Great Spirit for man and woman to live together in harmony." [46]

This advice might strike us as a bit odd. The Quaker speakers addressed their remarks specifically to men, even though their audience was mixed. They seemed to ignore the fact that Seneca women often initiated "divorce" and that "putting away" a spouse, in practical terms, often meant removing a husband's possessions from his wife's house, forcing the rejected man (not woman) to find a new dwelling. It is likely that Seneca women and men had expectations about their domestic partnerships—both how they were constituted and how they ended—that varied considerably from the ideas of their resident missionaries. In other words, Quaker observers misunderstood or misconstrued Seneca marriage and divorce, portraying women as victims when, in fact, they were empowered and willing collaborators in the dissolution of domestic bonds. [47]

On the other hand, it is possible that Quakers witnessed some abuse of women and advocated their own moral practices to address real social problems among the Senecas. Such mistreatment was most likely to occur during drinking sprees, particularly following men's trading journeys to sell furs or timber, when they took their pay in whiskey. Jackson recalled from his early days at Genesinguhta how "disagreable being in their Towns [was] on account of Liquor." And an old woman present when he recounted those memories "cry'd out" in agreement, "that was the truth." Women's residence in their own households, surrounded by family and clan, would help protect wives from the violence of drunken husbands. But by the early nineteenth century, Seneca residence patterns were in transition and had increasingly varied from older, matrilocal forms. Multifamily longhouses were increasingly rare, and Seneca people improvised their housing and family structures in the face of dislocation. Women may indeed have become more vulnerable to husbands' violence and suffered materially when men's commerce turned pelts or pine logs into whiskey rather than provisions. And when a large contingent returned with their liquid pay, a village could be transformed into hell on earth for as long as a week, until the kegs were drained. Prudent souls locked themselves up in their houses or hid in the woods, but others suffered from violence, exposure, accidents, and neglect. Abstinence and control of liquor supplies in Seneca villages helped curb this problem, which was very much reduced early in the nineteenth century, as Jackson's journal suggests. [48]

For Quakers, families played an essential role in promoting the holy conversation necessary for social, economic, and spiritual development, and therefore they placed a premium on stability and longevity, not to mention their particular sense of morality, in marriage. Friends shared some assumptions about marriage and proper domestic order, if not missionary approaches, with other Protestant denominations. In the 1830s, Asher Wright, a Presbyterian minister and skilled linguist, would establish himself at the Buffalo Creek Seneca reservation, and at his mission station he compiled an English-Seneca religious catechism. It ranged widely through Christian theology. After discussion of Adam and Eve, it asked, "What law did God make then?" The answer: "The law of marriage." Seneca catechists were queried, "Is that law broken when a man and woman live together as husband and wife without the ceremony of marriage?" The answer, of course, was, "It is." Sacred law was also "violated when a man and his wife part and marry other persons." Quakers held similar views, and in their own more circumspect way they sought to inculcate them among their proselytes at Allegany. The dangers were both spiritual and material. Friends found it difficult to imagine that "traditional" Indian domestic arrangements, and the family environments they created, could adequately supply the material needs or sufficiently nurture the seed of the Spirit in Seneca adults and, most important, their children. It likely struck them that such families would depress Senecas' economic competency and promote carnal talk rather than holy conversation.[49]

Yet if the Quaker correspondence between resident missionaries and the Indian Committee in the first three decades of the nineteenth century betrays some disappointment and frustration at the limits of Seneca transformation, that record nonetheless chronicles the remarkable general success of the Friendly program. Even the unsympathetic itinerant Congregational minister Jacob Cram could write in 1805, "From a very drunken, idle people, more so than any of the Seneca settlements," the Allegany Senecas "have become the most industrious. By many of them, it is looked upon unfriendly for a white person to offer them liquor." The rival missionary reported a functioning school, an Indian-run blacksmith shop, Indian coopers making buckets and churns, abundant livestock, men employing oxen and plows, the operation of a gristmill and sawmill, and progress in the practical domestic arts. Moreover, Cram observed, "the exertions in this settlement have had a favourable influence on the other Seneca settlements, in leading many to decline the use of strong liquors, and to employ themselves in the business of husbandry." Although the War of 1812 would create temporary havoc (including new, troublesome bouts with alcohol) as it engulfed the Senecas living on the borderlands of the United States and British Canada, the progress noted by Cram continued.[50]

Nonetheless, there were limits to the Quakers' success, as Senecas fell short of fully realizing Friendly hopes of Indian civilization. In retrospect, we might see Seneca "failure" as a greater Seneca success, on Native terms, in constructing a hybrid Seneca social, economic, and religious culture. With Quaker help—and sometimes in spite of Quaker prescriptions—in these years Senecas forged a new way to survive as Seneca. Of course, the Friends did not necessarily see it that way, particularly as they lamented the Senecas' reluctance to transform communally held tribal territory into individual private property.

Disturbing "Their Quiet Possession of Said Lands": Seneca Land Reform

At the turn of the nineteenth century and the beginning of the Quaker civilization program among the Senecas, the U.S. General Allotment Act (1887)—which broke up Indian tribal lands, carved them into individual homesteads, and ultimately resulted in the loss to Native people of nearly one hundred million acres—lay four score and seven years in the future. Still, the Quaker plan to divide Indian land into separate, family-owned plots echoed an already familiar refrain of reformers. In a 1819 letter on the subject to the Allegany Senecas, President James Monroe merely repeated similar appeals made by Washington and Jefferson and various philanthropists, as well as those scheming to acquire "surplus" lands unclaimed by individuals or to buy lands cheaply once freed of complex titles and regulations: "You cannot become civilized till you have advanced one step further—You know that among my white children, each has his own land separate from all others. You ought to do the same." Monroe urged the Senecas "to divide your land among families, in lots sufficiently large to maintain a family, according to its size." "By thus dividing your land," he wrote, "each one could then say, this is mine; and he would have inducements to put up good houses on it, and improve his land by Cultivation."[51]

Monroe hardly needed to elaborate that, by dividing their land, Seneca agriculturalists would declare not only that "this is mine" but also that all other, unallotted lands were not. "Civilization" meant consolidation of Native farms and farm families on a fraction of their residual homelands. The alchemy of transforming communal land into private property produced not gold but real estate, a huge surplus of land available for sale to white citizens. That was the point—the beauty of the process for architects of national expansion and American democracy like Thomas Jefferson, whose Empire for Liberty demanded vast tracts of "free" land to underwrite white Americans' liberty and opportunity. Civilization was good for the Senecas, they were told. But Senecas themselves understood—better than their Quaker Friends—that allotment in severalty would be devastating to Seneca national territory and sovereignty.

Private property held a sacred place in American ideology as the fount of political virtue and liberty. It gave owners a stake in society, insured their independence, and inspired them to industry because they (not a master) would reap the fruits of their labor. In an agrarian society, land was an essential resource, the basis of production and reproduction. Farmers and their families depended on land ownership for subsistence, to enable any aspirations for market production, and to create long-term family wealth that could be transferred through inheritance to children. The real world of the early republic was complicated, however, by the nascent growth of towns and cities, commerce, and manufacturing, and by debates over how such developments might advance (or undermine) the growth of the United States. In the countryside, rising populations and shrinking availability of land, or the control of speculators and landlords, constricted landownership and challenged yeomen's dreams. Many in fact did not (and would never) own land—not slaves, not most urban dwellers, not the increasing number of tenants, laborers, or working poor. But such facts did not compromise reformers' faith in their understanding of land as capital, as commodity, and as an anchor of morality and civility.[52]

Senecas of course agreed about the essential importance of land, but they thought about it in less abstract ways—not simply as capital to produce subsistence or wealth, but as *place*, as a particular homeland that bonded them to the landscape and each other. They remained wary of land division and individual ownership and resisted it strenuously. The Quakers initially encountered such resistance among the Oneidas, the first Iroquois people they sought to help. Missionaries reported to the Indian Committee in November of 1798 that Oneidas expressed "a fearfulness least the White People should entice individuals to sign away their lots and thereby involve them in difficulties." It was prudent to calculate that land was better protected if held collectively, though such commonly owned property could still be lost through fraud and bribery of Indian leaders, even at negotiations officially supervised by the United States government. Like the Oneidas, Senecas exhibited considerable skepticism and reticence with regard to Friendly suggestions. Missionary recommendations to divide land into family allotments, encouraging statements about the progress of "the idea of distinct property," and admonishments about Seneca failures to realize this critical goal fill the Quaker records. Twenty years after the advent of their enterprise, the Friends continued to prod the Senecas to adopt the institution and practice of private property. But, typically, each time they introduced the subject or pushed it on their hosts, "many questions arose."[53]

What would happen if allotments claimed were already being worked by others? What would happen if fields were split, separated, or occupied by others? Seneca women asked the Quaker missionary Jonathan Thomas at Tunesassa, "how will we know where our fields lay promiscuously & in confused divisions and all shapes & lines splitting and separating them & perhaps occupied by others, without a consideration for them?" Seneca men were equally concerned that allotment and private ownership might affect other land uses, especially the harvesting of natural resources, such as game or timber, which men cut from the nation's land and rafted downstream to sawmills and markets. Individually assigned lots might not contain good bottomland for planting or pines for cutting. Senecas thus responded that their land "was better owned in common." On the occasion of this debate in 1819, Thomas fought off discouragement. The idea "gains ground," he noted unrealistically, and would perhaps take hold fully in a year or two.[54]

The Friends had to acknowledge that Seneca land was imperiled, even if they sought not to dispossess Native people but to protect them. Indeed, among the obstacles to their agrarian reform program was the uncertainty among the Indians regarding their ability to retain their property—Seneca farmers would hardly invest time and labor in agricultural improvements on lands they might soon lose. Quakers campaigned to defend Seneca land and fight Seneca removal to the West, a threat that surfaced and created turmoil in 1817. As Halliday Jackson explained, "a measure of this kind would not only tend to unsettle the Indians in their agricultural pursuits, but if carried into effect, would entirely frustrate the plan of their Civilization, and render of little avail the labours of Friends for twenty years." In fact, this new danger encouraged the Quakers to advance even more strenuously their idea of division of Seneca lands into individual lots, buttressed now with restrictions against the sale, lease, or transfer of those lands to white people. And President Monroe's letter to the Allegany Senecas was solicited to back that effort. Although the plan won some support, it was again abandoned in the face of strong local Native opposition.[55]

The Seneca endeavors to protect their territory, resist allotment in severalty, and support ownership in common were broad based. They were also gendered. Women rejected land division and private property even more vehemently than men. The Quaker observer Jonathan Thomas noted their particular opposition in 1819: "the women seemed to claim such parcels of land [that might be allotted] for planting corn, & potatoes, &c. on[,] and the Idea of a division into lots become very unpopular with them." In part, Thomas reported, this was "because they were sensible that clearing land was a hard task perform[ed] by them & much difficulty to get their men to do it." Despite some changes in the sexual division of labor, women still did much of the difficult work of farming, including the clearing of land (with assistance from men). As Thomas acknowledged, "it takes time & attention to chop, burn, fence & prepare it for crops." Women had considerable investment in their fields, therefore, which they "owned," not as real estate but as usufruct—that is, they possessed these plots as long as they worked them. They were the means of production, and women were the primary producers of food. Reorganization of the Seneca landscape would unsettle Seneca women to their material and social disadvantage. And prescribed male-dominated individual family farms (unpopular with Seneca men) cut against the grain of women's collective work as well as land ownership patterns. If men objected to the land reform plan's potential impact on their access to natural resources—particularly game and timber—women's opposition was even more literally *grounded*. When the idea again became the subject of discussions during a three-day council late in 1828, Seneca women spoke definitively: "they gave their voice for the land to continue as it at present was," the Quaker Joseph Elkinton wrote from Tunesassa, "the property of the nation, which was now concluded on." As the property of the nation—rather than of individual Senecas, particularly Seneca men—the land remained the property of Seneca women.[56]

The Friends' mission to the Senecas was a gift, a relatively disinterested humanitarian gesture of great significance. Although the Quaker civilization program could be overbearing at times, it was nonetheless appreciated by most Senecas who recognized its benefits. But the reception and use of a gift—even when graciously accepted—does not necessarily mirror the intentions of its giver. Senecas transformed themselves with the guidance of Quakers, finding new ways to feed themselves, organize social life, act effectively in a larger, more complicated white world, and understand and address the wishes of the Great Spirit. What they became in the process, however, were not Native Quakers or assimilated Christians but new model Senecas, and the Friends' noncoercive approach gave them the freedom to do so.

But the Quaker's program—like the new way of Handsome Lake—was a solution that created new problems. Seneca women and men had to consider the costs as well as the benefits of adopting or rejecting particular reforms. If the Friends' new agricultural regime might relieve women of great toil, would it also relieve them of status, power, and purpose? Would it replace communal horticultural work with new responsibilities and drudgery? Was spinning more satisfying than farming? Would the institution of private property entail the loss, not only of women's property, but of the Senecas' national territory? Could men be entrusted to love and cherish the land, to farm it to produce subsistence? If Seneca men turned fully toward agriculture, could the Senecas survive without the commodity production and cash that they produced by rafting timber, trading pelts, and working for wages? Would new marriage practices and the erection of patriarchal households really give women greater security, dignity, and refinement, or would they jeopardize the happiness, safety, and prosperity of women and their children? Quaker missionaries sought to persuade their hosts through reason and good example. They emphasized free choice. And the Senecas made their own choices. Those choices are the subject of Chapter 5—there we will examine the conflicts and ironies of the Quaker economic modernization program, probing how the Senecas addressed the new problems that Quaker solutions posed.

The Philadelphia Society of Friends' nineteenth-century mission could not escape the ethnocentrism and cultural condescension of its time, but its unique willingness to permit and accept the Senecas' choices—even those it saw as wrong—distinguished the Quakers from others and helped enable the Senecas to reinvent themselves and survive. Friendly toleration meant not only that Senecas could transform themselves secularly on their own terms; but it also buffered the Senecas' religious revitalization, as they fashioned a new, non-Christian spiritual life out of their traditions, one that might better suit their new post-Revolutionary world.

CHAPTER 5

From Longhouse to Farmhouse: Quakers and the Transformation of Seneca Rural Life

In respect to the Allegheny reservation I have given directions to lay the towns out in that quarter without paying attention to it for the present. I am very sorry the quakers in this business is likely to give us much trouble with this reservation.

—Joseph Ellicott, surveyor and Holland Land Company agent (1798)

You are very capable to calculate what is for your advantage and what is not.

—Quaker visitors to Allegany Senecas (1817)

SENECA WOMEN AND MEN faced difficult choices as they remade themselves and their economic lives. But such decisions—and the dilemmas they confronted—were not entirely specific to them as Native people. Senecas shared some of the problems other poor and middling Americans encountered as new markets, new commercial relations, new systems of manufacturing, new forms of natural resource extraction, and new kinds of rural agricultural production transformed economic and social life in the early American republic.

How, when, and at what pace the United States made the transition to capitalism in the countryside in the eighteenth and nineteenth centuries is a matter of considerable debate among historians, but the fact of that long-term alteration is well established. Profound economic change altered rural America as the United States itself expanded, conquering and incorporating new lands and increasingly orienting those territories and their inhabitants to participate in a national—and international—market economy. Natural advantages, "internal improvements" (roads, canals, and later railroads), and legal and financial innovations provided the infrastructure for commercial agriculture and rural manufacturing, which some Americans enthusiastically embraced. The United States remained predominantly rural and agricultural, particularly in the first half of the nineteenth century, and relative to other countries it continued to have a large number of freehold farmers—that is, property holders who presumably retained the autonomy to realize the Jeffersonian dreams of economic "competency" and virtuous citizenship.[1]

In retrospective terms, however, we can observe trends during this era that those who were swept up in them felt but could not fully see. Individual landownership would shrink—periodically offset by the convulsive expansion of United States territory and the transfer of Indian land to white Americans. And the mythic independence of American yeomanry would decline, as more Americans rented, resorted to wage labor, became attached to markets, exchanged money, paid interest, and entangled themselves in networks of credit. While some of these rural Americans were pioneers and colonizers, they and their descendants could also find themselves among the colonized, with some prospering and others suffering through the adjustments that economic transformation demanded.[2]

In the upper Susquehanna Valley, for example, white settlers sought opportunity in a place newly opened following the American Revolution and Native dispossession. But wealthy landowners dominated, controlling land and economic activity through lease, mortgage, and credit arrangements. "Few pioneers were able to climb the economic ladder to become property holders," according to historian Peter C. Mancall. In the land that James Fenimore Cooper immortalized in fiction, the real future belonged to men like his father, William Cooper, the founder of Cooperstown and the basis for his character Judge Marmaduke Temple in *The Pioneers: or, The Sources of the Susquehanna; a Descriptive Tale* (1823). In contrast to Judges Cooper and Temple, "early squatters became farm laborers or tenants or they moved on, like Natty Bumppo, seeking an independent life in a wilderness that proved elusive."[3] Among the places such settlers would move to was the "Holland Land Purchase," the vast tract of New York "frontier" land west of the Genesee River extending to the Canadian border, Lake Erie, and Pennsylvania—that is, surrounding Seneca lands. Meanwhile, the upper Susque-hanna would become a source of valuable natural resources—coal and lumber—commodities extracted by those toiling for wages and sold in distant markets to fuel urban and industrial development. Mancall concludes, "In making this valley of opportunity part of the Atlantic commercial world, those who directed economic change in the eighteenth century ensured that most valley residents would become dependents in an age of independence."[4] Such was the future for much of the American countryside.

It is worth emphasizing that the Senecas of western New York were rural people too. Their predicament was in many ways unlike that which faced white farmers; indeed they became "rural" in a very different way—not by spreading out from an expanding colonial metropole, but, instead, by having one envelop them. Yet Seneca dependency within the United States bore some resemblance to that growing dependency experienced by white Ameri-cans in the countryside. Ironically, the Senecas possessed material and cul-tural resources—tribal land, legal status, and community experience—that might offer a greater means than many white farming families could muster to retain a degree of social and economic autonomy. And Seneca people could use these resources as well to help conserve their cultural identity, political viability, and physical presence in New York, surviving in place rather than "moving on" like Cooper's fictional Leatherstocking, disappear-ing like his Native companions Chingachgook and Uncas—the Last of the Mohicans—or suffering removal to the trans-Mississippi West.[5]

The United States moved inexorably toward a capitalist economy in the nineteenth century, which would offer both opportunities and perils and embrace Indians as well as white Americans. The mentality of those who experienced this great transformation is difficult to reconstruct and the sub-ject of scholarly contention. It is likely that many found the novelties of emerging capitalism, perhaps paradoxically, both attractive and threatening. But whether white farmers and their families were protocapitalists or com-mitted to an older moral economy, or somehow both, they overwhelmingly organized their economic lives through a household mode of production. They worked to advance a simple goal—to preserve the integrity of their families and households and to pass on an ability to do the same to succeed-ing generations. Some have called this approach "subsistence-surplus produc-tion." It was characterized by engagement with local and sometimes distant markets, but on terms set by rural people themselves, within the context of a household economic structure and family goals. To achieve such ends generally required cooperation within households and local communities—with extensive exchange of work and goods—rather than complete self-sufficiency. As historian Christopher Clark concluded about western Massachusetts in this era (and by implication much of rural America), "'Independence' required 'interdependence' within households and between them."[6]

In their post-Revolutionary world, the Senecas cultivated just this sort of interdependence and selective engagement with distant markets (particularly by rafting lumber and pelts down the Allegheny River to Pittsburgh), in order to promote economic competency and a measure of "independence." Quaker missionaries sought to remake the Seneca world not merely (or even primarily) by renovating Native religious practice but especially by prescribing new gender roles, family structures, forms of landownership, and patterns of work. They too hoped to cultivate Seneca independence, but through economic isolation. In urging female domesticity and male agricultural toil, they pushed Seneca women to stay home and Seneca men to remain nearby—as farmers. Quakers perceived timber-cutting, market-oriented, Pittsburgh-bound, gallivanting Seneca men as a problem—one nearly as severe as the perils of spirituous drink, itself associated with Seneca trips down the river to Pennsylvania markets. Senecas knew they lived in a complicated, volatile economic universe. But their Friendly advisers failed to see the flexibility and utility—even the modernity—of their hybrid household production and exchange economy. Instead, like other white missionaries and observers, they suffered a blindness that stemmed from their prejudices, anxieties, and good intentions.[7]

Conflicted Quakers and the Market Revolution

Quakers offered an unrealistic, impractical, sometimes contradictory message to the Senecas. Their prescriptions about male individualism and agrarianism, female subservience and domesticity, and nuclear family self-sufficiency were well meaning and conventional but increasingly anachronistic. Would white settlers and farmers under similar circumstances have followed them? Philadelphia's hinterlands had been a center of commercial agriculture since the mid-eighteenth century, and Pennsylvania and New Jersey Quakers had long produced agricultural goods for market. Friends counted among their numbers many of the region's most prominent men of commerce and finance, and Philadelphia was itself embarked on a commercial and increasingly industrial revolution. Yet Quaker visitors to the Allegany reservation did not exactly imagine the Senecas as commercial farmers or future capitalists. Nor did they grasp that living Senecas did not embody a classic primitive past—as a people mired in "barbarism," a stage in the conventional Enlightenment continuum of progress toward "civility." In the midst of change, the Friends themselves were profoundly conflicted about the course of social and economic development in the United States. Quakers struggled to determine how they should respond, fit in, or pull back. Their vision for the Senecas entailed a simpler, more idealized life—a life that remained more isolated, self-sufficient, and utopian than the one available to most Americans, even themselves.[8]

For Quakers, the early nineteenth century was a time of religious, social, and economic turmoil, which would culminate in the 1827 schism separating American Friends into "Orthodox" and "Hicksite" factions. The bitter split emerged from differences over doctrine and authority and quite possibly the divergent social and economic positions of Orthodox and Hicksite Friends, at least among those associated with the Philadelphia Yearly Meeting. The factions' theological disputes and distinctive beliefs might appear obscure to outsiders, but they inspired considerable conflict, as did the personal clashes between Quaker leaders and their respective supporters. We might look more carefully here not at questions of theologies and personalities but at the Friends' struggle with the social, religious, and economic transformations of the early American republic, which was democratizing, evangelizing, and commercializing.

For the historical sociologist Robert W. Doherty, the history of the Society of Friends in the eighteenth century and beyond can be written in terms of the "struggle between Quaker ideals and worldly practice." Some Friends found new opportunities in response to economic changes and embraced them. Others found them unsettling, even corrupting, and "looked with nostalgia to a bygone world which was more congenial to them." According to Doherty, distinctions in material circumstances as well as worldview divided Hicksite and Orthodox Friends. The former were generally poorer, more rural, and less attached to the commercializing economy. In Philadelphia, Hicksites more often lived in marginal neighborhoods, were newer to the city, and as artisans were less likely to work as master craftsmen or own their own shops. Orthodox Friends, on the other hand, were generally wealthier, more urban, and more likely to work in prestigious professions or as master craftsmen. In Philadelphia, they more often resided in better neighborhoods. Orthodox Friends who lived in the countryside were more likely to engage in commercial agriculture, less likely to be debtors, but more likely to use the money they did borrow for commercial purposes. And Orthodox Friends, unlike Hicksites, were well represented among those investing in new speculative business enterprises—banks, navigation or canal companies, manufacturing ventures—and were more supportive of economic development generally. The leader of the schism, Elias Hicks, on the other hand, disapproved of man-made improvements, such as the Erie Canal. Hicks is reputed to have said, "If the Lord had intended there should be internal waterways, he would have placed them there, and there would have been a river flowing through central New York." If Orthodox Friends seemed willing to make peace with the early nineteenth-century secular world, Hicksite Quakers were more apt to draw back from that world, avoid association with non-Friends, and resist its new commercial dynamics.[9]

Subsequent scholars of Quaker history have challenged some of Doherty's specific claims about the socioeconomic basis of the Hicksite Schism, but there seems little doubt that the commercial transformation of the United States economy and society informed the controversy, providing a context for the debate among Friends about the essential meaning of Quakerism. Some worried: Had economic success among Friends led to wealth, luxury, and ostentation at odds with Quaker humility and simplicity, particularly in light of a consumer revolution that offered Americans an unprecedented world of goods, increasingly emblematic of the middle class? Embracing new economic opportunities might produce even greater wealth and worldliness and bring Quakers into more sustained contact with outsiders. And the market revolution might create, not merely unprecedented wealth, but also human misery inconsistent with Quaker humanitarian values. In trying to ameliorate such social and economic dislocation, Friends debated the appropriateness of collaboration with evangelical Protestants. These denominations rapidly increased in number and power in the early nineteenth century and seemed to favor approaches different from (and perhaps at odds with) those common among Friends. Quakers had done the work of benevolence for decades and were more interested in providing material relief than in simply sharing the Bible. Still, as historian Bruce Dorsey has shown, whether Quakers turned inward and became more sectarian (as Hicksites did), or whether they acted more publicly and cooperatively with mainstream Protestantism (the Orthodox approach), both factions engaged in benevolence, including work with Indians, though perhaps in different ways and for different reasons.[10]

Quaker reformers and activists found their Indian work important not only because it followed in the footsteps of William Penn and performed a significant public and humanitarian purpose but perhaps because it offered a useful outlet for expressing and ameliorating deeper anxieties about the changing world—how Friends might live in it and reshape it. Exclusive Quaker benevolent efforts and organizations, like the Philadelphia Indian Committee and its Seneca enterprise, did not aggravate tensions within the Society of Friends, as did those proliferating after 1810 that mixed Quakers and non-Quakers. But given the changing social and economic conditions of the early republic and the growth of discord within the Society of Friends, it is not surprising that Quaker missionaries might find themselves conflicted—or that their anxieties about America's commercializing society would be reflected in their prescriptions for the Senecas.[11]

Friends saw individual male property ownership and agriculture as essential to Seneca progress. But what exactly would this accomplish? Quaker missionaries seldom examined their assumptions, but we might: Would the Quaker program enhance the Senecas' ability to feed themselves? Were the Indians actually poor and hungry, and would this new economic regime guarantee their subsistence? Would it (should it) permit surplus production for the market? How closely would (should) Senecas resemble white settlers and farmers? Like other white American officials and reformers, including Quakers, the Philadelphia Friends among the Senecas were confident in their prescriptions and often unable or unwilling to see the Indians for what they were.

Quakers believed the Senecas to be in a distressed state, which the Indian appeals to the Friends in the 1790s that inspired the mission seemed to confirm. In a speech printed in a Quaker pamphlet to promote the subscription of funds for this purpose, Gayashuta, "an ancient Chief of the Senneca nation," contrasted an earlier time of plenty with contemporary misery. "When I was young and strong our country was full of game. . . . I and the people of my nation had enough to eat. . . . [H]unting was then not tiresome, it was diversion, it was pleasure." The Indians' natural wealth allowed them to act generously toward William Penn and his people and share the land. But now, Gayashuta lamented, he was old and feeble: "he wonders at his own shadow it is become so little." White people have driven away the animals, and young men "must hunt all day long to find game." He and others like him "are become poor, and are hungry and naked."[12]

Times and conditions had certainly changed by the 1790s, and the Senecas had indeed suffered deprivation, but Gayashuta's words were formulaic, part of a conventional Seneca (and broader Iroquois) discourse of pathos—of feeling, sensibility, humility, and regard—among allied parties. At the heart of Iroquois formal public discourse—internal and external—was condolence, which acknowledged the past, praised and lamented the passing of great leaders, and created the conditions for peaceful and productive action. Internally, the Condolence Council, composed of a series of rites, mourned the death of leaders, assuaged grief, restored sanity to the bereaved, recited the roll of chiefs, and elevated new ones to replace the deceased. Externally, diplomatic initiatives employed a similar format, with condolence at its center. Iroquois envoys acknowledged the perils of travel and expressed sorrow over the deaths suffered since the parties had last convened. They ritually removed obstructions along the paths that separated peoples, and they symbolically wiped away tears, unblocked ears, and unstopped mouths to allow clear, calm, and rational speech.[13]

Ceremonial grief and consolation thus infused diplomatic discourse and gave traditional Seneca (and more generally Iroquois) speech a melancholy tone. It emphasized death and decline as the basis for subsequent rebirth or requickening. In the Iroquois condolence ceremony, after the roll call of league chief titles—remembering revered, departed leaders as well as those who currently wore the "antlers" of office—an "outburst of lamentation follows," the nineteenth-century ethnologist Horatio Hale observed. "In recalling these memories of departed greatness," the Iroquois listener was "filled with grief and humiliation at the contrast presented by the degeneracy of his own days." The rite then ended mournfully and abruptly with the words "Now we are dejected in spirit." Seneca diplomatic speech could assume this "melancholy cast" even in the best of times. If this was a recitation of desolation and poverty, Hale noted, it was "doubtless so from the beginning, and before the decay of the Commonwealth or the degeneracy of the age." Hale translated the "doleful exclamation" *Enkitenlane* ("Now we are dejected in spirit") as "I am becoming poor," or "wretched," or "I am in a pitiable state." The ritualized nature of this Iroquois discourse, then—in which a Seneca speaker, even in times of plenty, might lament that he and his people were but a mere shadow of their former selves—should caution us against too literal a reading of Gayashuta's 1790 appeal to the Philadelphia Friends.[14]

Like other Native people, Senecas spoke publicly in formal, coded social language to their friends and allies to invoke reciprocity. Even among equals, parties might find themselves in momentary positions of dominance or weakness, for example, as hosts or as visitors. In such circumstances, hosts were required to show hospitality and generosity, while guests properly expressed deference and humility. In the late eighteenth century, Senecas and Philadelphians were no longer equals. Seneca wealth and power had declined, though they were hardly powerless. And in the 1790s Seneca delegations made their way to Philadelphia (the nation's capital) in a delicate position, to engage in diplomacy and arrange for aid. They found themselves among Friends. Under the circumstances—and in light of their cultural patterns of diplomatic discourse—it should not be surprising to hear Senecas using phrases that bewailed their declension, poverty, and hunger. But Gayashuta's lamentation should not be taken at face value. It was an expression of conscious and formulaic self-deprecation. And it was uttered within the context of a long-standing alliance (reciprocal but no longer equal) designed to enable and promote acts of Friendly generosity—a generosity that both parties agreed the Quakers owed the Indians. A pathetic appeal, given the Senecas' less powerful position, was the polite way to garner the Friends' assistance.[15]

The Friends, however, took Seneca words literally. They mistook style for substance, symbol for reality. In addition to their exaggerated sense of the severity of Seneca poverty and starvation, they misapprehended its cause. Gayashuta's speech highlighted the decline of game and linked it with hunger among the Senecas. Similarly, Cornplanter in 1791 told the Friends (in a speech also published in the Quakers' promotional pamphlet), "The Senneca nation see that the Great Spirit intends they should not continue to live by hunting, and they look round on every side and enquire who it is that shall teach them what is best for them to do." Such comments functioned as rhetoric—that is, they deployed the available means of persuasion. They spoke about a male subsistence activity—hunting—and used the difficulties encountered in that pursuit to illustrate the broader troubles Seneca people faced.[16]

But the situation was less dire than such rhetoric suggested. Hunting was not insignificant; it was much more than mere "diversion" or "pleasure," the characterization used by Gayashuta, which played to white assumptions. Game food supplemented Seneca diet, and skins could be exchanged for goods or cash. An eyewitness account of conditions at Allegany, from Major John Norton (Teyoninhokarawen), the half-Cherokee, half-Scots deputy of the Mohawk leader Joseph Brant, sketched a picture of prospect and prosperity, not crisis, in 1809: "These people have an advantageous situation; although their Reserve is only half a mile on each side of the river, for forty miles in length, yet it takes in the most valuable kind of land. . . . It forms the most valuable hunting ground of any possessed by the Five Nations. They can conveniently take skins, meat and timber, to Pittsburgh, where they generally get a good price for these articles." Hunting would remain an important economic endeavor, his hosts suggested, and "many found it more to their interest to hunt than to work." One Seneca man noted "that for his part he had acquired all his property by hunting, and that with the produce of the Chase, he had hired people to build and work for him." Hunting remained viable, at least through the early decades of the nineteenth century—buoyant enough to produce not merely subsistence but a surplus of meat and skins to trade. And yet, in the same year that Norton visited Allegany and saw its bounty, Cornplanter conformed to standard rhetorical practice when he told a visiting Quaker delegation, "we were become reduced & in a State of Poverty, [and] I had a desire that my Friends, the Quakers, might come & set down by us."[17]

Seneca subsistence itself continued to be diverse, with farming, not hunting, the major contributor. Standard and not necessarily inaccurate complaints about the demise of game animals spoke only in limited ways to the question of actual food availability among the Senecas. Yet Quakers easily assimilated such words into a ready-made progressive scenario in which humans advanced from a primitive hunter state toward prosperity and civility by abandoning the chase and adopting agriculture. Cornplanter's speech thus confirmed what Friends were primed to hear—that the Senecas were a pathetic, backward people in need of help, that Cornplanter and his people could not live by hunting alone and were now ready to learn what Quakers might teach and to acquire the technology Friends might offer. The fact that Senecas did not actually subsist by hunting and were not actually starving, that they produced adequate supplies of food through farming—a production that allowed them to feed Quaker missionaries well when they first arrived in 1798—did not seem to challenge the Friends' assumptions and prescriptions. Perhaps surprisingly, such myopia continued to afflict Quakers not merely in Philadelphia but in their western New York mission as well.[18]

The Friends thus advocated a transition to agriculture for a nation of horticulturalists in order to feed a people who were not hungry. Women's agricultural labor already substantially provided Seneca subsistence, yet Quakers implicitly ignored and devalued that work, while explicitly committing themselves to the task of helping the Senecas feed themselves. They sought to relieve Seneca women of their excessive burdens as agriculturalists, yet they professed a commitment to teach these women industry—something presumably they already knew. In part, the illogic of such plans can be explained in terms of a gendered ethnocentrism typical of colonialism, even the well-meant colonialism of Friends. Quakers surely believed that intensive agriculture, employing draft animals and plows, using male labor, and growing preferred crops was more technologically advanced, more efficient, and more productive. In addition, Quakers saw significant social benefits in redirecting men—understood to be idle and subject to dissipation, in their pursuits of "diversion" and "pleasure"—into productive, toilsome, uplifting activity.[19]

The Friends' blindness regarding men's work mirrored their blindness about women's work. Though not farmers, men assisted in the heavy labor of preparing fields, and they contributed to the Seneca economy through hunting and logging—productive activities that generated critical items for exchange, and thus the means to procure the things Senecas could not make themselves. Were they idle? With the decline of game, presumably hunting now took more, not less, time, expertise, and effort. And logging pines, sawing boards and cutting shingles, gathering bark for tanneries, and rafting logs and processed timber products to market demanded considerable labor of Seneca men. Men's work, like women's, was seasonal and episodic, as it had always been, but the conventional stereotype of the lazy Indian man (and the Indian woman drudge) hardly seems apt. White settlers and farmers—the presumed models for the Senecas—did not themselves work year round in a sustained way, with the same intensity. Seasonal agricultural patterns on white farms produced long days (up to fourteen hours) and full weeks of work at active times of the year but permitted substantial leisure at other periods, typically during the winter months.[20]

What is idleness? For early nineteenth-century Quakers and other white middle-class Americans it was more than temporary lack of movement or activity. They infused the term with social and moral meaning, as conveyed in the old aphorism "idle hands are the devil's tools." In opposition to idleness, reformers promoted "industry," "habitual diligence in any employment," but particularly agriculture or "steady attention to business." And steady, regimented toil would be critical to synchronized production and labor discipline in the new American factories. Yet breaks from work might be construed more positively not as idleness but as rest or leisure. And Senecas—like working-class white Americans in the early republic, whether rural or urban—might have asked, does one live to work, or work to live? If comfort and material competency can be achieved through episodic bursts of activity, why should one work from dawn to dark, day after day?[21]

In the more densely settled regions of the country, in the places governed by the Philadelphia Yearly Meeting, for example, or in the northern New England states that sent many pioneers into western New York, increases in population and the declining amount (and degrading condition) of land for agricultural production pushed farmers to work harder, intensify and diversify production, and occasionally labor for wages in order to survive. This certainly required industry, even among those who did not embrace the logic of capitalist accumulation. Perhaps Quakers anticipated a Malthusian crisis of increasing population amid finite Seneca land-holdings, which would necessitate new forms of industry. No one articulated such a concern.[22] Nor did Friends explicitly advocate greater industry in agricultural production specifically to create surpluses that could be sold in markets to generate profits and capital—accumulating wealth to create more wealth—and to integrate into a national market economy. What *did* the Friends have in mind?

A Seneca Friendly Utopia

Quaker prescriptions for the Senecas oddly resembled the goals that Joseph Ellicott, representing the Holland Land Company, had for the settlers he sought for the company's holdings encompassing the entire southwestern edge of New York State, some 3.3 million acres that abutted or surrounded Seneca territories. As resident agent from 1800 to 1821 (he continued to serve the Ogden Land Company after it acquired the Holland Land Company's preemption rights in 1810), Ellicott hoped to recruit settlers who would advance the company's objective of substantial profit through land sales and rural economic development. For Ellicott and the company's proprietors, "the great objective" was "to get these lands settled and under improvement." Ellicott believed, "Whilever they remain in a state of nature they have no real value; because they are not productive to any individual, and their value will be enhanced in proportion to the extent and populousness of the settlement." According to the Holland Purchase's historian Charles E. Brooks, Ellicott viewed this social and economic development "as an evolutionary process," and the challenge was to compress this long, gradual progression—from hunting and pasturage, to agriculture and commerce—into a few decades. While actually promoting Native dispossession, men like Ellicott allowed themselves to believe—despite the evidence embodied in Seneca people and reservations all around them—that Indians had already passed from the scene. His task was therefore to repopulate the Holland Purchase progressively with seminomadic white improvers and herdsmen, who would then give way to permanent, industrious settlers and farmers, who in turn would transform the landscape into a place of commerce.[23]

Company agents distinguished between two types of pioneers. Good settlers were those willing to overcome the wild environment and alter it—"improve" it, in the conventional language of the day—by clearing, fencing, and cultivating land. Bad settlers were those who proved "lazy and dissolute," who merely squatted, living off the land without cultivating or enhancing it. "Their improvements are inconsiderable, and in many instances scarcely deserve the name. Large families, exhibiting all the appearances of poverty and misery, drag out a wretched existence without a chance of bettering their condition," one company agent complained in 1821. He referred to white pioneers here, but this was just the sort of evaluation that Senecas and other Indian people often earned from white missionaries and other reformers.[24]

To facilitate development, and to attract and enable the better sort of settler, Ellicott and his colleagues encouraged and helped finance the building of an infrastructure essential to communication, transportation, and commercial development. Markets played a critical role in the development project. New York Congressman Peter B. Porter observed in 1810: "The great evil . . . , under which the inhabitants of the Western country labor, arises from the want of a market. . . . The single circumstance, of the want of a market, is already beginning to produce the most disastrous effects not only on the industry but the morals of the inhabitants." Porter's critique mixed moral with social and economic concerns, and again, though applied to white pioneers, it resembled the criticism directed at Senecas: "Such is the fertility of their lands, that one half of their time spent in labor is sufficient to produce every article, which their farms are capable of yielding in sufficient quantities, for their own consumption, and there is nothing to incite them to produce more. They are, therefore, naturally led to spend the other part of their time in idleness and dissipation." Certainly white settlers and Senecas differed substantially from each other, but the fears expressed by Congressman Porter about the limited "improvement" of wild landscapes and wild men—whether white newcomers or Native inhabitants—and their reluctance to embrace capitalist logic and move from subsistence to surplus production, suggest commonalities in the experiences of both in the commercializing countryside of the early American republic.[25]

To address such concerns, the Holland Land Company worked to create markets and promote local manufacturing, particularly by building or subsidizing the construction of grist- and sawmills. The latter encouraged clearing and provided finished building materials; the former encouraged production of corn and especially wheat, which could be exchanged locally and traded in the marketplace. The company similarly invested in the local manufacture of salt, which could be traded to markets as distant as Montreal and Pittsburgh, in exchange for glass, iron, and hollowware, and it recruited blacksmiths, tavern and hotel operators, merchants and storekeepers, and others who might enable local agricultural development, manufactures, and commerce. Regional markets, adequate transportation, local processing and manufacturing, money and credit (Ellicott helped found the Bank of Niagara in 1816) would promote the economic development of the Holland Purchase, fundamentally transform its people and landscape, and advance the company's interests. In this increasingly less remote corner of New York, white pioneers of the Holland Land Purchase lived through (and sometimes resisted) the rural equivalent of the renovating impact of capitalism on working people in industrializing urban America.[26]

Friends among the Allegany Senecas shared some of the assumptions and objectives of men like Joseph Ellicott, himself a Maryland Quaker. They seemed to understand Seneca men just as Ellicott understood the Holland Land Purchase's white pioneers (Ellicott and his agents had little to say about women, who were critical to family success but were not property owners or farmers). Like those pioneers, Seneca men were asked to quickly traverse a series of stages from hunters and herders to farmers. They were instructed to "improve" their land, based on the notion that labor created value and affected by the misapprehension that the landscape was not already transformed by Seneca subsistence activity. Seneca property was not unaltered "wilderness"—it was productive and precious in different, culturally specific ways. Improvements not only made land more valuable in the Holland Land Purchase, but they advanced settlers' claims to ownership, even when they had not yet gained title.[27]

Quakers might have made a similar presumption and reasoned that an "improved" Seneca reservation would be less vulnerable to dispossession. Inherent in the Friends' prescribed transformation of Indian life was an implicit claim that such changes would promote Seneca security as well as happiness and prosperity. The possibility that they might have been correct in certain regards complicates assessments of Quaker colonialism. If Quakers misunderstood Seneca social and economic life and underestimated its utility, they did have a sense of how the Senecas and their lands would be evaluated by outsiders and would remain vulnerable to dispossession. In one significant way, of course, the Friends were dead wrong: the program of "civilization" and "improvement" had been designed not simply to help "poor" Senecas but to render their "surplus" lands more available for white expropriation. Improved individual holdings among the Senecas enhanced the quality and quantity of Seneca land destined, speculators hoped, for white possession. The Quakers' assumptions and logic pushed their program in a direction that Senecas themselves—based on their understanding of its flaws and true costs—partially and selectively adopted, but often discreetly and politely resisted.

In light of the world of rural, capitalist development all around them, the Quaker program takes on the appearance of a discrete, utopian version of the Holland Land Purchase for the Senecas, in which, with Friendly assistance, the Seneca tribe would function as proprietor and individual Indian "settlers" would become "farmers." Unlike the Holland Purchase owners and managers, the Seneca nation would function on a nonprofit basis, and, unlike the Holland Purchase settlers, individual Senecas would remain more stationary and isolated from the increasingly interconnected, commercial world, again with Quaker help, by engaging it only selectively and remaking their own, insulated version of social and economic modernity.[28]

The Senecas—not a land company or the Quakers—owned the land critical to their life, liberty, and pursuit of happiness. In contrast to white settlers of the Holland Purchase, Senecas did not need to acquire land; rather, they needed to retain what they held. In addition, according to the Friends, they needed to reorganize and "improve" it. Senecas did not prefer to treat land as a commodity. They differed from white pioneers and land agents, who understood land as capital and real estate, something to be bought and sold, whose worth was based not merely on its inherent properties (including its productive potential) but on its market value. But in other respects, Seneca rural development might look like economic development elsewhere. Quakers prescribed—and some Senecas accepted—the alteration of woodlands into farmlands, the enclosure of plots, fenced to exclude livestock, and the intensive cultivation of crops in plowed fields, nearby progressively improved farmsteads housing individual families. Roads carved their way through the wilderness, tied farms together, and enabled transportation of materials and produce. Sawmills produced lumber for building locally, and gristmills processed Seneca grain, while blacksmith shops fabricated and repaired necessary tools. As in the Holland Purchase, this rural transportation and manufacturing infrastructure emerged through subsidies, in this case financed and built by Quakers for Seneca use.[29]

Senecas benefited from the Friends' sawmill, for example, not only as an outlet for their harvested timber, but also as a source of processed boards, which they could buy at a substantial discount. They interrogated their Quaker patrons to insure that the mill was in fact run in a manner that aided them—and in a way that operated outside the logic of the market. As the Quaker visitor and former missionary Halliday Jackson reported in 1806, "The Indians . . . want to know how this Money ['rais'd by the Quakers to assist them'] was laid out, and whether these Mills was paid for out that Money, for you have built them Mills & the Indians buy Boards from you, and sometimes they cant tell whether you are helping them, or they helping you." The Friends replied, "these Mills cost a great deal of Money but that if ever they should be sold to other People, the money would be applied to the use of the Indians," and further "that none of the money rais'd for the benefit of the Indians would ever be applied to any other purpose." The Senecas were satisfied. Friends employed a white man to operate the sawmill, and they directed that "all the logs the Indians bring to the Mill are saw'd to the halves, and Boards are sold to such of them as want to buy at half a dollar pr. hundred feet which is about half the present Market price."[30]

But here the object seemed less to promote integration of the Seneca economy with the larger commercial world than to segregate it. If Congressman Porter had decried the lack of markets in the Holland Purchase, Quakers seemed unconcerned—perhaps even thankful—for their absence in areas proximate to their Seneca mission. While markets played an essential role in rural capitalist development, providing the opportunity for profit and the incentive for production itself, they could also afford the income and opportunity to consume the worst that the white world had to offer—wasteful luxury, ostentation, or dissipation—especially if men took their profits in alcohol. The Allegheny River reserve remained remote, even after construction of the Erie Canal, and thus Allegany Senecas lacked easy access to markets to buy supplies and materials or to sell agricultural produce. Such a limitation might have seemed like an advantage to the Friendly visitors, who could insulate Seneca neophytes from the influences of the corrupting white world. Quakers themselves would bestow the technology, tools, supplies, and incentives that markets might otherwise provide.[31]

This hybrid economy represented a sort of market production without markets, coupled with household production enabled by Quaker subsidies. Increased Seneca manufacturing and use of new technologies would have been encouraging to those Friends enthusiastic about the larger commercializing world. Seneca isolation from real markets and concentration on home-centered production, on the other hand, would have been more amenable to those Friends anxious about the market revolution. The Quakers seemed to dream of a new Seneca economic world that was a Friendly, Jeffersonian place, purged of markets, venders, and vice. We get a sense of its logic from the journals of two missionary Quakers, Halliday Jackson and John Philips, who recorded—and implicitly endorsed—the message of Erastus Granger, superintendent of Indian affairs, at New Amsterdam (Buffalo) in 1806. Granger, a Jefferson administration appointee, advised the Senecas to emulate the lives of idealized white rural Americans, not those who lived in the growing American towns and cities. Such places, he noted, were filled with "the Doctors, the Lawyers, Ministers & Merchants, which is a class of people I wish may never come among you." The Friends seemed to hope that social and economic seclusion would be possible in remote Allegany. Responding to a government inquiry in 1819, Joseph Ellicott attested to the apparent success of their approach: "It is an undoubted fact that the Indians now residing in the Allegany Reservation, who have been upwards of twenty years under the instruction of Friends delegated by the yearly meeting of Friends in Philadelphia, and have by their local situation been otherwise almost entirely excluded from intercourse with white people are more civilized and have acquired a better knowledge in the mechanical arts and husbandry than any other portion of the Seneca Nation."[32]

Seneca "self-sufficiency" was a practical goal that both Friends and Indians might find attractive, as would many rural white farming families. But Quakers seem to have ignored the fact that Senecas had already found their own path to self-sufficiency—an interdependent independence that engaged the market. As one Pittsburgh merchant noted in 1803, Seneca men "generally came down twice a year, with their canoes heavy loaded, with furrs, peltry, mogasons, deer hams, tallow, bear skins." Later in the journal, he wrote, "They have besides a sawmill, and being surrounded with lofty pine trees, they cut them into boards or scantling and float them down to Pittsburgh at the time of high water. And on these rafts they bring their peltry, furrs, and good canoes, to push up their return cargoes . . . and sometimes shingls, the latter of which I have bought for one dollar and fifty cents per thousand and paid for them in merchandize." Similarly, the Calvinist missionary Jacob Cram, passing through the Allegany Seneca reservation in 1805, reported that Senecas "have learnt the smith business, so as to do common work. Many are ingenious in house carpenter work. One learned how to make axes in three days. One learned to make sacks in two days. Two are good coopers in making buckets and churns." Cram commented as well on the Senecas' wealth of livestock, particularly their "great number of swine," noting "some have salted down pork for sale." Such industry and trade represented the exchange of raw materials (logs), processed items (furs, tallow, meat), finished goods (moccasins, boards, shingles), and sometimes labor by enterprising Seneca men for necessary supplies, things unavailable to Senecas locally (unless offered by Quakers), and perhaps even cash.[33]

In 1799, Quakers learned that kegs of beer were among the items transported home by Seneca men, and observers (and Senecas) would complain more generally about the trade in stronger spirits. Beer and whiskey were not available locally (except perhaps during treaty negotiations), certainly not from Quakers. Friends and reforming Senecas attempted to control the free market in liquor. Seneca consumption of alcohol had led to a good deal of trouble. Yet, ironically, its sale—not *to* Indians but *by* Indians to their white neighbors—could represent Seneca enterprise. In 1806, Quaker visitors to the Allegany reservation learned from their resident missionary colleagues "that one or two of their young Chiefs had introduc'd some Liquor in a Clandestine manner in order *to sell to the white people*, but the Indians in general was much oppos'd to such conduct." Quakers too sought to dampen rather than encourage this market exchange, both the local sale of liquor and the far-flung trade oriented toward Pittsburgh. In 1810, the Quaker missionary Halliday Jackson wrote in his journal, "a trade upon benevolent principles would be advantageously opened by friends with the Natives giving them more for their peltries than others and thus superseding the necessity of their going to a distant market. It should be a barter with *useful* supplies."[34]

Friends did often make necessary tools available (typically lending rather than selling them), and they provided raw materials for spinning. But as

Quaker authorities communicated to Senecas at Allegany in 1803, they opposed (and would continue to oppose) opening a store locally, which might have functioned as a marketplace, buying Seneca produce and vending necessary manufactured goods and supplies. At Cattaraugus a few days later, the Quaker visitors expressed a willingness to offer some more assistance (supplying additional blacksmith tools and another plow), but there were limits. They refused to contribute more oxen for the same reason they demurred when asked to become shopkeepers among the Senecas: the Friends sought to avoid Seneca dependency, "as they must learn to help themselves."[35]

Of course, the way Senecas helped themselves—a way suited to the changing conditions of their world—was to trade with Pittsburgh, amid Friendly criticism of the practice, and to accept Quaker aid while tolerating their conflicted, impractical advice. A visiting Quaker delegation told them in 1817, "we have been made very sorry in observing the large quantity of excellent pine timber cut and preparing for rafting and upon enquiring of our friends residing among you are informed they have advised you strongly against it." (They were more positive in their assessment of those Seneca homes that, by 1806, boasted "pannel Doors and glass Windows"—features most likely imported from Pittsburgh.) But the Friends' concerns and regrets did not lead to compulsion: "You are very capable to calculate what is for your advantage and what is not. We therefore desire you would take into consideration whether you would not have been in a better situation generally if you had employed the same time which you have spent in cutting and rafting timber in cultivating your good land, which would . . . produce a plentiful supply for yourself and cattle." For Quakers, it was "evident [that] their attention in cutting and rafting pine timber has much retarded their progress in agriculture." But for Senecas, indeed capable of calculating their own advantages, such production and exchange were essential and superior to the prescribed course of "progress" in agriculture, already well managed by women.[36]

While appreciating Quaker material and technical aid, Senecas must have wondered how long Friendly subsidies would continue. And Quakers were reluctant to establish markets locally that might simultaneously enable Seneca commercial exchange and expose Senecas to predatory or corrupting commerce. Given the nature of their land, the distance of markets, and the limits of transportation networks, commercial agriculture was hardly feasible. Meanwhile, subsistence farming thrived, improved by technical innovations, though still superintended and practiced by women. The extraction and trade of renewable natural resources (lumber, forest products, pelts), as well as partially processed and finished goods, seemed to Senecas a better means of gaining critical items they could not manufacture themselves. Quakers complained about such trade, as we have seen, on numerous levels, but their arguments must have seemed unconvincing to Senecas. They asked Seneca men, in a sense, to give up the labor and enterprise that could generate salable products for the marketplace for alternative work that would not produce surplus and marketable commodities and was already performed well by others (women). To avoid dependency, which Quakers proscribed, Senecas rejected the advice about male agriculture that they prescribed.

Ironically and impractically, the Friends seem to have preferred that Senecas pursue a sort of commercial farming detached from the market, made possible by Allegany's remoteness and propped up by their own, inconstant offering of supplies and equipment, profits and incentives, usually available only through markets. The Friends thus asked that Senecas decrease their standard of living in the interest of a mechanical adherence to a stereotypical Indianness born of ethnocentrism and good intentions. Such an approach simultaneously expressed, even before the Hicksite schism erupted, a Quaker-Orthodox confidence in the new commercial, capitalist world as well as a Quaker-Hicksite aversion to materialism and the market. It was less a recipe for self-sufficiency and "progress" than it was for dependence and decline.

Women and the Perils of Domestic Industry

Where did women figure in these plans? The Quaker men who founded the Seneca mission welcomed female Friends to their outpost in the summer of 1805, expressing satisfaction that the newcomers would not only assist in transforming Seneca society but also relieve Quaker men of their own domestic duties. As Halliday Jackson later wrote, "from the first settlement to this time, in addition to the various calls of the Indians, and their out-door labours, they [that is, male Friends] had all their domestic and culinary services to perform,—except some little aid received at times, by hiring some of the Indian women." The female missionaries, Rachel Cope and Hannah Jackson, in addition to their domestic service to Quaker men, would specialize in the renovation of Seneca women. As Indian men increasingly assumed the burdens of agriculture, the Friends hoped, Indian women would be afforded "more time to turn their attention to the business of the house, and the concerns more properly allotted to females, in all civilized societies." Quaker women would teach both by direct instruction and through their own example, as Seneca women visited Quaker domiciles. There, Indian women would learn "industry, economy, and [a] superiour mode of living"; they would be encouraged "to imitate the more useful and rational economy of our women friends," Halliday Jackson noted, which included spinning, knitting, and soap-making.[37]

Gender-specific incentives had been offered by Quakers to Seneca women as well as to men to encourage prescribed social and economic transformation. After some initial trouble obtaining spinning wheels and procuring flax, Seneca women began to make a bit of progress, according to the missionaries' report. By early 1806, some were making soap and "some have Spun and Knit a little, and appear Desirous to improve." Later in February 1806, Friends wrote, "a few have made considerable progress, and have now a small Piece ready for the loom." But Rachel Cope and Hannah Jackson also observed that some Senecas proved skeptical or objected to this new domestic production, and it became the subject of general debate in a council in 1807. After a vigorous appeal by Quaker spokesmen and mature consideration by Indian leaders, Senecas tentatively endorsed this new female project, while allowing individual Indian families the option of accepting or rejecting Quaker instruction in the domestic arts.[38]

In the following years, Quakers reported uneven progress. In October 1808, for example, the Friends related that among the Indian women and girls "not much advancement hath been made in spinning the latter part of the season." But in March 1810, Quaker chroniclers noted, "More has been done the present winter at spinning by them than has been heretofore in one year." By the next winter, the Friends could describe substantial advances in women's spinning: "Out of 110 Women residing on this reserve, upwards of 50 have come forward to learn to spin, 25 of which are capable of making good yarn, four of their number had 90 y. [yards] wove within two years part, those four now have yarn sufficient to make 36 yds more, ten of them have purchased wheels for themselves, two of the foremost of them have spun and wove 21 y. of linsey, it was a particular satisfaction to us that they were prevailed upon to weave it themselves." Meanwhile, men's improvement in agriculture was frustratingly slow—"so slow that we sometimes conclude that they are not ripe for trade." "On the whole," the Friends admitted in February 1811, "our service here (except for the spinning) does not amount to encouragement sufficient to calculate to reside long amongst them, without a change in our arrangements with the native, unless a revival taken place amongst them in the spirit of improvement in mechanical arts more than has been of late."[39]

If the Senecas' advances in spinning and related domestic employments seemed uniquely positive to Quakers, this "progress" was as much cyclical as linear. In the fall of 1808, female instruction and domestic industry had lagged in part because Seneca women and girls remained occupied, "having been much employed in the labour of the fields."[40] As Quaker reports repeatedly acknowledged, Seneca women would continue to farm, fitting in other tasks around this central occupation. In any October, not merely in 1808—at the end of the harvest—Seneca women would have little time to spin or weave.[41] Not surprisingly, Friends most frequently reported Seneca successes in the domestic arts during the winter season, when women were free of agricultural work. Farming itself persisted as a female occupation, critical culturally and socially as well as economically. Women's planting, cultivation, and harvesting continued to be highly ritualized among the Senecas, as it had been for generations, women spiritually aligned with their "Great Three Sisters"—corns, beans, and squash—as they were physically connected in the fields where they grew. New crops—whether food (wheat), fodder for livestock (oats or hay), or raw material for manufacturing cloth (flax)— sometimes grown by men, lacked this traditional religious status and cultural place.[42]

Women worked in the fields not because men were lazy but because their horticultural tasks gave women purpose, power, and status, while they contributed fundamentally to Seneca subsistence. It is possible that women could have produced a surplus for the marketplace, and women were not averse to trade, though the limitations of the landscape and distance from markets made it less likely. Senecas did on occasion trade surplus corn to neighboring whites, but such transactions did not necessarily make these Indian farmers "market oriented." Trade took place on terms defined by rural producers themselves—among Indians as well as rural whites—to serve their own goals: family and community independence and competence. Opportunity and motive for classic commercial agriculture were limited, and in any case Quakers apparently did not imagine Seneca women engaged in such an enterprise or embodying such a role. Occasional trade in agricultural produce was, for Senecas, as it was for nearby white farmers, more characteristic of a subsistence-surplus household economy than a new, market-centered commercial regime.

Giving up farming in this era would have cost women plenty, while depressing the Senecas' standard of living. Women's primary role as producer and provider of food and their connection to the land where food was gathered and cultivated were intricately woven into Seneca cultural life. To replace women as farmers would require a radical reknitting of Seneca culture. Women were the proprietors and stewards of Seneca land, and they acted as a force for its preservation. Women's as well as men's economic and ecological practice made collective, rather than individual, private ownership preferable, indeed critical.[43]

Senecas rejected Quaker proposals for division of their lands in severalty (individual, private property) in gendered ways. Seneca women observed that "our fields lay promiscuously or in confused divisions and all shapes & lines splintering & separating them & perhaps occupied by others." Individuals maintained claims to particular parcels as they used them, but particular "ownership" was momentary or transitory—"confused" to outsiders but broadly sensible to Native people. Collective ownership was superior because it offered flexibility over time and space and fit the subsistence needs of Senecas generally. Seneca women and men rejected ownership in severalty because they continued to favor extensive over intensive production—a diverse rather than a specialized, or simplified, economic (and ecological) strategy.[44]

Modern ecologists see extensive farming, which more closely mimics nature, as the more prudent and sustainable. Land wears out and needs rest; extensive production spreads and thus lessens human impacts, while intensive agriculture potentially mines the soil and degrades it. Clearing new land was difficult and required collective effort, and allowing land to remain fallow demands cooperative restraint. Native people required various terrains to cultivate, gather, or extract resources and produce food. Senecas thus told Quakers, "Many think that if divided into lots they cannot do this & that lots that may fall to them will not have within its lines bottom lands for planting, and pine for rafting & say [therefore, the lands are] better owned in common." The Friends' recommended changes in Seneca ownership and land use thus found little support among Seneca women. To accept such transformation, women would have been required to remake cultural life, abandon their stewardship role, reduce their social status and power, substitute individual, more isolated, work patterns for collective ones, and accept a new economic regime likely to erode their people's standard of living and bonds of community.[45]

Quakers nonetheless remained hopeful that Seneca women would leave the fields to men, and they continued to overstate Seneca advancement in the transformation of agricultural labor. But as we have seen, such progress was not what it appeared to be. Men assisted women in the hard work of clearing new fields, and some acquired skill in plowing, which could be understood as field preparation rather than cultivation itself. As such, plowing seems to have become a specialized job for some Seneca men, a means to earn wages. With plows and oxen scarce, Native people pooled their resources and employed those with specialized skills and access to scarce tools to plow their fields. According to one report, an enterprising young Seneca man had plowed some twenty-two acres in 1819, earning from various Native employers a rate of two dollars per acre. Despite Friends' hopes, from a Seneca perspective, male plowing produced cash, not corn or wheat.[46]

Similarly, apparent success in animal husbandry among men did little to challenge women's ascendancy in the control of land and in agriculture generally. Various Quaker observers heralded the novel increase of livestock (though Iroquois communities had long supplied their meat through raising stock as well as hunting). In 1805, a Friend noted, "they have a number of fat cattle to sell this fall and hogs in abundance." Swine proved especially useful, as they did for so many early Americans, both Indians and whites. They were easily managed, could fend for themselves, multiplied rapidly, and could be raised for sale or salted for consumption. Seneca swineherds ultimately would not impress Quakers and others as sufficiently advanced (white herders often fell below the threshold of "civility" as well). Nor were Quakers impressed by Seneca success in raising horses. In 1809, they told residents at Cattaraugus, "We are pleased to observe some increase in the number of your cattle, but if you had more Cows and Oxen and fewer Horses, you would find advantage in it." "They have more horses than is of any advantage to them," one Friend complained in 1817. In fact, some horses might have been traded locally, and they were useful to Seneca men in hauling timber, advancing the very enterprise that Quakers believed distracted men from real agricultural toil. In any case, male livestock management was not understood as agricultural work by Senecas and did little to displace Seneca women from their fields of corn, beans, squashes, potatoes, and other vegetable crops, the core of their subsistence. Instead, such male labors further enabled traditional women's agricultural work.[47]

The domestic arts and industry prescribed by Quakers for Seneca women would thus augment, not replace, their agricultural labors. Seneca women had traditionally managed their own households, within multifamily longhouses that were organized on a matrilineal, matrilocal basis—that is, embracing senior women, their female offspring, and their spouses and families (with men marrying into their wives lodges). And many characteristics of this communal, maternal order would persist even as Senecas shifted to smaller houses occupied by single families. We need not presume, as Quakers did, that such households lacked "useful and rational economy" or could not match the Friends' own "superiour mode of living." Still, Senecas were not averse to aid and technological innovation, and they could see some advantages in Quaker instruction and the domestic manufacturing they recommended. Foremost among these recommendations was the practice of spinning thread and weaving cloth—the "homespun" that could clothe Indian as well as white rural families. Seneca women traditionally performed the skilled work of tanning skins and fabricating clothing, and much earlier in the eighteenth century they had begun to acquire manufactured cloth and use it to make garments for themselves and their families. They would continue to work in leather and cloth, even producing moccasins for sale, including them in the cargo men rafted to Pittsburgh (as we have seen above). The production of cloth itself, though, was something new. Was such female industry in fact practical and advantageous?[48]

The ability to produce their own fabric might have struck Seneca women as a considerable benefit, potentially raising their standard of living and enhancing Seneca self-sufficiency. The Quakers had offered bounties to encourage production of linen and woolen cloth (or linsey-woolsey, a combination of the two), under particular conditions that encouraged male agriculture and female domesticity. Linen, it was stipulated, should be manufactured "out of flax raised on her own or her husband's land, and spun in her own house." Similarly, woolens and linsey were to be made from the wool of a woman's own or her husband's sheep, and "spun in her own house."[49] All this was easier said than done. But if some women were willing to spin and weave, few among the Senecas—female or male—seemed committed to producing much flax or tending sheep. The raw materials for this domestic industry would have to come from elsewhere, from the Friends themselves. As would the tools of the trade—spinning wheels and looms—lent or given to Seneca women, or later sold to them in subsidized fashion. After women Friends had established themselves at Tunesassa among the Allegany Senecas, and thus were able to offer female instruction, they acknowledged the shortage of raw materials locally: "wool we dont expect you can get a great deal of yet, but we saw some flax of your own raising and our friends have a little wool and flax which they will be willing to give you to begin with and next year you can raise more flax." (The next years would not yield much Native flax, let alone wool.) In their appeal, the Quakers told the Senecas, "A house is built for such of your girls to work in as incline to be instructed and some wheels provided." In short, Quakers provided much of the incentives, raw materials, and equipment for Seneca domestic manufacturing—nearly everything but the labor itself. This was a recipe for colonial economic dependence.[50]

Seneca women were prepared to work, but they would need to assimilate the new tasks of spinning and weaving into their broader work lives in ways consistent with their habits and greater responsibilities. Seneca women preferred to work communally. They organized their new employment along such lines, led by senior women. Spinning became most intolerable (the drudgery of it aside) when it became a solitary enterprise—when group instruction and work ended and when the increase of spinning wheels no longer required sharing of equipment and common labor. In this regard, Seneca women were not completely unlike white rural women. They frequently complained of the loneliness and confinement of cloth work and appreciated "spinning frolics" and quilting bees that brought women and girls together sociably. Seneca women, also like their white counterparts, sometimes specialized in their domestic manufacturing or "changed work," sharing the larger economic burdens of womanhood among neighbors while dividing up or trading particular tasks. In 1806, Quakers promised the Senecas that "our friends will assist you in getting it [the flax and wool they might spin] made into Cloth." Apparently, although many learned to spin, only one Seneca woman ever became proficient at weaving (a more specialized skill among white rural women as well). This expertise eventually allowed her to trade her cloth beyond her own village, to neighboring white settlers.[51]

Like rural white women and men, Senecas would make rational choices about the relative economy of home production versus consumption of machine-made cloth. Spinning (if not weaving) was "a nearly universal occupation" among white farm women, "a very proper accomplishment for a farmer's daughter," wrote the New Jersey Quaker Susanna Dillwyn in 1790. "Given the significance of spinning in women's lives," then, as the historian Mary Beth Norton has observed, "it is not surprising that American men and women made that occupation the major symbol of femininity." It was that emblematic quality—as much as its practical economic value—that recommended spinning as "a very proper accomplishment" for Seneca girls and

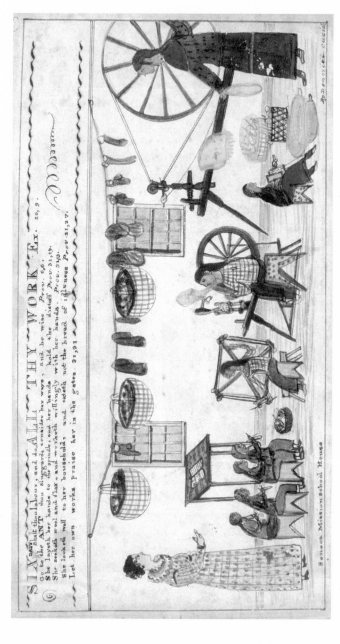

Figure 13. *Woman Teaching Indian Girls, Seneca Mission School House*, by the Tuscarora artist Dennis Cusick, ca. 1821. Here, in a scene from Buffalo Creek, Seneca girls and women—like those under the supervision of Quakers at Allegany—receive gender-specific training in spinning, carding, and knitting. The image includes several prescriptive biblical verses from Exodus and Proverbs, including the following: "She layeth her hands to the spindle, and her hands hold the distaff" (Proverbs 31:19); "She seeketh wool and flax, and worketh willingly with her hands" (Proverbs 31:13); and "She looketh well to her household, and eateth not the bread of idleness" (Proverbs 31:27, which the text mistakenly cites as 21:27). Courtesy of the Hirschl & Adler Galleries, New York.

women. But if the spinning wheel was the badge of domesticity and woman-hood, it was nonetheless destined for obsolescence. By the mid-eighteenth century, most women in northern seaboard towns and cities had already abandoned the production of their own cloth in favor of cheaper imported textiles manufactured in England. The boycotts and economic nationalism of the American Revolutionary era temporarily revived domestic manufacture in urban areas, but as commerce returned and grew machine-produced cloth would become an increasingly more available and attractive item for con-sumption, not merely in cities but in the countryside as well.[52]

Friendly prescriptions for Seneca women (and white missionary pro-grams generally) ignored such trends, however. Quakers' efforts to transform Indian women and their work expressed as many conflicts and concerns as their attempts to remake men's labor and the larger Seneca economy. They reflected their own misgivings about the course of commercial and industrial development—about the growth of consumption and luxury on the one hand, and misery and poverty on the other. They betrayed growing anxieties about how Quakers themselves might live in such a world (or apart from it), in simplicity rather than corruption. And they reflected as well female Friends' particular challenges as middle-class women, capable and increas-ingly well-educated and committed to public service in an age that did not yet support women's social, legal, economic, or political equality. The Seneca mission might be a place where conflicted Quaker women could create and reaffirm a traditional, idealized, reassuring world of gentle patriarchy and domesticity, while legitimately acting beyond their own domestic sphere and doing Seneca women good. Their enterprise might be a means of engaging the world while remaining apart, in remote southwestern New York, and creating a model for more general reform that stressed fundamental Quaker values of family nurturance and discipline.[53]

While Quaker women worked to transform poor Senecas, they were laboring to instruct and assist the poor of Philadelphia. Comparing these projects is suggestive. As historian Margaret Morris Haviland has shown, in the late eighteenth century, Quaker women confronted the newly misfortu-nate of Philadelphia and sought to cast over them "the veil of charity." Fe-male Friends were disturbed by the real problems of economic dislocation associated with the rise of manufacturing in the early republic (the working poor and destitute made up at least a third of the population), and they were driven to perform acts of material benevolence that utilized their talents but were consistent with women's caregiving functions. Quaker women thus organized a number of charities in the 1790s, which continued to operate through the early nineteenth century. In 1795, they founded the Female Society for the Relief and Employment of the Poor as well as the Society for the Free Instruction of African Females. In 1798, they formed the Aimwell School Association. These Quaker women hoped to assist their charges materially and "allure them into the Path of Virtue." The practical training—"guarded education"—they offered to urban black women bore some resemblance to the instruction offered to Senecas. It included visitation, vocational training, and relief. It sought to teach reading, writing, and ciphering. It stressed piety, honesty, responsibility, frugality, and self-sufficiency. Quaker women handed out spinning wheels and sewing work.[54]

In 1798, the same year that Quakers commenced work at Allegany, they embarked on a novel experiment in Philadelphia when they established a "House of Industry" (opened January 1799). Its female founders wrote, "We are induced to believe a benefit would arise in providing a house containing several commodious apartments, purchasing a quantity of Flax, Wool, some large & small Wheels and other utensils necessary in spinning and appropriating one of the rooms & such utensils to the use of a number of spinners who might be made comfortable by one fire, and supplied with food at a much lower rate than would be possible by distributing a portion to each family." Though Friends ultimately hoped to restrict Seneca women to their own homes, where they would practice the domestic arts within the confines of new patriarchal households, in fact the instruction and early spinning that occurred at Allegany bore some resemblance to the Philadelphia House of Industry. Seneca women were not destined—not in Quakers' minds—to become wage earners in a workshop or factorylike setting, as seemed to be the case in Philadelphia. But at Tunesassa beginning in 1806, Friends did similarly endow a Seneca house of instruction and work.[55]

At Tunesassa as in Philadelphia, Quakers afforded a common manufacturing facility, the raw materials, the tools and equipment, and the instruction and support necessary for production. In both places, their benevolent enterprises utilized economies of scale by consolidating work and training. The point in Tunesassa was not, as in Philadelphia, to provide women regular paid work, but rather to instruct collectively and then redeploy women in their own households. Still, both places advanced a reformist agenda, designed to transform poor women—to make them "clean and decent," to regulate their "conversation," to teach them habits of industry, and to console and correct, not to convert. The group experience proved amenable to

Seneca women, as did the chance to produce goods or cash to augment their families' lives.[56]

But they remained skeptical. One Seneca doubter, Johnson Silverheels, asked in 1806, "we want to know what these Girls are to get for working there." And they did not ultimately share the Quakers' goal of domestic manufacturing situated within individual households. Seneca women and girls might well have preferred the wage work characteristic of the Philadelphia House of Industry, which could be performed collectively and incorporated strategically without upsetting the basic organization of their social and working lives. In Philadelphia, though the House of Industry did not employ complex machinery or synchronized production, Quaker women seemed to look forward to new forms of labor organization and discipline that would become common as working people—girls and women among them—increasingly toiled for wages in factories. In Tunesassa, Quaker women seemed to look backward, using a modern, consolidated form of instruction and production to achieve a traditional end for Seneca women—domesticity, which removed rather than integrated women into a commercial economy. It did not work. Senecas never embraced the Quakers' ultimate purpose, failed to produce the requisite raw materials, proved unenthusiastic about individual ownership of spinning wheels, rejected solitary spinning, and by the 1820s abandoned homespun altogether, as machine-produced textiles became the more economical choice.[57]

Seneca women thus negotiated a course distinct but not completely dissimilar from the one traveled by white rural women. Unlike white farming women, Senecas provided the bulk of their families' subsistence through their work in the fields, and they would continue to do so. Seneca women never devoted themselves to spinning and weaving in a way comparable to their rural white counterparts. Spinning flax fit Seneca women's seasonal work schedules, but spinning wool—usually done after shearing in the spring—conflicted with their agricultural responsibilities. And no Seneca women (or Seneca men, for that matter) aspired to become shepherds, an unpromising, ruinous occupation in the Allegany landscape of that era. In western Massachusetts at the very beginning of the nineteenth century, inventories suggest that three-fourths of rural families could make their own yarn and one-third their own cloth. The rate of domestic manufacturing was never this high among the Senecas. But the premiums offered by the Hampshire, Franklin, and Hampden Agricultural Society to rural white women to produce various kinds of cloth suggest that artificial incentives were required here as well as on the Allegany reservation. White women in the Massachusetts countryside faced increased labor demands, as families struggled to maintain their household viability and independence. In addition to spinning and weaving, women were responsible for increased dairy production, and many were bearing more children. In the second decade of the nineteenth century, fertility rates seem to have declined, and women's household production was reorganized, with most households abandoning textile production between 1815 and 1830, according to historian Christopher Clark. As a sign of the times, the annual Northampton cattle show's report on domestic manufacturing in 1831 complained about the dearth of entries of plain cloth submitted for its competition, attributable, it said, to a "diversion of female industry . . . from household manufacturing." Increasingly, the show would feature the products of local textile mills, and the cloth used by rural people would be factory-made and store-bought.[58]

By the 1820s, the Senecas had a made a similar choice, both in the interest of tradition (allowing women to retain their traditional work and status) and novelty (accepting new market relations, specialized trade, and wage work for men). Seneca innovation and hybridity, not the Quakers' prescriptions, would permit Senecas generally to remain self-sufficient and independent in an ever more interconnected, commercialized world. Ironically, Friendly efforts to redeploy men in agricultural production and women in "domestic industry" were designed to fix a subsistence system that was not broken and break a system of market exchange that was critical to the Senecas' own household exchange economy. The Friends' conflicts and anxiety about capitalist transformation, and their internal struggle about the direction of Quakerism itself, made it difficult for them to appreciate the utility of Seneca adjustments or the real nature of their own contribution to Seneca survival. The idealized vision of self-sufficient Seneca yeomen and spinners was anachronistic from the start. Its passing eclipsed a conflicted Quaker nostalgia that Senecas themselves prudently dismissed, even as they benefited materially from Quaker relief, instruction, and tolerant counsel. Like those white settlers who increasingly encroached on Indian lands in New York, the Senecas adjusted to change in order to serve a fundamental goal of economic competence and intergenerational social survival.[59]

CHAPTER 6

Seneca Repossessed, 1818–1826

Artful men may apply to [the general government] for the appointment of a commissioner to hold a treaty; and by false but plausible representations, and perhaps, too, aided by certificates of men apparently disinterested, obtain their request: the poor oppressed Indians "having no comforter."
—Timothy Pickering to the Indian Committee, Philadelphia Yearly Meeting (1817)

But I returned and considered all the oppressions that are done under the sun; and behold the tears of such as were oppressed, and they had no comforter; and on the side of their oppressors there was power, but they had no comforter. Wherefore I praised the dead that are already dead more than the living that are yet alive; but better than they both is he that hath not yet been, who hath not seen the evil work that is done under the sun.
—Ecclesiastes 4:1–3

I think the whiskey did it.
—Tommy Jemmy in Liverpool (1818)

AUGUSTUS FOX, A western New York entrepreneur and sometime impresario, had occasion to write a young English Quaker women, Elizabeth Fothergill, in August 1819. We will hear more about both soon, because they played important roles in the early career of the notorious Tommy Jemmy, before his execution of the alleged witch Kauquatau in 1821. Fothergill cared deeply about the Senecas' welfare. Now she learned about a disturbing "division amongst the Indians." Fox reported that it had been "caused first by Missionaries, who have come among them, endeavouring to prevail on them to lay aside the religion of their fathers, and embrace a new one." "[S]ome of them appear to comply," Fox wrote, "whilst the great majority of the nation oppose it, and urge the indispensable obligation of serving the Great Spirit, according to the customs of their fathers." But worse, Fox observed, "The government has been trying to purchase their lands, which they refuse to sell, but not withstanding which, it has troubled their minds very much."[1]

As the 1820s approached, the Senecas were living in an agitated, divided world. Religious controversy, exacerbated by new missionary intrusions, was unsettling. But more than that, it was dangerous—it made a united response to the new, more intensified efforts to dispossess them more difficult. Seneca minds were "troubled" because their very existence was imperiled—especially by the benign sounding efforts to "purchase" their lands. In the years approaching the United States' fiftieth birthday, the Senecas successfully parried unprecedented challenges—new assaults on their tribal lands, their sovereignty, their national identity and integrity, their presence in New York State. It was a time characterized by one Quaker missionary as "the blackness of darkness." The Senecas' nativist revival, the patronage of the Friends, their resourcefulness and renewed cultural resources, and some luck allowed them to prevail, to see new dawns. They avoided removal, contested the legal diminishment of their property rights, collected annuities that helped them survive, retained and restored a land base in New York, and won an ambiguous but significant victory in the landmark legal case *New York State v. Tommy Jemmy*. As the sun rose over the Empire State and the United States, and Americans celebrated their country's jubilee, the sun did not set on the Senecas.

The Blackness of Darkness: Seneca Division and Repossession

In the Treaty of Fort Stanwix in 1784, the United States government treated the Indians as "a subdued people . . . overcome in a war." Such conquest had no actual basis in fact. Great Britain had claimed only sovereignty over Indian territory within its colonies—not property rights—and following its defeat in the Revolution it could not convey rights it never claimed. The first secretary of war, Henry Knox, quickly realized that an Indian policy of military reduction would prove difficult and costly; conciliation would be cheaper, more effective, and consistent with national honor. In practice, therefore, the new federal government proceeded to purchase rather than simply to confiscate Indian land. But it retained a sense of its full dominion over Native territories. By the Treaty of Canandaigua in 1794, it began to refer to Indian lands as "reservations"—the more clearly delineated, shrinking tracts reserved for Indians, surrounded by non-Indian state and federal territory. The extent to which white jurisdictions and even white land "ownership" might penetrate these reservations was a matter of some ambiguity.[2]

With the Intercourse Act of 1790 and follow-up legislation, the federal government asserted its role as ultimate authority in Indian affairs (to the detriment of state claims), and it imposed its control over all Native land sales, which now could take place only within the context of public treaties, held under the authority of the United States. Private concerns could acquire an exclusive right to purchase Indian land—called the right of preemption— but they could not execute these sales without the consent of the federal government. As the legal scholar Stuart Banner observes, restrictions on Indians' ability to sell their land—even if they chose not to sell it at all— diminished Native ownership rights. "When Indian land could be bought and sold with the Indians still on it, the Indians' right to the land started to feel, to the buyers and sellers, less like fee simple ownership." Technically, all that was being bought and sold was the exclusive right to purchase Indian land in the future, not the land itself. But increasingly, American property law constructed Indians as mere tenants, not as conventional owners of their own land. Holders of preemption rights seemed to acquire, Banner writes, "a fee simple title subject to the Indians' [temporary] right of possession, rather than [merely] a contingent right to own the land in fee simple in the future." Such legal developments raised troubling questions: Who actually possessed Seneca land, and what was the nature of that possession? Who were the "real" owners of the residual homelands Senecas "possessed" in the early nineteenth century?[3]

From 1798 to 1809, the Holland Land Company held the preemption rights to Seneca reservation land, which technically offered nothing more than the opportunity to purchase whatever property—if any—the Senecas proved willing to sell. The Senecas in fact exhibited little interest in selling any land, at least without considerable manipulation and coercion, and in

1810 the company sold its preemption rights—at fifty cents per acre, for nearly 200,000 acres—to the well-placed former U.S. congressman David A. Ogden, who, with the backing of family members, created the Ogden Land Company. Ogden's investment amounted to nearly $90,000, with the potential to generate millions, but with no guarantees. He and his investors thus commenced a campaign to transfer Seneca land—through political influence and manipulation—to their business concern in order to sell it at a considerable markup to white settlers.[4]

The War of 1812 temporarily derailed these efforts, as the borderlands were enflamed and the development of western New York halted. But with the end of the war in 1815, new pressure mounted for the Senecas, as the Ogden Land Company sought to cash in through Seneca dispossession. The company worked in concert with state and federal officials, who exhibited less concern for Native "rights" than for economic development, civilization, and progress. Particularly valuable to the company were Seneca lands near the expanding town of Buffalo and along the Genesee River, south of where the city of Rochester would materialize.[5]

Before the war, Rochester did not exist, while Buffalo was a village of about a thousand residents. With the construction of the Erie Canal, both would become bustling metropolises. Buffalo, the western terminus of the canal and vital trade nexus with the West, required additional land to grow, available only to the east—the location of the Senecas' Buffalo Creek reservation. As the Erie Canal ran through central New York, it opened up the rich agricultural lands of the Genesee country, which quickly emerged as a national and international breadbasket. And, like Buffalo, Rochester became an instant city, a vibrant processing and manufacturing center, based on its access to the canal, a vast agricultural hinterland, abundant natural resources, and the substantial water power of the Genesee River. Proposals circulated to consolidate the Senecas in one reserve—the Allegany reservation, the place deemed most remote and least valuable—to remove them from the paths of white progress and profit. The Senecas themselves rejected such plans, whether to relocate them to a proximate site or to a distant one across the Mississippi River.[6]

The Senecas' Quaker patrons eyed these developments with concern, and they advocated a familiar response in defense of Indian territory and autonomy. As we have seen, nearly from the beginning, Friends advised Senecas to divide their collective property into individual patriarchal family plots as a means to promote male agriculture and female domesticity. Individual male ownership of property was the cornerstone of their "civilization" program. Increasingly, Quakers saw it as the foundation of Seneca national survival itself, especially given their belief that Seneca leaders—too easily corrupted—were the weak link in the chain protecting Seneca lands. The Friends therefore advocated allotment in severalty with greater insistence than ever before, even at the risk of alienating their Seneca hosts. Much was at stake. As Halliday Jackson later recalled, the threat of removal would not only tend to unsettle the Indians in their agricultural pursuits, but . . . entirely frustrate the plan of civilization, and render of little avail the labours of Friends for twenty years past . . . in promoting their advancement toward a civilized state."[7]

If Senecas believed that collectivity offered strength, the Quakers—in good faith—reached a somewhat different conclusion, though they too sought to protect the Indians' homeland. As we have seen, the Senecas resisted allotment for a variety of reasons—its inconsistency with subsistence and commercial activities, its frustration of gender arrangements, its impracticality and logistical problems, as well as the likelihood in their view that it would enable, not impede, alienation of land. But Quakers believed that broad individual distribution of property would attach Seneca people even more firmly to their land and present obstacles to those who attempted to buy it, assuming that hundreds of individual negotiations with unwilling sellers would be more difficult for unscrupulous purchasers to manage than a single large acquisition arranged with a small group of irresolute, bribable chiefs. History would prove, disastrously, that allotment would in fact be a key tool in the erosion of tribal lands and sovereignty; and it should not have been difficult for Quakers to predict that future. But they pressed on with their prescriptions, unable apparently to overcome their own prejudices about what constituted civilized life. Although most Senecas remained skeptical and opposed, the Quakers believed some were willing to follow the advice of Friends. Their reports to the Philadelphia Indian Committee from Tunesassa and Cattaraugus were guarded but hopeful.[8]

Those hopes would be unfulfilled. Despite rising resistance, in spring of 1818 the survey of the Allegany reservation was set to proceed. It was directed by Cotton Fletcher, formerly in the employment of the Holland Land Company. His connection was sure to excite suspicion. When Fletcher arrived to begin his work in August, he was prevented and expelled. Those chiefs who continued to support the land division requested that their Philadelphia Friends "obtain a written instrument from the President of the United States having the seal affixed to it, strengthening (as they say) their title to their lands so that they may be easy themselves and their children after them."⁹

But what the Senecas received from Washington only aggravated the controversy. In a letter read aloud by the local Indian agent at a Buffalo Creek Council in September of 1818, the U.S. secretary of war, John C. Calhoun, communicated the unwelcome advice that the Senecas should accept removal west of the Mississippi—to Arkansas! And he did so, purportedly, on behalf of the president; his reply was to be "Interpreted to the six Nations as a Letter from their Father the President, written by his Secretary of War."¹⁰ President Monroe followed up with a personal, clarifying communication, as the Senecas requested. His letter was heartening to some but puzzling and less than reassuring for most Senecas. Monroe endorsed the Quakers' civilization program and specifically advocated allotment: "By thus dividing your land, each one could then say, this is mine; and he would have inducements to put up good houses on it, and improve his land by Cultivation." Was it a positive sign that Monroe's laconic correspondence made no mention of Arkansas, or did his neglect of the subject simply mask nefarious plans to remove the Senecas to a trans-Mississippi reservation? Did the president imply that failure to comply with allotment would trigger forced relocation? This was a mixed message—particularly in conjunction with the one from Calhoun and Jasper Parrish, the interpreter and U.S. subagent to the Six Nations—one that inspired confusion and consternation.¹¹

The Philadelphia Friends had been asked to intercede, not only with the president, but with the governor of New York as well. Whether they did so or not is unclear, but a New York Assembly resolution, passed on March 4, 1819, offered a disturbing reply. It "resolved . . . that his Excellency the Governor be required to co-operate with the government of the United States in such measures as may be deemed most advisable, in order . . . to induce the several Indian tribes within this state to concentrate themselves in some suitable situation, under such provisions, and subject to such regulations as may [be] judged most effectual to secure to them the best means of protection and instruction in piety, and agriculture, and gradually to extend to them the benefits of civilization." Such legislation advanced the Ogden Land Company's interests by proposing to consolidate Seneca population and thus open large tracts of land to sale and development, while it advanced New York State efforts to extend its jurisdiction over Native people and their lands. Threateningly, the resolution "authorized and requested [the governor] to take such measures, either with or without the co-operation of the government of the United States."[12]

Meanwhile, David A. Ogden, on behalf of the Ogden Land Company, petitioned the president to enlist his support in Seneca removal, or at least their concentration in a single reserve. Ogden characterized the company, presumptuously, as the "Proprietor" of the lands presently "occupied by the Remains of the Seneca Nation of Indians." Ogden here inflated his company's legal status—to the rank of owners—and demoted the Senecas to mere occupants. He then outlined a simple, increasingly familiar, and (for the Senecas) dangerous plan, which Ogden "understood to be approved and recommended by the Government." It entailed "collecting the scattered Tribes of the Seneca Nation, so as to form them into one or more compact Settlements, in order to their more easy and economical Instruction, to purchase at a fair Price, such Lands as they could not possibly use or improve, and to convey to their Use upon equitable Terms, the preemption Right in an adequate Portion of those which they might wish to retain for the Purpose of a permanent Seat."[13] Ogden invoked myths and prejudices about Native life and landscape common to white audiences, and he painted his proposal in a fashion that emphasized its benevolence and justice. The Indians were scattered and as yet uncivilized, and government actions would promote their welfare and instruction economically, compensate them equitably, and promote development by transferring wasted lands to others for improvement.

Ogden's memorial conveyed a clear sense of frustration, however. He wrote President Monroe in the wake of firm Seneca refusals to sell the lands the Ogden Company claimed to own. Indeed they declined even "to listen to these overtures" and took offense that Ogden had broached the subject. Ogden expressed shock that the Seneca nation assumed "an unqualified Title to the Lands they occupy," a title they believed had been secured to them in 1794 by the Treaty of Canandaigua. The Senecas produced the document in Ogden's presence, cited it directly in rejecting his claims, and suggested that Ogden's appearance on such business itself constituted a violation of the treaty.[14]

But, Ogden asked, did the Pickering treaty in fact diminish his company's proprietary rights? If it did—illegally in his view—then the company deserved indemnification; if it did not—as Ogden believed—then officials should offer clarification and confirm the company's rights. The Pickering treaty could not, in his view, "enlarge" Seneca ownership—to the detriment of the Ogden Land Company—after it had been legally reduced and transferred. Resolving this confusion quickly was critical. It had encouraged the Senecas to resist "any change in their Location"; it had undermined Ogden's efforts to procure "the relinquishment of the Native claim"; it had encouraged the Indians, Ogden claimed, "to waste the timber and assume the Right of making Sales to other Indians Tribes in a manner highly prejudicial to the rights of the proprietors of the preemption Title"; and it had enabled the Senecas "to lease their Lands to White People."[15]

Ogden's complaints highlight the radical extent of this threat to Seneca sovereignty, land, and resources. His interpretation—one increasingly mainstream in American legal opinion—treated the Senecas as mere tenants. Not only did it deny them an unqualified ownership of their reserves; it undermined their ability to use or develop their land and resources autonomously. Transfers of land to all non-Senecas, including their own Iroquois kinspeople, would be illegal. Leasing arrangements were similarly prohibited. Seneca extraction and sale of natural resources—principally timber—was likewise constrained or proscribed—not in the interest of conservation, of course, but to preserve the rights of others to exploit and profit from this landscape once the Senecas' actual possession had been relinquished.[16]

Interested parties sought expert legal opinions on this important matter. One came from Richard Harrison, the prominent New York City attorney who taught at Columbia, where David A. Ogden's brother and business associate, Thomas Ludlow Ogden, was his student. Harrison largely endorsed David Ogden's claims. As did the U.S. attorney general William Wirt in an ambiguous yet devastating opinion. Wirt granted that the Senecas' land title, "however narrow," was nonetheless "a title in fee simple." Senecas held "a title of perpetual inheritance because it will be admitted on all hands that neither the present occupants nor their heirs so long as the nation subsists can be rightfully driven from their possessions." But that "fee simple" title was of a peculiar sort, according to Wirt—"a legal anomaly" because the Senecas, he believed, lacked "the right of alienation." Like Harrison, Wirt denied the Senecas the right to lease as well as to sell their land, and he found even greater restrictions in the ways that Senecas might legally use their property. He wrote, "They have no more right to sell the standing timber, the natural production of the soil as an article of traffic than they have to sell the soil itself." Wirt believed that the Senecas might use their land for "the purpose of subsistence" but not commerce. Cutting and selling timber would "waste" or destroy the value of their reserves; therefore, not only was logging without the Senecas' permission illegal—it was "a trespass against their right"—but even timber harvesting by the Senecas themselves or their lessees was prohibited because it violated the rights of the preemption title holders. Wirt concluded, "the special property which the Indians have in the timber may entitle them to the damages for cutting it down yet that general property which would authorize a sale of the timber can not . . . be legally inferred."[17]

Though justified in legal terms and supported by humanitarian claims, this unfavorable interpretation of Seneca possession struck at the heart of their hybrid exchange economy and imperiled Seneca national existence. Ogden and others presented Senecas as a backward people, but in fact it was their innovation and success in accommodating the new economic realities of the early republic—engaging in extensive market exchange, amassing land and developing its resources, and promoting economic development through leasing—that made them an obstacle to concerns such as the Ogden Land Company. "The History of every Indian Tribe on the Atlantic Coast without exception," Ogden wrote, "proves that they cannot long exist in their savage character in the Neighborhood of civilized Society." Ogden hoped that President Monroe would help him fulfill such a prophecy, but in fact it was Seneca civility, not savagery, that made the Senecas problematic. The extinction that most concerned Ogden was his own.[18]

The Senecas themselves would have admitted that the exploitation of natural resources within their reservations in some instances was damaging, and their leasing arrangements with white neighbors could sometimes work out badly. They frequently complained about timber theft by white poachers, for example, and urged enforcement of New York laws which prohibited trespassing and illegal timber cutting. White squatters sometimes expropriated tribal resources and could be difficult to expel. But the Senecas required protection not from themselves, as men such as Ogden asserted, but from outsiders. And they sought to preserve their land base and the ability to use their land autonomously and resourcefully. Ogden, on the other hand, challenged their ownership, sought to restrain their "destruction" of lands he claimed, and, casting them as backward and irredeemable, recommended removal to "Lands remote from settlement."[19]

Leasing, in particular, made economic sense for the Senecas—as a way to compensate for their limited labor and technological resources, to circumvent the constraints imposed on their ownership rights, and to promote economic development and produce cash. And such benefits accrued while Senecas retained their land—both as sacred space and as capital. White tenant farmers could "improve" tribal land, demonstrate advanced agricultural techniques, and pay rent, generating Seneca income. As a group of Christian Seneca chiefs later explained to President John Quincy Adams, "We have a great deal of land, all fit for fence and plow, which we cannot improve for a great many years. Our old people also live on some of this land. We want our Father the President, to say that we may lease such lands for the benefit of the Nation, and of such poor people." Similarly, the Senecas entered into leasing arrangements that permitted local whites to operate sawmills on Seneca property. Though officially proscribed, such partnerships enabled both Natives and newcomers to raise capital for further economic development. But Seneca entrepreneurial activity violated the ethnocentric expectations of officials and reformers and challenged the Ogden Land Company's interests. A petition to the New York State legislature later complained that such leasing on Seneca reservations placed Indians in "the relation of Landlord to a tenantry of white citizens."[20]

Whether Senecas sought to pursue such "improvement" strategies or preferred other land uses, they generally agreed that their remaining property—even when not under direct cultivation—was not surplus. As Red Jacket replied to David Ogden in July 1819, "You told us that we had large and many unproductive tracts of land. We do not view it so. Our seats are considered small; and if left here long by the great Spirit, we shall stand in need of them. We shall want timber. Land after improvement of many years wears out. We shall want to renew our fields; and we do not think that there is any land in any of our reservations but what is useful." Red Jacket concluded, "We will not part with any, not one of our reservations.[21]

Though Senecas largely sought *not* to sell their land, limitations imposed on their possession nonetheless depressed their land's value and undermined the Senecas' ability to realize its appreciation; indeed, such restrictions on how Senecas might use their land, along with white encroachment, could even prove coercive, making sales more likely. Yet the Senecas held out against this pressure. A letter from Friends at Cattaraugus reported David A. Ogden's failure in discussions with the Senecas: they "have intirely refused any negotiation . . . and say they are determined never to move to the westward." As Augustus Fox made clear in a letter to Elizabeth Fothergill in August 1819, the Senecas completely rejected Ogden's legal claims and pretensions: "Red-jacket told the United States' agent & a gentleman that owns the Prescription [that is, preemption] right (speaking of the Indians) that 'We don't make land: the Great Spirit made this land, & gave it to our fathers, who handed it down to us to sit down upon. You tell us that Mr. O[gden] has a prescription right to our reservations. You surprise us: this is new to us. God gave us this Land; and if Mr. O. had come down from Him, with his blood & flesh upon his bones, then we might be disposed to believe he has a prescription right, for we derived our rights from the Great Spirit.'"[22]

Meanwhile the Ogden Land Company reorganized and President Monroe ordered an inquiry into the situation, preparatory to another effort to extinguish Seneca land title, concentrate Senecas on smaller reserves, and remove them west of the Mississippi.[23]

The Friends remained concerned. Quaker missionaries at Cattaraugus reported encroaching white settlers. The Senecas' possession of "so large a portion of open lands of superior quality induce frequent applications from many of their neighbors for privilege to settle among them[,] flattering the Indians with the prospect of an easy method of obtaining large increase of crops & by permitting them as tenants to cultivate their Lands." For Quakers, the problem was not merely the evil influence of degenerate whites or the potential for Seneca dispossession. They worried in addition that such arrangements encouraged idleness and enabled the avoidance of Seneca male agriculture and industry. And they remained largely blind or opposed to Seneca entrepreneurial behavior. They reported, "such expectation [related to white tenancy] has induced many of the Indians to favour their wishes, and a number of [white] families of inferior grade had lately obtained a partial grant to move onto the Reservation." Men like Ogden sold land; other white grandees rented or leased it; but Quakers expected Senecas to cultivate it themselves, through their own manly toil. The Friends sought to dissuade the Indians from allowing such practices. Some Seneca chiefs agreed. With a certain amount of relief, the Quakers reported, "part of the families who had taken possession, the Indians have been prevailed upon to order off." This result served the Ogden Land Company interests as well—why should white farmers buy land from Ogden when they could lease it from Seneca proprietors? For the company, the Seneca nation was not merely an obstacle; it was a potential competitor. The Philadelphia Indian Committee did not cooperate with the likes of David A. Ogden, but the Quakers' involvement in these controversies and the unprecedented (and uncharacteristic) pressure they brought to bear on Seneca men and women to accept allotment implicated them in the growing crisis. Tension mounted among the Senecas, and factionalism festered.[24]

These years also saw the increased presence of evangelical missionaries at Buffalo Creek, Cattaraugus, and other Seneca reserves, even at Allegany, where Cornplanter momentarily welcomed a Presbyterian mission. Factions divided along religious lines—separating Handsome Lake adherents and religious conservatives from those who accepted various new evangelical Protestant faiths. But the major fault line ran between those committed to "civilization" (particularly its valorizing of private property) and those favoring "tradition" (in fact a new, hybrid "traditional" way of life that selectively adapted new technologies and economic relations). For many, a resurgent nativism offered the best response to the escalating threats they faced, both external and internal.[25]

The Reverend Timothy Alden, proselytizing among the Senecas on behalf of the Society for Propagating the Gospel in the summer of 1818, witnessed the emergence of such nativism firsthand. While at Cattaraugus, Alden heard of a council taking place at Tonawanda that included representatives from all the Seneca communities. He inquired about its purpose. The "chief warriour," Wendungguhtah, told him, "they are all met together upon the same business as you are on"—that is, evangelism. But in this case their object was promoting the gospel of Handsome Lake. Alden pushed on to Tonawanda, where he was welcomed but not allowed to preach, given the pressing business at hand. "The great object of this council was," Alden observed, "to revive the moral instruction formerly received from Goskuk-kewaunau Konnedieyu [that is, Handsome Lake], the prophet as he was called. . . . The Indians seem now to think much of those instructions, and are desirous of having them recalled to mind, and re-delivered for the benefit of the rising generation. Many speeches were made, in which, the lessons inculcated by the prophet, were recounted, and their importance urged by various, persuasive, energetic, appeals."[26]

The Tonawanda convocation represented a revived nativist revivalism, which promoted solidarity and resistance to the latest threats to Seneca land, culture, and sovereignty. This nativism, drawing inspiration from the teachings of Handsome Lake, but powered as well by "traditionalists" such as Red Jacket who did not necessarily embrace the *Gaiwiio*, opposed those Senecas who placed more faith in the prescriptions of white missionaries and officials. Through the early 1820s, Seneca nativism grew. The Quaker missionary and schoolteacher Joseph Elkinton reported in December 1820 that *Gaiwiio* adherents had even removed the irons from a Quaker-built sawmill and sold them to secure the funds to repair their ceremonial house at Cattaraugus.

Was this an antimodern, anti-"civilization" protest, an act of expediency, or both? The unsettlement and rancor within Seneca communities stemmed less from religious differences than from the difficult and unresolved question of how Senecas might survive as Senecas. And the Quakers for the first time found themselves in the middle of these internal struggles.[27]

As the Allegany chief Governor Blacksnake, a nephew and lifelong supporter of Handsome Lake, protested to Elkinton, his "people did not know why friends had told them the name of a Seneca would in a few years only be known in history, if they did not endeavour to take hold of improvements, and many of their people were not pleased with such language being told them." At the heart of the controversy was allotment, and the Quakers' imprudent and intrusive advocacy of the program, which imperiled their mission. For Blacksnake, it was a life or death issue. The Senecas "felt no objection to being killed if that was to be their lot, which they thought very little worse than losing their lands would be, which they considered very probable." Blacksnake noted "that it had now been twenty years since friends came amongst them, that their people had become more & more divided since that time & had now become two parties." He complained "that friends had recommended them to divide their reservation & each family have separate farms, which measure the Indians had undertaken & found it a bad one & did not accomplish, that the Quakers still advised them to it, notwithstanding they were aware of the difficulties that had been made in the Nation, by the proposition & state." For Blacksnake, that made the Quakers complicit, "as much as if friends had been in great measure the cause of the difficulties & divisions among the Indians."[28]

By this time, Elkinton himself had begun to face hostility and harassment and felt increasingly uncomfortable in Cold Spring: "I often think it is like 'blackness of darkness' & feel glad when I get away from the village." Elkinton here referenced the epistle of Jude: "And the angels which kept not their first estate, but left their own habitation, He hath reserved in everlasting chains under darkness unto the judgment of the great day. . . . Raging waves of the sea, foaming out their own shame; wandering stars, to whom is reserved the blackness of darkness for ever" (Jude 1:6, 13). Had the Allegany reservation become a hell on earth, a place of chaos and fear? Or perhaps Elkinton meant to quote a more ancient biblical verse: "Whoso curseth his father or mother, His lamp shall be put out in blackness of darkness" (Proverbs 20:20). If so, who had pronounced the curse, and who was being subjected to punishment? Did Seneca rejection of their Quaker patrons' prescriptions constitute such a curse? In a single potent phrase, drawing on these biblical allusions, Elkinton conveyed to his Friendly associates in Philadelphia the darkness and dangers of his Seneca milieu—a roiled, tumultuous world in which the woman Kauquatau could be executed as a witch.[29]

Although the Friends were discouraged, even vacating their mission for a brief time, they persevered, as most of the Senecas hoped they would.[30] They pulled back from their aggressive advocacy of allotment and returned to their earlier circumspection, even if they continued to favor division of Seneca lands into family plots and continued to pursue their larger "civilization" program. The revival of Handsome Lake's teachings would continue and during the following decades be codified by the faithful, particularly by Blacksnake at Allegany and Jemmy Johnson at Tonawanda. Resurgent Seneca nativism, and the relative success of Red Jacket's defense of Tommy Jemmy and Seneca sovereignty (as we will see) pointed the way to Seneca survival. Serious travails lay in the not-too-distant future. But Cornplanter, Handsome Lake, Red Jacket, and numerous others, including those chiefs like Pollard who converted to Christianity, helped their people forge the necessary tools of survival for the Senecas. They would face new encroachment and dispossession, along with persistent threats of removal, but the Senecas preserved a land base within the Empire State, and maintained at least a semiautonomy, as the American "frontier" moved west.

From 1819 though the mid-1820s, the letters that traveled between western New York and Washington, D.C., told the same story: continued white encroachment on Seneca lands; continued Seneca leasing arrangements considered illegal by the Ogden Land Company and numerous white officials; continued foot-dragging by Seneca leaders regarding removal proposals; and continued Seneca refusal to entertain Ogden offers to buy their lands.[31]

Opinion remained divided on Seneca reservations, but by 1826 at least some Seneca leaders had concluded that a limited sale of land might secure their people's survival without removal. In November 1826, a group of Christian Seneca chiefs told the federal subagent Jasper Parrish that, "having agreed how much of our land we would sell for the benefit of the Nation, we required of the proprietors a bond, that they would hereafter ask of us no more. With this we are satisfied, being determined to live and die at the homes of our fathers, and if we find we have more land than we want we can offer it for sale ourselves." In short, these Seneca chiefs envisioned a final treaty and land cession to end all treaties and land cessions. The agreement offered "land for peace"—it would diminish their landholdings but allow Senecas to remain in New York, living peacefully in possession of their residual reserves. Not all were willing to engage in such a compromise, but the negotiations proceeded—with considerable disagreement and subsequent charges of intimidation and fraud. Ultimately, in the 1826 treaty the Senecas lost their remaining lands in central New York and saw their reservations at Buffalo Creek, Tonawanda, and Cattaraugus substantially reduced in size. In all, the Seneca land base shrank by roughly 87,000 acres. Seneca chiefs, however, secured a promise that they would "forever after be left in quietness upon that subject." And the treaty stipulated that any future discussion of land cessions could be initiated only by the president or the Senecas.[32]

A United States commissioner later appointed to investigate fraud allegations surrounding the 1826 treaty, Richard Montgomery Livingston, reported in July 1828, "The Indians en masse are opposed to a removal—Schemes having such an object in view are looked upon with abhorrence." Yet the Ogden Land Company would not go away. In response, a council of prominent Seneca chiefs issued a firm declaration in November 1832: "We Chiefs of the Seneca Nation Being assembled at the Council House at Buffalo Creek promise, Covenant and Pledge ourselves this day that we will never sell our said lands so long as we continue to be chiefs of this nation. And we further promise that so long as our nation continues to exist we will remain on these Reservations in the state of New-York now occupied by the said Seneca Nation." Red Jacket had died in 1830, but others—including Black Snake, Big Kettle, and the elderly Cornplanter, along with the notorious Tommy Jemmy—stepped forward to lead Seneca resistance.[33]

Yet in 1838, the Senecas would lose an additional 102,069 acres—all their remaining New York lands, except a one-mile-square reservation at Oil Spring—and were nearly removed to a trans-Mississippi reservation in Kansas. The Treaty of 1838 must rank among the most corrupt proceedings in the history of the United States. In response, Quaker advocates worked diligently to expose official duplicity, publicize their fraud, and redress the enormous injury perpetrated by the treaty. With Quaker assistance, the Senecas later managed to restore their reservations at Allegany and Cattaraugus in the federal Supplemental Treaty of 1842, and in 1856 the Tonawanda band of Senecas successfully purchased a remnant of their lost lands as a reservation and reestablished themselves in northwestern New York. The Senecas did not disappear, thanks to their revitalized cultural strength and their ability to manipulate white factionalism, exploit the ambiguities of American federalism and its divided authority, invoke the benevolence of patrons such as the Quakers, and fashion a hybrid economy serviceable within a world of emerging capitalism.[34]

"All the World's a Stage": Tommy Jemmy and the Empire State

On November 4, 1825, the Erie Canal officially opened, with Governor De Witt Clinton presiding at a grand ceremony in New York Harbor at Sandy Hook. Here Clinton emptied a keg of Lake Erie water into the bay, carried by the first canal boat to traverse the entire state from west to east, suggesting that New York City was now the imperial emporium of the western world, linking the upper interior of North America—and its incalculable economic potential—with the Atlantic world.[35] The governor and political architect of the canal made this maiden voyage on the *Seneca Chief*, a canal boat whose name evoked a romantic past.

Who was the eponymous "Seneca Chief"? Cornplanter perhaps, who still lived on his tract near the Allegany reservation, or his half brother, the Seneca prophet Handsome Lake, who had died in 1815, just two years before New York State shoveled its first spades of dirt to excavate the 363-mile ditch? A better candidate was Red Jacket, the most celebrated and admired of Seneca leaders, even though his most famous speeches, widely published in newspapers, pamphlets, and books, excoriated Christian missionaries, just as his 1821 defense of Tommy Jemmy had flayed the hypocrisy of condescending white critics. Red Jacket's fame in fact was international. When the Revolutionary general and protégé of George Washington, the Marquis de Lafayette, returned and toured the United States on the eve of its fifty-year national jubilee, he traveled along much of the nearly completed Erie Canal, and in Buffalo in June 1825 Red Jacket was among those dignitaries on hand to greet the French hero. Red Jacket charmed the "Nation's Guest." They both seemed avatars of an earlier era, helping Americans to celebrate their past as they turned a corner into a glorious future.[36]

As it turns out, there was another Seneca chief who had achieved an international celebrity of sorts—Soonongise, or Tommy Jemmy. Tommy Jemmy had not merely traveled east from Buffalo to New York but, from 1817 to 1819, had ventured across the Atlantic Ocean to Great Britain as a performer in the Storrs and Company Indian Show. Anticipating both Barnum and Buffalo Bill, Walter Brigham of Chautauqua, acting as financial manager, and Augustus Carlton Fox, interpreter and "showman"—a person "already known as a skillful hand in managing the wild men"—headed the enterprise, "a speculation" funded by businessmen from Buffalo and Canandaigua. They arrived in Liverpool on the last day of January 1818, their first stop in a grand tour of Europe that was meant to include the British Isles and a visit to Paris. A Buffalo chronicler later remarked, "The Indians were a splendid set of fellows, and they knew it, and were wonderfully set up by their knowledge and the notice they attracted and attention they received. . . . They were novelties, shown off in their native costumes, with brilliant feathers, and bright-hued garments, and wild ways—and John Bull was wonderfully taken by them."[37]

The troupe never saw Paris. It was reported that the manager Augustus Fox sometimes found himself "at his wits' end to keep them [the Indians] anywhere in bounds." On one occasion, allegedly after excluding Tommy Jemmy from a visit to a display of exotic animals in Liverpool, Fox and Brigham faced the irate Seneca chief "in a threatening state of jealous wrath and—whiskey-ness, with a knife in his hand." Fox reportedly fended him off with a chair, and Tommy Jemmy stalked away. But not before impaling his knife in the impresario's door. A meeting among the Seneca performers ultimately restored peace, and Tommy Jemmy was alleged to have concluded, "I think the whiskey did it." What actually inspired such rage is not clear. Perhaps it was the whiskey, or perhaps Tommy Jemmy and others grew frustrated with their treatment as spectacles or specimens. Or perhaps the incident itself is apocryphal.[38]

The broadside that shouted to the inhabitants of Leeds in the English Midlands in April 1818, trumpeting the upcoming exhibition of "WILD INDIAN Savages, From the Borders of Lake Erie, In the Western Wilds of North-America," advertised the appearance of a "Chief & Six Warriors." According to newspaper accounts, that "chief" was a "Colonel Thomas, or Long Horn"—a more dignified appellation for Tommy Jemmy than drunkard or murderer. The *Leeds Mercury* listed him as Se-nung-gise, or "Long Horns," age forty-one, which made him twice as old as some of the other Native performers, who ranged in age from eighteen to twenty-four. Tommy Jemmy would have been a toddler when General John Sullivan rampaged through his Seneca homeland during the American Revolution in 1779. Perhaps he was carried by his mother or scrambled to keep up with his fleeing family, as they abandoned their burning village and escaped west toward refuge at Buffalo Creek. Three decades later, Tommy Jemmy fought on the

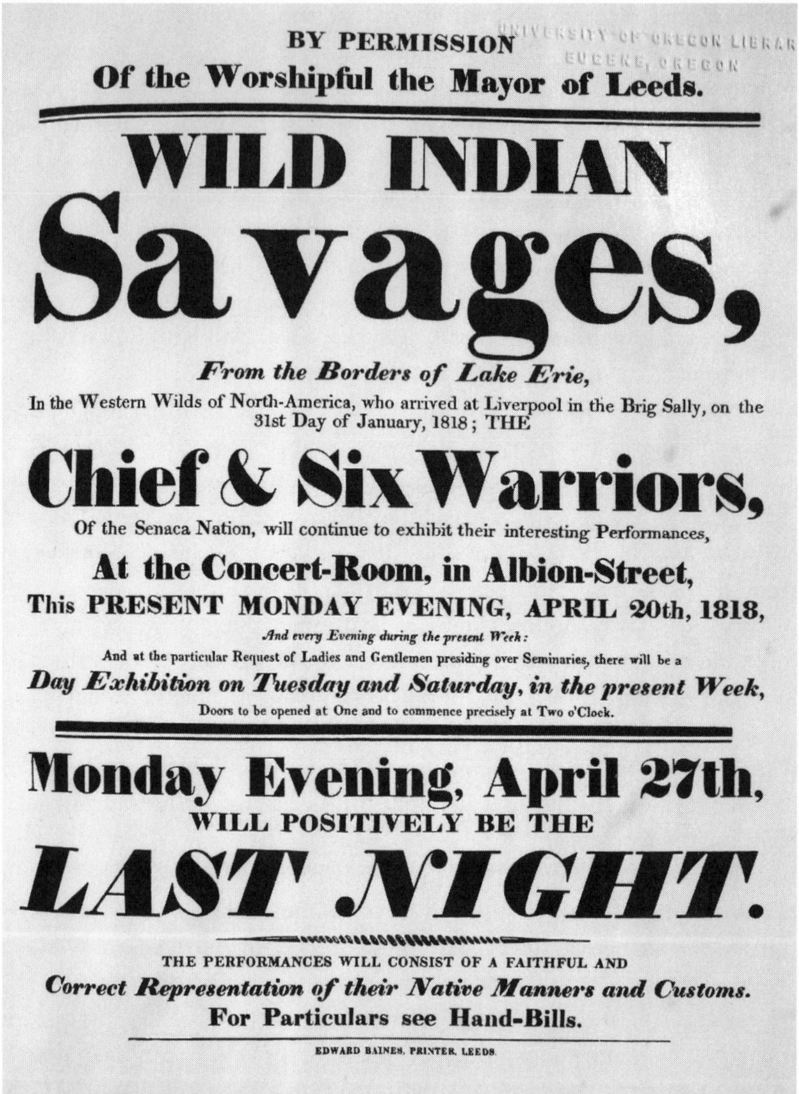

Figure 14. Advertisement for the Indian show featuring Tommy Jemmy and his Seneca compatriots, appearing in Leeds for a one-week engagement in April 1818. From Carolyn Thomas Foreman, *Indians Abroad, 1493–1938* (Norman: University of Oklahoma Press, 1943). Reprinted by permission of the University of Oklahoma Press.

other side—against the country he was now visiting. He was a veteran of the War of 1812, having served the United States in its borderland war with British Canada along with other Buffalo Creek Senecas, including Red Jacket, Young King, Captain Pollard, and Farmers Brother. Tommy Jemmy was never as prominent as these chiefs. He may have commanded other Seneca men during the indecisive conflict, but it is not likely that he ever achieved the high rank of "colonel." Still, "Colonel Thomas" had a nice ring to it and reflected his stature in the troupe.[39]

On stage the Seneca men played to the English crowd's ethnocentric expectations. The *Leeds Intelligencer* wrote, "The Seneca Nation, no Doubt, has existed for many Centuries, yet the Manners and Customs of the People remain in their primeval State, who seem happy in their original Simplicity." It's not surprising that English audiences, any more than nineteenth-century white Americans, would consign Indians to such demeaning noble savagery, which misunderstood Seneca history and neglected and obscured the dramatic alterations of Seneca lives, landscapes, and culture in the post-Revolutionary period. But behind the scenes, we can see the Seneca performers as much more than primitive curiosities or beasts. From Liverpool they visited Manchester, and after Leeds they proceeded to York and then to London for an extended engagement. Along the way, they met with English Quakers, the Friends of their Philadelphia Friends and allies. They were supplied with books and offered instruction in reading, and reportedly they "were quick of apprehension and made good progress in their lessons." The "aged chief" Tommy Jemmy did not acquire literacy himself, but he encouraged his young colleagues and acted as their "monitor." According to the *Leeds Mercury*, "a more pleasing scene cannot be exhibited than to behold an Indian Chief, heretofore deemed but a small remove in his nature from the beast in his native forest, laying down his tomahawk, and instructing his warriors in the rudiments of the English language." Despite the condescending tone and ethnocentric assumptions of such praise, Tommy Jemmy nonetheless emerges here as something other than the unruly, besotted madman who allegedly planted his dagger in Augustus Fox's hotel room door, if not in the manager's hyperventilating chest.[40]

Indeed, the chief emerges from the pages of Elizabeth Fothergill's contemporary journal as a dignified, self-possessed man of the world. Fothergill, a young Quaker woman living at Fulford, near York, received word of the celebrated Seneca troupe from a Friend at Leeds, and she soon made their acquaintance as they paused at York for several performances during three weeks in May 1818. She first encountered Tommy Jemmy, "the eldest one, the Chief," at the Freemason Coffeehouse, where she interrupted his game of billiards. "He came up to me in a friendly manner, and shook hands, then with the same ease & composure, going on with his game," she wrote. Later, at a retreat on a country estate that included some seventy guests, many of them Quakers, she was impressed with his carriage and public speech, in which he thanked his host for the day, his Quaker patrons, and the Great Spirit. "The chief used little or no action in speaking, but looked impressively toward the person he was addressing, keeping his mouth nearly in one position . . . , the lips little employed in the Seneca Indian language."[41]

When they adjourned to the garden, Tommy Jemmy "goodnaturedly" allowed gawking guests to examine his tomahawk—actually a calumet, a ceremonial peace pipe in the form of a hatchet. With admirers in tow, he walked the paths "with a manly independent air." Fothergill described Tommy Jemmy as nearly six feet tall. "He called himself an old man, though his years, I understood, did not exceed 42 or 43. He appeared vigorous and healthy, but bore the marks of care and hardship evidently in his face, the expression of which was very stern, if he chose to be so; yet it is often relaxed into friendliness and cheerful good-humour." Age had cost Tommy Jemmy some of his teeth, she observed, but the chief, with his prominent brow, deep-set eyes, well-formed nose, strong chin, and full lips, remained an impressive presence.[42]

Fothergill noted Tommy Jemmy's grace and leadership: "His manners were very easy and affable with the young train of Indians attending him, never assuming any state toward them, though if he had occasion to direct or advise them, they paid him all due respect." Tommy Jemmy and his compatriots were well dressed, in their dark brown and blue coats, dark blue pantaloons, white shirts of printed cotton, plumed turbans, red girdles or sashes, and moccasins—"soft leather slippers." In his "Indian garb," the chief had a "very striking and formidable effect," the Quaker woman observed. While the younger men pursued their studies by day, Tommy Jemmy would don his show regalia and ride about York, in order to promote the Indians' evening performances.[43]

During one of these excursions, at Whitsuntide, with holiday crowds thronging the streets, Tommy Jemmy endured what Fothergill called "a very unpleasant incident." Some unruly thug assaulted the chief, striking him across the shoulders and sending him sprawling. "In an instant, he started up on his feet," Fothergill wrote, "and with great indignation brandished his tomahawk to meet the assailant." But by then, the "cowardly desperadoe had fled, or disappeared in the crowd." The affronted Tommy Jemmy rose in self-defense, not in mindless fury, and as he was sped away he "expressed his opinion strongly that our magistrate ought to take cognizance of it [the assault] and punish such behaviour as it deserves." Fothergill was most impressed by Tommy Jemmy's restraint, which displayed the character, not of a firebrand, but of a composed, cautious leader. "He . . . showed, I think, considerable prudence and self-command in the midst of this warm excitement, by refraining from any rash act, such as striking any one near himself, or throwing at random his tomahawk amongst the crowd, which perhaps a more passionate man would have done, although the consequences might have been his own loss and detainment." Was this a man who would kill lightly?[44]

It is unlikely that the Indian theatrical excursion of 1818–19 was designed by Senecas to serve any strategic or diplomatic purpose, but it did become an opportunity to parley with English Quakers and perhaps prod additional relief from them or their Philadelphia coreligionists. The group met with Friends in Leeds on April 20, 1818, and these Quakers offered them a lengthy "talk." In addition to expressing welcome, friendship, and the oneness of all people, the speech offered counsel, which resonated with the advice American Quakers had been offering from the beginning of their mission. This Friendly guidance was a well-meaning but predictable mix of recommendations Senecas already embraced along with ethnocentric suggestions reflecting little understanding of Seneca circumstances. The English Friends also offered a critique of the Indian Show, perhaps taking its melodramatic humbug a bit too literally: "Brothers, . . . You came to show our Countrymen how you make war,—how you use the bow and arrow, how you fight your battles—how you scalp the slain,—and then how you make peace again,—We your Brethren the Quakers do not want to learn these things. Brothers. The love from the great Spirit in our hearts teaches us to love each other—it does not teach us to fight and kill one another." From there, the Quakers made their pitch for abandoning the hunt (misunderstood to be the primitive Senecas' chief means of subsistence), accepting agriculture (misunderstood to be largely absent among the Senecas), embracing female domesticity, and accepting temperance. Oxen and chains, plow and scythe, wheel and the loom, hammer and the anvil: "These are the weapons that will overcome your enemies.—take fast hold of them and your enemies will flee before you.—Let these tools never fall out of your hands." The English Friends hoped that the

Seneca delegation might carry their ponderous advice back to their people, particularly emphasizing enclosure of land, male agriculture, female domestic industry, and literacy, to allow Senecas to read the Good Book. But the Friends of Leeds also conveyed a conditional offer of relief: "Brothers. If you need more ploughs and oxen,—if you want more saws and hammers;—if you want more wheels and looms, we think our brothers in your country will send you them;—but if they can not send all you may have need of tell them to send us word and we will try to help them."[45]

Tommy Jemmy and his troupe obtained a copy of the speech, which they carried with them back to western New York, where Seneca kinsmen used it diplomatically to garner additional aid from their Philadelphia patrons. At a council at Cattaraugus in December 1819—in the midst of tensions related to proposed allotment, concentration, and removal—they told their resident Quakers that "Several of our young men have lately been induced to cross the great waters expecting to receive some advantage from their Journey." While abroad, "they were met by a number of our Friends . . . who appeared much pleas'd to see them." Those Quakers "made great enquiry about our situation, and on finding we had land enough but many still poor and needy they gave them a great deal of good counsel and sent a long talk to our Nation." They recommended, "if we were in need of help to apply to our Friends the Quakers in america, and if they should not be able to afford relief, they on the other side of the Water Stood ready to consider our condition and tender such aid as we might stand in need of." Perhaps playing one body of Friends off another, and willing to endure tedious lectures if they generated material assistance, the Senecas concluded delicately, "We know it is a great thing to trouble our brothers after so much kindness, but hope when they understand the tale we have received they will excuse the liberty we have taken and if it should not be agreeable to their feelings to notice our request [for additional livestock] we wish them to write to our friends on the Other side of the Water and let them know we stand ready and shall be very thankful to receive the help they have promised."[46]

In England, the Indian Show had drawn considerable, enthusiastic audiences, but "matters went so adversely on account of great expenses, that notwithstanding the great success of the exhibition as a show, Brigham fell far behind in money matters, and, being in debt and in danger of imprisonment on account of it," he was replaced and returned to the United States. When their summer run at London's Drury Lane Theatre concluded, the Seneca troupe also returned to western New York, forced to beg and borrow the money required to pay their passage home. They arrived on April 22, 1819. Within three years, Tommy Jemmy's use of a knife would be better documented, when he publicly slit the throat of a convicted "witch" in April of 1821, in a contested performance that some critics called "murder" and others "justice."[47]

It is hard to imagine De Witt Clinton's Erie Canal barge named for the infamous Tommy Jemmy, but the *Seneca Chief*—like many names of boats— might have been as much a joke as an expression of imperial nostalgia. Did this *Seneca Chief* represent "the last of his race," as it moved east along the revolutionary superhighway of its day, the greatest public works project in American history until passage of the Interstate Highways Act in the mid-twentieth century? In fact, real, living Seneca Indians accompanied the governor and other notables on the grand inaugural passage in the fall of 1825, but they rode behind, on a boat improbably called *Noah's Ark*. There were two Seneca boys onboard, and in retrospect perhaps they presaged the Senecas' survival amid the floodtide of expansion and transformation that washed over their reservations in western New York and the early American republic. But *Noah's Ark* fell behind the *Seneca Chief* and the rest of the ceremonial fleet, never actually arriving in New York City. It was just as well.[48]

For many white New Yorkers the disappearance of the Senecas or other Native people might be tragic, but it was an inevitable by-product of progress. In classic tragedy, after all, noble protagonists are undone by their own fatal flaws. Indian demise was a foregone conclusion, even while technically preventable. Senecas themselves strove to ensure that the fait accompli was never actually accomplished. But white New Yorkers—to give their new world a mythic pedigree and perhaps to express some exculpatory nobility— named places and things after antiquities, the ancients of both the old world and new. Thus they founded a Rome, New York, near Oneida Lake, a Syracuse, New York, on Onondaga Lake, and an Ithaca, New York, on Lake Cayuga, all on or linked to the Erie Canal. And they named a canal boat the *Seneca Chief*. As a Quaker advocate for the Senecas wrote later, in 1840, "Unless something is done, and done effectually, in a little time no vestige will remain of this once powerful race, except the beautiful names they have conferred on our noblest rivers and loftiest mountains." Or, we might add, on their most lucrative mercantile vessels. "These may, for ages after they cease to exist, remain to attest the beauty of their language; but every thing else regarding them will be lost in oblivion, and the indelible stigma of their utter extermination be for ever fastened upon our country."[49]

In 1825, white Americans, like the Senecas, were in the process of reinventing themselves. Indians were obstacles, foils, sometimes partners in that creative process, as Americans took stock of their first fifty years as a nation and plunged headlong into a brave new world of commercial and industrial expansion, while, paradoxically, they began to express some misgivings about the fate of the republic. Why did the country, after only fifty years, require a Great Revival, a burning-over, a bracing course of benevolent reform? What—and who—needed reformation? After ending its colonial period with a successful War for Independence, had the United States itself become a colonial power, and who was being colonized—rural and working people, whites as well as blacks and Indians? What was the meaning of American liberty and democracy? These were the questions that lingered during the decade of America's jubilee and intensified in the 1830s. And the Seneca homeland was at the center of it all. The Erie Canal celebration signaled the end of the frontier era for New York and projected a great national geopolitical future. Where did Senecas fit in? They had not moved, yet the Senecas now resided in the Empire State. There they established a fragile but enduring semi-sovereignty, gave up land but fended off complete dispossession, and resisted removal. In the process, they managed to overcome both internal division and relentless external pressure, drawing on their characteristic resourcefulness and the new cultural tools developed under the guidance of Handsome Lake and their Philadelphia Friends.

Imperial New York

New York well deserved the nickname "the Empire State," earned in this era.[50] New Yorkers embraced an imperial objective that dramatically transformed the state in the fifty years after the American Revolution. As early as 1807, rural newspapers such as Canandaigua's *Genesee Messenger* projected fantastic economic progress through "internal improvements"—specifically by means of a canal that used existing waterways to breach the North American East-West divide, allowing New York to supplant Philadelphia as the greatest port of the continent and ensuring that New Orleans would not monopolize the future commerce of the American interior. Such a canal would enhance the value of millions of acres, allow commercial agricultural production for distant markets, and generate substantial "remittances for its imported merchandize." New York would be the gateway for expansion: "It would greatly facilitate emigration to the western new lands." The author of this prophetic vision, Jesse Hawley (employing the nom de plume "Hercules"), further predicted the rise of New York City: "This port, already of the first commercial consequence in the United States, would, shortly after, be left without a competition in trade, except by that of New-Orleans. In a century its island would be covered with the buildings and population of its city." Moreover, in western New York, other cities would burgeon—like Buffalo: "The harbor of Buffaloe would exchange her forest for a thicket of marine spars." "To sum up the whole in a sentence," Hercules wrote, "if the project be but a feasible one, no situation on the globe offers such extensive and numerous advantages to inland navigation by a Canal, as this!"[51]

From Buffalo to Albany to Manhattan, the canal did create a channel of trade connecting the Great West, New York City, and the Atlantic world. The effects of territorial expansion, enveloping white settlement, and economic development on the Senecas little concerned white New Yorkers. Even before the end of the War for Independence, they had coveted the rich lands of Iroquoia, and New York State representatives and officials pressed their own claims of sovereignty and authority against those of the United States in an effort to acquire them.[52]

New York had rushed to assert its dominion over the landscape invaded and destroyed by General John Sullivan in 1779. New Yorker John Jay, then serving in Congress, wrote Governor George Clinton, "Would it not be proper for New York to establish Posts in that Country, and in every respect treat it as their own. In my opinion, our State has had too much Forbearance about these matters." In 1783 the state legislature sought to expropriate Iroquois lands to compensate New York soldiers for their military service. Though the plan was challenged by Congress, New York continued to avow its sovereignty within its own borders and frustrate the general government's conduct of Indian affairs, as it did at Fort Stanwix in 1784. Meanwhile, even those serving the state and the national governments in official capacities—such as Philip Schuyler and his land speculating brother, Peter Schuyler—sought to circumvent not only federal statutes but New York State law as well, contained in the 1777 state constitution, which stipulated that land negotiations be conducted only with the authority and consent of the legislature.[53]

Quickly following the Fort Stanwix treaty, the New York State legislature had moved to promote "settlement of the waste and unappropriated lands" within the state, even arranging to advertise and distribute such lands *before* New York had gained title. And efforts by citizens and officials of New York to dispossess the Iroquois continued throughout the 1780s and 1790s. By the time the Six Nations accepted the Canandaigua treaty in 1794, Oneida-Iroquois lands in central New York had been reduced from some five or six million acres to one-quarter of a million acres, for example, and the state illegally acquired more than one hundred thousand acres more within a few months following (and in violation of) the agreement. Ironically, the Oneidas had sided with the Americans in the Revolution and placed their trust in "friends" such as Philip Schuyler. With friends like this, the Oneidas' brethren, the Senecas, were prudent to choose other patrons.[54]

The phenomenal growth of the white population in the central, then western parts of New York State increasingly surrounded the Six Nations and threatened to push them into oblivion, or at least to a trans-Mississippi reservation. (Some ended up in Wisconsin, others in Kansas and Oklahoma.) Most whites—whether nationalist or state-focused—assumed the Iroquois would disappear, as their landholdings dissolved, not only through legal, illegal, or "extralegal" acquisition, but through the encroachment that undermined Native people's subsistence. New York thus planted the "roots of dependency" among the Iroquois, according to a logic well expressed by Philip Schuyler, who saw the remnants of the Six Nations in New York as "no obstacle to our future": "for as our settlements approach their country, they must from the scarcity of game, which that approach will induce to, retire further back, and dispose of their lands."[55]

Senecas endured this ordeal through resourceful adaptation, the revitalization of Handsome Lake, and the earnest help of the Quakers. The Senecas suffered, but the decline of game did not fundamentally undermine their subsistence; they relied most heavily not on hunting but on the agricultural work of women, now assisted by new technology and the help of Native men. Seneca woodlands, even when devoid of game, retained their value because forests remained a valuable source of lumber and timber products, produced and exchanged by Seneca men. Seneca women adapted domesticity to their existing patterns of work, continued to farm, and became modest consumers of manufactured cloth and other goods. Even the more proximate white population, though it sometimes violated Seneca property rights, poached Seneca resources, and abused Seneca people, could provide localized markets, wage labor, or even a pool of white labor or tenants for the Seneca

Figure 15. *Talk with the Indians at Buffalo Creek, 1793*, sketch by the British officer C. A. Pilkington, who attended the proceedings. The Quakers' faithful presence as witnesses and protectors of Seneca interests is depicted in this illustration (purported to be "the earliest known Buffalo picture") of a 1793 negotiation that preceded the Treaty of Canandaigua of 1794. Seated in the center, from left to right, are Beverly Randolph, General Benjamin Lincoln, and Colonel Timothy Pickering, the chief U.S. representative and soon to become U.S. secretary of war and secretary of state. They listen to a Seneca orator, through the translation of an interpreter (likely Horatio Jones). Standing in the center, literally looking over the shoulders of the federal officials, is a group of plainly clad Friends. General Israel Chapin, hands in pockets, stands to the Quakers' immediate left, while various British officers stand to the interpreter's right. From Frank H. Severance, ed., *Publications of the Buffalo Historical Society 6* (1903): facing 497.

subsistence-surplus exchange economy. But a pervasive myth of the vanishing Indian—achieved programmatically through assimilation or removal—discouraged white Americans from accommodating (or even contemplating) a perpetual Native presence within New York or any other American state. Yet New Yorkers had no choice but to confront the persistence of the Senecas in western New York, who maintained there a land base, a tenuous sovereignty, legal rights, and their own social order.

New York's presumption that its law was paramount within its borders—that it therefore exercised sovereignty over Indian people residing within the state—met a challenge in 1802. In a murder case involving a Seneca man from Buffalo Creek, which in some ways anticipated the travails of Tommy Jemmy, we see the confrontation of state and tribal authority. Here the Senecas deployed the ambiguity of federalism to their advantage, playing the general government against the state, forcing New York to justify its dominion, not merely over the Indians but also against Washington, D.C.[56]

In midsummer 1802, a Seneca man named Stiff-Armed George (or Seneca George) was accused of the assault and murder of a white man, John Hewitt, in an incident that occurred near Buffalo Creek on July 25. The details are murky, and, as in many such disputes, different parties offered different versions of the event. Apparently, following a drunken altercation outside a tavern, George had been followed and roughed up by two men. In defense he pulled a knife and stabbed his assailants, mortally wounding Hewitt. The criminal proceedings against George raised much larger questions, including the nature of Seneca sovereignty and the federal relationship among tribes, states, and the national government. In three August speeches to the governor of New York in Albany, the Seneca orator and leader Red Jacket protested the arrest and judicial procedures Stiff-Armed George faced. Two decades before Tommy Jemmy confronted his murder indictment, then, Red Jacket began to rehearse the arguments he would employ on behalf of the Senecas in 1821.[57]

Red Jacket observed that Indians and whites were held to unequal standards and, more important, that Indians were not answerable to New York State but "to the United States only under our existing treaties with them." He declared to Governor George Clinton, "although it is true that this crime was committed within the Limits of your State, we know of no Treaty with the state by which we are bound to give satisfaction; but we are perfectly willing to treat with the United States and to give them satisfaction in the same manner we have heretofore received when we were the injured party." He asked, "Did we ever make a treaty with the state of New-York, and agree to conform to its laws?" Red Jacket answered his own rhetorical question: "No. We are independent of that state of New-York." In essence, the Senecas asserted that the affair was a matter of diplomacy rather than criminal law. He told the governor, "We hope . . . you will use your influence to settle this business in a peaceable way, and keep the chain of friendship bright between us." But the trial proceeded.[58]

Red Jacket had hoped that his persuasion might forestall a trial. But, comprehending that he might fail, he pushed for bail, protested the injustice of the death penalty, and pleaded extenuating circumstances. "Imprisonment for an Indian is worse than death," he argued, urging the acceptance of a bond "for any reasonable sum to deliver up the prisoner at the time of trial." When the request was refused, he commented, "You may doubtless think your Laws are right, but to us in this case they appear particularly hard." "We have uniformly done whatever we could to preserve peace and good order." Yet the state's judges would not even allow the Senecas "to keep our friend . . . till the wounds & bruises, he had received in the affray, were healed." Red Jacket suspected that a request for bail was in fact not inconsistent with New York law and might have been granted to a non-Indian defendant. And he observed that whites accused of killing Indians were never punished with death, even though their crimes were more heinous and premeditated. Stiff-Armed George did not act in cold blood but "under intoxication and passion." Moreover, "the prisoner was always a good civic man when sober, and the next relation to the first chief of our nation, as were also some of those Indians formerly killed by the white people." Red Jacket's pleading seemed to have little effect.[59]

Stiff-Armed George was convicted in a state court of oyer and terminer at Canandaigua on February 23, 1803. Yet jurors in the case surprisingly petitioned the State for a pardon, despite their finding of guilt. They were convinced that "had not the said George been pursued & beaten before any wound was given by him . . . fatal consequences would not have ensued." And they recognized the existence of extenuating circumstances—including a general pattern of "wanton & unprovoked attacks on several of the Indians of the Seneca Nation, which have had a great tendency to influence their minds." Even earlier, though not as quickly as Red Jacket might have preferred, Secretary of War Henry Dearborn wrote to Governor Clinton on behalf of the president recommending clemency should the defendant be convicted. Dearborn affirmed Red Jacket's claim that unruly whites had previously murdered Senecas at Buffalo Creek, including a member of the defendant's own family, and that they had largely escaped punishment. A pardon, Dearborn suggested, "would perhaps be no more than justice to the Indians requires, and . . . it would undoubtedly have a good effect on the minds of the Indian Nations generally." The governor—in an act of mercy and diplomacy—granted these requests and pardoned Stiff-Armed George.[60]

Technically, Stiff-Armed George's conviction signaled a failure for Seneca claims of independence. Yet in winning a pardon and asserting their sovereignty, Senecas won an important if partial victory. They did so by pitting federal and state governments against each other, and by appealing to some New York citizens to take the Indian side against other white New Yorkers. The Senecas not only invoked federal treaty and law, but they managed to elevate the Stiff-Armed George case above normal state criminal proceedings, getting the secretary of war to intercede on their behalf in the interests of peace on the new nation's borderlands. Red Jacket and other Seneca advocates proved able to engage some of New York's and the republic's white citizens, challenging them to act nobly and mercifully, rising to meet the standards of their own self-image as a virtuous, just, and benevolent people.

Following a paper victory, Governor Clinton's pardon avoided a jurisdictional confrontation and trouble, both with Senecas and the national government. This turn of events reflected the residual power of the Senecas— physical as well as moral. The state of New York saved face, and its citizens' act of mercy allowed them to think well of themselves. Mercy presupposes the legitimacy of the sanctions imposed and the authority imposing them; suspension of sanctions is a noble performance, a magnanimous act of benevolence that confirms authority itself. Did New York State hope to win the deference of Senecas and cement its dominion through this condescension? Red Jacket and the Senecas, without acknowledging New York's supremacy, managed to save the life of Stiff-Armed George and a measure of their own autonomy. The improvised solution of the case settled little, however, and the contest over order, sovereignty, and legality in New York emerged more starkly in the early 1820s in *State v. Tommy Jemmy*.[61]

Witchcraft, Murder, or Capital Punishment? *State v. Tommy Jemmy*

By 1821, Tommy Jemmy had settled back into life at Buffalo Creek. He was now a notable figure, a man of the world, a seasoned and responsible leader of his people, a Seneca chief. He and other members of the Indian Show troupe might, indeed, have received "some advantage from their Journey" across the Great Waters. That meeting between his delegation and English Friends in Leeds lent Tommy Jemmy a bit of distinction as a diplomat, while it offered the Senecas some leverage with their American Friends. But in the spring of 1821, things began to go badly. A near relative fell ill, and then she died—a disconcerting turn of events for Tommy Jemmy. Discussions with other chiefs determined the cause of her demise: witchcraft. The council identified the offending "witch" and imposed a sentence of death. Just in time: this evil woman had been implicated in "the death of various individuals of . . . [the] tribe, who had perished by the sorceries of the defunct." Now she must die. Tommy Jemmy had not been assigned the task of executing the woman implicated, Kauquatau, once she had been returned to the Senecas' jurisdiction. But the official executioner faltered—"either his hand failed, or his conscience smote him, and he declined the fulfillment of his bloody commission," wrote William Leete Stone, the nineteenth-century New York editor, writer, and politico. Tommy Jemmy, by reputation a man quick with the knife, stepped in to perform the melancholy duty. New York authorities immediately indicted him for the capital crime of murder, consistent with their sense of dominion, morality, enlightenment, and justice. On Saturday, May 5, 1821, Tommy Jemmy found himself in the Erie County jail.[62]

So began the landmark case, *New York State v. Tommy Jemmy*. Pitted against each other were the sovereignty claims of New York and the Senecas, not to mention their divergent cultural systems. The trial and its aftermath would answer (ambiguously) jurisdictional questions critically important in the Senecas' efforts to survive autonomously—not in the West but within the Empire State. It would influence the developing understanding of American federalism and the Indians' place within the larger federal structure of divided power and sovereignty. Significantly, its proceedings would galvanize the Senecas, stoking their efforts to build solidarity and national strength in the face of this threat of extermination—not merely to the individual Tommy Jemmy but to the Senecas generally. The trial would not signal an end to witchcraft belief among the Senecas, or even among some rural whites, who persisted in their supernaturalism even after it had been labeled "superstition." If Tommy Jemmy's offense made the Senecas look backward to outsiders, his defense could not have achieved its success if the Senecas had not been an adaptive, innovative people.[63]

The Senecas opened with the protest that New York lacked jurisdiction, but the State moved forward, pushing to establish its control of criminal matters within its borders and to assert its own particular moral and legal standards. Given that the "crime" occurred in Seneca territory, and that both the victim and perpetrator of the act in question were Indians—in contrast to the Stiff-Armed George case—New York was raising the stakes. Raising them further was the realization that the Senecas, despite their decline in power, retained some means to frustrate enforcement of New York State decrees and to disrupt peace and order with violence. Two decades earlier, before Stiff-Armed George faced New York justice, the state had prosecuted George Peter, a Brothertown Indian, for the murder of his wife in Oneida County. Peter was convicted and then hanged on March 26, 1802, as historian Alan Taylor notes, becoming the first Indian executed by the state of New York. But the Brothertown Indians were a relatively vulnerable and powerless group, unlike the Senecas and their Iroquois confederates (who could potentially mobilize "might" as well as "right"). And the subsequent Stiff-Armed George case had raised as many questions as it had answered about state jurisdiction and Seneca sovereignty.[64]

The Tommy Jemmy affair surprised white New Yorkers. Its revelation of continued witch-hunting was odd and disturbing. More bewildering was the fact that the defendant in the case, Tommy Jemmy, was a Seneca chief, one who "possesses more than a common share of intelligence," a Native cosmopolitan who had seen London if not Paris. And yet he showed no remorse. Indeed, he "appears not to be conscious of having done any thing criminal or improper in the murder he has perpetrated." This "murder" flouted New York law and white New Yorkers' sense of progress and civilization.[65]

A sense of excitement and apprehension surged through the village of Buffalo as the circuit court session commenced on July 9, 1821. Two days later, Judge Joseph C. Yates presided at a court of oyer and terminer to consider the matter of Tommy Jemmy. "This case awakened much interest," a reporter wrote, "particularly among the Indians, great numbers of whom thronged the court house during the trial, and manifested great anxiety for the result." According to another reporter, the judge "directed that a convenient part of the court room should be allotted to the Indians," represented by their principal leaders, including Red Jacket and Captain Pollard. Tommy Jemmy was officially represented by A. H. Tracy and S. M. Hopkins, but Red Jacket, as we have seen, stole the show as virtual cocounsel. Years later, the prominent Buffalo citizen Orlando Allen recalled that Red Jacket sat next to Tommy Jemmy's attorneys throughout the trial, taking a leading role even in jury selection, Red Jacket "scanning with his piercing eye the lineaments of every talesman who had been summoned as a juror, suggesting who should be accepted and who challenged." Purportedly on one occasion, he even made a prospective juror remove his glasses, "shutters from the window of his soul," so that "he might look within for the evidence of honesty or guile."[66]

Tommy Jemmy initially declared himself not guilty, but on the next day his counsel amended that plea to challenge the court's authority directly, arguing again that the Senecas, as parties to a sovereign and independent state, possessed the power to "lawfully exercise the exclusive right to try and punish members of their own nation for offences committed against other members of the nation within their territory." In short, they claimed, Tommy Jemmy's deed—inappropriately termed "murder" by the State—was a lawful act beyond the jurisdiction of New York State courts. Heman B. Potter, the district attorney, and John C. Spencer prosecuted the case, bringing to bear the best legal talent available in the state. Potter was a graduate of Williams College and, after moving to Buffalo from Columbia County, founded the leading law firm in the new city. Spencer had begun his law practice in Canandaigua in 1809 and rose to become district attorney for the five western counties and assistant New York attorney general. He had been elected to the United States Congress and served from 1817 to 1819, and he currently sat in the New York State Assembly. Later he would serve as United States secretary of war and secretary of the treasury in President John Tyler's administration. Against them, Red Jacket and other witnesses offered not merely brilliant "sarcastic philippic" but a systematic presentation of arguments and evidence, including the several treaties concluded between the United States and the Seneca nation. Without deliberating for more than a few minutes, the jury found "a verdict that all the allegations contained in the prisoner's plea were true." Hoping to forestall defeat, the prosecution quickly moved "to arrest the judgment," and the court agreed to suspend its proceedings, transferring the case to the State Supreme Court. The inconclusive trial thus ended, with a white jury persuaded of the Senecas' relative sovereignty if not civility—a victory for the Senecas and Tommy Jemmy. Had he gotten away with murder? The answer was "no"—either his act was lawful and just (it was not murder), or his act of murder remained subject to New York justice.[67]

In mid-August 1821, the case of Tommy Jemmy came before the bar of the New York Supreme Court, which required the defendant to "answer further, notwithstanding the verdict of the jury." John C. Spencer again represented "the people"—that is, the white citizens of the state, certainly not its Native inhabitants—and claimed that the acquitting jury erred when it offered judgments on law rather than simply fact. The fact of Seneca sovereignty, according to Spencer, had not been established. Indeed, he asserted (presumably on the dubious basis that colonization itself vacated Indian sovereignty) that the Senecas had not claimed or exercised sovereignty since 1620. Moreover, during the American Revolution, the Senecas had been enemies of the United States and had been conquered, subsequently acknowledging that conquest and subjection.[68]

On behalf of Tommy Jemmy and the Senecas, Thomas J. Oakley countered Spencer's arguments. Oakley was no less impressive an advocate than Spencer. A Yale graduate, Oakley began his legal practice in Poughkeepsie and was himself elected to the United States House of Representatives, serving from 1813 to 1814. Like Spencer, he then served in the New York State Assembly, but he had also been New York State attorney general, just ending his term in 1821. Oakley would be elected again to the U.S. Congress and ended his career as chief justice of the New York City Superior Court. The former attorney general now argued, against Spencer, that the findings of a jury in a capital case are, indeed, conclusive on the court, both as law and fact. More significant, Oakley rejected Spencer's assertions contesting Seneca sovereignty. The Senecas clearly had maintained their independence throughout the colonial period. Even Seneca defeat in the American Revolution did not imply a change of government or law, Oakley noted. Moreover, echoing Red Jacket, he affirmed, "if jurisdiction was acquired over them by conquest, it was that of the United States and not of this state, and that the United States had never ceded it to this state."[69]

Newspaper accounts summarized the discussions as "a very thorough examination of all the laws, treaties, documents, and public history relating to the Indians." The court acknowledged, "there was considerable difficulty in the question" and adjourned to consider the case. It set bail at one thousand dollars, precluding Tommy Jemmy's immediate release from jail. But in the end the Supreme Court discharged the prisoner; it was powerless to conclude, definitively, that the Senecas lacked the autonomy they claimed or that, under the circumstances, Tommy Jemmy's act precisely fit the definition of "murder." As Stone wrote, "the court, not liking to make a decision recognizing the independent jurisdiction of the Indians in such cases, and yet being unable to deny to them the existence of a qualified sovereignty,—perceiving, moreover, very clearly that the case was not one of murder, as the Indians 'understood it,'—liberated of the prisoner."[70]

The broader implications of the Tommy Jemmy case became clear when news reached Buffalo—news widely reprinted in eastern newspapers—that other Native people were employing a comparable defense when indicted for murder. An October 23, 1821 story reported that Ketaukah, a Chippewa Indian charged with the death of a Dr. Madison near the Manitoowach River on the west side of Lake Michigan, had been tried by the Territorial Supreme Court at Detroit. "The principle involved in this trial relative to the sovereignty of the Indian tribes, was somewhat similar to that in the case of Tommy Jemmy." The defense "interposed a plea to the jurisdiction of the court," contending that the accused was a member of an independent Indian nation, which retained "exclusive jurisdiction of all offences committed within the limits of its territory." As in the Tommy Jemmy trial, arguments and documents were submitted to prove that these Indian nations had been recognized "as distinct communities, independent of the United States, competent to form alliances, declare war, make peace, and to do all other acts incident to a sovereign people." In this instance, the alleged murder occurred on Indian land, but its victim was a non-Indian, thus distinguishing it from the Tommy Jemmy affair. Nonetheless, Ketaukah's unsuccessful defense challenged the court's assertion of authority and the trial itself—construing it as an illegitimate intervention in the internal affairs of a foreign nation. At best, it claimed, settling such a murder required diplomacy, not unilateral action by the Michigan Territory. But Ketaukah lost his case and his life, as did Kewabiskim, a Menominee man tried under similar circumstances for the murder of Charles Ulrick at Green Bay. Both men were executed on December 27, 1821.[71]

In New York, Governor De Witt Clinton sought to clarify the state's position and establish its authority by proposing a legislative fix. Following his lead, on April 12, 1822, the New York Assembly disposed of the defendant Tommy Jemmy by officially pardoning him, even though he had not actually been convicted of any crime. And it specifically claimed state criminal jurisdiction over Indian tribes within its boundaries. Embedded in a "whereas" clause, the legislation asserted that "the sole and exclusive cognizance of all crimes and offences committed within this state, belongs of right to courts holden under the constitution and laws thereof, as a necessary attribute of sovereignty, except only crimes and offences cognizable in the courts deriving jurisdiction under the constitution and laws of the United States."[72]

This remedy nonetheless perpetuated the ambiguities of the case. The state of New York was forced to recognize Seneca sovereignty, after a fashion, as it attempted to extinguish that sovereignty by legislation. In an earlier clause, the bill acknowledged, "The Senecas, and other tribes of Indians residing within this state, have assumed the power and authority of trying and punishing, and in some cases capitally, members of their respective tribes for supposed crimes by them done and committed in their respective reservations, and within the state."[73] Was this Native assumption of power and authority legal or illegal? On what basis did Indians assume it? And did such power and authority continue, in light of the ongoing relationship between Indian tribes and the federal government, as well as the dominance of federal over state authority under certain circumstances, which the legislation acknowledged?[74]

The New York Assembly and Senate's unorthodox (and gratuitous) pardon of Tommy Jemmy seemed to condone or somehow excuse a homicide it condemned, or at least it seemed to acknowledge a complexity and set of extenuating circumstances that muddied the clear moral denunciation of the act. "It is deemed by the legislature expedient to pardon him," the bill said. The unusual pardon was expedient, but it left many questions unanswered: How did New York stand on the "civilization" program for its Native denizens? Did it countenance witchcraft and violence? In striving to clarify and strengthen its own sovereignty, would New York in fact bring greater order, safety, and peace to the lives of Senecas as well as its white citizens? Or was the legislation asserting a new state order as destructive as it was constructive, undermining not merely Seneca sovereignty and jurisprudence but challenging United States authority as well? New York State acted energetically here to close a door it wanted to believe had never been open.[75]

But was the door to Seneca autonomy still open? The ambiguity of the law, and of American federalism, opened the possibility that Senecas might yet escape New York legal jurisdiction and thereby challenge the state's exercise of complete dominion within its borders. While Senecas rejected New York's overreaching, the federal government remained silent. Had New York successfully dissolved the Senecas and their territory into a single, state-dominated social and legal order? Only time would tell, and at least initially, the Michigan Territory murder cases of 1821 seemed to affirm New York's position. As did the trial of George Corn Tassel in Georgia in 1830. Corn Tassel was a Cherokee man arrested and tried in a state court for a crime he allegedly committed on Cherokee lands against another Indian named Sanders. The court found Corn Tassel guilty and sentenced him to hang. The Georgia superior court upheld the decision, arguing that state sovereignty demanded that states have full criminal and civil jurisdiction over Indian tribes within their boundaries. The court cited New York's 1822 legislation. William Wirt, the former U.S. attorney general, appealed the Georgia decision to the United States Supreme Court, which then ordered the state to appear before it in January 1831. But Georgia too sought a legislative solution to its problem, and in a special session convened on December 22 it defied the U.S. Supreme Court by ordering Corn Tassel's execution to proceed. Two days later, Georgia disposed of the case and defendant himself, hanging the unfortunate George Corn Tassel.[76]

Three days later, Wirt initiated another, more famous proceeding—*Cherokee Nation v. Georgia*—filing it directly in the United States Supreme Court as a lawsuit involving a foreign nation and a state. The Marshall Court ultimately held that the Cherokees were not a foreign nation and therefore the Court lacked jurisdiction, an apparent victory for Georgia (and New York). But in a dictum, Marshall defined the Cherokees and other tribes as "domestic dependent nations" whose relationship with the federal government "resembles that of a ward and a guardian." This decision, along with another in *Worcester v. Georgia* in 1832 that went against the state, found the Cherokees (and by implication other Indian nations) to be distinct communities, occupying their own territory, with primary responsibility for their own internal affairs. If they were subordinate to the federal government, such nations were *not* subsidiary to state government—they were outside of their control altogether.[77]

Yet the denouement of these cases is as instructive as the violent end of George Corn Tassel—"legally" murdered by Georgia in defiance of the Supreme Court—with important implications for our understanding of the contested terrain of western New York State. Georgia, attempting to destroy Cherokee sovereignty and expropriate Native territory, had prohibited the presence of missionaries on Cherokee lands, except when licensed by state officials. The Reverend Samuel Worcester and others refused to obtain such a permit and went to jail, offering the grounds for Wirt's test case. Yet after the missionary's (and the Cherokees') legal victory—reversing and annulling Worcester's conviction—Georgia refused to release him. Worcester remained in prison for a year and a half, before accepting a deal requiring him to abandon the Cherokees and pledge allegiance to the state of Georgia in exchange for his freedom and pardon by the governor of Georgia.[78] Such was the victory for Cherokee sovereignty, and such was the performance of the federal government's trusteeship of an American Indian people, most of whom were subsequently removed from Georgia via the infamous Trail of Tears.[79]

President Andrew Jackson was sympathetic to Georgia's claims. Despite the Supreme Court's rulings, he remained convinced that Indians could not constitute sovereign nations; he might have agreed with Chief Justice Marshall that they were domestic dependents, but he understood the tribes to be dependent not merely on the national government but on the states as well. "I have been unable to perceive any sufficient reason why the Red man more than the white, may claim exemption from the municipal laws of the state within which they reside," he wrote. Jackson was unable to defend the federal authority that Marshall found embedded in the Constitution, and, in any case, he was disinterested in doing so. Jackson was not the president to fulfill the general government's obligation to the Indians, or to constrain states that overstepped their authority. The overlapping orders in places like western New York remained murky.[80]

On the one hand, in 1822 Tommy Jemmy and the Senecas won. The Seneca defendant escaped conviction, and his people established the sovereignty of their reservations, encircled though they were by the state of New York. Federal law and the Senecas' own residual if greatly diminished power proved significant, while the subsequent New York legislative act declaring state jurisdiction over civil and criminal matters on Indian reservations within the state proved legally empty, or at least technically unconstitutional, as the *Cherokee* and *Worcester* cases demonstrated in the following decade.

On the other hand, in 1822 "victory" was provisional and vulnerable. Extralegal—or even illegal—forces proved more powerful than federal law and court rulings in places like New York and Georgia. In a sense, these incidents supported the adage "might makes right," although white Americans did not see it this way. States believed that civil and criminal jurisdiction followed sovereignty over land, and they imagined themselves to possess such sovereignty. It did not matter apparently that in New York the Iroquois had not been conquered, at least not by New York, nor had Senecas divested themselves of their remaining territory or the right of self-government within their homelands. Nonetheless, white citizens, speculators, and officials of the state acted as if Seneca sovereignty had been extinguished, and they worked to fulfill their prophecy of Seneca dispossession and disappearance. Such colonialism assumed an aura of legality, as the United States proved disinterested in challenging the Empire State in its attempts to erode Seneca sovereignty and assert its jurisdiction. The federal government, New York, and private concerns holding "preemption rights" to Seneca land often coop-erated—to the detriment of the Senecas—but they could also work at cross-purposes, especially when pushed by politically astute leaders such as Red Jacket, Seneca advocates like the Quakers, and other white Americans pursu-ing their own self interests.[81]

Behind the Frontier

How did Senecas survive in this complex, dynamic, and equivocal legal and extralegal universe? To what extent were they actually subjected to New York criminal justice, in violation of their own legitimate but unenforceable sovereignty? According to legal historian Sidney Harring, the majority of nineteenth-century Indian criminal cases were never reported; nationally, thousands of Indians were pulled into local courts, tried, sentenced, sent to prison or executed. Was this true for Senecas? Perhaps, but they likely bene-fited from haphazard enforcement of federal regulations and state law, cir-cumventing a legal system the state of New York believed it had legitimately established.[82]

Separate worlds with separate but overlapping orders continued to exist simultaneously in western New York, though white power and Seneca power were hardly symmetrical. And the economies of Senecas and white New York continued to be intermingled. To obliterate the Seneca presence promised to be too costly, too violent. White New Yorkers, in any respect, could be satis-fied that their dominion substantially prevailed, even if Seneca reservations continued to dot the landscape. This dominion was achieved and maintained primarily through diplomacy, evasion, fraud, and wishful thinking, not through violence. Yet violence lurked under the surface and in people's mem-ories, supporting the social order. The threat of force, or the public memory of violent coercion, was more important than actual military conquest. As Cornplanter had reminded President Washington in 1790, at the Treaty of Fort Stanwix the United States delegates "told us that we were in your hand, and that, by closing it, you could crush us to nothing." Such strength gave white Americans the power, if not the moral authority, to dictate the terms of Indian relations. But it also invited white citizens and officials to act hon-orably, according to their political and religious principles, and some—such as the Quakers—sometimes accomplished good, both because of and despite their good intentions.[83]

The Senecas in the 1820s endured both the "blackness of darkness" and a certain redemption and transcendence. Under increasing pressure from settlers, land companies, scheming officials, and invasive missionaries, they adjusted, devised a hybrid subsistence-exchange economy, lost ground but defended themselves against dispossession, and conserved a tenuous autonomy and sovereignty. They revived and continued their revitalization project and began to formally canonize the Code of Handsome Lake. Some embraced Christianity, but Christians and "traditionalists" and followers of the *Gaiwiio* alike forged enough solidarity to endure as Senecas. Their struggle to survive would continue, and fresh challenges would emerge. But as the United States celebrated its fiftieth birthday, the Senecas could observe that the nation's birth had not resulted in their own death.

In early June 1825, the Marquis de Lafayette, on his triumphant, sentimental return to America, approached Buffalo from the south and west, having visited nearly all twenty-four of the far-flung United States, even the newest and most western one, Missouri. Lafayette, Washington's virtual son and an enduring symbol of the Revolutionary generation, was the nation's guest on the eve of its jubilee. Among his most ancient hosts was Red Jacket. Red Jacket represented the past, as did Lafayette. But the fact that they both remained present was significant and celebrated persistence—of people, principles, and fraternal relations. The two men had a brief interview, which Lafayette's chronicler Auguste Levasseur turned into humor. "Time has much changed me," Lafayette was said to have remarked to Red Jacket, after recalling their last meeting, in 1784 at Fort Schuyler. Red Jacket exclaimed, "time has been less severe on you than me; he has left you a fresh countenance, and a head well covered with hair; whilst as for me—look!" The chief then untied his headscarf and displayed his completely bald pate. For Levasseur, the joke was on the simple Indian who was not able to understand how civilized people repaired "the injuries of time"—in this case, with a wig. Levasseur wryly observed, all "were cautious not to explain the error; and perhaps did right, for he might have confounded a wig with a scalp, and wished to have regarnished his head at the expense of that of one of his neighbors." Levasseur thus managed to portray Red Jacket (like Tommy Jemmy) simultaneously as a noble and ignoble savage—dignified, eloquent, and primitively haughty, yet ignorant and unpredictable, and not to be trusted with a scalping knife. In fact, both men were gracious and well-spoken, both resourceful and devoted leaders, both decidedly worldly.[84]

RED JACKET.
SENECA WAR CHIEF.

Published by Campbell and Burns

Figure 16. *Red Jacket, Seneca War Chief,* ca. 1840, on stone by C. Corbould, from a painting by C. B. King, printed by C. Hallmandel, ca. 1835. Courtesy of the Library of Congress, Prints and Photographs Division, Washington, D.C.

Levasseur expressed regret that he could not linger a bit longer: "I wished much to have visited the large village inhabited by the . . . [Senecas], a short distance from Buffalo," but other "agreeable" entertainments detained them and they could not "spare the time" before proceeding to Niagara Falls and pushing into the new Erie Canal. So Lafayette left the Senecas behind as he headed east, while white Americans left them behind as they pushed increasingly west, to Missouri and beyond the Mississippi. For the Senecas, assuming a less conspicuous place in the growing republic might have its advantages. As we have seen, the canal boat carrying De Witt Clinton and his party inaugurating the opening of the Erie Canal later that year was called the *Seneca Chief.* In fact, Red Jacket already had a ship named for him—a merchant schooner first launched in June 1820. The cargo vessel *Red Jacket* would begin its life in the service of the British-American boundary commission on the Detroit River and in Lake Huron; later it would serve the western commerce that was transforming New York and the United States. At the ship's dedication, Red Jacket reportedly said, "You have a great name given to you,—strive to deserve it. Be brave and daring. . . . [F]ear neither the swift winds nor the strong waves. Be not frightened nor overcome by them, for it is by resisting storms and tempests that I, whose name you bear, obtained my renown." The Senecas had resisted storms, and they would continue to survive tempests.[85]

Conclusion

The day of the great HO-DE-NOH-SAU-NEE is now far spent. The last rays of the setting sun have cast their light upon the gaudy feathers of their head-dresses, upon their bright necklaces and their buckskin suits. The ancient music is hushed. . . . The laughter of the children does not ring through the silent forest; the voices of the wild animals do not resound. . . . —all these native voices that the Indian so well loved, all are still, they are part of the silent past.

—Inscription by Ha-non-da-a-suh, Moses Shongo (1903)

Currently, the Seneca Nation occupies sovereign land set aside by the Treaty of Canandaigua in 1794. . . . [It] has over 7,300 enrolled members and holds title to five territories in Western New York, specifically, the Cattaraugus, Allegany, Oil Spring, Niagara Falls, and Buffalo Creek territories. . . . The Seneca Nation continues to support its own people and the surrounding communities with a variety of cultural, educational and economic efforts, including Seneca Niagara Casino & Hotel, Seneca Allegany Casino & Hotel and Seneca Gaming and Entertainment in Irving. . . . The Seneca Nation endeavors to preserve its rich cultural heritage and welcomes the opportunity to share it with the global community. . . . Come see why Seneca Allegany Casino & Hotel is where the action is!

—Seneca Allegany Casino & Hotel Web site (2009)

IN 1903 IN Buffalo, when volume 6 of the *Publications of the Buffalo Histori-cal Society* first appeared, thoughts of death must have loomed over that west-ern New York metropolis. Just two years earlier in their fair city—perhaps as the Historical Society's editors prepared their volume on the Niagara Fron-tier, the Genesee Country, and "the pathos of a vanished folk," that is, the Iroquois—Buffalonians witnessed the assassination of United States Presi-dent William McKinley, shot and killed by an anarchist, Leon Czolgosz. Buffalo, poised to demonstrate its status as a major transportation and manu-facturing center, and (city fathers hoped) the focus of international attention as the host of a world's fair, the Pan-American Exposition of 1900, instead suffered ignominy and shame. The exposition lost money, boosters lamented the toll taken on their city's reputation by McKinley's murder, and even Jumbo, the nine-ton elephant starring in the exposition's animal show, proved unruly and, in an unfortunate accident, was electrocuted—the won-ders of a new technology gone terribly wrong. So perhaps this was an auspi-cious moment for Buffalonians to turn from the perils of progress to a romantic past, sentimentally recalling the death of another people in order to obscure present anxieties about their own prospects, to imagine a better fu-ture, looking forward from the early nineteenth rather than from the early twentieth century.[1]

In a foreword to the volume, set off with a melancholy header showing a coffinlike pedestal entombed in overgrown foliage, Moses Shongo's inscrip-tion echoed the classic language of the "last of the Mohicans" genre. Pre-sented as the dying words of a Seneca leader, it read, "Here, at the Western Door . . . the people of the Great League gave up their worldly customs to join their now spiritual forefathers. It is to their memory . . . that the tablet is engraved above the entrance to the grand hall of the Buffalo Historical Society:

NEH-KO, GAH-GIS-DAH-YEN-DUK.
OTHER COUNCIL FIRES WERE HERE BEFORE OURS.

Was the society's nostalgic indulgence also meant to be cautionary? Was it implied that other council fires might some day be kindled after their own was quenched? Would the rise of the Empire State see its own fall? For the present, turn-of-the-century historians and memorialists concentrated on the decline of western Iroquois civilization. Shongo's inscription concluded, "Few and scattered are the remnants of the once-powerful confederacy; fewer still they who know its customs. 'A few more suns, and my people will only live in history.' This saying of one of our great chieftains is now fulfilled.'"[2]

Such an imperial elegy was premature, as it was when delivered ever earlier by Philip Freneau, James Fenimore Cooper, and others. Despite their ordeal, Senecas remained in New York State—they were not extinguished in the early republic, in the Gilded Age, or even in the twentieth century. Certainly, they were reduced in number, scattered, and forced to change many of their customs and to develop new forms for old institutions, such as their storied league. If they maintained a connection with their forefathers and foremothers, the Senecas had not literally joined them in the grave. Their past was not silent; they lived not only in history but in the present; indeed, their survival stems in part from the rebirth they fashioned for themselves in the early republic. This book has chronicled a critical chapter in the ongoing contradiction of the much-prophesied Seneca death, tracing Seneca revitalization and reform in the fifty-year period following United States Independence. Iroquois council fires were not permanently extinguished, and the flame of Seneca society and culture continued to burn in the half century after the American Revolution, even as white land speculation, agricultural and commercial and then industrial development, legal encroachment on Native sovereignty, and Christian revivalism spread throughout New York State and beyond. Senecas survived the 1826 jubilee, and they survived through the Centennial of 1876, the Bicentennial of 1976, and the commencement of the twenty-first century. Today the Seneca nation endures, on its own lands but also beyond, with a third of its people living off-reservation across the country. Seneca reserves remain discrete but also integrated into the cultural worlds of the United States and Canada, and the Seneca economy remains resourceful, today focusing especially on tourism and gaming. The Senecas' endurance, resourcefulness, and resilience (and perhaps their continued fragility) are expressed in classic twenty-first-century fashion—on the Seneca nation's Web site.[3]

Let us return briefly to where we began, with the trial of Tommy Jemmy. We might conclude that, by the 1820s, Senecas had come a long way in their cultural transformation. They had "advanced" to such a degree that their witch-hunting had begun to resemble the late seventeenth-century Salem witch trials. Ironies abound in the history of early national America, which inaugurated a new colonial era under United States auspices—such as the Cherokee demonstration of their advanced state of civilization through their successful adoption of slave-based plantation agriculture, before they were "removed" by belligerent and covetous Georgians. As we have seen, Tommy Jemmy's celebrated trial, and the New York State legislation that tried to fix its unsettling result in 1822, became a footnote in the infamous story of Cherokee removal.[4] Unlike most Cherokees, however, the New York Senecas persisted in their ancient homeland, and that persistence—not yet assured but enabled by their purposeful transformation and revitalization in the early republic—is perhaps the most important fact of nineteenth- and twentieth-century Seneca history. Like Tommy Jemmy, the Senecas lost some battles but survived.

In 1842, in preparation for negotiation of a new federal treaty that would restore Seneca reservations at Allegany and Cattaraugus, the United States commissioner of Indian affairs T. Hartley Crawford wrote instructions to the U.S. representative Ambrose Spencer. The seventy-seven-year-old Spencer was the father of Secretary of War John C. Spencer, who had been Tommy Jemmy's prosecutor. The elder Spencer was an equally lofty political figure—a graduate of Harvard, a member at various times of the New York Assembly and Senate and the U.S. House of Representatives, a former New York State attorney general, a mayor of Albany, and a justice of the New York Supreme Court. While in Congress, Spencer had been a vocal opponent of the Indian Removal Act of 1830. Commissioner Crawford urged "a conciliatory spirit" in his instructions to Spencer. Although Spencer's charge was to repair the damage of the 1838 treaty, Crawford nonetheless claimed that his office had proceeded then with good intentions: "The general government was concerned only to relieve a flourishing and thriving part of the territory of New York from the *incubus* of an Indian population, and to remove the Indians themselves out of the way of temptation that surrounds them." *Incubus* was a peculiar word for Crawford to use to describe the Senecas of western New York. Were they an "evil spirit," a "person or thing that oppresses or burdens"? Were they a "nightmare" or a "demon," as the term implies? Crawford's unguarded correspondence adds another dimension to our understanding of a "Seneca Possessed."[5]

How was Seneca—the place and its people—possessed? Like Salem, Massachusetts, in 1692, as Red Jacket suggested in 1821, Seneca country was a site of contention, as it was claimed, redeemed, and transformed, and as new forms of economic enterprise, beliefs, and ways of life struggled to prevail. Western New York, like eastern Massachusetts, was colonized by outsiders and possessed in culturally specific ways. Amid conflicts over land, modes of production, and political power, both places were "possessed" by their indigenous devils. That is, the residents of Salem and of Seneca communities struggled among themselves, as they tried to accommodate their changing worlds, control their destinies, and define the particular natures of their social, cultural, and spiritual landscapes. This story, of Seneca possession and repossession—of attempted conquest, consolidation, and ongoing, complex negotiation *across* cultural frontiers as well as *within* the worlds such frontiers distinguished and joined—forces us to rethink the story of Indian-white relations. In the midst of their rise and fall, death and rebirth, Native people like other Americans struggled bitterly and acted creatively as they imagined and sought alternative futures. The Senecas' unique historical experience in this era occurred within a larger context of American growth and transformation—of rural people increasingly tied to national and international commercial networks, pushed west as pioneers but also pulled into growing industrial towns and cities, enveloped in a world of new social prescriptions, unruly democratic politics, and revived, evangelical Protestantism.

Our story has been about possession—about dominion, spirit, and mastery. We might also consider, in the end, the Senecas' ultimate self-possession, which allowed them to determine their own dynamic history, to maintain and remake "tradition," to define not only their past but their future. The Seneca prophet invented a "new way" that possessed a particular Iroquois past and became the "Old Way of Handsome Lake." The Seneca orator Red Jacket sought to possess even the alien history of Salem, and by playing on cultural conflicts within white society he (and Handsome Lake) found ways to conceal and protect Iroquois "traditional" life as it was being remade. White missionaries, speculators, and government officials, meanwhile, worked to force Senecas and other Native people into an imperial history of alleged human advancement, Christian progress, and capitalist economic development. Sometimes with good intentions, too often with bad, they sought the end of Seneca history, achieved through Seneca cultural transformation and disappearance—it was a contest of dominion, spirit, and mastery. They failed, and Seneca history continues.

NOTES

1. William L. Stone, *The Life and Times of Red-Jacket, or Sa-Go-Ye-Wat-Ha; Being the Sequel to the History of the Six Nations* (New York: Wiley and Putnam, 1841), 316; the incident is treated at 316–22. See also Robert W. Bingham, *The Cradle of the Queen City: A History of Buffalo to the Incorporation of the City* (Buffalo, N.Y.: Buffalo Historical Society, 1931), 386–88. Cooper's classic *Last of the Mohicans* was first published later that decade, in 1826.

2. The classic account of Seneca revitalization is Anthony F. C. Wallace, *The Death and Rebirth of the Seneca* (New York: Knopf, 1970), a work to which the analysis here is indebted; some of what I argue in these pages is implicit in Wallace's account, but Wallace's purpose was different. I build on the pathbreaking work of Wallace to examine the gendered nature and implications of Handsome Lake's revitalization program, including the feminization of Seneca witch-hunting, which it encouraged, as well as the post-Revolutionary predicaments of both Senecas and Quakers in the early republic. Elisabeth Tooker, "On the Development of the Handsome Lake Religion," *Proceedings of the American Philosophical Society* 133.1 (1989): 35–50, offers some valuable correctives to Wallace. While recognizing the importance of Seneca—and more generally, Iroquois—revitalization, Tooker and others caution that its achievements should not be overstated. Iroquois communities differentially shared in this renaissance, and each continued to struggle internally and externally in the face of continued colonialism. For an insightful analysis of the Iroquois predicament following the American Revolution, which focuses particularly on the Oneidas, see J. David Lehman, "The End of the Iroquois Mystique: The Oneida Land Cession Treaties of the 1780s," *William and Mary Quarterly*, 3d ser., 47.4 (1990): 523–47. Though the "Iroquois mystique had magnified the power and influence of the Confederacy" and the Revolution had taken a significant toll on Iroquois strength, real or imagined, Lehman argues nonetheless that the demise of the Iroquois has been exaggerated (525). Also critical for understanding the Oneida experience is Karim Michel Tiro, "The People of the Standing Stone: The Oneida Indian Nation from Revolution through Removal, 1765–1840" (Ph.D. diss., University of Pennsylvania, 1999).

3. Stone, *Life and Times of Red-Jacket*, 318. We know little about the victim of this

execution beyond her sex and her alleged crime of witchcraft. The murder was reported in the *Spirit of the Times* (Batavia, N.Y.), May 11, 1821, and the *Ontario Repository* (Canandaigua, N.Y.), May 15, 1821. Tommy Jemmy, the Seneca executioner, was well-known locally for his travel to England with the Storrs & Co. Indian Show in 1818. Thanks to Paul Johnson for generously sharing newspaper clippings detailing these events. Note that Tommy Jemmy, unlike Handsome Lake, was a "Pine Tree Chief"—an earned, honorary leadership status—not one of the approximately fifty hereditary (and higher-status) league chiefs among the Six Nations Confederacy.

4. "Murder," from the *Niagara Journal* (Buffalo, N.Y.), May 8, 1821, in the *New-York Evening Post*, May 15, 1821.

5. Red Jacket's speech was recorded originally in the *Albany Argus* and widely reprinted under various headlines, including "Indian Justice" and "Eloquence of Red Jacket." See the *American Mercury*, August 7, 1821, for example, or the *Essex Register* or the *Salem Gazette*, August 8, 1821, which reprints a story from Buffalo's *Erie Gazette*. See also Stone, *Life and Times of Red-Jacket*, 320–21; Bingham, *Queen City*, 387–88. Bingham gives the number of "witches" executed, according to Red Jacket, as "thousands," an even greater exaggeration. At Salem during the 1692 witch crisis, twenty were executed, and four others died while in prison, most of them women. See Paul Boyer and Stephen Nissenbaum, eds., *The Salem Witchcraft Papers: Verbatim Transcripts of the Legal Documents of the Salem Witchcraft Outbreak of 1692*, 3 vols. (New York: Da Capo Press, 1977), 1:3.

6. Although the history of the early national United States is ripe for a systematic reappraisal in light of the recent historiography of postcolonialism, I wish only to make the simple point that colonialism—especially with regard to Native people such as the Senecas—did not cease after the success of white Americans' successful colonial revolt. Though much less prominently considered in "postcolonial" analysis than other continents, North America too—even after its "colonial period"—has experienced the continued impact of colonialism and imperialism. Scholars of the United States are increasingly joining in such studies. See, for example, Jack P. Greene, "Colonial History and National History: Reflections on a Continuing Problem, *William and Mary Quarterly*, 3d ser., 64.2 (April 2007): 235–50, and the comments that follow in this edition. American independence advanced Seneca dependence, and the "Empire for Liberty" envisioned by Jefferson and others would be based on western expansion, that is, persistent colonialism. Thus, students of American Indian history find themselves examining the ongoing adjustments of *colonial* rather than postcolonial subjects, even as the subaltern status of Senecas and others was constructed in relation to white postcolonial actors. For a useful introduction to the work of the Subaltern Studies Group, which stresses its importance for historical study, see the forum devoted to the subject in the *American Historical Review* 99.5 (December 1994): 1475–1545, especially Frederick Cooper, "Conflict and Connection: Rethinking Colonial African History," 1516–45. See also Bill Ashcroft, Gareth Griffiths, and Helen Tiffin, *The Empire Writes Back: Theory and Practice in Post-Colonial Literatures*, 2d ed. (London: Routledge, 2002); Robert J. C. Young, *Postcolonialism: An Historical Introduction* (Malden, Mass.: Blackwell, 2001).

7. See Matthew Dennis, *Red, White, and Blue Letter Days: An American Calendar* (Ithaca, N.Y.: Cornell University Press, 2002), esp. 81–118. Andrew Burstein, *America's Jubilee: How in 1826 a Generation Remembered Fifty Years of Independence* (New York: Knopf, 2001), analyzes the post-Revolutionary generation's collective efforts to memorialize their nation and define their own place in it on the occasion of the United States' fiftieth anniversary.

8. See, for example, Robert Troup to Jasper Parrish, Geneva, N.Y., August 24, 1810, manuscript collections (HM 8900), Huntington Library, San Marino, Calif., which describes the Ogden Land Company's efforts to promote the concentration of Seneca communities on a single reservation and the removal of many to the West, in Arkansas or perhaps Michigan Territory. See also Carl Benn, *The Iroquois in the War of 1812* (Toronto: University of Toronto Press, 1998); Alan Taylor, *The Divided Ground: Indians, Settlers, and the American Revolution* (New York: Knopf, 2006), analyzes the construction of this border and its implication for Native people in the period leading up to the War of 1812.

9. The historical literature on the social and economic transformation of early nineteenth-century America is extensive. See, for example, James A. Henretta, "Families and Farms: *Mentalité* in Pre-Industrial America," *William and Mary Quarterly*, 3d ser., 35 (January 1978): 3–32; Christopher Clark, "Household Economy, Market Exchange, and the Rise of Capitalism in the Connecticut Valley, 1800–1860," *Journal of Social History* 13 (Winter 1979): 169–89, and Clark, *The Roots of Rural Capitalism: Western Massachusetts, 1780–1860* (Ithaca, N.Y.: Cornell University Press, 1990); Charles Sellers, *The Market Revolution: Jacksonian America, 1815–1846* (New York: Oxford University Press, 1991). Useful overviews of the transition to capitalism debate are provided by Allan Kulikoff, "The Transformation to Capitalism in Rural America," *William and Mary Quarterly*, 3d ser., 46 (January 1989): 120–44; Michael Merrill, "Putting 'Capitalism' in Its Place: A Review of Recent Literature," *William and Mary Quarterly*, 3d ser., 52 (April 1995): 315–26; Naomi R. Lamoreaux, "Rethinking the Transition to Capitalism in the Early American Northeast," *Journal of American History* 90.2 (September 2003): 437–61; Christopher Clark, "The View from the Farmhouse: Rural Lives in the Early Republic," *Journal of the Early Republic* 24 (Summer 2004): 198–207. On early industrialization, see Herbert G. Gutman, *Work, Culture, and Society in Industrializing America: Essays in American Working-Class History* (New York: Knopf, 1976); Alan Dawley, *Class and Community: The Industrial Revolution in Lynn* (Cambridge, Mass.: Harvard University Press, 1976); Thomas Dublin, *Women and Work: The Transformation of Work and Community in Lowell, Massachusetts, 1826–1860* (New York: Columbia University Press, 1979); Paul Faler, *Mechanics and Manufacturers in the Early Industrial Revolution: Lynn, Massachusetts, 1780–1860* (Albany: State University of New York Press, 1981); Jonathan Prude, *The Coming of Industrial Order: Town and Factory Life in Rural Massachusetts, 1810–1860* (New York: Cambridge University Press, 1983). And see Jack Larkin, *The Reshaping of Everyday Life, 1790–1840* (New York: Harper and Row, 1988); the changing, early nineteenth-century world of work, leisure, and spectacle is brilliantly surveyed in Paul E. Johnson, *Sam Patch, the Famous Jumper* (New York: Hill and Wang, 2003).

10. Frederick Jackson Turner first propounded his "frontier thesis" in a paper, "The Significance of the Frontier in American History," delivered at the American Historical Society's annual meeting in 1893, during the Columbian Exposition in Chicago, a World's Fair commemorating the four hundredth anniversary of Columbus's voyage in 1492. Turner famously declared (and lamented) the end of a significant chapter in American history corresponding to the closing of the "frontier." Though much critiqued and caricatured, Turner's thesis has shown astonishing persistence in American popular discourse as a means to explain American history, identity, and exceptionalism. Turner posited a historical trajectory in which America moved from east to west, from savagery and barbarism to civility, from hunting to herding to agriculture to industrial production, and from wilderness to rural enclaves to cities. Historians have successfully challenged the explanatory utility of the thesis on numerous empirical grounds and pointed out its profound ethnocentric implications.

11. Carla Gardina Pestana, "The City upon a Hill Under Siege: The Puritan Perception of the Quaker Threat to Massachusetts Bay, 1656–1661," *New England Quarterly* 56.3 (September 1983): 323–53; Melvin B. Endy, *William Penn and Early Quakerism* (Philadelphia: University of Pennsylvania Press, 1973); Richard S. Dunn and Mary Maples Dunn, eds., *The World of William Penn* (Philadelphia: University of Pennsylvania Press, 1986); Richard Bauman, *For the Reputation of Truth: Politics, Religion, and Conflict among the Pennsylvania Quakers, 1750–1800* (Baltimore: Johns Hopkins Press, 1971); Sydney V. James, *A People Among Peoples: Quaker Benevolence in Eighteenth-Century America* (Cambridge, Mass.: Harvard University Press, 1963); Thomas D. Hamm, *The Transformation of American Quakerism: Orthodox Friends, 1800–1907* (Bloomington: Indiana University Press, 1988); Robert W. Doherty, *The Hicksite Separation: A Sociological Analysis of Religious Schism in Early Nineteenth-Century America* (New Brunswick, N.J.: Rutgers University Press, 1967); Bruce Dorsey, "Friends Becoming Enemies: Philadelphia Benevolence and the Neglected Area of American Quaker History," *Journal of the Early Republic* 18.3 (Fall 1998): 395–428; Margaret Morris Haviland, "Beyond Women's Sphere: Young Quaker Women and the Veil of Charity in Philadelphia, 1790–1810," *William and Mary Quarterly*, 3d ser., 51.3 (July 1994): 419–45.

12. Seneca Falls, New York, was the site of a convention in 1848 that helped launch the struggle for women's suffrage in the United States. Veterans of the anti-slavery movement, Elizabeth Cady Stanton and Lucretia Mott, a Quaker, organized the event and held it in Stanton's hometown, once the homeland of the Six Nations of the Iroquois. The convention adopted a "Declaration of Sentiments," which paraphrased the Declaration of Independence and extended its language to explicitly address women's rights. It declared, for example, "We hold these truths to be self-evident: that all men and women are created equal." See Gail H. Landsman, "The 'Other' as Political Symbol: Images of Indians in the Woman Suffrage Movement," *Ethnohistory* 39.3 (Summer 1992): 247–84.

13. See especially Stuart Banner, *How the Indians Lost Their Land: Law and Power on the Frontier* (Cambridge, Mass.: Harvard University Press, 2005). A very small Seneca removal did occur in 1846, with some sixty-six Senecas joining other Iroquois on a Kansas

reservation. The venture proved disastrous and lasted only a year, with the death or return of all but two Seneca migrants; see Thomas S. Abler and Elisabeth Tooker, "Seneca," in William C. Sturtevant, gen. ed., *Handbook of North American Indians*, 20 vols. projected (Washington, D.C.: Smithsonian Institution, 1978–) (hereafter *HBNAI*), vol. 15, *Northeast* (1978), ed. Bruce G. Trigger, 511. In addition, some Senecas and Cayugas established a reservation in northeastern Oklahoma; they were composed of descendants from autonomous Senecas who had moved into the Ohio Country in the eighteenth century and later established themselves at Sandusky. In the early nineteenth century, they were joined by some Senecas and Cayugas from Buffalo Creek. A treaty established a reservation for the group in northwestern Ohio, but after passage of the Indian Removal Bill of 1830, in 1831–32 these Senecas and their kinspeople were removed west of the Mississippi River to Indian Territory. See William C. Sturtevant, "Oklahoma Seneca-Cayuga," in ibid., 537–43.

14. The classic work on religious revivalism in nineteenth-century western New York is Whitney R. Cross, *The Burned-Over District: A Social and Intellectual History of Enthusiastic Religion in Western New York, 1800–1850* (Ithaca, N.Y.: Cornell University Press, 1950). Eric Hobsbawm and Terence Ranger, eds., *The Invention of Tradition* (Cambridge: Cambridge University Press, 1983), esp. 1–14, comment on the process through which communities, through ritual or symbolic practices, seek to inculcate certain values and norms by repetition so as to cultivate a sense of continuity with the past, particularly during moments of considerable stress. Senecas invented their Old Way of Handsome Lake and transformed it into "tradition" during the first half of the nineteenth century. Not surprisingly, however, the prophet and his code—like other new religious figures and their creeds—have never fully escaped "history."

15. Paul Boyer and Stephen Nissenbaum, *Salem Possessed: The Social Origins of Witchcraft* (Cambridge, Mass.: Harvard University Press, 1974).

16. Banner, *How the Indians Lost Their Land*, 182–83.

17. William Makepeace Thackeray, *Vanity Fair: A Novel Without a Hero* (originally London, 1848), Modern Library edition (New York: Modern Library, 2001), 3, 252–53.

CHAPTER 1. COLONIAL CRUCIBLE AND POST-REVOLUTIONARY PREDICAMENT

1. "Murder," *Niagara Journal*, May 8, 1821. The "murder" was also reported in the *Spirit of the Times*, May 11, 1821, and the *Ontario Repository*, May 15, 1821.

2. In the colonial period, prosecution of "murders" could create diplomatic crises, though rarely, and typically only if they involved the killing of whites by Indians. See, for example, James H. Merrell, *Into the Woods: Negotiators on the Pennsylvania Frontier* (New York: W. W. Norton, 1999), 42–53, which explores the complicated diplomacy forced by the killing of a fur trader, John Armstrong, by the Delaware man Mushumeelin in February 1744 in a dispute over debts and a horse. Merrell notes, "Ordinarily, their deaths [those of Armstrong and his two servants] would have attracted little attention" (45). The

context of impending war between Britain and France and the necessity of placating Native allies changed things. Even in this extraordinary context, when they attempted to extend white justice to Indian suspects, white authorities could not act autonomously. Prosecution had to be negotiated, to avoid an "international incident." As a Conestoga man aptly named Civility had remarked earlier in the context of an effort to ban sales of rum among the Indians in the 1720s, his "Concern . . . was not so much for fear of any Accident among the Indians themselves, for if one Indian should kill another they have many ways of making up such an Affair." Instead, he was apprehensive "lest a Christian should be ill used by any Indian intoxicated" (167). In short, white prosecution of alleged Indian crimes was not a matter of routine justice until white power allowed authorities to assert jurisdiction. Earlier such prosecutorial efforts were fraught, or they were nonexistent, as Native people settled their own criminal affairs, without white interference. Similarly, Stuart Banner, *How the Indians Lost Their Land: Law and Power on the Frontier* (Cambridge, Mass.: Harvard University Press, 2005), argues that Indian-white property disputes during the colonial era were typically resolved by colonial governors and legislatures, not by courts: "colonial officials tended to conceive of the complaints as raising questions of diplomacy rather than law" (70). See Alan Taylor, *The Divided Ground: Indians, Settlers, and the American Revolution* (New York: Knopf, 2006), esp. 317–22, on New York State's efforts to demote Indian sovereignty (in ways that also challenged federal power) by imposing the common law of murder in Indian cases—first in those involving cross-cultural murder, then in homicides among Indians.

3. "Murder," *Niagara Journal*, May 8, 1821, reprinted widely, as in the *New-York Evening Post*, May 15, 1821. On these events and their larger context, see Matthew Dennis, "Sorcery and Sovereignty: Senecas, Citizens, and the Contest for Power and Authority on the Frontiers of the Early American Republic," in John Smolenski and Thomas J. Humphrey, eds., *New World Orders: Violence, Sanction, and Authority in the Colonial Americas* (Philadelphia: University of Pennsylvania Press, 2005), 179–99.

4. "Murder," *Niagara Journal*, May 8, 1821.

5. New York State's court system is complicated. During the early nineteenth century, courts of oyer and terminer (meaning to "hear and determine") met in each county at least once a year and had jurisdiction over crimes punishable by life imprisonment or death. Justices of the Supreme Court of Judicature, traveling on circuits individually, presided at these courts. In addition, the justices sat together in two terms each year hearing arguments and ruling on points of law raised during pleading in the Supreme Court or during circuit court trial proceedings. The Supreme Court also reviewed numerous cases appealed from the county-level civil and criminal courts by writs of error, and from courts of justices of the peace by writs of certiorari. The Constitution of 1822 changed some of these arrangements, including the organization of the Supreme Court; it reduced the number of justices from five to three and divided the state into eight judicial circuits, each presided over by an appointive circuit judge. These circuit judges presided over civil trials in the circuit courts and criminal trials in the courts of oyer and terminer. The Supreme Court was not the court of last resort. Above it at the time of Tommy

Jemmy's trial was the Court of Errors (made up of the state senators, the lieutenant governor as senate president, the chancellor, and the justices of the Supreme Court). It reviewed cases brought up by writ of error from the Supreme Court and by appeal from the Court of Chancery, and it was also empowered to try government officials who had been impeached by the assembly. See *"Duely and Constantly Kept": A History of the New York Supreme Court, 1691–1847* (Albany: New York State Court of Appeals and the New York State Archives, 1991), esp. 9–10.

6. See ibid.; William L. Stone, *The Life and Times of Red-Jacket, or Sa-Go-Ye-Wat-Ha; Being the Sequel to the History of the Six Nations* (New York: Wiley and Putnam, 1841), 321–22. See also Robert W. Bingham, *The Cradle of the Queen City: A History of Buffalo to the Incorporation of the City* (Buffalo, N.Y.: Buffalo Historical Society, 1931), 388; Christopher Densmore, *Red Jacket: Iroquois Diplomat and Orator* (Syracuse, N.Y.: Syracuse University Press, 1999), 96–97 (Densmore erroneously records the equally prominent John C. Spencer, not Oakley, as Tommy Jemmy's attorney; Spencer was opposing counsel); *Albany Argus*, August 17, 1821. On the ramifications of the case for Indian law, see Sidney L. Harring, *Crow Dog's Case: American Indian Sovereignty, Tribal Law, and United States Law in the Nineteenth Century* (Cambridge: Cambridge University Press, 1994), esp. 37–38. Banner, *How the Indians Lost Their Land*, offers a definitive discussion of the transformation in the legal understanding of Indian sovereignty, particularly as it pertained to land ownership.

7. Banner, *How the Indians Lost Their Land*, 123, 203, 214–15.

8. Governor De Witt Clinton had previously indicated his wish that the Senecas be treated like other New York Indians—that is, with diminished sovereignty, subject to the state's jurisdiction. See, for example, message from Clinton to the assembly, February 4, 1821, Legislative Assembly Correspondence and Legislative Action Files, 1794–1827, Assembly Papers, vols. 32–34, microfilm series A1818, reel 2, New York State Archives (NYSA), Albany, N.Y. The bill, "An Act declaring the jurisdiction of the Courts of this State and pardoning Soo non gize otherwise called Tommy Jemmy," was passed by the assembly and endorsed without comment by the New York Council of Revisions, a body made up of Governor Clinton, Chancellor Kent, and Supreme Court Justice Yates, empowered to rule on the constitutionality of state legislation, on April 12, 1822. See *Laws of the State of New-York, Passed at the Forty-fifth Session of the Legislature* (Albany: Cantine and Leake, 1822), 202, and the Minutes of the Council of Revisions, 1778–1824, vol. 5, 299–300, microfilm A0027, NYSA. A copy and transcription of the New York State legislation is among the Philadelphia Yearly Meeting Indian Committee Records, Quaker Collection, Special Collections, Haverford College, Haverford, Pennsylvania (hereafter cited as I.C. Records), box 3, dated April 12, 1822.

9. Banner, *How the Indians Lost Their Land*, 219–21; in *Cherokee Nation v. Georgia*, Justices Smith Thompson and Joseph Story dissented, arguing that Cherokees *were* a foreign state, and thus the court should have jurisdiction in the case (220). And see Harring, *Crow Dog's Case*, 26–34. The principle that American Indians were subject to their own laws would be more definitively established in *Ex parte Crow Dog* (1883). The chal-

lenge to New York came in a felony assault case on the Tuscarora reservation, *Cusick v. Daly* (1914), in which a state court of appeals held that *Crow Dog* preempted New York State in the area of criminal jurisdiction over Indian reservations (38). Tribes' independence from state authority and jurisdiction would erode over time, culminating in 1952 in Public Law 280, which extended state criminal jurisdiction over reservations in certain states. For a good overview of the tangled jurisdictional history enmeshing the Senecas, New York State, and the United States, see Laurence Hauptman, *Historical Background to the Present Day Seneca Nation-Salamanca Lease Controversy: The First Hundred Years, 1851–1951* (Albany: Nelson A. Rockefeller Institute of Government, State University of New York, 1985). The ambiguity surrounding the relationship between tribes, states, and the federal government dates to the Articles of Confederation (ratified 1781), which stated in Article IX, "The United States in Congress assembled shall have the sole and exclusive right and power of . . . regulating the trade and managing all affairs with the Indians, not members of any States, provided that the legislative right of any State within its own limits be not infringed or violated." But were Senecas "members" of New York, and what constituted infringement of legislative rights by the federal government within the limits of New York? Jack Rakove, "American Federalism Before the Constitution," in Jack P. Greene, ed., *The American Revolution: Its Character and Limits* (New York: New York University Press, 1987), 88–103, calls Article IX "ambiguous" and "baffling."

    10. Barclay to Cadwallader Colden, in *The Letters and Papers of Cadwallader Colden*, vol. 8, *Additional Letters and Papers, 1715–1748,* Collections of the New-York Historical Society, vol. 67 (New York, 1937), 279. In fact, *ongwehoenwe* is better translated as "the people" or "original people," a self-designation similar to those of other Native people of North America. Nonetheless, Barclay and others did not err in attributing to the peoples of the Iroquois a pride and self-confidence that outsiders could find disconcerting.

    11. Matthew Dennis, *Cultivating a Landscape of Peace: Iroquois-European Encounters in Seventeenth-Century America* (Ithaca, N.Y.: Cornell University Press, 1993); Daniel K. Richter, *The Ordeal of the Longhouse: The Peoples of the Iroquois League in the Era of European Colonization* (Chapel Hill: University of North Carolina Press, 1992); and Francis Jennings, *The Ambiguous Iroquois Empire: The Covenant Chain Confederation of Indian Tribes with English Colonies from Its Beginning to the Lancaster Treaty of 1744* (New York: W. W. Norton, 1984); the latter two works are especially insightful about the eighteenth-century Iroquois experience. See also Dean R. Snow, *The Iroquois* (Oxford: Blackwell, 1994). The origin of the Five Nations Confederacy is a matter of some controversy, but the Iroquois League—including the Mohawks, Oneidas, Onondagas, Cayugas, and Senecas—was certainly functioning by the early seventeenth century, when European colonization began in earnest in the region of the Iroquois homeland. A century of colonialism proved unsettling to numerous Native peoples throughout the Northeast and Southeast and produced various new social amalgamations and political alliances. Among those suffering dislocation were the Tuscaroras of North Carolina. Defeated in the Tuscarora War between 1711 and 1713, they migrated north and found refuge among the Five Nations. In 1722 or 1723 the Tuscaroras were formally adopted into the Iroquois League, and the Confederation became known as the Six Nations of the Iroquois.

12. My point is not that Iroquois women and men understood or experienced the intrusion of European colonists literally as witchcraft, though some of the persons and material culture they encountered in the process did seem to some Iroquois to be implicated in witchcraft. See, for example, the charges made against the Jesuit missionary Isaac Jogues, executed by Mohawks in 1646 as a witch; a Jesuit chronicler wrote, "sickness having fallen upon their bodies, . . . and worms having perhaps damaged their corn, . . . these poor blind creatures have believed that the Father had left a Demon among them, and that all our discourses and all our instructions aimed only to exterminate them" (Reuben Gold Thwaites, trans. and ed., *The Jesuit Relations and Allied Documents*, 73 vols. [Cleveland: Burrow Brothers, 1896–1901], 30:229, 31:73–75). On the "ethically neutral" quality of sacred power, which could come from a variety of provenances, see Karim Michel Tiro, "The People of the Standing Stone: The Oneida Indian Nation from Revolution through Removal, 1765–1840" (Ph.D. diss., University of Pennsylvania, 1999), 91.

13. For a general overview of the impact of colonists, their ideas, and their material culture, see Colin G. Calloway, *New World for All: Indians, Europeans, and the Remaking of Early America* (Baltimore: Johns Hopkins University Press, 1997); James Axtell, *The Invasion Within: The Contest of Cultures in Colonial North America* (New York: Oxford University Press, 1985); Daniel K. Richter, *Facing East from Indian Country: A Native History of Early America* (Cambridge, Mass.: Harvard University Press, 2001). On alcohol, see Peter C. Mancall, *Deadly Medicine: Indians and Alcohol in Early America* (Ithaca, N.Y.: Cornell University Press, 1995).

14. Contact between the people of the Five Nations of the Iroquois and Europeans commenced, at least indirectly, through the European materials that filtered into Iroquoia, as early as the second quarter of the sixteenth century. As archaeologist James W. Bradley, *Evolution of the Onondaga Iroquois: Accommodating Change, 1500–1655* (Syracuse, N.Y.: Syracuse University Press, 1987), suggests, European products were converted into traditional forms, and, initially at least, continuity rather than change characterized life among the Onondaga Iroquois he studied (see esp. 80). The advent of European people, their material culture and technologies, would precipitate greater changes in the future, but the larger pattern of assimilating foreign objects, ideas, and people on Iroquois terms would continue as long as Iroquois people retained a modicum of autonomy and power. On the impact of warfare, pestilence, and proselytizing among the Iroquois, see Dennis, *Cultivating a Landscape of Peace*, especially "Epilogue: Iroquois Reconstruction," 257–71; Richter, *Ordeal of the Longhouse*; Axtell, *Invasion Within*.

15. See especially William Starna, "Mohawk Iroquois Population: A Revision," *Ethnohistory* 27 (1980): 371–82; Dean R. Snow and Kim M. Lanphear, "European Contact and Indian Depopulation in the Northeast: The Timing of the First Epidemics," *Ethnohistory* 35 (1988): 15–33; Snow, *The Iroquois*, 94–100, 109–11.

16. Thwaites, *Jesuit Relations*, 31:73–75, 121–23; and see Dennis, *Cultivating a Landscape of Peace*, 92, 262–63; Richter, *Ordeal of the Longhouse*, 188, 232, 266.

17. The classic account is Jennings, *Ambiguous Iroquois Empire*; and see Daniel K. Richter and James H. Merrell, eds., *Beyond the Covenant Chain: The Iroquois and Their*

Neighbors in Indian North America, 1600–1800 (Syracuse, N.Y.: Syracuse University Press, 1987); Richter, *Ordeal of the Longhouse,* 206–54; Dennis, *Cultivating a Landscape of Peace,* 268–71; Richard Aquila, *The Iroquois Restoration: Iroquois Diplomacy on the Colonial Frontier, 1701–1754* (Detroit: Wayne State University Press, 1983), 85–128; Timothy J. Shannon, *Indians and Colonists at the Crossroads of Empire: The Albany Congress of 1754* (Ithaca, N.Y.: Cornell University Press, 2000), 19–24; Anthony F. C. Wallace, "The Origins of Iroquois Neutrality: The Grand Settlement of 1701," *Pennsylvania History* 24 (1957): 223–35; Richard Haan, "The Problem of Iroquois Neutrality: Suggestions for Revision," *Ethnohistory* 27 (1980): 317–30; J. A. Brandão and William A. Starna, "The Treaties of 1701: A Triumph of Iroquois Diplomacy," *Ethnohistory* 43.2 (Spring 1996): 209–44.

18. Wallace, *Death and Rebirth of the Seneca,* 111–14; Jane T. Merritt, *At the Crossroads: Indians and Empires on a Mid-Atlantic Frontier, 1700–1763* (Chapel Hill, N.C.: University of North Carolina Press, 2003), 303–4. Francis Jennings, *Empire of Fortune: Crowns, Colonies, and Tribes in the Seven Years War in America* (New York: W. W. Norton, 1988), 426–73, assesses the aftermath of the war.

19. Thwaites, *Jesuit Relations,* 43:291. The Jesuits were a driving force in the colonization of New France, unlike the clerics of New Netherland, where commerce was king. New Netherland's mercantile goals were best served by toleration—Dutch colonists sought to get along to get ahead. This served the interests of the Iroquois, who remained culturally confident *and* interested in acquiring items of European manufacture.

20. See Daniel K. Richter, "Iroquois Versus Iroquois: Jesuit Missions and Christianity in Village Politics, 1642–1686," *Ethnohistory* 32 (1985): 1–16. On Caughnawaga/Kahnawake, see William N. Fenton and Elisabeth Tooker, "Mohawk," in William C. Sturtevant, gen. ed., *Handbook of North American Indians,* 20 vols. projected (Washington, D.C.: Smithsonian Institution, 1978–) (hereafter *HBNAI*), vol. 15, *Northeast* (1978), ed. Bruce G. Trigger, 469–71.

21. Hugh Hastings, ed., *Ecclesiastical Records of the State of New York,* 7 vols. (Albany, 1901–16), 2:1018; Richter, *Ordeal of the Longhouse,* 222–23; Tiro, "People of the Standing Stone," 91–98, 101; James P. Ronda, "Reverend Samuel Kirkland and the Oneida Indians," in Jack Campisi and Laurence M. Hauptman, eds., *The Oneida Indian Experience: Two Perspectives* (Syracuse, N.Y.: Syracuse University Press, 1988), 23–30. On the Mohawk diaspora, see James W. Paxton, "Kinship, Communities, and Covenant Chains: Mohawks and Palatines in New York and Upper Canada, 1712–1830" (Ph.D. diss., Queen's University, Ontario, Canada, 2006).

22. For a magisterial account of these broad developments, see Richard White, *The Middle Ground: Indians, Empires, and Republics in the Great Lakes Region, 1650–1815* (Cambridge: Cambridge University Press, 1991). Fred Anderson, *Crucible of War: The Seven Years' War and the Fate of Empire in British North America, 1754–1766* (New York: Knopf, 2000), is the classic treatment of the subject.

23. "Proceedings of a General Congress of the Six Nations, etc.," March 4–8, 1768, in Samuel Eliot Morison, ed., *Sources and Documents Illustrating the American Revolution, 1764–1788,* 2d ed. (London: Oxford University Press, 1929), 60–61.

24. Colin G. Calloway, *The American Revolution in Indian Country: Crisis and Diversity in Native American Communities* (Cambridge: Cambridge University Press, 1995). The standard account of the Six Nations' participation in the Revolution is Barbara Graymont, *The Iroquois in the American Revolution* (Syracuse, N.Y.: Syracuse University Press, 1972). Karim Tiro offers important revisions to both Calloway's and Graymont's accounts; see Tiro, "A 'Civil' War? Rethinking Iroquois Participation in the American Revolution," *Explorations in Early American Culture* 4 (2000): 148–65. Indians quickly acquired a role in an emerging national myth of the United States as savages against which Americans might construct their own identity. Note, for example, the depiction of Indians in later celebrations of George Rogers Clark's July Fourth capture of Kaskaskia in 1778. Clark was enshrined as an Illinois state hero. See Jessie Palmer Weber, comp., *The Centennial of the State of Illinois: Report of the Centennial Commission* (Springfield: Illinois State Journal Co., 1920), 14, 29, 223–40. At the official July Fourth celebration for Illinois' centennial year (1918), Wallace Rice's poem "The Freeing of Illinois" lumped evil British and savage Indians together against the forces for freedom. "On Independence Night," the bold Clark and his men approach Kaskaskia, take the post, drag down the British flag and hoist the Stars and Stripes. "Forever freed by Clark's bold deed from tyrants overblown / These lovely lands of Illinois become Virginia's own" (234). Indians are represented as tyrants and usurpers of land possessed legitimately by white settlers; celebrating Illinois pioneers as exemplars of American nationalism on Independence Day thus denigrates Indians as the villains in the United States' political creation story. The U.S. Constitution would grant Native Americans a conditional sovereignty and recognize certain rights, though it proved difficult to claim and protect them; see especially Banner, *How the Indians Lost their Land*, and Charles F. Wilkinson, "Indian Tribes and the American Constitution," in Frederick E. Hoxie and Peter Iverson, eds., *Indians in American History: An Introduction*, 2d ed. (Wheeling, Ill.: Harlan Davidson, 1998), 105–20.

25. Edward Countryman, "From Revolution to Statehood (1776–1825)," in Milton M. Klein, ed., *The Empire State: A History of New York* (Ithaca, N.Y.: Cornell University Press, 2001), offers an excellent, brief analysis of this history; see esp. 230, 234. See also Countryman, *A People in Revolution: The American Revolution and Political Society in New York, 1760–1799* (Baltimore: Johns Hopkins University Press, 1981); and Taylor, *The Divided Ground*.

26. Countryman, "From Revolution to Statehood," 242–45; Graham Hodges's entry, "New York in the American Revolution," in Richard L. Blanco, ed., *The American Revolution, 1775–1783: An Encyclopedia*, 2 vols. (New York: Garland, 1993), esp. 1236–37; Peter C. Mancall, *Valley of Opportunity: Economic Culture along the Upper Susquehanna, 1700–1800* (Ithaca, N.Y.: Cornell University Press, 1991), 149–55. On Sullivan's expedition, see Joseph R. Fischer, *A Well-Executed Failure: The Sullivan Campaign against the Iroquois, July-September 1779* (Columbia: University of South Carolina Press, 1997), but see also Tiro, "Rethinking Iroquois Participation," 157–61.

27. Mancall, *Valley of Opportunity*, 155–59, quotation at 156; Countryman, "From Revolution to Statehood," 258–59.

28. Quoted in Graymont, *Iroquois in the American Revolution*, 99.

29. Quoted in Calloway, *Revolution in Indian Country*, 29–30.

30. Graymont, *Iroquois in the American Revolution*, 113.

31. Tiro, "Rethinking Iroquois Participation," 149–51; Kirkland quoted in Calloway, *Revolution in Indian Country*, 33; and see Graymont, *Iroquois in the American Revolution*, 113, which sees the extinguishing of the council fire in more catastrophic terms.

32. James E. Seaver, ed., *A Narrative of the Life of Mrs. Mary Jemison* (1824; new ed., Syracuse, N.Y.: Syracuse University Press, 1990), 53–55 (all subsequent references are to this edition unless otherwise indicated); Tiro, "Rethinking Iroquois Participation," 151–52; Thomas S. Abler, ed., *Chainbreaker: The Revolutionary War Memoir of Governor Black-snake* (Lincoln: University of Nebraska Press, 1989), 87–88; Abler, *Cornplanter: Chief Warrior of the Allegany Senecas* (Syracuse, N.Y.: Syracuse University Press, 2007), 42–45. See also Calloway, *Revolution in Indian Country*, 24, 33–34; Graymont, *Iroquois in the American Revolution*, esp. 104–28 on the end of neutrality and fractures within the league, and 129–56 on the disaster surrounding the 1777 campaign.

33. Abler, *Chainbreaker*, 130, and *Cornplanter*, 42–45; Tiro, "Rethinking Iroquois Participation," 153. Tiro convincingly argues that Iroquois on each side acted purposefully to minimize the impact of the war on their Iroquois opponents through surreptitious diplomacy and avoidance of battles in which they would face Indian, as opposed to white, opponents. In short, the Iroquois sought to make this "civil war" among the Six Nations as "civil" as possible.

34. Calloway, *Revolution in Indian Country*, 51–52; George Washington, *Writings*, ed. John Rhodehamel (New York: Library of America, 1997), 350–51.

35. Seaver, *Narrative of the Life of Mrs. Mary Jemison*, 54, 57–58, 60.

36. Washington, *Writings*, 365.

37. Fischer, *A Well-Executed Failure*, 192–94; Abler and Tooker, "Seneca," 507–8; Graymont, *Iroquois in the American Revolution*, 213; Wallace, *Death and Rebirth of the Seneca*, 141–48. On the origins of the name "Town Destroyer," I follow Wallace and others, rather than William N. Fenton (*The Great Law and the Longhouse: A Political History of the Iroquois Confederacy* [Norman: University of Oklahoma Press, 1998], 117n.), who argues that the designation dates from the Seven Years' War, not from the Revolution.

38. See Wallace, *Death and Rebirth of the Seneca*, 144, 168, 194–96. Some of these villages, especially in the Ohio Country, would have identified themselves as "Iroquois" more reluctantly than Six Nations leaders or imperial officials would have liked. On the contention between the Six Nations and their "client" communities, and the declining influence of the former over the latter, see especially Michael N. McConnell, *A Country Between: The Upper Ohio Valley and Its Peoples, 1724–1774* (Lincoln: University of Nebraska Press, 1992). Kayangaraghta quoted in Fischer, *A Well-Executed Failure*, 192.

39. Snow and Lanphear, "European Contact and Indian Depopulation," 15–33, is a good, brief treatment of the initial demographic disaster that European colonization initiated in North America. Some natural increase in nonplague years and incorporation of

outsiders, especially Native refugees dispersed by warfare (in some cases by the Iroquois themselves), allowed Six Nations' population to recover, though not to aboriginal levels. See also Richter, *Ordeal of the Longhouse*, 58–59, 65–66, 114, 173, 188, 256, 331 n. 19, 355–56 n. 60. Elisabeth Tooker, "The League of the Iroquois," in *HBNAI*, 15:421, contains a table, "Iroquois Population Estimates by Fighting Men, 1660–1779." Note also that migration of loyalist Iroquois to Canada accounts for some of the population loss among Iroquois in the new republic.

40. For a summary analysis of Seneca history and geography, see Abler and Tooker, "Seneca," 505–17; see 507–13 for assessment of the post-Revolutionary period through the mid-nineteenth century and for maps of the Seneca reservations. See also Elisabeth Tooker, "Iroquois Since 1820," in *HBNAI*, 15:449–65. For a contemporary description of the Allegany and other Seneca communities, see *The Journal of Major John Norton, 1816*, ed. Carl F. Klinck and James J. Talman (Toronto: Champlain Society, 1970), 7–11.

41. Abler and Tooker, "Seneca," 509. Every metaphor has its limitations—the Seneca "purgatory" was not a realm for the dead, as in Christian theology, but of living if desperate Seneca people. Referring more broadly to suffering short of everlasting damnation, the term *purgatory* can suggest any place or condition of suffering or torment, especially one that is temporary. In his fourteenth-century work *The Divine Comedy* (1308–21), in its second *cantica*—*Purgatorio*—Dante gave purgatory a physical location on earth. Sinners who labored to free themselves of their sins resided there temporarily, rather than in Hell, hoping, striving for ultimate deliverance—salvation. Senecas had not died, nor had they "sinned" in this sense, but they had experienced a hellish war and found themselves in a torturous state from which they hoped to escape—not through death but through transcendence. In the 1780s and 1790s, like the denizens of Dante's *Purgatorio*, their fate seemed uncertain.

42. Mary Jemison conveyed her story to James Seaver in 1823, who edited it and first published it in 1824. Citations here come from the Syracuse University Press, 1990, edition cited above.

43. The tawdry adventures of Ebenezer Allen are described in Seaver, *Narrative of the Life of Mrs. Mary Jemison*, 64–76; Daniel J. Brock, "Allan (Allen, Allin), Ebenezer," in *Dictionary of Canadian Biography* (hereafter *DCB*), 5 vols. (Toronto: University of Toronto Press, 1966–), 5:13–15. See also the entry for Ebenezer Allan in Frank H. Severance, "The Tale of Captives at Fort Niagara," *Publications of the Buffalo Historical Society*, ed. Frank H. Severance (hereafter *PBHS*), 9 (1906): 237. The sketch characterized Allen as a "murderer" and "Bluebeard of the backwoods."

44. Seaver, *Narrative of the Life of Mrs. Mary Jemison*, 66–71; quotation at 70–71. Brock argues that Allen's resentment at his dismissal by the British Indian Department at the end of the war led to his independent activity in the peace negotiations between the American government and the Six Nations, which in turn led to his arrest and imprisonment for ten months. Allen complained about his "most cruel and inhuman" treatment "imprisoned in a Detestable prison like A common Criminal" (*DCB*, 5:14).

45. Seaver, *Narrative of the Life of Mrs. Mary Jemison*, 71–72.

46. Ibid., 71–73. Jemison does say that Sally, Allen's "squaw," was a "slave" to his other wife, Lucy.

47. Ibid., 73–74.

48. Ibid., 74.

49. Stephen Mihm, "The Alchemy of Self: Stephen Burroughs and the Counterfeit Economy of the Early Republic," *Early American Studies* 2.1 (Spring 2004): 123–59, quotation at 124.

50. Seaver, *Narrative of the Life of Mrs. Mary Jemison*, 74–75; according to Jemison, Allen's foul life ended in 1814 or 1815, in a Delaware Indian town in Upper Canada. He left two white widows and numerous children "to lament his loss." See also George H. Harris, "The Life of Horatio Jones," *PBHS* 6 (1903): 493–94; the Senecas' final, unsuccessful appeal of Mary and Chloe's dispossession, made to the U.S. secretary of war, John C. Calhoun, came in 1823. Allen became embroiled in controversies in Upper Canada, in conflicts related to liquor vending, dubious land sales, and failure to pay debts. These problems might have made him an American sympathizer during the War of 1812—but were another manifestation of his faithlessness. Allen was imprisoned by the British and died soon after his release. According to Brock, he continued his polygamous ways in Upper Canada. Though one of his British commanders spoke favorably about him, one American historian called him a "'Tory bloodhound; with a character which combines the lasciviousness of a Turk with the blood-thirstiness of a savage." Brock concludes, "Allan was neither a saint nor a villain, but simply a product of the frontier" (*DCB*, 5:15)—a telling comment on the nature of the Seneca new world on the borderlands of the early American republic.

51. The name of Jemison's Genesee lands, Gardeau or Gardow (in Seneca, *Ga-da-oh* or *Kau-tau*), meant "down and up," or valley and hillside.

52. Seaver, *Narrative of the Life of Mrs. Mary Jemison*, 107–11. The trusted white neighbor was Thomas Clute, brother of Jellis Clute, a key associate in the Ogden Land Company, a private firm holding the "preemption" rights to Seneca land and dedicated to obtaining it, through questionable means if necessary. On the Ogden Land Company, see especially Mary H. Conable, "A Steady Enemy: The Ogden Land Company and the Seneca Indians" (Ph.D. diss., University of Rochester, 1994).

53. Seaver, *Narrative of the Life of Mrs. Mary Jemison*, 119–24; Thomas Clute, Jellis Clute, and their partner Micah Brooks, acting on behalf of the Ogden Land Company, sought and obtained leases to Jemison's land and pushed her to legalize her conveyance, which required the approval of the United States government and the Seneca nation. A meeting between Seneca chiefs, representatives of the United States, and other interested parties accomplished this task at a council in September of 1823, and Jemison signed over all but a small portion of her reservation for an annuity of three hundred dollars a year. These developments, including the sale of all remaining Gardeau land not previously sold by Jemison, are examined in Conable, "A Steady Enemy," 83–84; and Laurence M. Hauptman, *Conspiracy of Interests: Iroquois Dispossession and the Rise of New York State* (Syracuse, N.Y.: Syracuse University Press, 1999), 149–52. And see Harris, "Life of Horatio

Jones," 503. The federally sanctioned sale of Gardeau (Jemison's reserve) in 1826 (though never ratified by the U.S. Senate) conveyed thousands of acres for $4,286, representing about thirty cents per acre.

54. Seaver, *Narrative of the Life of Mrs. Mary Jemison*, 81–87, quotation at 85.

55. Ibid., quotations at 87. Jesse was intimate with whites and had adopted many of their customs, which may have antagonized his brothers; the brothers might also have been jealous of the special regard Mary had for Jesse as her youngest son (see 104–7). On John's violent end, see 112–13.

356. Ibid., 83. Thomas's assessment might have been affected by his brother's confounding of conventional Iroquois matrilocal residence patterns (in which a husband lived with his wife's family), though, as some scholars have recently observed, domestic arrangements were fluid among the Iroquois and perhaps poorly described by the culturally specific, fraught term *marriage*. On the problems of "marriage" as a cross-cultural, transhistoric concept, see Ann Marie Plane, *Colonial Intimacies: Indian Marriage in Early New England* (Ithaca, N.Y.: Cornell University Press, 2000).

57. Seaver, *Narrative of the Life of Mrs. Mary Jemison*, 82. Although witchcraft was increasingly associated with women among the Senecas, it remained available as a charge against men as well as women, as it had among white misogynist witch-hunters in an earlier era.

CHAPTER 2. HANDSOME LAKE AND THE SENECA GREAT AWAKENING

1. Whitney R. Cross, *The Burned-Over District: The Social and Intellectual History of Enthusiastic Religion in Western New York, 1800–1850* (Ithaca, N.Y.: Cornell University Press, 1950), 9.

2. The Second Great Awakening was a diverse movement, with variations by denomination, theology, liturgy, region, and social context. Considering Seneca revitalization in terms of the awakening does not therefore unduly attenuate its definition. The awakening lacks a single, comprehensive history, but see especially William G. McLoughlin, *Revivals, Awakenings, and Reform: An Essay on Religion and Social Change in America, 1607–1977* (Chicago: University of Chicago Press, 1978), 98–140; Nathan O. Hatch, *The Democratization of American Christianity* (New Haven, Conn.: Yale University Press, 1989); Jon Butler, *Awash in a Sea of Faith: Christianizing the American People* (Cambridge, Mass.: Harvard University Press, 1990); Mark A. Noll, *A History of Christianity in the United States and Canada* (Grand Rapids, Mich.: W. B. Eerdmans, 1992), 165–244; Noll, *America's God: From Jonathan Edwards to Abraham Lincoln* (New York: Oxford University Press, 2002), 159–421. The best local study of the awakening in New York remains Cross's *Burned-Over District*; but see also Michael Barkun, *Crucible of the Millennium: The Burned-Over District of New York in the 1840s* (Syracuse, N.Y.: Syracuse University Press, 1986); David L. Rowe, *Thunder and Trumpets: Millerites and Dissenting Religion in Upstate New York, 1800–1850* (Chico, Calif.: Scholar's Press, 1985).

3. Cross, *Burned-Over District*, 3.

4. The encroachment of Christian settlers, of course, also helped produce the economic and social crisis that Handsome Lake's revival was designed, in part, to address.

5. See especially Karim Michel Tiro, "The People of the Standing Stone: The Oneida Indian Nation from Revolution through Removal, 1765–1840" (Ph.D. diss., University of Pennsylvania, 1999), esp. 147–50, 155–80, 190–99 on the Oneidas' religious revivalism and syncretism and on Kirkland's career among the Oneidas. As Tiro demonstrates, the Oneidas' traditionalism was equally syncretic—innovative, not static.

6. See particularly Frank H. Severance, ed., "Narratives of Early Mission Work on the Niagara Frontier and Buffalo Creek," *Publications of the Buffalo Historical Society*, ed. Frank H. Severance (hereafter *PBHS*), 6 (1903): 163–380. Robert F. Berkhofer Jr., *Salvation and the Savage: An Analysis of Protestant Missions and American Indian Response, 1787–1862* (1965; New York: Athenaeum, 1976), is a good general treatment. See also "Summary Report of Mr. Cram's Late Mission," and "Extracts from Rev. Mr. Cram's Journal," *Massachusetts Missionary Magazine* 3.10–12 (March–May 1806): 383–95, 433–37, 470–74; quotation at 384. This chronicle well illustrates the extent and variety of, and the competition between, Christian missionaries proselytizing among the Senecas and other Iroquois.

7. Cross, *Burned-Over District*, 8–13.

8. Ibid., 40–51, esp. 40–42, 47 (quotation at 41).

9. Ibid., 40–51; Butler, *Awash in a Sea of Faith*, 242.

10. See, for example, Paul E. Johnson, *A Shopkeeper's Millennium: Society and Revivals in Rochester, New York, 1815–1837* (New York: Hill and Wang, 1978); and see Johnson and Sean Wilentz, *The Kingdom of Matthias: A Story of Sex and Salvation in Nineteenth-Century America* (New York: Oxford University Press, 1994). On the Millerites and New York millennialism, see Rowe, *Thunder and Trumpets*; Barkun, *Crucible of the Millennium*. Strong currents of anticlericalism also enabled Indian critiques of Christianity.

11. Henry R. Howland, "The Seneca Mission at Buffalo Creek," *PBHS* 6 (1903): 125–33.

12. "Red Jacket to Reverend Alexander, 1811," reprinted in Christopher Densmore, *Red Jacket: Iroquois Diplomat and Orator* (Syracuse, N.Y.: Syracuse University Press, 1999), 141–42.

13. "Red Jacket's Reply to Reverend Cram, 1805," in Densmore, *Red Jacket*, 139. Cram reported about a November meeting with Red Jacket at Buffalo Creek but did not relate the particulars of the Seneca orator's speech; see "Extracts from Rev. Mr. Cram's Journal," 436, entry for November 12, 1805. See Matthew Dennis, "Red Jacket's Rhetoric: Postcolonial Persuasions on the Native Frontiers of the Early American Republic," in Ernest Stromberg, ed., *American Indian Rhetorics of Survivance: Word Medicine, Word Magic* (Pittsburgh: University of Pittsburgh Press, 2006), 15–33, which also discusses the problematic quality of Native American rhetoric mediated through non-Native sources.

14. "Red Jacket's Reply to Reverend Cram, 1805," 139–40. Red Jacket's speeches were frequently reprinted, even anthologized in the *American Speaker*, 3d ed. (Philadelphia: Abraham Small, 1816). The critical evaluations of Christianity by Red Jacket and others Native speakers could not have found their way into print without the sympathy

of white critics of particular denominations. Samuel Wood published a pamphlet, *Speeches Delivered by Several Indian Chiefs* (New York: Samuel Wood, 1810), for example, which contained an 1805 anticlerical speech of Red Jacket and a similar one by an anonymous Indian to a Swedish missionary in 1710. See also *Indian Speeches Delivered by Farmer's Brother and Red Jacket* (Canandaigua, N.Y.: James D. Bemis, 1809) and *Native Eloquence: Being Public Speeches Delivered by Two Distinguished Chiefs of the Seneca Tribe of Indians* (Canandaigua, N.Y.: James D. Bemis, 1811). Between 1822 and 1824, these speeches were reprinted by an explicitly anti-Calvinist and anti-missionary magazine, *Plain Truth*, published in Canandaigua, New York. White Americans expressing anticlerical views did not necessarily reject Christianity; they were often devout but partisan in attacking particular denominations and clergy. More generally, see Bruce Dorsey, *Reforming Men and Women: Gender in the Antebellum City* (Ithaca, N.Y.: Cornell University Press, 2002), 177–78; Gordon S. Wood, "Evangelical America and Early Mormonism," in Jon Butler and Harry S. Stout, eds., *Religion in American History: A Reader* (New York: Oxford University Press, 1998), 183.

15. Johnson, *A Shopkeeper's Millennium*, 137–39.

16. Halliday Jackson, "A Short History of My Sojourning in the Wilderness" was edited and published by Anthony F. C. Wallace as "Halliday Jackson's Journal to the Seneca Indians, 1798–1800," *Pennsylvania History* 19.2 (April 1952): 117–47, and 19.3 (July 1952): 325–49 (hereafter cited as "Jackson's Journal, 1798–1800"), quotation at 146. Jackson's language reflected his holy purpose and perhaps his sense of himself as a latter-day prophet, guided by an Inner Light. Note that Jackson became a Hicksite after the 1827 schism within the Society of Friends. Thomas D. Hamm, *The Transformation of American Quakerism: Orthodox Friends, 1800–1907* (Bloomington: Indiana University Press, 1988), 16, notes that Hicks and his followers had a heterodox position on the Bible—it remained important, but biblical revelations were considered far inferior to those still imparted to humans by the Holy Spirit. If this view undermined biblical authority, it perhaps also invited Quakers to draft new, Bible-like texts in their own times.

17. Wood, "Evangelical America," 180.

18. "Jackson's Journal, 1798–1800," quotations at 126, 133, 145.

19. Ibid., 137. Jackson uses "Columbia" here to refer to the United States. The yellow fever epidemic of 1798 was one of a series that afflicted Philadelphia and other eastern cities. Jackson later learned that 3,500 deaths had occurred in Philadelphia, "and many were Slain [by the disease] in the Villages round about, even of the Valliants of Israel were fallen not a few" (143). Jackson also quotes here Psalm 91:5–6, suggesting that the faithful might triumph over these trials: "Thou shalt not be afraid . . . . Nor for the pestilence that walketh in darkness; nor for the destruction that wasteth at noonday." Jackson perhaps imagined the Friends as angels to the Senecas, following the subsequent if unquoted passage: "For He will give His angels charge over thee, To keep thee in all thy ways" (Psalm 91:11).

20. "Jackson's Journal, 1798–1800," 134.

21. Ibid., 134–35.

22. Ibid., 135; on Wilkinson, see especially Susan Juster, " 'Neither Male nor Female': Jemima Wilkinson and the Politics of Gender in Post-Revolutionary America," in Robert Blair St. George, ed., *Possible Pasts: Becoming Colonial in Early America* (Ithaca, N.Y.: Cornell University Press, 2000), 357–79. Most likely, Jackson first learned of Wilkinson from Philadelphia newspaper reports, laced with suggestions of sexual scandals, that commented on her tour of the city in the early 1780s. They accused her of "having separated men from their wives, wives from their husbands, and made confusion wherever [she has] been" (364). I do not mean to suggest that Handsome Lake learned his behavior from Jemima Wilkinson, only that his later resurrection and role as a prophet were less unusual developments in the context of his time and place than we might expect.

23. "Jackson's Journal, 1798–1800," 145–46. In addition, the executed "witch" was denied proper funeral rites; instead, her executioners "digged a hole in the Earth and put her therein for there was no mourning over her" (145).

24. Ibid. See *The Oxford English Dictionary* (Oxford: Oxford University Press, 1971), s.v. "smite." For example, see 1 Samuel 6:19, referring to Saul's acts of smiting: "And he smote the men of Bethshemesh, because they had looked into the ark of the Lord, even he smote of the people fifty thousand and threescore and ten men: and the people lamented, because the Lord had smitten many of the people with a great slaughter."

25. "Jackson's Journal, 1798–1800," 145–46. On the persisting belief in witchcraft and supernatural practice—in divining rods, fortune-telling, magically healing—see Butler, *Awash in a Sea of Faith*, 228–33. Note that a Philadelphia mob attacked a woman for sorcery in May 1787 and later stoned her to death—that is, during the time of the Constitutional Convention (ibid., 228); Wood, "Evangelical America," 185. Handsome Lake's first vision, according to Jackson's version, revealed "there were some very bad people among us who would pison others but one of them was lately killed" ("The Visions of Connudiu or Corn-Planters Brother," in "Jackson's Journal, 1798–1800," 342).

26. "Jackson's Journal, 1798–1800," 141 and 345. Some have referred to Handsome Lake as a Seneca Lazarus, referring to the biblical figure whose story is told in the Gospel of John. The analogy is not exact. Cornplanter was not a Jesus figure to Handsome Lake's Lazarus, and the latter had been "dead" a few hours, not four days. Neither Cornplanter nor Handsome Lake proclaimed, "I am the resurrection, and the life: he that believeth in me, though he were dead, yet shall he live: And whosoever liveth and believeth in me shall never die" (John 11:25–26). But Handsome Lake's resurrection did give him and his prophecy credibility, if not divinity, among many Senecas. Quaker observers were more skeptical but not dismissive.

27. "Jackson's Journal, 1798–1800," 341–42, 344, and 146–47. Jackson was not present during Handsome Lake's first vision, though he witnesses subsequent visions. Joel Swayne was likely present; according to Jackson, he "was exercis'd at the village of Cornplanter" during these events (ibid., 145–46). Jackson's account of the first vision is based on the eyewitness account of Henry Simmons (344–49). On Handsome Lake and his new religion, as codified by his followers, see Arthur C. Parker, "The Code of Handsome Lake, the Seneca Prophet," New York State Museum Bulletin 163 (1913), reprinted as book

2 in William N. Fenton, ed., *Parker on the Iroquois* (Syracuse, N.Y.: Syracuse University Press, 1968), esp. 9–13.

28. "Jackson's Journal, 1798–1800," 344. In a later vision, angels told Handsome Lake that "because the White people have learning they . . . think they have the mind of the Great Spirit in their Books and he wishes the Indians to have these things written in a Book that they may keep them in remembrance" (ibid.). In addition to the firsthand accounts of the Quakers, the emergence of the prophet Handsome Lake is noted in P. C. T. White, ed., *Lord Selkirk's Diary, 1803–1804* (Toronto: Champlain Society, 1958), 245–46. The codified Seneca version of the prophecies and teachings appears in Parker, "Code of Handsome Lake," esp. 21–26. These events are narrated in Anthony F. C. Wallace, *The Death and Rebirth of the Seneca* (New York: Knopf, 1970), chaps. 8 and 9.

29. Parker, "Code of Handsome Lake," 27–30.

30. Ibid., 66–68, quotation at 68. Handsome Lake's quotation of Christ's lament notwithstanding, the prophet did not reject all "the ways of the white man"; instead, he condemned mindless assimilation while favoring a particular, prescribed kind of selective adaptation of white beliefs and practices to Seneca "traditional" life. On Iroquois reverence for Washington, see Lewis H. Morgan, *League of the Iroquois* (orig. pub. as *League of the Ho-de-no-sau-nee, or Iroquois*, 1851; reprint ed., with intro. by William N. Fenton [Secaucus, N.J.: Citadel Books, 1962]), 256–57, 178–79. Washington had earned the title "Destroyer" for authorizing the ruthless campaign led by General John Sullivan that destroyed much of Iroquoia in 1779, during the Revolution. Handsome Lake's prophesying, including his divine conversations and communion with the dead, might strike us today as outlandish, but in their era they were no more eccentric than Swedenborgians, Mesmerists, Mormons, spiritualists, and other enthusiast Christians who spoke with God or had "séances" with the deceased; see Butler, *Awash in a Sea of Faith*, 234–35.

31. "Visions of Connudiu," and "Henry Simmons' Version," in "Jackson's Journal, 1798–1800," 342–43 and 346–48. Wallace, *Death and Rebirth of the Seneca*, 242–48, provides a summary analysis of the second vision of Handsome Lake.

32. Parker, "Code of Handsome Lake," 71–74. The apocalyptic nature of Handsome Lake's vision, related to crisis within Seneca communities, made the *Gaiwiio* "premillennial." "Postmillennialists" believed that the world would end gloriously after its reform and perfection, after a thousand-year reign of Christ. Premillennialists, on the other hand, predicted the catastrophic destruction of the world and an immediate return (or advent) of Christ—that is, the end of the world would precede, not follow, the Second Coming. See Barkun, *Crucible of the Millennium*, 19–20, 24–25; Rowe, *Thunder and Trumpets*, ix–x; A. F. C. Wallace, "Revitalization Movements," *American Anthropologist* 58 (1956): 264–81, stresses the rationalism of some millennialist movements, like the one among the Senecas, based on their reaction to extreme collective stress.

33. Parker, "Code of Handsome Lake," 71–74. See Quaker proscriptions against gaming and idleness in George S. Snyderman, ed., "Halliday Jackson's Journal of a Visit Paid to the Indians of New York (1806)," *Proceedings of the American Philosophical Society* 101.6 (December 1957): 565–88; quotation at 577.

34. Parker, "Code of Handsome Lake," 71–74; witch punishment quotation at 71–72; Butler, *Awash in a Sea of Faith*, 236–37.

35. Parker, "Code of Handsome Lake," 72–73.

36. Ibid., 72. As Cornelia Hughes Dayton, *Women Before the Bar: Gender, Law, and Society in Connecticut, 1639–1789* (Chapel Hill: University of North Carolina Press, 1995), demonstrates in another, not too distant context, legal codes and practices can reconcile the punishment of men as well as women with patriarchy, male privilege, and the double standard; Sharon Block, *Rape and Sexual Power in Early America* (Chapel Hill: Omohundro Institute of Early American History and Culture and the University of North Carolina Press, 2006).

37. Rape was generally infrequent among Indians, including the Iroquois; see Block, *Rape and Sexual Power*, 223–30, which offers an informed discussion, with important qualifications. On Wilkinson, see Juster, "Neither Male nor Female," 360, 364, 372. Juster notes that Wilkinson was unusual, as the resurrection of masculine power in the form of a prophet became a hallmark of antebellum religious reform. More typical, if such prophesy can be called typical, were men such as Robert Matthews, or the Prophet Mathias, who offered a "potent blend of populism and patriarchy, in which he castigated women as 'the capsheaf of the abomination of desolation—full of all devilty'" (372).

38. Merle H. Deardorff and George S. Snyderman, eds., "A Nineteenth-Century Journal of a Visit to the Indians of New York" [by John Philips, 1806], *Proceedings of the American Philosophical Society* 100.6 (December 1956): 582–612, quotation at 604. The Quakers' relatively weak Trinitarianism and doctrine of the Inner Light seemed more compatible with Seneca spirituality than were the beliefs and practices of creed-based Christians.

39. Anthony F. C. Wallace offers an authoritative synthesis of the origins and nature of Handsome Lake's religion in "Origins of the Longhouse Religion," in William C. Sturtevant, gen. ed., *Handbook of North American Indians*, 20 vols. projected (Washington, D.C.: Smithsonian Institution, 1978–) (hereafter *HBNAI*), vol. 15, *Northeast* (1978), ed. Bruce G. Trigger, 442–48. The Native Seneca ethnologist Arthur C. Parker noted, early in the twentieth century, that Senecas believed in "one Great and Supreme Being, who was their creator and preserver." "To him, however," Parker wrote, "they do not attribute the creation of the world. He is merely its protector, and sustainer" (misc. MS essay fragment, "Religion" [Freeman no. 530], in the Parker Collection, American Philosophical Society, Philadelphia). Handsome Lake's Supreme Being was no less a protector and sustainer than an earlier Iroquois Great Spirit, even though they did not attribute to this god the creation of the world or the Iroquois people themselves. Needless to say, these characteristics differentiated the Seneca god from the Christian Supreme Being. Note that Handsome Lake did not claim divine status himself. On the evaluations of the prophet by Kirkland and Doctor Peter, see *The Journals of Samuel Kirkland: Eighteenth-Century Missionary to the Iroquois, Government Agent, Father of Hamilton College*, ed. Walter Pilkington (Clinton, N.Y.: Hamilton College, 1980), 412–13, entries from July 20 and August 3, 1806.

40. L. F. S. Upton, *Micmacs and Colonists: Indian-White Relations in the Maritimes,*

1713–1867 (Vancouver: University of British Columbia Press, 1979), xiv; Anne-Christine Hornborg, "St. Anne's Day: A Time to 'Turn Home' for the Canadian Mi'kmaq Indians," *International Review of Mission* 91.361 (April 2002): 237–55; Dean Snow, *The Iroquois* (Oxford: Blackwell, 1994), 158–60. On Handsome Lake's modification of the Iroquois traditional rites, see, for example, William N. Fenton, *The Iroquois Eagle Dance: An Offshoot of the Calumet Dance*, Smithsonian Institution Bureau of American Ethnology Bulletin 156 (Washington, D.C.: U.S. Government Printing Office, 1953), esp. 32–33, 78–79, 102–4, 107, 143–44; with regard to the Eagle Dance, for example, Fenton wrote, "the prophet altered its purpose from a war and peace ceremony to a medicine society" (153).

41. Carla Gerona, *Night Journeys: The Power of Dreams in Transatlantic Quaker Culture* (Charlottesville: University of Virginia Press, 2004). In referring to Handsome Lake's dreams as "visions," I am not making this distinction (at least during his first "vision" he was asleep, or in a coma-like state). See Elisabeth Tooker, *Native American Spirituality of the Eastern Woodlands* (New York: Paulist Press, 1979), 89–90.

42. Gerona, *Night Journeys*, 3, 9, 18, quoted at 3. See also Wallace, *Death and Rebirth of the Seneca*, esp. 59–75, for its seminal work on dreams and dream interpretation in Seneca, and Iroquois, culture. And see Harold Blau, "Dream Guessing: A Comparative Analysis," *Ethnohistory* 10 (1963): 233–49; Matthew Dennis, *Cultivating a Landscape of Peace: Iroquois-European Encounters in Seventeenth-Century America* (Ithaca, N.Y.: Cornell University Press, 1993), 112–13.

43. Gerona, *Night Journeys*, 207–10, 224–25; Butler, *Awash in a Sea of Faith*, 222–23, 238–39, 242–43.

44. Henry Simmons's manuscript journal quoted in Wallace, *Death and Rebirth of the Seneca*, 23. Simmons similarly endorsed the dreams of a Seneca man that seemed to recapitulate Handsome Lake's vision, including the hellish punishments for drunkards, philanderers, wife beaters, and so forth. Simmons concluded, "the dream was true" and its message was confession of sin, repentance, and reform, as it was for Handsome Lake (225). For a similar argument about the empowering nature of divine communication, in this case through the visitation of angels (sometimes during dreams), see Elizabeth Reis, "Immortal Messengers: Angels, Gender, and Power in Early America," in Nancy Isenberg and Andrew Burstein, eds., *Mortal Remains: Death in Early America* (Philadelphia: University of Pennsylvania Press, 2003), 163–75. Reis emphasizes that angel visitation proved significant in authorizing those with limited power, particularly women in the nineteenth century. Men seemed more able to use angelic conversations to found new religions. Handsome Lake—who sometimes referred to the four messengers as angels—was in a privileged position as a league chief, though he had not served with any distinction, and as a Seneca he shared in their declining position vis-à-vis an expanding white society. See also Reis, "Otherworldly Visions: Angels, Devils, and Gender in Puritan New England," in Peter Marshall and Alexandra Walsham, eds., *Angels in the Early Modern World* (Cambridge: Cambridge University Press, 2006), 282–96.

45. Tiro, "People of the Standing Stone," 181–82; Alan Taylor, *The Divided Ground: Indians, Settlers, and the Northern Borderland of the American Revolution* (New York:

Knopf, 2006), 380. See Barbara Graymont, "The Tuscarora New Year's Festival," *New York History* 50.2 (April 1969): 143–63, on the pressures felt by Christian Tuscaroras in the wake of the great revival of the traditionalist religion around the time of Handsome Lake's first vision, which included the preaching of a prophet from the Six Nations Reserve in Canada. On Hiawatha and the Peacemaker, see Dennis, *Cultivating a Landscape of Peace*, esp. 76–115.

46. Tooker, *Native American Spirituality*, 69; Wallace, "Origins of the Longhouse Religion," 445, and see more extensively Wallace, *Death and Rebirth of the Seneca*. It is possible that the social breakdown perceived by Handsome Lake (and reflected in his own prevision drunkenness) was, for other Senecas, overstated. Dysfunctional desires, like Handsome Lake's prescriptions, could be expressed in dreams, but not all dreams were created equal. The prophet's power would reside, in part, in his ability to monopolize prophesying.

47. Parker, "Code of Handsome Lake," 9–10, 20–22; the "Time of Trouble" and "The Sick Man" precede "The Strange Death of the Sick Man" and his revival (23ff.). On alcohol among Native people, see generally Peter C. Mancall, *Deadly Medicine: Indians and Alcohol in Early America* (Ithaca, N.Y.: Cornell University Press, 1995). For an example of Six Nations' efforts to ban liquor, see petition to the legislature of New York, n.d. [between March 1798 and January 1800], Colonial and Early Statehood Records, microfilm A1823, "Petitions, Correspondence, and Reports Relating to Indians, 1783–1831," 40:323–25, NYSA; on this occasion the chiefs chided the legislature for its failure to enact prohibitions against the sale of liquor—called a "tyrant"—on reservations: "We were willing to let you have our Land when you needed—We are willing to maintain the chain of friendship with you—And we desire to live in peace—and to enjoy all our privileges—But how can we come to this so long as you as it were willing to see us destroyed by this Tyrant."

48. Parker, "Code of Handsome Lake," 9, writes that Handsome Lake's success as a temperance reformer "came not from an appeal to reason but to religious instinct"; "Jackson's Journal, 1798–1800," 343; see also Simmons's account, ibid., 347–48. See also "Account of a visit made by Penrose Wiley, John Letchworth, Anne Mifflin, Mary Bell & Co. to the Seneca Indians, settled on Allegany River," October 1803, Special Collections, Cornell University, Ithaca, N.Y.; in this account, by visiting Quakers, their temperance message had resonance because it echoed Handsome Lake: "What has been said agrees with what our Prophet has told us, therefore it must be true. He has told us that we should live in peace and good-will, and that if we drank Whiskey we should never go to Heaven." The liberal dispensing of alcohol at treaty negotiations was infamous for promoting fraud. Alcohol also functioned as a trade good that promoted Native American dependency and debt, cultivated consciously by white traders and officials to necessitate Indian payment in the form of land; see Richard White, *The Roots of Dependency: Subsistence, Environment, and Social Change among the Choctaws, Pawnees, and Navajos* (Lincoln: Nebraska University Press, 1983), esp. 58–59, 83–86. Most nativist movements since the eighteenth century—from the Delaware prophet Neolin to the Shawnee prophet Tensk-

watawa—had rejected alcohol; see, for example, Daniel K. Richter, *Facing East from Indian Country: A Native History of Early America* (Cambridge, Mass.: Harvard University Press, 2001), 180, 228. On white Americans' alcoholic consumption and its implications, see W. J. Rorabaugh, *The Alcoholic Republic: An American Tradition* (New York: Oxford University Press, 1979), esp. 10; petition to the legislature of New York, n.d., microfilm A1823, 40:323–25, NYSA.

49. "Jackson's Journal, 1798–1800," 347–48 and 143 (Jackson's biblical reference is unclear, but it might refer to Galatians 5:6); Parker, "Code of Handsome Lake," 41. In the spring of 1799, before Handsome Lake's visions, the Quaker missionary-schoolteacher Henry Simmons condemned "Dancing Frolicks" as "the Devil's works" in Cornplanter's village. A council agreed to abandon such dancing, "for some of them thought it must be wicked, because they had Learned it of white people, as well as that of drinking Rum and Whisky & getting Drunk, which they knew was Evil." Still, their ceremonial dances would continue. Simmons's journal quoted in Wallace, *Death and Rebirth of the Seneca*, 231. Among the sanctioned activities were the bowl game, a sacred ritual celebrated during the midwinter ceremony, and lacrosse; see also Snow, *The Iroquois*, 160–61. The prophet's denunciation of fiddle playing targeted a musical practice new to Seneca experience, and perhaps echoed prohibitions common among some evangelical Protestants against the "devil's music." According to Parker, "Code of Handsome Lake," 73 n. 1, the Indians "detest the 'fiddle' and 'fiddle dances' as things of great evil and assert that they produce as much wickedness as drunkenness."

50. Simmons in "Jackson's Journal, 1798–1800," 349. The "old Chief" refers here to Cornplanter, who in the immediate aftermath of the Sick Man's vision was Handsome Lake's chief spokesman.

51. Cross, *Burned-Over District*, 3. Unlike many Second Great Awakening religious movements, the *Gaiwiio* was not characterized by perfectionism—a commitment to individual perfection that, collectively, would issue in the millennium.

CHAPTER 3. PATRIARCHY AND THE WITCH-HUNTING OF HANDSOME LAKE

1. "Murder," *Niagara Journal*, May 8, 1821; "Indian Justice," *Erie Gazette*, July 17, 1821. The story was followed in Salem, Massachusetts, infamous for its witch-hunting in 1692; see the *Salem Gazette*, August 3, 1821. The same story, in the *Albany Argus*, carried a different, more positive headline: "Eloquence of Red Jacket."

2. I suspect that earlier witchcraft suspicions and accusations among the Iroquois were balanced by gender, and that post-Revolutionary Seneca witch-hunting demonized women in unprecedented fashion, but the available evidence does not permit any satisfactory quantitative analysis. The predominance of women among those accused and executed at Salem, and throughout the history of early New England, conditioned white Americans to see witchcraft as a female domain, as did centuries of misogynous witch-hunting and folk beliefs in Europe. See Jacob Sprenger and Heinrich Kramer, *Malleus maleficarum* [1485–86], ed. and trans. Montague Summers (1928; repr. New York: B.

Blom, 1970), 47; Keith Thomas, *Religion and the Decline of Magic* (New York: Charles Scribner's Sons, 1971), 520. For New England and its feminized understanding of witchcraft, see Elizabeth Reis, *Damned Women: Sinners and Witches in Puritan New England* (Ithaca, N.Y.: Cornell University Press, 1997), esp. chaps. 3 and 4; Carol F. Karlsen, *The Devil in the Shape of a Woman* (New York: W. W. Norton, 1987), esp. 47–52. On the aftermath of Salem, see Bernard Rosenthal, *Salem Story: Reading the Witch Trials of 1692* (Cambridge: Cambridge University Press, 1993), esp. 204–18; and see Gretchen Adams Bond, *The Specter of Salem: Politics and Memory in Nineteenth-Century America* (Chicago: University of Chicago Press, 2008), which examines the 1692 Salem witchcraft trials in American national memory. Red Jacket's reference to New England's history was not mere poetic license. Massachusetts was directly involved in the resettlement of western New York as a result of an agreement between the states of New York and Massachusetts, signed at Hartford, Connecticut, December 16, 1786, which capped negotiations over conflicting claims for western lands that had surfaced during the American Revolution. Massachusetts retained preemption rights on lands in western New York, while ceding to New York "the government, sovereignty and jurisdiction" over the disputed territory. See Frank H. Severance, "Journals of Henry A.S. Dearborn," *Publications of the Buffalo Historical Society*, ed. Frank H. Severance (hereafter *PBHS*), 7 (1904): 37, 39; Anthony F. C. Wallace, *The Death and Rebirth of the Seneca* (New York: Knopf, 1970), 153; J. David Lehman, "The End of the Iroquois Mystique: The Oneida Land Cession Treaties of the 1780s," *William and Mary Quarterly*, 3d ser., 47.4 (1990): 523–47, esp. 532–39, 541.

3. Jon Butler, *Awash in a Sea of Faith: Christianizing the American People* (Cambridge, Mass.: Harvard University Press, 1990), 90, 228–29. See also Christine Leigh Heyrman, *Southern Cross: The Beginnings of the Bible Belt* (Chapel Hill: University of North Carolina Press, 1997), 73–74, which traces the fight against supernaturalism within southern evangelical Protestantism through the antebellum period; increasingly they disparaged belief in witches, demons, and magic by associating it with African Americans.

4. According to Mary Jemison, at least among the Senecas living along the Genesee River, "women never participated" in drunken "frolics" until after the revolutionary war; thereafter, "spirits became common in our tribe, and has been used indiscriminately by both sexes," though intoxication remained more common among men than women; see James E. Seaver, ed., *A Narrative of the Life of Mrs. Mary Jemison* (1824; new ed., Syracuse, N.Y.: Syracuse University Press, 1990), 127. According to Anthony F. C. Wallace, *The Death and Rebirth of the Seneca* (New York: Knopf, 1970), 200, women in particular, as petty traders, obtained whiskey from whites and retailed it in their villages; women could thus be implicated in the alcohol crisis even if men predominated among village drunks.

5. With apologies to Barbara Welter, "The Cult of True Womanhood, 1820–1860," *American Quarterly* 18 (Summer 1966): 151–74. Since Welter named the "cult," others have applied, extended, and modified the concept. See especially Aileen S. Kraditor, ed., *Up from the Pedestal: Selected Writings in the History of American Feminism* (Chicago: Quadrangle Books, 1968), which introduced the phrase, "cult of domesticity" in the editor's introduction; Nancy F. Cott, *The Bonds of Womanhood: "Women's Sphere" in New En-*

gland, 1780–1835 (New Haven, Conn.: Yale University Press, 1977). See also Mary P. Ryan, *Womanhood in America from Colonial Times to the Present,* 3d ed. (New York: Franklin Watts, 1983), 113–65; Ryan, *Cradle of the Middle Class: The Family in Oneida County, New York, 1790–1865* (Cambridge: Cambridge University Press, 1981); Nancy Grey Osterud, *Bonds of Community: The Lives of Farm Women in Nineteenth-Century New York* (Ithaca, N.Y.: Cornell University Press, 1991). See Linda K. Kerber, "Separate Spheres, Female Worlds, Woman's Place: The Rhetoric of Women's History," *Journal of American History* 75 (1988): 9–39, for a critique of historians' use of the notion "separate spheres," which urges them to account for the dynamic relations between women's and men's roles and worlds. With regard to the shifting gender organization of Seneca communities, it is clear that the new gender prescriptions of Handsome Lake, the Quakers, and others, while having an important impact, are not necessarily descriptive of how life was actually lived. And while new sorts of tasks and spheres for men and women were promoted, the distinct lives of men and women continued to be defined and lived dynamically.

6. In contrast to the Christian revivals of the First and the Second Great Awakenings, there is little evidence that in Handsome Lake's revival women were more heavily represented than men among "church" members or active followers. We might expect the opposite but lack data to support such a conclusion.

7. Arthur C. Parker, "The Code of Handsome Lake, the Seneca Prophet," New York State Museum Bulletin 163 (1913), reprinted as book 2 in William N. Fenton, ed., *Parker on the Iroquois* (Syracuse, N.Y.: Syracuse University Press, 1968), 32–33. Admonitions against whiskey and against conventional Seneca sexuality and marriage practice, expressed by both Handsome Lake and Quaker missionaries, appear throughout the Quaker records. See, for example, The Philadelphia Yearly Meeting Indian Committee Records, Quaker Collection, Special Collections, Haverford College, Haverford, Pennsylvania (hereafter cited as I.C. Records), report to the Committee for Promoting the Gradual Improvement and Civilization of the Indians, October 19, 1809, box 2, which contains a speech of Conudiu (Handsome Lake) playing off of similar Quaker prescriptions.

8. George S. Snyderman, ed., "Halliday Jackson's Journal . . . of a Visit Paid to the Indians of New York (1806)," *Proceedings of the American Philosophical Society* 101.6 (December 1957): 565–88 (hereafter cited as Halliday Jackson's Journal [1806]), quotations at 580 and 577.

9. On the advent of women among the Quaker missionaries, see "To the Chiefs and others of the Seneca Nation residing on the Alleghany River," May 13, 1805, I.C. Records, box 2; Halliday Jackson, *Civilization of the Indian Natives; or, A Brief View of the Friendly Conduct of William Penn toward Them in the Early Settlement of Pennsylvania . . . and a Concise Narrative of the Proceedings of the Yearly Meeting of Friends, of Pennsylvania . . . since 1795, in Promoting Their Improvement and Gradual Civilization* (Philadelphia: Marcus T. C. Gould; New York: Isaac T. Hopper, 1830), 50. On the encouragement of soap making and Seneca cleanliness, see ibid., 51, 52 (quotation), 64, 76; after an 1814 visit, Jackson concluded that the Seneca women "appeared more cleanly in their persons and houses than they formerly did; and their manners, and general deportment, appeared to

be rising from that degraded state in which they had formerly lived, and becoming more assimilated to the modes and practices of white people" (64). See also Benjamin Cooper et al. to the Indian Committee, December 17, 1805, I.C. Records, box 2.

10. Parker, "Code of Handsome Lake," 31. The code's prescription that a "man and wife" should live together, establishing their own household, seemed to promote the common Quaker emphasis on a decentralized residence pattern, which placed individual families in separate farmsteads. Friends praised those at Cold Spring in 1801 who began to live in such a manner, while criticizing others for "huddling together in town" in the manner of unassimilated Indians (see "Extract of a letter from one of the Friends settled on the Alleghany River," February 28, 1801, I.C. Records, box 1). It became clear later, however, that the prophet supported residence in towns rather than on dispersed farmsteads, most likely for the same reasons New England Puritans idealized concentrated village settlement—it promoted ritual life and knit the community together in a web of mutual support and surveillance.

11. Parker, "Code of Handsome Lake," 30, 32.

12. Jackson, *Civilization of the Indian Natives*, 76, expressed the rhetoric of domesticity and separate spheres in the following quotation of a Quaker delegation speaking to a *mixed* audience of Senecas: "Brothers, the greatest kindness a man can do to his children, is to begin early, to learn them to be industrious, and to engage them in business suitable to their years. The boys ought to help their fathers in the fields—the mothers and daughters to be engaged in spinning—in making clothes, in cooking victuals, and in all the business that is suitable to their sex—their houses, their beds, their clothes, and every thing about them, should be kept clean and in good order." The Friends' record of success was mixed, but they did achieve some Seneca reform, especially when their program and the nativist one promoted by Handsome Lake dovetailed, as they often did.

13. "Halliday Jackson's Journal . . . (1806)," 582, 582 n. 29. Jackson characterized the council as unusually large: "This was the largest Counsel I had ever been at among them, a number of principal Women attended" (577). William N. Fenton, *The Iroquois Eagle Dance: An Offshoot of the Calumet Dance*, Smithsonian Bureau of American Ethnology Bulletin 156 (Washington, D.C.: U.S, Government Printing Office, 1953), 78, noted the role of a Seneca woman in reviving Handsome Lake's religion at Tonawanda, temporarily suspended with the prophet's death in 1815, when she encouraged her grandson to resume recitation of the prophet's teachings.

14. Wallace summarizes these arguments in "Origins of the Longhouse Religion," in William C. Sturtevant, gen. ed., *Handbook of North American Indians*, 20 vols. projected (Washington, D.C.: Smithsonian Institution, 1978–) (hereafter *HBNAI*), vol. 15, *Northeast* (1978), ed. Bruce G. Trigger, 445.

15. The famous Seneca leader Red Jacket of Buffalo Creek exemplified the factional and gendered divisions that Handsome Lake would encounter—though a nativist and supporter of much of the prophet's agenda, he nonetheless opposed Handsome Lake politically on numerous occasions, and significantly Red Jacket was often designated as a speaker for women; see Christopher Densmore, *Red Jacket: Iroquois Diplomat and Orator*

(Syracuse, N.Y.: Syracuse University Press, 1999), xvi. Late in his career, Handsome Lake was driven from the Allegany settlements and relocated at Tonawanda, where he lived for four years. In 1815, he journeyed to Onondaga, where he died. According to Fenton, based on historical research and fieldwork, the prophet "was plagued by the jealousy of rival village chiefs" (*Iroquois Eagle Dance*, 78). His efforts to standardize ritual and purge extraneous rites, orders, and societies met resistance as well. Based on a dream revelation, Handsome Lake decreed, "It is not right for you to have so many dances and dance songs. A man calls a dance in honor of some totem animal from which he desires favor or power. This is very wrong, for you do not know what injury it may work upon other people" (Parker, "Code of Handsome Lake," 39). Societies were overtly disbanded, but they sometimes continued surreptitiously, backed by rivals. In time, some of these societies incorporated Handsome Lake adherents and were assimilated into the prophet's new religion (Fenton, *Iroquois Eagle Dance*, 78–79).

16. Joseph-François Lafitau, *Customs of the American Indians Compared with the Customs of Primitive Times*, ed. and trans. William N. Fenton and Elizabeth Moore, 2 vols. (Toronto: Champlain Society, 1977), 1:241. The term *witchcraft* is used here to refer to all forms of malevolence (and *witch* refers to those who directed it) among the Iroquois. While the diverse practices and practitioners designated generally by such terms certainly varied, especially over time and across cultural boundaries, apparently the Iroquois themselves did not divide malevolent acts or distinguish terminologically between, say, those of *witches* and those of *sorcerers*. See Annemarie Shimony, "Iroquois Witchcraft at Six Nations," in Deward E. Walker Jr., ed., *Systems of North American Witchcraft and Sorcery* (Moscow: University of Idaho, 1970), 239–65, esp. 242–43. On Iroquois notions of *otkon* and *orenda* and witchcraft beliefs and practices, see Lafitau, *Customs of the American Indians*, 1:240–41; Wallace, *Death and Rebirth of the Seneca*, 84; Åke Hultkrantz, *The Religions of the American Indians*, trans. Monica Setterwall (Berkeley: University of California Press, 1979), 12; Daniel K. Richter, *Ordeal of the Longhouse: The Peoples of the Iroquois League in the Era of European Colonization* (Chapel Hill: University of North Carolina Press, 1992), 24–25; Dean R. Snow, *The Iroquois* (Oxford: Blackwell, 1994), 54, 96, 98; Matthew Dennis, *Cultivating a Landscape of Peace: Iroquois-European Encounters in Seventeenth-Century America* (Ithaca, N.Y.: Cornell University Press, 1993), 90–94. See also the following: George S. Snyderman, "Witches, Witchcraft, and Allegany Seneca Medicine," *Proceedings of the American Philosophical Society* 127.4 (1983): 263–77; David Blanchard, "Who or What's a Witch? Iroquois Persons of Power," *American Indian Quarterly* 6.3–4 (1982): 218–37; DeCost Smith, "Witchcraft and Demonism of the Modern Iroquois," and "Onondaga Customs," *Journal of American Folk-Lore* 1.3 (1888): 184–93 and 195–98, and "Additional Notes on Onondaga Witchcraft and Hon-do-i," *Journal of American Folk-lore* 2.7 (1889): 277–81; Lewis H. Morgan, *League of the Iroquois* (orig. pub. as *League of the Ho-de-no-sau-nee, or Iroquois*, 1851; reprint ed., with intro. by William N. Fenton [Secaucus, N.J.: Citadel Books, 1962]), 164–65; Annemarie Anrod Shimony, *Conservatism among the Iroquois at the Six Nations Reserve* (New Haven, Conn.: Department of Anthropology, Yale University, 1961), esp. 261–88; Bruce G. Trigger, *The Children of Aataentsic:*

A History of the Huron People to 1660, 2 vols. (Montreal: McGill-Queen's University Press, 1976), 1:66–67, 81, 424–25, 500, 534–44, 589–601, 646, 657, 696, 708, 715–19; Elisabeth Tooker, *An Ethnography of the Huron Indians, 1615–1649*, Bureau of American Ethnology Bulletin 190 (Washington, D.C.: U.S. Government Printing Office, 1964), 117–20. The latter two works focus on the culturally similar Iroquoians, the Hurons; most scholars of the seventeenth-century Iroquois, facing gaps in the documentary record, accept generalizations about Iroquois culture that draw on evidence from other related Iroquoians, especially the Hurons. The secondary works listed above base their discussion of Iroquoian witchcraft belief and practice in the seventeenth and eighteenth centuries on extensive contemporary references to such Native belief and practice. See especially Reuben Gold Thwaites, trans. and ed., *The Jesuit Relations and Allied Documents*, 73 vols. (Cleveland: Burrow Brothers, 1896–1901).

17. See especially Wallace, *Death and Rebirth of the Seneca*, 76–77, 84; Shimony, *Conservatism among the Iroquois*, 261–62: she observed firsthand, during her fieldwork in the late 1950s, "an almost paranoid undercurrent of suspicion, in which each person sees his health and good fortune and even his life threatened by someone or something."

18. On the underlying anxieties of Native American life, with important lessons for historians of the early American period, see A. Irving Hallowell, "Some Psychological Characteristics of the Northeastern Indians," in *Culture and Experience* (1955; New York: Schocken Books, 1967), 125–50. For Bressani's relation of 1653, see Thwaites, *Jesuit Relations*, 39:27. Note, however, that Handsome Lake would "suffer a witch to live," should she be willing to confess and repent. In this regard, he acted in way congruent with Puritan authorities at Salem, Massachusetts, in 1692. The law against witchcraft was derived from the Bible: "Thou shalt not suffer a witch to live" (Exodus 22:18).

19. "Notes on the customs of the Seneca Indians, c. 1890" (PA 47), Ely S. Parker Papers, Huntington Library, San Marino, Calif.

20. See Shimony, *Conservatism among the Iroquois*, 286–88; Blanchard, "Who or What's a Witch," 230; Lafitau, *Customs of the American Indians*, 243.

21. Parker, "Code of Handsome Lake," 29–30, 46, 72; whether the prophet's ban was new or a renewal of older proscriptions, it represented a significant (and gendered) effort to police the use of magic. On the gendered rivalry and hostility that could arise within the context of Iroquois matrilineal social organization, see the various tales in J. Curtin and J. N. B. Hewitt, "Seneca Fiction, Legend, and Myths," *32d Annual Report of the Bureau of American Ethnology* (Washington, D.C., 1918) and the Waugh Collection of Iroquois Folktales (APS Film 1375), American Philosophical Society, Philadelphia, which is described by Martha Champion Randle, "The Waugh Collection of Iroquois Folktales," *Proceedings of the American Philosophical Society* 97.5 (1953): 611–33. Randle analyzes gendered aspects of this material in "Psychological Types from Iroquois Folktales," *Journal of American Folklore* 65 (1952): 13–21.

22. The epic of the Peacemaker is conveniently summarized in Paul A. W. Wallace, *The White Roots of Peace* (Philadelphia: University of Pennsylvania Press, 1946). See also the discussion in Dennis, *Cultivating a Landscape of Peace*, esp. 91, 93–94. Atotarho, or

Adodarhonh (Thadodaho in Onondaga), is still the most important confederacy chief title among the Iroquois, the first Onondaga name in the roll call of the chiefs. See Tooker, "The League of the Iroquois: Its History, Politics, and Ritual," *HBNAI*, 15: 424, 427. On Adriochten, see *A Journey into Mohawk and Oneida Country, 1634–1635: The Journal of Harmen Meyndertsz van den Bogaert*, trans. and ed. Charles T. Gehring and William A. Starna (Syracuse, N.Y.: Syracuse University Press, 1988), 4, 31–32 n. 26. On the Jesuit priest Isaac Jogues's martyrdom, see Thwaites, *Jesuit Relations*, 30:229; 31:73–75. Scholars of Iroquois culture and history agree almost uniformly that Iroquois "witches" could be women *or* men; apart from the exception discussed below, scholars have not argued for any gender imbalance in such accusations. See, for example, Snow, *The Iroquois*, 98: "Witches, it was believed, could be either male or female"; or Shimony, "Iroquois Witch-craft at Six Nations," 243: "The belief in witches, both male and female, is a well-documented indigenous trait." Lafitau provides conflicting information on Iroquoian "witches"; he writes, with regard to "*Agotkon* or spirits," "there is a great number of them of both sexes. The women especially are suspected of playing a part in this little business" (*Customs of the American Indians*, 1:238). It is unclear who—Natives or European newcomers—were suspicious here. Further, one might wonder, does "little business" refer to minor or variant forms of sorcery or shamanism, suggesting a gendering of shamanistic practice? Finally, given Lafitau's larger agenda—a comparison of the *moeurs des sauvages amériquains* with the *moeurs des premiers temps*—it is not surprising to observe Lafitau "normalizing" the different practices of the Iroquois and other North American Natives, conserving a sense of their exoticism but rendering it more familiar and conventional. As Thomas Jefferson observed in a letter critiquing Lafitau (perhaps too harshly) in 1812, "unluckily Lafitau had in his head a preconceived theory on the mythology, manners, institutions and government of the ancient nations of Europe, Asia and Africa, and seems to have entered on those of America only to fit them into the same frame, and to draw from them a confirmation of his general theory. . . . He selects . . . all the facts and adopts all the falsehoods which favor his theory, and very gravely retails such absurdities as zeal for a theory could alone swallow" (Jefferson to John Adams, June 11, 1812, in *The Works of Thomas Jefferson*, ed. Paul Leicester Ford, 12 vols. [New York: G. P. Putnam's Sons, 1904–5], 11:250–51). Jefferson himself acknowledged, however, Native belief in "conjurers and witches" (252).

23. Parker, "Code of Handsome Lake," 61–62, 70 (Punisher's domain), 49 (apocalypse).

24. Ibid., 45. See also "Account of a visit made by Penrose Wiley, John Letchworth, Anne Mifflin, Mary Bell & Co. to the Seneca Indians, settled on Allegany River," October 1803, Special Collections, Cornell University, Ithaca, N.Y.: "We have renounced Whiskey," the Senecas informed the visiting Quakers. Cornplanter told them, "I believe the Good Spirit never intended the Grain which is given us to live on, should be made into Whiskey." Cornplanter even blamed drought on white whiskey-making: "The white people have taken so much water to make whiskey, is the reason the waters are now so dryed up."

25. Parker, "Code of Handsome Lake," 29 n. 3.

26. Ibid., 71–72.

27. Jefferson to Taylor, Philadelphia, June 4, 1798, in Thomas Jefferson, *Writings*, ed. Merrill D. Peterson (New York: Library of America, 1984), 1050. The juxtaposition of Jefferson and Handsome Lake is kismet, but it suggests the ubiquity of witchcraft as both a metaphor and, for some, a physical threat. Jefferson would have seen Adams and his administration as the witch-hunters. Ironically, some might later have been tempted to characterize the prophet's ascendancy in the same terms—as the reign of a witch-hunter. Witchcraft belief, and witch-hunting, continued into the twentieth century among the Iroquois; see Sidney L. Harring's analysis of the remarkable Iroquois witch-murder trials of the 1930s, "Red Lilac of the Cayugas: Traditional Indian Law and Culture Conflict in a Witchcraft Trial in Buffalo, New York, 1930," *New York History* 73.1 (January 1992): 65–94, which demonstrates the continued vitality of witchcraft belief among the Iroquois into the twentieth century. Harring tends to characterize Iroquois witchcraft as "traditional," and perhaps it was by the 1930s, but this is too vague a term to account for the transformations in Iroquois witchcraft belief and practice in the late eighteenth and early nineteenth centuries.

28. According to Halliday Jackson, *Civilization of the Indian Natives*, 42, by 1801 Handsome Lake had "acquired considerable influence in the nation, so as to be appointed high priest and chief Sachem in things civil and religious"; see also ibid., 47, 50. In a January 23, 1803, letter written by Quaker missionary Jacob Taylor for Handsome Lake to the Indian Committee, the prophet asserted, the "principal part of the Sineca Nation have agreed to be under his [the prophet's] Government—and nothing in the future of any Consequences that relates to the Sineca is to be transacted without the Knowledge and approbation of Conudiu [Handsome Lake]" (I.C. Records, box 2). Jonathan Thomas to Thomas Wistar, representing the Indian Committee, April 21, 1804, I.C. Records, box 2, noted that the prophet "does not pretend to have many visions of late, but his influence is great over most of the Indians of the Seneca nation and even to others of the six nations."

29. Halliday Jackson's account of the prophet's visions is in Anthony F. C. Wallace, ed., "Halliday Jackson's Journal to the Seneca Indians, 1798–1800," *Pennsylvania History* 19.2 (April 1952): 117–47, and 19.3 (July 1952): 325–49 (hereafter cited as "Jackson's Journal, 1798–1800"). Henry Simmons's version is in ibid., 345–48. Jackson's journal identifies the "witch" clearly as "a certain woman . . . whom they suspected to have a familiar Spirrit, because they say she had done much mischief by Pison [poison] and Witchcraft" (145); see also Jackson's "Visions of Connudiu" (ibid., 343), which mentions, during the recounting of Handsome Lake's second vision, the existence of "two people who lived in our village that would hurt others, but one was lately killed"; Simmons's version similarly recounts Handsome Lake's implication of "some very bad ones among them, who would poison others, but one of them lately killed, yet their [*sic*] remained one like her who was a man" (ibid., 345). If an accusation ever stemmed from this revelation against the latter, male "witch," it went unrecorded.

30. Wallace, *Death and Rebirth of the Seneca*, 261–62; Wallace raises the possibility that this legend may actually refer to the execution of June 13, 1799, but we cannot be sure. He also speculates on the reasons that more executions of "witches" have not come to light and suggests that they might have been minimized by the prophet's acceptance of confession and repentance among the accused (262). Both the search for witches' bodily marks and the ability of indicted "witches" to escape death through confession support Red Jacket's alignment of Seneca witch hunts with those of Salem, Massachusetts, in 1692. On confession at Salem, see Reis, *Damned Women*, 121–63.

31. There is much that we will never know about the Handsome Lake–era witch hunts, and conclusions about their scope and nature must remain tentative. Precisely how many were accused, how many were executed, which lineages, clans, and villages were most heavily represented, how many were women and how many were men—answers to these questions may ultimately be unanswerable. Nonetheless, Seneca traditions should not be dismissed as "mere" folktales and "superstition"; not only do independent documentary sources corroborate pieces of such traditions, but oral cultures in general, and Iroquois people in particular, have demonstrated considerable powers of memory. Without texts as aids, Senecas and other Native people cultivated the art of memory, committed themselves to it collectively, and insured its conservation through recitation. As one ethnographer of the Iroquois has commented, "most men and women were walking archives." With memory and truth a collective rather than an individual possession, knowledge may well have been slower to change than in literate societies—that is, details and meanings may well have been more faithfully memorialized over long periods of time. Seneca recollections of events like the Handsome Lake witch hunts, recorded in folk narratives, deserve careful scrutiny. On the processes and powers of Iroquois memory, see William N. Fenton, "Structure, Continuity, and Change in the Process of Iroquois Treaty Making," in Francis Jennings et al., eds., *The History and Culture of Iroquois Diplomacy: An Interdisciplinary Guide to the Treaties of the Six Nations and Their League* (Syracuse, N.Y.: Syracuse University Press, 1985), 13, 34 n. 28. See Walter J. Ong, *Orality and Literacy: The Technologizing of the Word* (London: Methuen, 1982), esp. 57–68 on oral memorization; James Axtell, *The Invasion Within: The Contest of Cultures in Colonial North America* (New York: Oxford University Press, 1985), 14–15, discusses the implications of orality in the face-to-face worlds of American Indians in the colonial period. For example, the Quaker John Philips, visiting the Allegany Senecas in 1806, was impressed by his interlocutors' powers of recall in their reply to a lengthy speech. He wrote, "after Speaking Softly together a Little while to my astonishment the Chief warrior arose and made a Long Speech and a perticular Reply to all that was Read adverted to Every part of it and enlarged thereupon Considerably"; Merle H. Deardorff and George S. Snyderman, eds., "A Nineteenth-Century Journal of a Visit to the Indians of New York" [by John Philips, 1806], *Proceedings of the American Philosophical Society* 100.6 (December 1956): 608.

32. See Seaver, *Narrative of the Life of Mrs. Mary Jemison*, 128, on the accusation against Jamison; on the accusation against the woman cousin of Big Tree, see 159–60; here, gender and kinship as well as other factors combined to render the women vulnerable to accusation of witchcraft.

33. On the Seneca-Munsee witch crisis, see Jackson, *Civilization of the Indian Natives*, 42–43; "Joseph Ellicott's Letter Books," *PBHS* 26 (1926): 122–23 ("sundry old women . . ." quotation); "A Message from the People called Quakers of Pennsylvania to Corn-planter and the other Chiefs of the Seneca Nation settled on the Allegeny River," May 1801, I.C. Records, box 1 (quotation of Quaker advice); Henry Drinker, Nicholas Waln, Thos. Stewardson to "Friend," n.d., I.C. Records, box 1; "A Message from the People called Quakers of Pennsylvania, the children of Onas, to the Muncey Tribe of Indians settled at Cataragus," May 23, 1801, I.C. Records, box 1; William Wallace and Henry Baldwin to Thomas McKean, governor of Pennsylvania, April 14, 1801, I.C. Records, box 1; Jonathan Thomas, Joel Swaine [Swayne], Jacob Taylor to the Committee, June 28 and August 3, 1801, I.C. Records, box 1. In a letter "To David Mead and other Friends, from the 2 Principal Chiefs of Muncy and others," April 11, 1801, I.C. Records, box 1, Munsee leaders ambiguously stated, "The Cornplanter took one of our Chiefs and kept him all winter on account of the Witchcraft of his daughter as he Blamed our nation for it." Clearly, the Allegany Senecas blamed the Munsees generally, but the line "the Witchcraft of his daughter" can be taken to refer to the bewitchment of Cornplanter's daughter or, alternatively, as witchcraft allegedly inflicted by the hostage chief's daughter. See also Wallace, *Death and Rebirth of the Seneca*, 255–59, 261; Deardorff and Snyderman, "A Nineteenth-Century Journal," 592.

34. Report of the committee visiting the Seneca missions, December 14, 1803, I.C. Records, box 2. On Seneca suspicions of Munsees as predisposed toward witchcraft, see Deardorff and Snyderman, "A Nineteenth-Century Journal," 592; Parker, "Code of Handsome Lake," 27 n. 3, notes that some Senecas believe that "witchcraft was introduced among them by some Algonquin tribe which they adopted"; and see Wallace, *Death and Rebirth of the Seneca*, 256. On the complex meaning of the symbolic transformation of Delawares into "women," see Dennis, *Cultivating a Landscape of Peace*, 108–10, esp. 109 n. 79.

35. Jane T. Merritt, *At the Crossroads: Indians & Empires on a Mid-Atlantic Frontier, 1700–1763* (Chapel Hill: University of North Carolina Press, 2003), 170–74, 192–97, 201; quotation at 192. See also Daniel K. Richter, *The Ordeal of the Longhouse: The People of the Iroquois League in the Era of European Colonization* (Chapel Hill: University of North Carolina Press, 1992), 243–44, 274–76.

36. Merritt, *At the Crossroads*, 192–97; quotations at 193.

37. Benjamin Cope et al. to the Committee from Cattaraugus, August 12, 1810, I.C. Records, box 2. On the institutionalization of confession and repentance, see Parker, "Code of Handsome Lake," 69. A Seneca chief named Gahighque, or "Sunfish," was said to have killed a "witch" in front of the longhouse at Cold Spring on the Allegany reserve about 1808, "about the last such killing there," wrote Deardorff and Snyderman, "A Nineteenth-Century Journal," 598 n. 18. Late in 1806, the missionary Samuel Kirkland, commenting on Handsome Lake and his impact among Oneidas and Onondagas to whom he ministered, wrote about the prophet's use of confession: "The prophet insists upon oral confession & when it is entire, give absolution, insisting at the same time

upon their persevering in reformation" (*Journals of Samuel Kirkland: Eighteenth-Century Missionary to the Iroquois, The Government Agent, Father of Hamilton College*, ed. Walter Pilkington [Clinton, N.Y.: Hamilton College, 1980], 419).

38. Parker, "Code of Handsome Lake," 46–47. The incident is described in Wallace, *Death and Rebirth of the Seneca*, 291, which clarifies that the two women accused died as a result of the lashes they received. A drawing by the Seneca artist Jesse Cornplanter illustrates the event (see Figure 9). The Jesse Cornplanter drawings are in the New York State Library, Albany.

39. Parker, "Code of Handsome Lake," 46, 58.

40. Ibid., 27–29 n. 3, 114 n. 1.

41. See Densmore, *Red Jacket*, esp. 56–59; Granville Ganter, ed., *The Collected Speeches of Sagoyewatha, or Red Jacket* (Syracuse, N.Y.: Syracuse University Press, 2006), esp. 110–11. Arthur C. Parker's papers contain notes from Aurelia Jones (December 1905), who talked about an older relative—an interpreter for Red Jacket at Buffalo Creek. According to Jones, his relative "Always said Cornplanter and H[andsome] L[ake] enemies [with Red Jacket]. Jealous because R. J. could talk better. . . . C. P. said R. J. knew too much too young to speak unless told what to say. . . . H. L. scolded R. J. C. P. said H. L. would be head sachem by and bye." Misc. notes, including copy of pencil, Arthur C. Parker Papers, box 1, folder 30, New York State Library, Albany. Similarly, another of Parker's informant told him, "They say Red Jacket was a medicine man. He did not like H. Lake"; see Parker Papers, box 1, folder 32.

42. "Account of the Seneca Prophet, or the Man of the Great Spirit," *Christian Observer* (Boston), 7.2 (February 1808): 135; Wallace, *Death and Rebirth of the Seneca*, 259–60; Laurence M. Hauptman, *Conspiracy of Interests: Iroquois Dispossession and the Rise of New York State* (Syracuse, N.Y.: Syracuse University Press, 1999), 133–34.

43. Parker, "Code of Handsome Lake," 68.

44. De Witt Clinton, *Discourse Delivered before the New-York Historical Society, at Their Annual Meeting, 6th December, 1811* (New York: James Eastburn, 1812), reprinted in William Campbell, ed., *The Life and Writings of De Witt Clinton* (New York: Baker and Scribner, 1849), 205–66, quotations at 241–42; "Religious Intelligence," including "Account of the Seneca Prophet, or the Man of the Great Spirit," *Christian Observer*, February 1808, 136. Other white observers similarly saw Handsome Lake as a charlatan; see, for example, the journal of the Reverend Samuel Kirkland, who termed the prophet "an imposter," though he did not condemn him publicly (*Journals*, 412). Handsome Lake's claims of direct revelation were particularly unacceptable (undermining the truth of the Bible as holy writ); Kirkland was skeptical, to say the least, of the prophet's ability to conjure up such revelations as needed: "if he wants a new revelation to answer any particular purpose, he can at any time cover his head with a Bearskin for an hour or two, then lay it aside, muse awhile, & then disclose the communication which have been made to him" (418).

45. See Wallace, *Death and Rebirth of the Seneca*, 202–6, 259–60; Stone, *Life and Times of Red-Jacket*, 166–67. It should be noted that Red Jacket himself was a believer in

witchcraft and caused the execution of at least one (female) victim; we have already seen his role in the defense of Tommy Jemmy, the witch-killer in 1821. Though the prophet's accusation against Red Jacket is embedded in the Code of Handsome Lake, both Red Jacket and Handsome Lake became prominent opponents of the alienation of Seneca land, though at various times each had advocated and profited from land sales, directly or indirectly. Though relatives and allies, Handsome Lake and Cornplanter would later have their own falling out.

46. In addition to the problems of poor documentation, it is possible that some accused "witches" escaped inscription in the historical record because they confessed, relented, and reformed, and thus escaped execution. In contrast to Puritan New England—the Salem crisis aside—Seneca "witches" who confessed were rehabilitated and reintegrated into the community. For another example of witch-hunting (and an execution averted) among the nearby Tuscaroras, see *Memoir of the Late Rev. Lemuel Covell, Missionary to the Tuscarora Indians and the Provinces of Upper Canada; Comprising a History of the Origin and Progress of the Missionary Operations in the Shaftsbury Baptist Association, up to the time of Mr. Covell's Decease in 1806. Also a Memoir of Rev. Alanson L. Covell . . . . by Mrs. D. C. Brown, Daughter and Sister of the Deceased*, 2 vols. in 1 (Brandon, Vt.: Telegraph Office, 1839). Covell's memoir recounted, "On arriving at the Indian station [in 1803], Mr. Covell found his red friends in much trouble and agitation. A woman was about to be executed, burned alive, as a witch" (136). The missionary was able to help stop the tragedy and restore civil harmony. As he reported, emphasizing his own—and God's—heroic action, "The poor savages were melted by the exhibition of God's wonderful love, and unmerited kindness. The execution was abandoned, the poor prisoner set free, the hostile chiefs reconciled, and the whole community rejoiced" (136–37).

47. The 1808 execution is mentioned in Deardorff and Snyderman, "A Nineteenth-Century Journal," 598 n. 18; Cornplanter's speech appears in a report to the Indian Committee, October 19, 1809, Philadelphia Yearly Meeting Indian Committee Minutes, Quaker Collection, Special Collections, Haverford College, Haverford, Pennsylvania, 10 vols. (hereafter I.C. Minutes), 1:307–10; Joel Swain [Swayne] et al. to the Committee, August 16, 1810, I.C. Records, box 2, provides a follow-up. The gender of the alleged witch is unknown. Wallace, "Origins of the Longhouse Religion," *HBNAI*, 15:447, concludes that "gradually popular sentiment congealed against him [the prophet] on the witchcraft issue. He was accused of using it to remove political rivals, like Red Jacket, and in general of assuming a dictatorial stance not congenial to Iroquois taste. He himself came finally to the opinion that he had gone too far and virtually dropped the persecutory mode of handling suspected witches."

48. "One of the Friends in Seneca Country," January 1802, quoted from the Logan Papers, Historical Society of Pennsylvania, in Snyderman, "Witches, Witchcraft, and Allegany Seneca Medicine," 276 n. 21. On good and bad spirits, see also Jackson, *Civilization of the Indian Natives*, 65.

49. "One of the Friends in Seneca Country"; Jackson, *Civilization of the Indian Natives*, 65. For the veiled threat against uncooperative Senecas, see Friends at Tunesassah

to the Indian Committee, February 3, 1807 (message delivered to Senecas January 31, 1807), I.C. Records, box 2.

50. On continuing belief in the devil's power, which accompanied the rejection of spectral evidence at Salem, see Reis, *Damned Women*, 55–92. In the long run, however, Reis argues, Satan became a less proximate force in the daily lives of New England Puritans after the Salem crisis. And among both the Puritans of Massachusetts Bay and the Senecas of western New York, no major witchcraft outbreaks occurred after their respective crises.

51. See Carla Gardina Pestana, "The City upon a Hill under Siege: The Puritan Perception of the Quaker Threat to Massachusetts Bay, 1656–1661," *New England Quarterly* 56 (1983): 323–53; Pestana, *Quakers and Baptists in Colonial Massachusetts* (Cambridge: Cambridge University Press, 1991), 149, 123–24, 129. Though Quakers were not uniformly accused as witches, they were understood (especially early in the seventeenth century) to be heretical lunatics and agents of the devil; when arrested as dissidents they were sometimes examined for "witches' teats," showing their familiarity with Satan. See also Christine Leigh Heyrman, *Commerce and Culture: The Maritime Communities of Colonial Massachusetts, 1690–1750* (New York: W. W. Norton, 1984), 108–17, on the implication of Quakers, or those associated with them, in the Essex County witchcraft trials. On the informally yet persistently held relationship between Quakers and witchcraft in New England, see also Karlsen, *Devil in the Shape of a Woman*, 122–25.

52. Report of a visit to Tunesassah and Cattaraugus to the Indian Committee, October 19, 1809, I.C. Minutes, 1:307. The delegates here exaggerated; while the range of those charged expanded wildly and embraced court officials and other people of prominence, including the judge Nathaniel Saltonstall, Dudley Bradstreet, the Andover justice of the peace, the minister Samuel Willard, and the wives of Governor Phipps and Increase Mather, no judges were formally charged or executed. It was the case, however, that accusers could find themselves among the accused. It is likely that such accusations undermined the credibility of the witch hunt. Given the accusation he had faced, Red Jacket may have understood this point from personal experience.

53. Thomas Stewardson et al., report on visit to Senecas to the Indian Committee, October 16, 1817, I.C. Records, box 3.

54. Tooker, "Development of Handsome Lake Religion," observes that support for Handsome Lake was hardly universal, that his teachings continued to be controversial after his death in 1815, and that the path to institutionalization was not smooth. She dates the revivals of Handsome Lake's teachings to the 1820s and especially the 1860s, in contrast to Wallace, *Death and Rebirth of the Seneca*, who dates the renaissance to the 1840s.

55. See also "Account of a visit made by Penrose Wiley, John Letchworth, Anne Mifflin, Mary Bell & Co."; during this visit to the Allegany Senecas, Seneca women were prominent in meeting with the Quakers and representing their views. The Friends reported, for example, "Cornplanter's sister, a Chiefess, with a grave Countenance, on behalf of her sisters, spake." Such public address by women occurred even at Cold Spring, where Handsome Lake was particularly influential; there "the women were solid and

attentive" in council, "and a few of their principal women, seeing the state the men were in did not wait for them to offer any thing; but consulting a few minutes together, spoke through a Chiefess."

56. Tooker, "Iroquois Since 1820," *HBNAI*, 15: 452. The Code of Handsome Lake was first formally recorded by Ely S. Parker in 1845 and again in 1848. As Tooker notes, economic and social change in Seneca life did not necessarily change the principles of Native religion but did alter the importance of certain rites. This could actually enhance women's religious role, given the continued importance of women in subsistence and domestic life, and given the way in which reservations, like the prereservation clearing or village (rather than more extensive prereservation territories), became the focal point of Seneca life. Women (along with men) served as faithkeepers; they acted prominently in medicine societies, some of which were exclusively female (others exclusively male). Rights to land and annuities continued to be inherited through the matrilineage, and hereditary chieftainships continued to be held in clans, with nomination and succession through female lineages. Finally, women continued to produce a substantial amount of the food consumed by their families, in their gardens, even after men began to assume a larger role in agriculture. For those who followed the Longhouse religion, all of these activities were integrated with rites of thanks and praise (ibid., 456–63).

57. See Annemarie Shimony, "Iroquois Religion and Women in Historical Perspective," in Yvonne Yazbeck Haddad and Ellison Banks Findly, eds., *Women, Religion, and Social Change* (Albany: State University of New York Press, 1985), 397–418; quotation at 415. On assimilation of older rites, which Handsome Lake opposed, and those favored by the prophet, after his death—a rapprochement among Seneca religious "traditionalists," see Fenton, *The Iroquois Eagle Dance*, esp. 78–79; for an example of a woman "Fortune Teller" successfully assisting a sick baby girl at Allegany in the 1940s, see ibid., 33.

58. Fenton, *The Iroquois Eagle Dance*, 41–43. Arthur C. Parker's papers contain other suggestive fragments attesting to the ongoing belief in witchcraft. See, for example, "Various notes, while at John Kennedy's, summer of 1903. Cattaraugus Reservation." These include reference to "who lived on flats back of Silverheels Farm." Parker reported that "Dondeh"—that is, George D. Jimeson—"Told about witch bone [drawing included in notes] from leg of deer. Old lady witched a man. Med. man knew who did it. Found bone in mans groin. Poulticed and took out from bandages. Found a hair wrapped around it. Threw it right through door. Bone went to witches house and through wall. Struck in witch. Next morning she was very sick and confessed" (Parker Papers, box 1, folder 32). For a dramatic demonstration of continued belief in witchcraft (and the execution of a "witch") among an Iroquois people in Buffalo in the early 1930s, see Harring, "Red Lilac of the Cayugas."

59. Witch hunts were prominent among other Native peoples who experienced the turmoil of the late eighteenth and early nineteenth centuries. As with the Senecas, Native prophets rose to prominence in part through their campaigns to rid their communities of "witches." See Gregory Evans Dowd, *A Spirited Resistance: The North American Indian Struggle for Unity, 1745–1815* (Baltimore: Johns Hopkins University Press, 1992), esp. 38–

40, 136–38. In the first decade of the nineteenth century, the Shawnee prophetic leader Tenskwatawa claimed special powers, granted by the Great Spirit, to discover witches, and like other witch-hunters he deployed this power against those who would challenge his own brand of nativism, especially those associated with whites and their "civilizing" mission. On the Shawnee witch hunts, see also Alfred A. Cave, "The Failure of the Shawnee Prophet's Witch-Hunt," *Ethnohistory* 42.3 (1995): 445–75; R. David Edmunds, *The Shawnee Prophet* (Lincoln: University of Nebraska Press, 1983), 42–48. Richard White, *The Middle Ground: Indians, Empires, and Republics in the Great Lakes Region, 1650–1815* (Cambridge: Cambridge University Press), 504–10, points out Tenskwatawa's emphasis on gender distinctions and the perceived threat that missionaries sought "to reduce Indian men to the status of women" (507). Central to the prophet's message was a gender system, according to White, "that emphasized the subordination of Indian women to Indian men"; thus, White notes, "the women who dominated the initial visionary outbreak largely vanished after 1806" (508). In an odd way, then, one might conjecture that Shawnee and Delaware witchcraft was "feminized" to the extent that the victims of their witch hunts were predominantly those who had been "reduced" to women by perceived or actual complicity with whites.

60. The witch-hunting of Handsome Lake and its defense by Red Jacket might also suggest the power of fear in constructing solidarity among a people—as painfully reinforced by the twentieth century's Cold War and, more recently, the United States after September 11, 2001.

CHAPTER 4. FRIENDLY MISSION

1. "Prophet of Alleghany," *Port Folio*, January 1811, 62. Note that the story behind this quotation is highly suspect; it reflects a view biased toward evangelical missionaries and their enterprise and may well invent incidents and dialogue. Still, it is convincing in its conviction that Handsome Lake rejected these missionary efforts and in its clear hostility toward the prophet.

2. George S. Snyderman, ed., "Halliday Jackson's Journal . . . of a Visit Paid to the Indians of New York (1806)," *Proceedings of the American Philosophical Society* 101.6 (December 1957): 565–88 (hereafter cited as Halliday Jackson's Journal [1806]), 565–88, quotations at 579 and 575.

3. The Quaker program of "civilization" among the Senecas can be reconstructed from records and minutes of the Committee Appointed by the Yearly Meeting of Friends Pennsylvania, New York, &c for Promoting the Improvement and Gradual Civilization of the Indian Natives, or "Indian Committee," of the Philadelphia Yearly Meeting, housed in the Quaker Collection, Special Collections, Haverford College, Haverford, Pa. The ten boxes of diaries, reports, and correspondences (I.C. Records), as well as the ten volumes of minutes (I.C. Minutes) and other manuscripts are also available on microfilm at the American Philosophical Society (film 824, reels 1–12). In addition to the Quaker Indian Committee records and minutes, see the published writings of participants, includ-

ing Halliday Jackson, *Civilization of the Indian Natives; or, a Brief View of the Friendly Conduct of William Penn toward Them in the Early Settlement of Pennsylvania . . . and a Concise Narrative of the Proceedings of the Yearly Meeting of Friends, of Pennsylvania . . . since 1795, in Promoting Their Improvement and Gradual Civilization* (Philadelphia: Isaac T. Hopper, 1830); Anthony F. C. Wallace, ed., "Halliday Jackson's Journal to the Seneca Indians, 1798–1800," *Pennsylvania History* 19.2 (April 1952): 117–47, and 19.3 (July 1952): 325–49 (hereafter cited as "Jackson's Journal, 1798–1800"); Merle H. Deardorff and George S. Snyderman, eds., "A Nineteenth-Century Journal of a Visit to the Indians of New York" [by John Philips, 1806], *Proceedings of the American Philosophical Society* 100.6 (December 1956): 586–612; George S. Snyderman, ed., "Halliday Jackson's Journal . . . of a Visit Paid to the Indians of New York (1806)," *Proceedings of the American Philosophical Society* 101.6 (December 1957): 565–88 (hereafter cited as Halliday Jackson's Journal [1806]). More generally, see Frank H. Severance, "Narratives of Early Mission Work," *Publications of the Buffalo Historical Society*, ed., Frank H. Severance (hereafter *PBHS*), 6 (1903): 165–380. Quotation from I.C. Minutes, vol. 1, March 8, 1796. The Reverend Jacob Cram's journal offers a firsthand account of the Quaker mission at Allegany; "Summary Report of Mr. Cram's Late Mission," *Massachusetts Missionary Magazine* 3.10–12 (March–May 1806): 383–95, 433–37, 470–74, esp. 390–94. The Cherokee-Scot (and adopted Mohawk) John Norton reported similarly in 1816 at Cattaraugus (an expansion of the Allegany mission "to promote the same end"), "The Friends (or People called Quakers) are about commencing a Settlement in the Neighborhood, with an intention of instructing these People in Agriculture, and the necessary Arts" (*The Journal of Major John Norton, 1816*, ed. Carl F. Klinck and James J. Talman [Toronto: Champlain Society, 1970], 8).

4. "Summary Report of Mr. Cram's Late Mission," 394 (italics in original). On the revival of the white dog ceremony at Oneida, see Karim Michel Tiro, "The People of the Standing Stone: The Oneida Indian Nation from the Revolution through Removal, 1765–1840" (Ph.D. diss., University of Pennsylvania, 1999), 192–93; on the earlier Quakers' mission to the Oneidas, and its nondogmatic, nonacquisitive quality, see ibid., 186–89. The Reverend Samuel Kirkland was, like Cram, frustrated by the Quakers; according to Kirkland, "Whatever the reason, the Quakers, since they first came among the Oneida, have invariably taken part with the pagans" (quoted in ibid., 187).

5. See generally Robert F. Berkhofer, Jr., *Salvation and the Savage: An Analysis of Protestant Missions and American Indian Response, 1787–1862* (1965; New York: Atheneum, 1976). The evolving middle-class definition of civilization, often in the context of reform activities, has been explored in a vast array of studies; see, for example, Bruce Dorsey, *Reforming Men and Women: Gender in the Antebellum City* (Ithaca, N.Y.: Cornell University Press, 2002); Richard Bushman, *The Refinement of America: Persons, Houses, Cities* (New York: Knopf, 1992); Stuart B. Blumin, *The Emergence of the Middle Class: Social Experience in the American City, 1760–1900* (New York: Cambridge University Press, 1989); Mary P. Ryan, *Cradle of the Middle Class: The Family in Oneida County, New York, 1790–1865* (New York: Cambridge University Press, 1981); Paul E. Johnson, *A Shopkeeper's Millennium: Society and Revivals in Rochester, New York, 1815–1837* (New York: Hill and Wang,

1978); Ronald G. Walters, *American Reformers, 1815–1860* (New York: Hill and Wang, 1978); Alisse Portnoy, *Their Right to Speak: Women's Activism in the Indian and Slave Debates* (Cambridge, Mass.: Harvard University Press, 2005).

6. Berkhofer, *Salvation and the Savage*, 4.

7. Rebecca Larson, *Daughters of Light: Quaker Women Preaching and Prophesying in the Colonies and Abroad, 1700–1775* (New York: Knopf, 1999), 25; Indian Committee to Cornplanter, April 28, 1798, I.C. Records, box 1.

8. Jackson, *Civilization of the Indian Natives*, 80–84.

9. Henry Drinker, Thomas Wistar, and Thomas Stewardson to Secretary of War Henry Dearborn, Philadelphia, December 31, 1801, in Letters Received by the Office of the Secretary of War Relating to Indian Affairs, microfilm series M-271, 1800–1823, 4 rolls, National Archives, Washington, D.C. (hereafter LRNA M-271), roll 1, 1800–1816 (this and other letters were part of a series of documents submitted to the secretary of war in 1812 by the Philadelphia Society of Friends in its role as Seneca advocates); Philip E. Thomas to A. H. Sevier, Baltimore, Second Month [February] 4, 1840, in Society of Friends, *The Case of the Seneca Indians in the State of New York: Illustrated by facts; printed for the information of the Society of Friends, by direction of the Joint Committees on Indian Affairs, of the four Yearly Meetings of Friends of Genesee, New York, Philadelphia, and Baltimore* (Philadelphia: Merrihew and Thompson, 1840), 56–57.

10. Beginning in the 1820s, Hicks began to produce a series of primitive paintings under the general title of *The Peaceable Kingdom*, referring to the biblical verses of Isaiah 11:6–9. Hicks would paint as many as one hundred versions of the scene. These engaging but enigmatic folk images typically quoted a famous painting by Benjamin West, *Penn's Treaty with the Indians* (first exhibited in London in 1775), which had been widely reproduced in inexpensive prints and had become ubiquitous on all sorts of everyday objects, from candle screens, trays, curtains, and quilts, to plates, crockery, and glassware. See Ellen Starr Brinton, "Benjamin West's Painting of Penn's Treaty with the Indians," *Bulletin of Friends' Historical Association* 30 (Autumn 1941): 99–131. On Edward Hicks, see Carolyn J. Weekley, with the assistance of Laura Pass Barry, *The Kingdoms of Edward Hicks* (Williamsburg, Va.: Colonial Williamsburg Foundation, 1999). Note that many critics have understood these images as comments not merely (or even primarily) on Quakers' relations with Indians but with each other at the time of the Friends' devastating schism with Elias Hicks—Edward Hicks's cousin—at its center in 1827–28. On the tarnishing of the Peaceable Kingdom ideal by real world events, see William Pencak and Daniel K. Richter, eds., *Friends and Enemies in Penn's Woods: Indians, Colonists, and the Racial Construction of Pennsylvania* (University Park: Pennsylvania State University Press, 2004); Jean R. Soderlund, ed., *William Penn and the Founding of Pennsylvania 1680–1684* (Philadelphia: University of Pennsylvania Press, 1983); J. William Frost, "'Wear the Sword as Long as Thou Canst': William Penn in Myth and History," *Journal of the Friends' Historical Society* 58.2 (1998): 91–113; Anne Cannon Palumbo, "Averting 'Present Commotions': History as Politics in *Penn's Treaty*," *American Art* 9.3 (1995): 28–55; Jon Parmenter, "Rethinking William Penn's Treaty with the Indians," *Proteus* 19.1 (2002): 38–44; Laura Rigal, "Framing the

Fabric: A Luddite Reading of Penn's Treaty with the Indians," *American Literary History* 12.3 (2000): 557–84; Jeremy Engels, "'Equipped for Murder': The Paxton Boys and 'The Spirit of Killing All Indians' in Pennsylvania, 1763–1764," *Rhetoric & Public Affairs* 8.3 (2005): 355–81.

11. Richard Bauman, *For the Reputation of Truth: Politics, Religion, and Conflict among the Pennsylvania Quakers, 1750–1800* (Baltimore: Johns Hopkins Press, 1971); Jane T. Merritt, *At the Crossroads: Indians & Empires on a Mid-Atlantic Frontier, 1700–1763* (Chapel Hill: University of North Carolina Press, 2003), esp. 198–231; Steven Craig Harper, *Promised Land: Penn's Holy Experiment, the Walking Purchase, and the Dispossession of Delawares, 1600–1763* (Bethlehem, Pa.: Lehigh University Press, 2006); Peggy Robbins, "A Walk of Injustice," *Pennsylvania Heritage* 14.3 (1988): 32–37; Anthony F. C. Wallace, *King of the Delawares: Teedyuscung, 1700–1763* (Syracuse, N.Y.: Syracuse University Press, 1990).

12. Bauman, *For the Reputation of Truth*, 77–97.

13. Ibid.; Frank H. Severance, "Quakers among the Senecas," *PBHS* 6 (1903): 165–68; Anthony F. C. Wallace, *The Death and Rebirth of the Seneca* (New York: Knopf, 1970), 220–21. See also the commemorative volume, G. Peter Jemison and Anna M. Schein, eds., *Treaty of Canandaigua 1794: 200 Years of Treaty Relations between the Iroquois Confederacy and the United States* (Santa Fe, N. Mex.: Clear Light Publishers, 2000), 260–94, which reprints an account of the proceedings from the journal of the Philadelphia Quaker William Savery, 260–94.

14. Jackson, *Civilization of the Indian Natives*; Timothy Pickering to Captain Israel Chapin, superintendent of the Six Nations, Philadelphia, February 15, 1796, LRNA M-271, roll 1 (this copy of Pickering's 1796 letter was part of the correspondence supplied by the Quaker advocates Henry Drinker, Thomas Wistar, and Thomas Stewardson in December 1801 to secretary of war, Henry Dearborn at his request); Deardorff and Snyderman, "A Nineteenth-Century Journal," 582–612, esp. 583–90; Bauman, *For the Reputation of Truth*, 202–14; Wallace, *Death and Rebirth of the Seneca*, 220–21.

15. Report of Henry Knox on the Northwest Indians, June 15, 1789, *American State Papers: Documents, Legislative and Executive, of the Congress of the United States, Selected and Edited under the Authority of Congress*, 38 vols. (Washington, D.C.: Gales and Seaton, 1832–61), class 2, *Indian Affairs*, 2 vols., 1:13–14; see also report of July 7, 1789, ibid., 53.

16. Melvin B. Endy, *William Penn and Early Quakerism* (Philadelphia: University of Pennsylvania Press, 1973); Richard S. Dunn and Mary Maples Dunn, eds., *The World of William Penn* (Philadelphia: University of Pennsylvania Press, 1986); Larson, *Daughters of Light*; Carla Gardina Pestana, "The City upon a Hill under Siege': The Puritan Perception of the Quaker Threat to Massachusetts Bay, 1656–1661," *New England Quarterly* 56.3 (September 1983): 323–53; Sydney E. Ahlstrom, *A Religious History of the American People* (New Haven, Conn.: Yale University Press, 1972), 205–13, 378–79; Jon Butler, *Awash in a Sea of Faith: Christianizing the American People* (Cambridge, Mass.: Harvard University Press, 1990), 118–20, 126–27.

17. Berkhofer, *Salvation and the Savage*, 58–59, notes that Quakers "did not encour-

age Indians to form First Day Meetings until sufficiently under the exercise of the spirit." Given the Quakers' limited evangelizing and circumspection, not surprisingly, "membership was long in coming and difficult to determine."

18. As we have seen, Handsome Lake in particular seemed to endorse two critical aspects of the Quaker program—temperance and a shift toward patriarchal families, tied especially to male agricultural production on family farms. The Senecas, despite their willingness to follow the guidance of both reformers, proved resistant to such male-centered agricultural production and developed an alternative hybrid economy, as we will see in Chapter 5.

19. For a brilliant analysis of marriage as a critical focus of colonialism, see Ann Marie Plane, *Colonial Intimacies: Indian Marriage in Early New England* (Ithaca, N.Y.: Cornell University Press, 2000). On colonial efforts to assimilate Indians in general, see Robert F. Berkhofer Jr., *The White Man's Indian: Images of the American Indian from Columbus to the Present* (New York: Knopf, 1978); see also Berkhofer, *Salvation and the Savage*. On the gendered nature of such assimilation campaigns, see Theda Perdue, "Southern Indians and the Cult of True Womanhood," in Walter J. Fraser Jr. et al., eds., *The Web of Southern Social Relations: Women, Family, and Education* (Athens: University of Georgia Press, 1985), 35–51; Mary E. Young, "Women, Civilization, and the Indian Question," in Mabel E. Deutrich and Virginia C. Purdy, eds., *Clio Was a Woman: Studies in the History of American Women* (Washington, D.C.: Howard University Press, 1980), 98–110. Diane Rothenberg, "The Mothers of the Nation: Seneca Resistance to Quaker Intervention," in Mona Etienne and Eleanor Leacock, eds., *Women and Colonization: Anthropological Perspectives* (New York: Praeger, 1980), 63–87, deals directly and provocatively with the gendered Seneca-Quaker encounter; see also Nancy Shoemaker, ed., *Negotiators of Change: Historical Perspectives on Native American Women* (New York: Routledge, 1994), which offers essays probing the question of how European settlement of the Americas affected the gender balance within Native societies.

For specific examples (among many) of various aspects of the Quaker "civilization" program, see (regarding hostility to communal ownership of property and encouragement of individual family ownership) "Extract of a letter from one of the Friends settled on the Alleghany River," February 28, 1801, I.C. Records, box 1, or Jonathan Thomas to Thomas Wistar, representing the Indian Committee, April 21, 1804, I.C. Records, box 1. Regarding Quaker hostility to collective patterns of work, especially female agriculture and male aversion to it and preference for lumbering, see, for example, Jonathan Thomas to Thomas Wistar, March 17, 1819, I.C. Records, box 3. On Quaker condemnation of whiskey, see, for example, Henry Simmons, Joel Swayne, and Halliday Jackson to the Committee, June 16, 1799, I.C. Records, box 1, or "Copy of a Speech delivered to Cornplanter . . . at a Council," September 14, 1799, I.C. Records, box 1. On Quaker criticism of Seneca marriage customs, see, for example, report on visit to Seneca missions, October 16, 1817, I.C. Records, box 3.

20. "Jackson's Journal, 1798–1800," 1:126.

21. These events can be followed in the I.C. Minutes, vol. 1; Joshua Sharpless and

John Pierce to Thomas Wistar, May 11, 1798, I.C. Records, box 1; copy of Friends' speech "To Cornplanter, and all our Indian brothers of the Seneca Nation, now living on the Allegany River," May 22, 1798, I.C. Records, box 1, emphasis added.

22. Speech of Friends "To Cornplanter, and all our Indian brothers of the Seneca Nation, now living on the Allegany River," May 22, 1798, I.C. Records, box 1. Such incentive offers, with similar prescriptions, would continue. See, for example, Jacob Taylor, Stephen Twining, and Hannah Jackson to the Committee, from Cattaraugus, February 22, 1812, I.C. Records, box 2.

23. Alexandra Harmon, "American Indians and Land Monopolies in the Gilded Age," *Journal of American History* 90.1 (June 2003): 106–33, analyzes the ironies of the "broad bilateral and intercultural discourse about economic culture, political economy, and race" revealed in debates over the allotment of Indian land in severalty (107). By the late nineteenth century, arguments against collective tribal ownership of land emphasized not merely the disincentive to work and "progress" allegedly inherent in such common ownership arrangements but also the supposed debilities caused by appropriation of tribal lands by individual enterprising tribal members, acting selfishly on their own behalf. Ethnocentric attitudes toward Native people and white predominance of power allowed reformers to attack "monopoly" in Indian societies in a manner never possible in their own society—through a radical expropriation and redistribution of property. Meanwhile, collective ownership and legal privilege became entrenched in American business in the modern "corporation." Ironically, as white reformers sought to abolish Indian collectives, the states passed general incorporation acts, encouraging the pooling of capital and limiting of individual liability, or responsibility. Note also that, for the Senecas and other Indians, there was no mention of the political rights conventionally associated with adult, white, male ownership of property.

24. On openness to technological innovations, "improvement" (i.e., sawmills, gristmills, roads), Western education, and moral reform, see, for example, "Extract of a letter from the Friends at Genesinguhta," January 16, 1800, I.C. Records, box 1; "Extract of a letter from Genesinguhta," September 3, 1800, I.C. Records, box 1; "Extract of a letter from one of the Friends settled on the Alleghenny River," February 28, 1801, I.C. Records, box 1; "Copy of a letter from five of the Cattaraugus Indians to the Friends settled at Genesinguhta," 1799 (no month or day indicated), I.C. Records, box 1; "Speech of Conidiu [Handsome Lake] on behalf of the Seneca Nation of Indians residing on the Alleghanny River . . . ," August 30, 1803, I.C. Records, box 2; excerpted Quaker documents sent to the secretary of war, December 1812, LRNA M-271, roll 1.

25. On different Allegany Seneca attitudes toward accommodation and acculturation, see, for example, Jonathan Thomas to Thomas Wistar, April 21, 1804, I.C. Records, box 2; Friends at Tunesassah to Thomas Wistar, February 1, 1807, I.C. Records, box 2; Friends at Tunessassah to the Indian Committee, February 3, 1807, I.C. Records, box 2. On the apparent willingness of some men to adopt the farming practices (intensive plow agriculture on individualized plots of land), see "Report of Baltimore Friends Yearly Meeting Indian Committee," October 15, 1804; Jackson, *Civilization of the Indian Natives,*

43–44. On the continued tendency of women to work communally, even at new tasks like spinning, see Friends at Tunesassah to the Committee, March 21, 1810, I.C. Records, box 2. On factionalism arising from contention over religion and land, see report of "Committee appointed to visit the Indian Nations on their reservations at Allegany & Cattaraugus," October 17, 1822, I.C. Records, box 3; "Copy of letter from Joseph Elkinton, Tunesassah," December 26, 1828, I.C. Minutes, vol. 1, 239–40; Jackson, *Civilization of the Indian Natives,* 75–83.

26. Simmons et al. to Indian Committee, July 29, 1798, I.C. Records, box 1; Simmons et al. to the Indian Committee, n.d., I.C. Records, box 1.

27. Simmons et al. to Indian Committee, June 16, 1799, I.C. Records, box 1; account by Joshua Sharpless et al. of visit to Allegany and Cattaraugus, November 16, 1799, I.C. Records, box 1; "Copy of Speech delivered to Cornplanter," September 14, 1799, I.C. Records, box 1; "Extract of a Letter from the Friends at Genesinguhta," January 16, 1800, I.C. Records, box 1. A transcript of a Quaker journal from September 13, 1801, sent to the secretary of war, December 1812, LRNA M-271, roll 1, noted, "Some families have lately left their large village called Je-ne-sha-da-go, [relocated at] . . . Genesangoughta & are clearing land near the latter place. Their thus settling separate & detached from each other is already manifestly more to their advantage than living together in villages." According to the entry, "One young Chief observed, 'When I lived at Jeneshadago, I could do no good, now I have left it I can work & make farm.' They also begin to have ideas of distinct property; each family consider the lots they clear, fence & cultivate as their own."

28. Jefferson to Brother Handsome Lake, November 3, 1802, in Thomas Jefferson, *Writings,* ed. Merrill D. Peterson (New York: Library of America, 1984), 556.

29. The idea of establishing their mission off-reservation was suggested late in 1802 (see Taylor and Swayne to the Indian Committee, December 11, 1802, I.C. Records, box 1); correspondence in 1803 details the implementation of the plan, summarized as well in the annual reports to the Yearly Meeting for the benefit of Friends in England (see I.C. Records, box 2); "Speech of Conidiu [Handsome Lake]," August 30, 1803, I.C. Records, box 2.

30. "Speech of Conidiu [Handsome Lake]," August 30, 1803, I.C. Records, box 2. This entry contains the remarks of Cornplanter as well as the prophet. The prophet and Handsome Lake stressed the similarities rather than the difference between their reforms and those of the Quakers, whom they hoped to retain as advocates and patrons.

31. "Report of Committee Visiting the Mission," December 14, 1803, I.C. Records, box 2; Jonathan Thomas to Thomas Wistar, April 21, 1804, I.C. Records, box 2; John Pennock et al. to the Indian Committee, June 9, 1804, I.C. Records, box 2; "Report of Baltimore Friends Yearly Meeting Indian Committee," October 15, 1804, I.C. Records, box 2.

32. "To the Chiefs and others of the Seneca Nation," May 13, 1805, I.C. Records, box 2; Benjamin Cope et al. to the Indian Committee, December 17, 1805, I.C. Records, box 2. These female missionaries were preceded by a delegation of Quaker women—the first to visit the Allegany Senecas in 1803; see "Account of a visit made by Penrose Wiley,

John Letchworth, Anne Mifflin, Mary Bell & Co. to the Seneca Indians, settled on Allegany River," October 1803, Special Collections, Cornell University, Ithaca, N.Y. The Quaker women promised their Seneca sisters that they would "inform the Brethren of your wish [for domestic instruction from women Friends], who have direction of these things. And enquire among the Sisters if any feel it their duty to come, and if any do, I doubt not they will be encouraged."

33. "Extract of a Letter from One of the Friends," February 28, 1801, I.C. Records, box 1; "Report of Committee Visiting the Mission," December 14, 1803, I.C. Records, box 2. In October 1803, a delegation of Quaker women were well received in Allegany, where they made an appeal that became increasingly formulaic: "of the necessity there is of continuing increasingly to turn . . . to [male] Agriculture & other useful employments; And by doing so, their women would have time to learn planting, and the management of Dairies; & Men and Women could learn weaving; By which they might have suitable changes of raiment, and keep themselves clean. Thus men and women, filling up their several departments in business, and helping one another, would maintain that order, in which consists the harmony and true peace of Society." This was the essence of holy conversation in an earthly peaceable kingdom. See "Account of a visit made by Quaker women."

34. Appendix to letter, Benjamin Cope et al. to Indian Committee, December 17, 1805, I.C. Records, box 2.

35. Snyderman, "Halliday Jackson's Journal . . . (1806)," 579–81, quotation at 581; Deardorff and Snyderman, "A Nineteenth-Century Journal," 605–6. Silverheels denied his family Quaker instruction in reading and spinning.

36. Friends to the Indian Committee, January 14, 1807, I.C. Records, box 2; summary of yearly reports (1807), I.C. Records, box 2. Silverheels later came to support the Quaker program for Seneca women. This message of women's "liberation" from inappropriate toil—promoted by Quakers and endorsed by Handsome Lake—represented the other, apparently more benign, side of the patriarchy advanced by both. Still, resistance would emerge as Seneca women in particular saw liabilities unnoticed or understated by the Friends and the prophet.

37. Snyderman, "Halliday Jackson's Journal . . . (1806)," 583; and see the Quaker journal excerpts sent to the secretary of war, December 1812, LRNA M-271; as early as 1802, the Quaker observers noted, "The Indians have exhibited not only proofs of ingenuity, but industry in constructing their houses. The work is done by themselves, even making the sashes, shingles & putting on roofs with very little assistance from our friends except their advice & the use of their tools. Glass[,] nails & some articles of ironmongery they procure from Pittsburg [sic]."

38. Snyderman, "Halliday Jackson's Journal . . . (1806)," 577–78. Jackson's older but less experienced Indian Committee colleague John Philips was less impressed: "though our friends think there is much improvement in Cleanliness amongst the Indians yet I think there is abundant Room for more for I could not have thought that any Creatures possest of Rational sence would have Lived in so much filth" (Deardorff and Snyderman, "A Nineteenth-Century Journal," 606).

39. On the subject of cleanliness in American history see Suellen Hoy, *Chasing Dirt: The American Pursuit of Cleanliness* (New York: Oxford, 1995), and Richard L. Bushman and Claudia Bushman, "The Early History of Cleanliness in America," *Journal of American History* 74 (March 1988): 1213–38.

40. Plane, *Colonial Intimacies*, esp. 4–8, 12, 178–80.

41. This social organization is conveniently summarized in William N. Fenton, "Northern Iroquoian Culture Patterns," in William C. Sturtevant, gen. ed., *Handbook of North American Indians*, 20 vols. projected (Washington, D.C.: Smithsonian Institution, 1978–) (hereafter *HBNAI*), vol. 15, *Northeast* (1978), ed. Bruce G. Trigger, 309–14. A recent historical archaeological study, Kurt A. Jordan, "Seneca Iroquois Settlement Pattern, Community Structure, and Housing, 1677–1779," *Northeast Anthropology* 67 (2004): 23–60, suggests the long-term flexibility and adaptability of Seneca communities, which concentrated or dispersed opportunistically, to take advantages of ecological, economic, or political opportunities. While the late eighteenth and early nineteenth centuries saw greater dispersion and a shift in housing types, particularly away from classic longhouses to "short longhouses" and "cabins," these adaptations were not unprecedented, nor did they represent acculturation or "cultural decline."

42. See, for example, Barry J. Levy, "'Tender Plants': Quaker Farmers and Children in the Delaware Valley, 1681–1735," *Journal of Family History* 3 (1978): 116–35, reprinted in Stanley N. Katz, John M. Murrin, and Douglas Greenberg, eds., *Colonial America: Essays in Politics and Social Development*, 5th ed. (Boston: McGraw-Hill, 2001), 240–65.

43. Levy, "'Tender Plants': Quaker Farmers and Children," esp. 243–44; Larson, *Daughters of Light*, 164–71.

44. See Barry Levy, *Quakers and the American Family: British Settlement in the Delaware Valley* (New York: Oxford, 1988), esp. 12–13; Larson, *Daughters of Light*, 133–71; Marilyn J. Westercamp, *Women and Religion in Early America, 1600–1850: The Puritan and Evangelical Traditions* (London: Routledge, 1999), 81–84.

45. Quaker disapproval extended also to sexual activity that preceded marriage. Generally, however, Quaker disapproval was expressed less through direct criticism than in the prescription of new sexual and marital norms. See, for example, report of Quaker committee's visit to Seneca reservations, October 17, 1822, I.C. Records, box 3. Black Snake's simple reply to the Quakers on that occasion reflected some twenty years of subtle instruction about patriarchal marriage: "we understand we should be tender & true to our wives, & that they should learn the ways of the white people." Years earlier, Cornplanter had acknowledged—telling Quakers what they wished to hear—"We are very sensible that it is displeasing to the Great Spirit for Husbands & Wives to separate" (substance of interaction at conference between Quakers and Senecas at Cold Spring Settlement, September 25, 1809, "Indians," September 25, 1809, folder, Historical Society of Pennsylvania, Philadelphia, in Francis Jennings, ed., *Iroquois Indians: A Documentary History of the Diplomacy of the Six Nations and their League* [hereafter *DHSN*], 50 microfilm reels [Woodbridge, Conn.: Research Publications, 1985], reel 45).

46. Deardorff and Snyderman, "A Nineteenth-Century Journal," 601; Snyderman, "Halliday Jackson's Journal . . . (1806)," 577.

47. It might strike us as ironic that, while the Quakers' prescribed reforms of Seneca marriage sought to protect women because women were perceived as disadvantaged and weak, Handsome Lake's complementary reforms at times demonized Seneca women because they were too strong and thus could thwart his reformation.

48. It is difficult to reconstruct the internal dynamics of Seneca families from such a temporal and cultural distance. We do not really know whether, or to what extent, Senecas had maintained "traditional" family structures or how precisely they continued to cultivate social harmony within their households. Critical, prescriptive messages from outsiders—even sympathetic observers—are not enough to make us conclude that Seneca families were in fact dysfunctional (to employ an anachronistic term), or to answer the question begged by such a formulation: functional or dysfunctional according to whom, on whose terms? See Snyderman, "Halliday Jackson's Journal . . . (1806)," 583; Simmons et al. to Indian Committee, June 16, 1799, I.C. Records, box 1, on the heavy presence of liquor in the community following the spring trade and the misery caused as a result; see also Deardorff and Snyderman, "A Nineteenth-Century Journal," 589. The turmoil of the War of 1812 seemed to make alcohol temporarily more prevalent and problematic among the Senecas.

49. English-Seneca Religious Catechism, ca. 1835, Buffalo Creek Reservation, Seneca Mission Station, Ely S. Parker Papers, box 1, PA 30, Huntington Library, San Marino, Calif. David A. Ogden—a self-interested observer if there ever was one, who was intent on acquiring Seneca land—claimed that the Buffalo Creek Senecas had descended into the moral turpitude that the Quaker- or Baptist-prescribed morality, centered on marriage and family, were designed to prevent. In a memorial to the president, he emphasized "the debased condition of the Seneca Indians; and especially those composing the Tribe which resides in the immediate vicinity of the Village of Buffaloe. The mendicity, drunkenness and idleness of these Indians, the indecency of their dress and the open and venal prostitution of their Women have absolutely rendered them an intolerable Nuisance, insomuch as to retard materially the growth of that important place." See David A. Ogden, "Memorial of David A. Ogden to the President of the United States, regarding removal of Senecas," ca. 1819, David Ogden Papers, Clements Library, University of Michigan, Ann Arbor, in *DHSN*, reel 46.

50. "Summary Report of Mr. Cram's Late Mission," 393–94. On the impact of the War of 1812, see Jackson, *Civilization of the Indian Natives*, 60–62.

51. James Monroe to the Seneca Indians living on the Allegany Reservation, January 15, 1819, I.C. Records, box 3. Of course, Monroe's claim that all his white "children" (presumably, he is referring to adult males here) owned their own land was untrue and became even less true over time. It is worth noting as well that in 1819 the African American population was approaching two million, most of them enslaved. As such they owned no land; indeed, legally they themselves were property. On the history of allotment, including allotment before "Allotment"—that is, the policy embodied in the General Allotment Act of 1887—see Stuart Banner, *How the Indians Lost Their Land: Law and Power on the Frontier* (Cambridge, Mass.: Harvard University Press, 2005), 257–90, esp. 258–63.

Henry Dearborn, secretary of war, had guaranteed the Senecas, in a letter March 14, 1802, "all lands, claimed by and secured to said Senecas . . . shall be and remain the property of the said Seneca and . . . all persons, citizens of the United States, are hereby strictly forbidden to disturb said Indian Nations in their quiet possession of said lands"; see Maris B. Pierce Papers, box 1, folder 2, Buffalo and Erie County Historical Society (BECHS), Buffalo, N.Y.

52. Thomas Jefferson offered a classic statement of the connection between property, virtue, and independence in his "Query XIX: Manufactures," *Notes on the State of Virginia* (1787), in *Writings*, 290–91:

> Those who labour in the earth are the chosen people of God, if ever he had a chosen people, whose breasts he has made his peculiar deposit for substantial and genuine virtue. . . . Corruption of morals in the mass of cultivators is a phaenomenon of which no age nor nation has furnished an example. It is the mark set on those, who not looking up to heaven, to their own soil and industry, as does the husbandman, for their subsistance, depend for it on the casualties and caprice of customers. Dependance begets subservience and venality, suffocates the germ of virtue, and prepares fit tools for the designs of ambition. . . . [G]enerally speaking, the proportion which the aggregate of the other classes of citizens bears in any state to that of its husbandmen, is the proportion of its unsound to its healthy parts, and is a good-enough barometer whereby to measure its degree of corruption.

53. Jacob Taylor et al. to the Indian Committee, November 26, 1798, I.C. Records, box 1; Jonathan Thomas et al. to the Indian Committee, March 17, 1819, I.C. Records, box 3. In 1812, the Quakers initiated a two-year incentive program that granted premiums (one dollar per acre) to individuals who "would enclose lots of land in a regular manner, not less than five Acres and as much larger as they found convenient and plant or sow the same in sufficient good order"; see Jacob Taylor et al. to the Indian Committee, February 22, 1812, I.C. Records, box 2.

54. Jonathan Thomas et al. to the Indian Committee, March 17, 1819, I.C. Records, box 3.

55. Jackson, *Civilization of the Indian Natives*, 67–72; report of Thomas Stewardson et al. to Indian Committee, October 16, 1817, I.C. Records, box 3. The Quaker Indian program was predicated on the protection of Indian lands, without which they saw little hope in promoting acculturation and "progress." The Indian Committee noted in its prospectus commencing their work, "The present appears to us a favourable period for carrying on this good work—the boundaries of some of the tribes are fixed by treaty—their lands cannot now be so easily alienated as heretofore, and evil communication with traders and others is intended to be prevented by Government" (Thomas Wistar, for the Indian Committee, "Epistle directed to the Quarterly and Monthly Meetings belonging to the said Yearly [Philadelphia] Meeting," November 3, 1795, in the promotional pamphlet, *At a Yearly Meeting for Pennsylvania, New-Jersey, Delaware and the Eastern Parts of Maryland and Virginia held at Philadelphia in the Ninth and Tenth Months, 1795* [Philadel-

phia: Samuel Sansom, 1795], 4). Similarly, Quakers were alarmed on behalf of Senecas when David A. Ogden acquired the preemption rights to Seneca lands from the Holland Land Company in 1810: if the Senecas were dispossessed, "not only the large amount of money already expended for their improvement and the exertion of many individuals for fifteen years will be in great degree lost, but an experiment which if persevered in, presented so fair a prospect of ameliorating their condition and ultimately of attaching them by the ties of Interest, Gratitude and Religion to the Government of this Country, will be frustrated"; see Indian Committee to the Secretary of War, Philadelphia, December 19, 1811, LRNA M-271, roll 1. Of course, Quakers and Indians might differ in their strategies for preventing the alienation of land or on the long-term desirability of corporate ownership.

56. Jonathan Thomas to the Indian Committee, March 17, 1819, I.C. Records, box 3; copy of Joseph Elkinton letter, December 26, 1828, I.C. Minutes, 2:239. Note that Iroquois men traditionally did assist women in field clearing; see, for example, Arthur C. Parker, "Iroquois Uses of Maize and Other Food Plants," *New York State Museum Bulletin* 144 (1910), reprinted as book 1 in William N. Fenton, ed., *Parker on the Iroquois* (Syracuse, N.Y.: Syracuse University Press, 1968), 21. Thomas wrote in 1819 that opposition to allotment "is so strong that these debates rise into warm sentiments." Note that the New York Senecas ultimately evaded inclusion in the General Allotment Act of 1887; at the time they reported "agriculture flourishes, the houses and farms of the Indians are constantly improving, the people are contented and prosperous, and there are no paupers to be a burden on the community"—all this based on a property system in which "lands are owned in common, controlled by national councils, and are permanently inalienable"; quoted in Banner, *How the Indians Lost Their Land*, 265.

CHAPTER 5. FROM LONGHOUSE TO FARMHOUSE

1. This and the following paragraph are informed by a wealth of historical literature. Among the most important contributions are Michael Merrill, "Cash Is Good to Eat: Self-Sufficency and Exchange in the Rural Economy of the United States," *Radical History Review* 3 (Fall 1976): 42–71; James A. Henretta, "Families and Farms": *Mentalité* in Pre-Industrial America," *William and Mary Quarterly*, 3d ser., 35.1 (January 1978): 3–32; Christopher Clark, "Household Economy, Market Exchange, and the Rise of Capitalism in the Connecticut Valley, 1800–1860," *Journal of Social History* 13 (Winter 1979): 169–89 and Clark, *The Roots of Rural Capitalism: Western Massachusetts, 1780–1860* (Ithaca, N.Y.: Cornell University Press, 1990). And see Charles Sellers, *The Market Revolution: Jacksonian America, 1815–1846* (New York: Oxford University Press, 1991). Winifred B. Rothenberg's work challenged these historians, arguing that farmers were capitalists from the start, or at least much sooner than earlier imagined; see *From Market-Places to a Market Economy: The Transformation of Rural Massachusetts, 1750–1850* (Chicago: University of Chicago Press, 1992). Useful overviews of the debate are provided by Allan Kulikoff, "The Transformation to Capitalism in Rural America," *William and Mary Quarterly*, 3d ser., 46.1

(January 1989): 120–44; Michael Merrill, "Putting 'Capitalism' in Its Place: A Review of Recent Literature," *William and Mary Quarterly*, 3d ser., 52.2 (April 1995): 315–26; Naomi R. Lamoreaux, "Rethinking the Transition to Capitalism" in the Early American Northeast," *Journal of American History* 90.2 (September 2003): 437–61; Christopher Clark, "The View from the Farmhouse: Rural Lives in the Early Republic," *Journal of the Early Republic* 24 (Summer 2004): 198–207; Janet A. Reisman, "Republican Revisions: Political Economy in New York after the Panic of 1819," in William Pencak and Conrad Edick Wright, eds., *New York and the Rise of American Capitalism: Economic Development and the Social and Political History of an American State, 1780–1870* (New York: New-York Historical Society, 1989), 1–44.

2. White pioneers played a complex role—a role more complicated than American myth acknowledges—as heroes and villains, victims and victimizers, and the various positions in between. The challenges of assessing such folk is even more thorny if the category "pioneer" is not marked as male, but instead includes women and children, who possessed less agency than white men. At the forefront of expansion, pioneers exploited the opportunities provided by "free" land and sometimes the labor of slaves and other unfree people, yet they themselves could be exploited by landlords and speculators and bear the brunt of Indian frontier violence. Sympathetic figures as victims, they are much less sympathetic as avatars of colonialism and borderland violence. Nuanced treatment of "pioneers" is rare, but see Patrick Griffin, *American Leviathan: Empire, Nation, and Revolutionary Frontier* (New York: Hill and Wang, 2007).

3. Peter C. Mancall, *Valley of Opportunity: Economic Culture along the Upper Susquehanna, 1700–1800* (Ithaca, N.Y.: Cornell University Press, 1991), 235. And see Alan Taylor, *William Cooper's Town: Power and Persuasion on the Frontier of the Early American Republic* (New York: Knopf, 1995).

4. Mancall, *Valley of Opportunity*, 238. The white settlement and development of the far western New York region is expertly analyzed in Charles E. Brooks, *Frontier Settlement and Market Revolution: The Holland Land Purchase* (Ithaca, N.Y.: Cornell University Press, 1996). On the successors to the preemption rights controlled by the Holland Land Company—David A. Ogden, his brother, and associates—who became the chief land speculators and opponents of the Senecas after 1810, see Mary H. Conable, "A Steady Enemy: The Ogden Land Company and the Seneca Indians" (Ph.D. diss., University of Rochester, 1994).

5. Note that some Senecas did suffer removal—those who had moved into Ohio in the eighteenth century subsequently agreed to treaties in 1831 (following Andrew Jackson's Removal Bill of 1830) to relocate west of the Mississippi, in "Indian Territory." In their exodus, the group of Senecas and other Native people experienced hardships typical of removal generally, including a dramatic death rate (25–30 percent). Other Senecas and Cayugas moved from New York to a reservation in Kansas between 1846 and 1852, following a disastrous 1838 treaty (most of the Seneca survivors of this relocation eventually returned to New York). See William C. Sturtevant, "Oklahoma Seneca-Cayuga," in William C. Sturtevant, gen. ed., *Handbook of North American Indians*, 20 vols. projected

(Washington, D.C.: Smithsonian Institution, 1978–) (hereafter *HBNAI*), vol. 15, *Northeast* (1978), ed. Bruce G. Trigger, 537–43. On efforts to remove the New York Senecas in conjunction with the devastating Treaty of 1838 (and successful Seneca resistance to removal), see Conable, "A Steady Enemy," esp. 96–111, 135–38, 139–65, 249–82.

6. Clark, *Roots of Rural Capitalism*, 12, 84; quotation at 24. Brooks, *Frontier Settlement and Market Revolution*, makes a similar point in the context of his study of the white settlement and transformation of western New York in the early nineteenth century, analyzing the territories that abutted or encompassed Seneca settlements in this era. Brooks's fine study, however, does not consider the Senecas' ongoing presence.

7. For analysis of a similar well-intentioned myopia among Quaker missionaries, see Daniel Richter, " 'Believing That Many of the Red People Suffer Much for the Want of Food': Hunting, Agriculture, and a Quaker Construction of Indianness in the Early Republic," *Journal of the Early Republic* 19.4 (Winter 1999): 601–28.

8. On capitalist development in Pennsylvania and its environs, see, for example, Thomas M. Doerflinger, "Rural Capitalism in Iron Country: Staffing a Forest Factory, 1808–1815," *William and Mary Quarterly*, 3d ser., 59.1 (January 2002): 3–38; and see Donna J. Rilling, "Sylvan Enterprise and the Philadelphia Hinterland, 1790–1860," *Pennsylvania History* 67.2 (Spring 2000): 194–217.

9. Robert W. Doherty, *The Hicksite Separation: A Sociological Analysis of Religious Schism in Early Nineteenth-Century America* (New Brunswick, N.J.: Rutgers University Press, 1967), 22, 24, 48–49, 62, 67–68; Hicks quoted at 28. For Sydney V. James, *A People Among Peoples: Quaker Benevolence in Eighteenth-Century America* (Cambridge, Mass.: Harvard University Press, 1963), 271–72, the "leading trait" among American Friends at the turn of the nineteenth century was an "increased devotion to simplicity"; the ideal— and a point of contention—was the shunning of great wealth and power in favor of a simpler life available to common, hardworking men.

10. Bruce Dorsey, "Friends Becoming Enemies: Philadelphia Benevolence and the Neglected Area of American Quaker History," *Journal of the Early Republic* 18.3 (Fall 1998): 395–428; see esp. 402, 414–15. Hicksites came to dominate the Seneca mission later in the nineteenth century.

11. Ibid., 416, 404.

12. *At a Yearly Meeting for Pennsylvania, New-Jersey, Delaware and the Eastern Parts of Maryland and Virginia held at Philadelphia in the Ninth and Tenth Months, 1795* (Philadelphia: Samuel Sansom, 1795), quotations at 5 and 6.

13. Horatio Hale, *Iroquois Book of Rites* (Philadelphia: D. G. Brinton, 1883). On condolence in Iroquois history and culture, see Matthew Dennis, *Cultivating a Landscape of Peace: Iroquois-European Encounters in Seventeenth-Century America* (Ithaca, N.Y.: Cornell University Press, 1993), esp. 79–84.

14. Hale, *Iroquois Book of Rites*, 80–81, 164–65.

15. See Richter, "Believing That Many of the Red People Suffer," esp. 624–25, for provocative and instructive analysis of Baltimore Quakers and their skewed understanding of Indians and their discourse in the Old Northwest, which occurred at the same time as

the Philadelphia Quakers' work with the Senecas. For useful comparative analysis among other Native people and white interlocutors, see Elizabeth Vibert, *Traders' Tales: Narratives of Cultural Encounters in the Columbian Plateau, 1807–1846* (Norman: University of Oklahoma Press, 1997), esp. 144–58, 163–204; Mary Black-Rogers, "Varieties of 'Starving': Semantics and Survival in the Subarctic Fur Trade, 1750–1850," *Ethnohistory* 33 (Fall 1986): 353–83; Bruce White, "'Give Us a Little Milk': The Social and Cultural Meaning of Gift-Giving in the Lake Superior Fur Trade," *Minnesota History* 48 (Summer 1982): 60–71. On reciprocity and gift giving among unequal parties, see Peter Hulme, *Colonial Encounters: Europe and the Native Caribbean, 1492–1797* (London: Routledge, 1986), esp. 147–48, which draws on the still instructive, classic work of Marcel Mauss, *The Gift: Forms and Functions of Exchange in Archaic Societies*, trans. Ian Cunnison (London: Cohen and West, 1970).

16. This is not to say that Senecas did not suffer distress, especially in the immediately aftermath of the Revolution, but that Seneca diplomatic speech as well as the shock of intercultural encounters could lead white reformers, officials, and missionaries (and subsequent historians) to misunderstand or overstate the misery of the "poor Indian." The familiar construction in Western, Christian discourse of the poor Indian—in Alexander Pope's famous lines (*Essay on Man* [1733–34]), "Lo! The poor Indian, whose untutor'd mind / Sees God in clouds, or hears him in the wind"—expressed a variety of feelings and assumptions (condescension, nobility, and pity) as well as demands for philanthropic action; see Laura M. Stevens, *The Poor Indian: British Missionaries, Native Americans, and Colonial Sensibility* (Philadelphia: University of Pennsylvania Press, 2004), esp. 18–21. On Seneca rhetoric, see Matthew Dennis, "Red Jacket's Rhetoric: Postcolonial Persuasions on the Native Frontiers of the Early American Republic," in Ernest Stronmberg, ed., *American Indian Rhetorics of Survivance: Word Medicine, Word Magic* (Pittsburgh: University of Pittsburgh Press, 2006), 15–33. For another example of this white discourse of Indian poverty and hunger, to which Indians adapted, see the speech of Governor William Hull at a council (which included visiting members of the Six Nations) at Brownston, Michigan Territory, September 26, 1810, Erastus Granger Papers, Penfield Library, State University of New York at Oswego: "We need not tell you how often you are disappointed in the chase and the hunger and malnourishment as consequences of it. Cultivate and you never will be disappointed. You will be pleased to receive the fruits of your labor." Digitized version available at http://www.oswego.edu/library2/archives/digitized_collections/granger2/sept2 61810.htm

17. *At a Yearly Meeting . . . 1795*, 6; *The Journal of Major John Norton, 1816*, ed. Carl F. Klinck and James J. Talman (Toronto: Champlain Society, 1970), 9; substance of interaction at conference between Quakers and Senecas at Cold Spring Settlement, September 25, 1809, in Francis Jennings, ed., *Iroquois Indians: A Documentary History of the Diplomacy of the Six Nations and their League* (hereafter *DHSN*), 50 microfilm reels (Woodbridge, Conn.: Research Publications, 1985), reel 45.

18. Richter makes a compelling, similar case for Baltimore Quakers and their relationship with Native people in the Old Northwest in "Believing That Many of the Red

People Suffer Much." Also instructive is the work of Diane Brodatz Rothenberg, "Friends Like These: An Ethnohistorical Analysis of the Interaction between Allegany Senecas and Quakers, 1798–1823" (Ph.D. diss., Department of Anthropology, City University of New York, 1976).

19. An example of the commonly held sense of human progress—which placed white Americans among the civilized and Indians further back in a stage of barbarism—was expressed by two Quaker missionaries to Senecas at Cattaraugus in June 1807; in this case, though, they hopefully placed Senecas on the same path to civilization: "Brothers, We know your customs are different from ours, and we don't expect you can leave them off at once, and learn the good ways of the white people—our forefathers once lived much like the Indians by hunting and clothed themselves with the skins of wild beasts. But as they became enlightened they gradually left of [off] the old Customs which they found was not so good, and took to Cultivating the Land, and by industry and steady attention the[y] soon learned many other usefull things, which now makes them live more comfortable. We want our Indian friends should also learn those good ways of living which would make their lives more comfortable and happy"; see Jacob Taylor and Joel Swain [Swayne] to Indian Committee, Cattaraugus, June 20, 1807, in Maris B. Pierce Papers, box 2, folder 4, Buffalo and Erie County Historical Society (BECHS), Buffalo, N.Y.

20. Brooks, *Frontier Settlement and Market Revolution*, 3; Robert Gallman, "The Agricultural Sector and the Pace of Economic Growth: U.S. Experience in the Nineteenth Century," in David C. Klingaman and Richard K. Vedder, eds., *Essays in Nineteenth Century Economic History: The Old Northwest* (Athens: Ohio University Press, 1975), 56.

21. On the work ethic, see Daniel T. Rogers, *The Work Ethic in Industrial America, 1815–1920* (Chicago: University of Chicago Press, 1978). And see Herbert G. Gutman, *Work, Culture, and Society in Industrializing America: Essays in American Working-Class History* (New York: Knopf, 1976), esp. 1–78. On the changing, early nineteenth-century world of work, leisure, and spectacle, see Paul E. Johnson, *Sam Patch, the Famous Jumper* (New York: Hill and Wang, 2003).

22. Quakers did express concern about a colonial corollary to Malthusian analysis: that is, a finite (or even diminishing) population facing a shrinking land base, eroded through colonial dispossession.

23. Brooks, *Frontier Settlement and Market Revolution*, 13, 19, 22–23, Ellicott quoted at 22. In a sense Ellicott and his Holland Land Company colleagues did make the Senecas disappear, at least from their concerns. In 1798, working as a surveyor for the company, Ellicott wrote his superiors, "In respect to the Allegheny reservation I have given direction to lay out the towns in that quarter without paying any attention to it for the present." He lamented Quaker "interference in this business," who in protecting their interests proved "very detrimental to the proprietors of the land adjoining this ridiculous reservation" (*Reports of Joseph Ellicott as Chief of Survey [1797–1800] and as Agent [1800–1821] of the Holland Land Company's Purchase of Western New York*," ed. R. W. Bingham, 2 vols. [Buffalo, N.Y.: Buffalo Historical Society, 1937–41], 1:37). In 1810, the Holland Land Company sold its right to purchase Seneca reservations to David A. Ogden, who formed

the Ogden Land Company with other investors. Thereafter, Senecas would deal with the Ogden Land Company, which was committed to Seneca dispossession, resorting even to corruption and fraud, as in the 1838 negotiations that (temporarily) liquidated all the remaining Seneca reservations; see especially Conable, "A Steady Enemy"; and see Abler and Tooker, "Seneca," in *HBNAI*, 15:511.

24. Brooks, *Frontier Settlement and Market Revolution*, 28–29.

25. Ibid., 32–36; Porter quoted at 28. Porter's career is detailed in Laurence M. Hauptman, *Conspiracy of Interests: Iroquois Dispossession and the Rise of New York State* (Syracuse, N.Y.: Syracuse University Press, 1999), 121–43; Hauptman called Porter "the Bashaw of the Border," who, despite his claims to be a friend of the Indian, was in fact one of the greatest promoters of their dispossession in the interest of western New York's economic development.

26. Brooks, *Frontier Settlement and Market Revolution*, 39, 41–45. On the transition to industrial capitalism, see especially E. P. Thompson's classic essay "Time, Work-Discipline, and Industrial Capitalism," *Past and Present* 38 (1967): 56–97; Gutman, *Work, Culture, and Society in Industrializing America*.

27. Brooks, *Frontier Settlement and Market Revolution*, 57.

28. It was important as well to Senecas that the Quaker mission operated as a non-profit enterprise. Quaker economic disinterestedness was essential to their credibility. In the summer of 1806, for example, Henry Abeal (the chief Cornplanter's son) queried a visiting delegation of Friends about the financial arrangements of their assistance program: "The Indians have understood there was a large sum of Money raisd by the Quakers to assist them, & they want to know how this money was laid out." The Friends satisfied their Seneca audience with the following reply: "now they might see how a great deal of money had been expended, & we still wish'd to keep a little in Bank to assist them more, but that none of the money rais'd for the benefit of the Indians would ever be applied to any other purpose." George S. Snyderman, ed., "Halliday Jackson's Journal . . . of a Visit Paid to the Indians of New York (1806)," *Proceedings of the American Philosophical Society* 101.6 (December 1957): 565–88 (hereafter cited as Halliday Jackson's Journal [1806]), 581.

29. See, for example, the visiting Quaker delegations' congratulations offered to the chiefs at Cattaraugus, September 15, 1814 for such "improvements," Maris B. Pierce Papers, box 2, folder 4, BECHS; see also Henry Drinker et al. to Secretary of War Henry Dearborn, Philadelphia, December 31, 1801, and abstract of journal of Friends, September 18, 1801, in Letters Received by the Office of the Secretary of War Relating to Indian Affairs, microfilm series M-271, 1800–1823, 4 rolls, National Archives, Washington, D.C. (hereafter LRNA M-271), roll 1, 1800–1816.

30. Snyderman, "Halliday Jackson's Journal . . . (1806)," 581, 572–73.

31. Ibid., 587–88. For an assessment of the Allegany reservation lands, their remoteness, and their value, see Joseph Ellicott to Morris I. Miller, Batavia, June 7, 1819, included among documents sent by Miller to John C. Calhoun, secretary of war, Utica, July 25, 1819, regarding negotiations with the Senecas to acquire their land and effect their concentration or removal, LRNA M-271.

32. Snyderman, "Halliday Jackson's Journal . . . (1806)," 587–88; Merle H. Deard-orff and George S. Snyderman, eds., "A Nineteenth-Century Journal of a Visit to the Indians of New York" [by John Philips, 1806], *Proceedings of the American Philosophical Society* 100.6 (December 1956): 582–612, quotation at 612; Ellicott to Morris, June 7, 1819, LRNA M-271.

33. John Wrenshall, "The Journal of John Wrenshall," 1816 (Pittsburgh Historical Society of Western Pennsylvania), quoted in Diane Rothenberg, "The Mothers of the Nation: Seneca Resistance to Quaker Intervention," in Mona Etienne and Eleanor Lea-cock, eds., *Women and Colonization: Anthropological Perspectives* (New York: Praeger, 1980), 71. Rev. Jacob Cram, "Summary Report of Mr. Cram's Late Mission," *Massachusetts Missionary Magazine* 3.10 (March 1806): 393. On rafting and its economic importance and environmental impact, see Michael Williams, *Americans and Their Forests: A Historical Geography* (Cambridge: Cambridge University Press, 1989), esp. 96–100. Around Buffalo Creek, at least, Senecas also gathered bark and sold it to Buffalo tanneries, the city's first industry to expand beyond local markets; see Conable, "A Steady Enemy," 16, 33.

34. Halliday Jackson's journal, 1810 (emphasis in original), quoted in Rothenberg, "Mothers of the Nation," 83n. On the illicit sale of liquor to local whites by enterprising Senecas, see Snyderman, "Halliday Jackson's Journal . . . (1806)," 573 (quotation, emphasis added); later, the Quakers formally advised the Senecas: "we desire that you will not buy *or sell it* [whiskey] any more for fear of offending the Great Spirit" (577, emphasis added).

35. Reply to Speech of Conidiu (Handsome Lake) on behalf of the Senecas, Jacob Taylor and Joel Swaine [Swayne], August 30, 1803, in The Philadelphia Yearly Meeting Indian Committee Records, Quaker Collection, Special Collections, Haverford College, Haverford, Pennsylvania (hereafter cited as I.C. Records), box 2.

36. Report on visit to Senecas, October 16, 1817, I.C. Records, box 3. Note that Quakers also expressed a conservationist concern, warning, "if you go on destroying it [timber resources] for a few years more at the rate you now are, you will have little of it left for yourselves or your children." Panel door and glass windows reported in Snyder-man, "Halliday Jackson's Journal . . . (1806)," 582.

37. Halliday Jackson, *Civilization of the Indian Natives; or, a Brief View of the Friendly Conduct of William Penn toward Them in the Early Settlement of Pennsylvania . . . and a Concise Narrative of the Proceedings of the Yearly Meeting of Friends, of Pennsylvania . . . since 1795, in Promoting Their Improvement and Gradual Civilization* (Philadelphia: Isaac T. Hopper, 1830), 50–51.

38. Addenda report to the Indian Committee, December 17, 1805 (appended February 22, 1807), I.C. Records, box 2; Friends to Indian Committee, February 14, 1807 (posted April 7, 1807), I.C. Records, box 2.

39. Friends to the Indian Committee, October 28, 1808, March 21, 1810, and February 12, 1811, I.C. Records, box 2.

40. Ibid., October 28, 1808.

41. The normal season for spinning and weaving among rural white women was December to May; see Mary Beth Norton, *Liberty's Daughters: The Revolutionary Experience of American Women, 1750–1800* (Boston: Little, Brown, 1980), 17.

42. On Iroquois women's farming and the rituals surrounding it, see Arthur C. Parker, "The Iroquois Use of Maize and Other Food Plants," New York State Museum Bulletin 144 (1910), reprinted as book 1 in William N. Fenton, ed., *Parker on the Iroquois* (Syracuse, N.Y.: Syracuse University Press, 1968), esp. 21–39; see also Elisabeth Tooker, "Women in Iroquois Society," in Michael K. Foster, Jack Campisi, and Marianne Mithun, eds., *Extending the Rafters: Interdisciplinary Approaches to Iroquoian Studies* (Albany: State University of New York Press, 1984), 109–23, esp. 116–17, 121; and see Rothenberg's perceptive analysis in "Mothers of the Nation," esp. 79–80.

43. Tooker, "Women in Iroquois Society," 116, 121. Of course, eventually Seneca and other Iroquois men did successfully reconcile agricultural work with an evolving Iroquois culture; Parker wrote in 1910, "The Iroquois man gradually became the man with the hoe and thought it no disgrace. This was hardly the case, however, a century ago" ("Iroquois Uses of Maize," 24).

44. Friends to Indian Committee, March 17, 1819, I.C. Records, box 3. One Philadelphia Quaker wrote his father in London regarding Seneca agricultural practice: "the little corn they raised was planted in one common field or clearing, & . . . this was done by the females of the Village, it has been an object with friends to endeavour to persuade them to disperse themselves & cultivate separate Lots"; see Samuel Emlen to William Dillwyn, Westhill (Philadelphia), May 8, 1811, Library Company of Philadelphia manuscript, in *DHSN*, reel 45.

45. Friends to Indian Committee, March 17, 1819, I.C. Records, box 3; Parker, "Iroquois Uses of Maize," 27–33; on historical Iroquois agricultural landscapes and their sustainability, see also Dennis, *Cultivating a Landscape of Peace*, 27–32.

46. Friends to Indian Committee, I.C. Records, box 2, February 12, 1811; Rothenberg, "Mothers of the Nation," 77. Note that male help in field preparation was not an innovation; it was a traditional male activity. See Parker, "Iroquois Uses of Maize," 21; Tooker, "Women in Iroquois Society," 115.

47. Friends to Indian Committee, November 2, 1805, I.C. Records, box 2; Amos Lee, John Brown, Thomas Stewardson, William Allinson to the Seneca Nation of Indians at Cattaraugus, November 29, 1809, Maris B. Pierce Papers, box 2, folder 4, BECHS; Friends to Indian Committee, I.C. Records, October 16, 1817, box 3; and see Rothenberg, "Mothers of the Nation," 77–78. In 1806, Halliday Jackson observed firsthand: "They have a good stock of Cattle and abundance of Swine—They have several horses among them, but the greater part of their farming and Drawing of logs &c. is done with Oxen." Snyderman, "Halliday Jackson's Journal . . . (1806)," 582. Livestock as a source of Indianwhite conflict, and as a focus of white criticism of Native economic practices, extends from the seventeenth to the twentieth century. See Virginia D. Anderson, "King Philip's Herds: Indians, Colonists, and the Problem of Livestock in Early New England," *William and Mary Quarterly*, 3d ser., 51 (1994): 601–24; and Richard White, *The Roots of Dependency: Subsistence, Environment, and Social Change among the Choctaws, Pawnees, and Navajos* (Lincoln: University of Nebraska Press, 1983).

48. See Dennis, *Cultivating a Landscape of Peace*, 109. Women's production of moc-

casins was critical—practically and symbolically—in enabling (or preventing) Seneca and other Iroquois men to go to war. Here, women's production of moccasins enabled men's commerce rather than warfare or diplomacy.

49. Speech of Friends "To Cornplanter, and all our Indian brothers of the Seneca Nation, now living on the Allegany River," May 22, 1798, I.C. Records, box 1. As noted above, incentive offers such as these continued, with similar prescriptions. See, for example, Jacob Taylor, Stephen Twining, and Hannah Jackson to the Committee, from Cattaraugus, February 22, 1812, I.C. Records, box 2.

50. Snyderman, "Halliday Jackson's Journal . . . (1806)," 576. In an accounting of Seneca livestock in 1819, the Quaker Jonathan Thomas wrote, "Sheep none (too many dogs & wolves)." He noted, "Women Spiners about 40 or 50 but little flax & not much spining done. several now have flax laying long undressed . . . there is frequent enquiries for seed, none to be had much nearer than Pittsburgh perhaps if to be sold there would excate [?] to sow"; Thomas to the Indian Committee, Tunesassa, March 1819, I.C. Records, box 3.

51. Norton, *Liberty's Daughters*, 15–20; Snyderman, "Halliday Jackson's Journal . . . (1806)," 576; report to the Indian Committee, September 20, 1811, I.C. Records, box 2. In 1809, the Quaker missionaries told Seneca men, "If many of you were to do more work on your Farms than you now do and were to encourage your Wives and Daughters to learn how to Spin Flax, wool &c, and two or three of them how to Weave; we believe you would find great advantage from it." They promised, "For one year from this time Jonathan Thomas is willing to Weave all the yarn that your Women Spin and no charge will be made for the Weaving, . . . if two or three of your women will learn to weave in that time—for you know it is our practice to put you in the way of doing your own work and not to do it for you—if none of your women learn to weave whilst Jonathan is here, his being among you will not be of that advantage we could wish"; see "Speech to Senecas settled on and near the Allegheny River," substance of interaction at conference between Friends and Senecas at Cold Spring Settlement, September 25, 1809, in *DHSN*, reel 45.

52. Norton, *Liberty's Daughters*, 15–18, quotations at 16–17, 18.

53. For exploration of these themes among other early national middle-class women, see Christine Stansell, *City of Women: Sex and Class in New York, 1789–1860* (New York: Knopf, 1986); Mary Ryan, *Cradle of the Middle Class: The Family in Oneida County, New York, 1790–1865* (New York: Cambridge University Press, 1981).

54. Margaret Morris Haviland, "Beyond Women's Sphere: Young Quaker Women and the Veil of Charity in Philadelphia, 1790–1810," *William and Mary Quarterly*, 3d ser., 51.3 (July 1994): 419–46, esp. 423–28.

55. Ibid., 429.

56. Ibid., 432–33.

57. Ibid., 433; Rothenberg, "Mothers of the Nation," 78–79. In contrast to Philadelphia's House of Industry, Seneca women and girls provided their own meals and child care. Silverheels quoted in Deardorff and Snyderman, "A Nineteenth-Century Journal," 604.

58. Clark, *Roots of Rural Capitalism*, 96, 132, 141–42. Men more than women would have been culturally more likely to adopt sheepherding among the Senecas, but sheep presented particular liabilities—they required intensive protection against wolves and poachers, for example, and were environmentally destructive in ways that swine, cattle, and horse were not.

59. It is not as if Senecas themselves were unconflicted about the capitalist transformations of the country. Unlike some of his white revivalist contemporaries, Handsome Lake never offered an explicit critique of capitalism, but he rejected some of its chief rewards—excessive and destructive consumption, particularly of liquor—and he favored subsistence rather than market production, cooperation and sharing rather than individual accumulation and enrichment. According to Halliday Jackson, Handsome Lake had advised "that they might farm a little bit . . . but must not sell anything they raised on their land, but give it away one to another, and especially to their old people; and, in short, enjoy all things in common." Some Friends might have endorsed the prophet's commitment to simplicity and his rather modest economic goals, but others in the Philadelphia Yearly Meeting had made fortunes through modern business enterprise and leaned toward further integration into (not detachment from) the new commercial capitalist world around them. See Jackson, *Civilization of the Indian Natives*, 43; Jonathan Thomas to Thomas Wistar, April 21, 1804, I.C. Records, box 2. On the contrasting economic styles among the Friends involved in the Indian mission, see Chapter 4. Compare, for example, the simple farmer and future Hicksite Halliday Jackson, on the one hand, and, on the other hand, the future Orthodox Quakers Thomas Wistar and Thomas Stewardson, the latter a rich and successful capitalist who owned some $61,000 worth of commercial paper, including interests in the Bank of North America, the Bank of Pennsylvania, the Schuylkill Navigation Company, the Newmarket Manufacturing Company, and the Chesapeake and Delaware Canal Company. See Doherty, *The Hicksite Separation*, 67–68.

CHAPTER 6. SENECA REPOSSESSED

1. Fox to Fothergill, August 1, 1819, included in Elizabeth Fothergill, "Account of Seven American Indians of the Seneca Nation Who Visited York during Three Weeks in the Month of May, 1818," 145–46, New-York Historical Society, New York, N.Y. This manuscript book was compiled by Fothergill from her journal, ca. 1835 or 1836.

2. Stuart Banner, *How the Indians Lost Their Land: Law and Power on the Frontier* (Cambridge, Mass.: Harvard University Press, 2005), 123. Remaining unclear was the critical question of whether Indian land had technically been forfeited to the United States and granted back to Indian nations, or whether it was truly residual—that is, it had never been forfeited and remained fully under the ownership and sovereignty of its original Native proprietors. See also Robert F. Berkhofer, Jr.'s classic *The White Man's Indian: Images of the American Indian from Columbus to the Present* (New York: Knopf, 1978), 141–45.

3. Banner, *How the Indians Lost Their Land*, 135–36, quotation at 163. The earliest

court opinions adopting this new view of Indian property rights—that the government, not the tribes, was fee simple owner of unsold Indian land—emerged in state courts in the first decade of the nineteenth century (168–70). In New York, the principle that Indians were not—and never had been—owners of their unsold land was established in *Van Gordon v. Jackson* (1809).

4. See Joseph Ellicott to Jacob Taylor, the Quaker missionary, May 29, 1809, The Philadelphia Yearly Meeting Indian Committee Records, Quaker Collection, Special Collections, Haverford College, Haverford, Pennsylvania (hereafter cited as I.C. Records), box 3. The best study of the Ogden Land Company is Mary H. Conable, "A Steady Enemy: The Ogden Land Company and the Seneca Indians" (Ph.D. diss., University of Rochester, 1994); on Ogden's acquisition of preemption rights and the formation of the Ogden Land Company, see 53–54. And see Laurence M. Hauptman, *Conspiracy of Interests: Iroquois Dispossession and the Rise of New York State* (Syracuse, N.Y.: Syracuse University Press, 1999), 147; Diane Brodatz Rothenberg, "Friends Like These: An Ethnohistorical Analysis of the Interaction between Allegany Senecas and Quakers, 1798–1823" (Ph.D. diss., City University of New York, 1976), 217–55.

5. Conable, "A Steady Enemy," 56–76.

6. Ibid.; Hauptman, *Conspiracy of Interests*, 163–64, 147; Rothenberg, "Friends Like These," 231.

7. Indian Committee to Jacob Taylor, Philadelphia, November 12, 1816, I.C. Records, box 3. The Quakers consulted Timothy Pickering, Revolutionary War general, former U.S. secretary of state, U.S. senator, and negotiator of the 1794 Treaty of Canandaigua, who encouraged them to advocate an allotment plan for the Senecas—a well-intentioned proposal, with some safeguards for the Senecas, but one that the Senecas wisely resisted. See Timothy Pickering to Thomas Stewardson and Thomas Wistar, February 8, 1817, I.C. Records, box 3. Halliday Jackson, *Civilization of the Indian Natives; or, a Brief View of the Friendly Conduct of William Penn toward Them in the Early Settlement of Pennsylvania . . . and a Concise Narrative of the Proceedings of the Yearly Meeting of Friends, of Pennsylvania . . . since 1795, in Promoting Their Improvement and Gradual Civilization* (Philadelphia: Isaac T. Hopper, 1830), 67.

8. On the course of allotment in American history, see Banner, *How the Indians Lost Their Land*, 257–90. For a fine case study of the devastating process in another context, see Emily Greenwald, *Reconfiguring the Reservation: The Nez Perces, Jicarilla Apaches, and the Dawes Act* (Albuquerque: University of New Mexico Press, 2002).

9. See Jacob Taylor to the Indian Committee, November 15, 1816, and 1818 Indian Committee Report, I.C. Minutes, vol. 2; report from Cattaraugus Council in October 1817, I.C. Records, box 3; Jackson, *Civilization of the Indian Natives*, 68–72; Rothenberg, "Friends Like These," 243; Jonathan Thomas at Tunesassah to the Committee, August 24, 1818, I.C. Records, box 3.

10. Copy of letter read and delivered to the Six Nations of Indians in Council at Buffalo by Jasper Parrish, subagent, September 19, 1818, in I.C. Records, box 3. On Parrish and Seneca protests against his performance as subagent, see Hauptman, *Conspiracy of*

Interests, 137–38, 152; "Petition to Secretary Calhoun for a New Agent," February 5, 1820, and "Petition to Remove Jasper Parrish and Jones, and Refusal to Move to Green Bay," May 3, 1823, in Granville Ganter, ed., *The Collected Speeches of Sagoyewatha, or Red Jacket* (Syracuse, N.Y.: Syracuse University Press, 2006), 222–24, and 233–38. See also "The Story of Jasper Parrish," in *Publications of the Buffalo Historical Society* (hereafter *PBHS*), 6 (1903): 527–38. Parrish was finally let go by Justus Ingersoll, the new superintendent for New York; he explained to Commissioner of Indian Affairs Thomas McKenney, "Mr Parrish is not my choice. My objections are various. One is the charge proffered against him & with strong probability of truth, that he accepted money from the purchasers of Indian Land, under circumstances . . . irreconcilable with official integrity"; Ingersoll to McKenney, Medina, New York, September 9, 1829, in Letters Received by the Office of Indian Affairs, microfilm series M-234, 1824–80, 962 rolls, National Archives, Washington, D.C. (hereafter LRNA M-234), roll 832, Six Nations Agency, 1824–34.

11. James Monroe to the Seneca Indians living on the Allegany reservation, January 15, 1819, in I.C. Records, box 3; Rothenberg, "Friends Like These," 244–46. James Robinson, a Christian Seneca chief at Allegany, later acknowledged that "his party were afraid to oppose the views of the President," to whom "they looked for safety respecting the holding of their lands." Robinson and other Senecas worried, "if they should be driven off from their present possessions and sent to the westward the Indians that were there were very warlike and no doubt many of them would lose their lives if they went there." See letter from Tunesassah, September 16, 1821, Philadelphia Yearly Meeting Indian Committee Minutes, Quaker Collection, Special Collections, Haverford College, Haverford, Pa., 10 vols. (hereafter I.C. Minutes), vol. 2.

12. Jonathan Thomas to the Committee, August 24, 1818, and In Assembly [New York], March 4, 1819, Resolution on Indian Affairs, in I.C. Records, box 3. See "Resolution of the New York State Senate to concur with the United States in encouraging the Indians within New York to concentrate themselves in suitable locations so as to secure their protection, obtain instruction in piety, and agriculture, and gradually to extend to them the benefits of civilization," and report of the committee of the New York legislature, about Indian lands, presented in Assembly, March 4, 1819, in Legislative Assembly Papers, 41:149 and 143–48, New York State Archives (hereafter NYSA), Albany, N.Y.

13. Ogden, "Memorial of David A. Ogden to the President of the United States, regarding removal of Senecas," ca.1819, in Francis Jennings, ed., *Iroquois Indians: A Documentary History of the Diplomacy of the Six Nations and their League* (hereafter *DHSN*), 50 microfilm reels (Woodbridge, Conn.: Research Publications, 1985), reel 46. Among the ironies of the proposal is the implication that the Senecas would need to buy Ogden's preemption rights to their remaining land—essentially purchasing land they already owned and had never sold.

14. Ibid. This interpretation of Native ownership—that is, that the Senecas actually owned the land they retained in their reservations and possessed all the rights associated with such ownership—fundamentally threatened the economic interests of those holding the preemption rights in those lands, the Ogden Land Company. The 1794 Pickering

treaty seemed to contradict Ogden's allegedly superior claims, derived, he argued, from an earlier title conveyed to his company indirectly by Massachusetts. (Massachusetts had settled its colonial land claims with New York at a conference at Hartford in 1786, where Massachusetts secured preemption rights in western New York, while New York established its sovereignty over those lands.) As Ogden acknowledged, the treaty's third article held that the lands in question were "the Property of the Seneca Nation." It promised that the United States would not disturb the Senecas and would guarantee them "the free use & enjoyment thereof, but it shall remain theirs until they choose to sell the same to the People of the United States who have the right to purchase." On the Hartford conference, see Edward Countryman, "From Revolution to Statehood," in Milton Klein, ed., *The Empire State: A History of New York* (Ithaca, N.Y.: Cornell University Press, 2001), 262. On the Pickering treaty, see also G. Peter Jemison and Anna M. Schein, eds., *Treaty of Canandaigua 1794: Two Hundred Years of Treaty Relations between the Iroquois Confederacy and the United States* (Santa Fe, N.M.: Clear Light Publishers, 2000).

15. Ogden, "Memorial."

16. Ibid.

17. "Copy of Mr. Harrison's opinion" [April 1819], Indian Collection, BOO-2, box 1, folder 2, Government and business, land claims and treaties, Buffalo and Erie County Historical Society (BECHS), Buffalo, N.Y. Harrison largely endorsed David Ogden's claims, arguing for example that Seneca land sales to their Cayuga kinspeople were illegal and thus void. With regard to natural resource production, Harrison wrote, "The Indians can certainly cut timber for their own use; they can also cut it to clear the land for actual cultivation by themselves. In short, they have a right to the timber so far as such right is essential to the free use and enjoyment of the land. But where more destruction of timber takes place than is required for the use of the Indians and particularly where the destruction is for the purpose of sale, I am of [the] opinion that the Proprietors under Massachusetts /as the legal owners of the Land/ [that is, the Ogden Land Company] may bring actions . . . against the purchasers or restrain them by Injunction." Harrison also rejected the Senecas' right to lease their land to whites. Note the impact of the treaty process, which increasingly redefined Iroquois people, not only as members of individual tribes (e.g., Senecas), but as members of particular reservations and communities (e.g., Allegany vs. Buffalo Creek Senecas). Thus Cayugas, who could be real and fictive kinspeople of the Senecas (e.g., members of the same clans) were alienated by white authorities, defined as non-Senecas, and thus deemed unable legally to "own" Native lands within Seneca reserves.

U.S. Attorney General William Wirt similarly concluded that the Treaty of Canandaigua did not divest the legal titles of New York, Massachusetts, or grantees under them settled and established in the convention of 1786, "nor are the preexisting rights of the Indians in any manner enlarged by that treaty." "Copy of the Opinion of Wm. Wirt, Atty. General," March 26, 1819, LRNA M-271, roll 2, 1817–19. The legal historian Stuart Banner, *How the Indians Lost Their Land*, 183–85, has shown the fallacy in the legal reasoning—based on faulty historical analysis—of numerous jurists in the early republic. Wirt and others erroneously assigned proprietary rights to "the Christian Sovereigns of Europe" as they colonized America in order to reassign such sovereignty and ownership rights to their successors, the state and federal governments.

Going against this grain was a later opinion expressed by Robert Montgomery Livingston, appointed to investigate fraud in the treaty negotiations of 1826. Livingston objected, "It cannot be that the Company can say to the Indians 'when the right of preemption was granted your Hunter condition was a Guarrantee [*sic*] to the purchasers that you should always remain wandering & never till the ground or cut the timber (which until recently was as valueless except to cover the game—as the game is now & could not have entered into the estimate at the time of the Purchase).' " Unlike others, Livingston recognized Seneca social and economic transformation. "The Company seeks to restrict the Indians to their *aboriginal use* of the their acknowledged right of occupancy. I *assumed* the liberty of telling the Indians that they had the right of occupancy in perpetuity unrestricted as to the *mode* of occupying and that as they had left the Hunter State & adopted the Agricultural they had the right to fell their trees to make room for the plough—that it would be advancing their Interests so to do—that the trees cut with such intentions would be theirs." R. M. Livingston to Peter B. Porter, secretary of war, Buffalo, July 4, 1828, LRNA M-234, roll 832.

18. Ogden, "Memorial." Claiming concern about Seneca extinction, Ogden dismissed all previous attempts at civilizing them, especially those of religious societies, such as the Quakers, who in fact opposed Ogden and his associates as Seneca advocates. Ogden called for government intervention—a radical experiment in social transformation to be imposed on the Senecas. Such action would benefit the Indians, he claimed, and promote greater public good:

> To the State of New York, these Indians are becoming a heavy Incumbrance, retarding the progress of civilization & Improvement; and detracting from the public resources and prosperity. No Taxes are charged on the Reservation; neither do they bear any part of the Burden of Roads & other objects of local Improvement. These extensive Tracts being situated principally along the Western Frontier, the acquisition of a dense and hardy white Population, in that quarter, would appear moreover to be an object of immense Importance to the United States. When it is considered that the Seneca Nation comprises little more than 2000 Souls, and that they retain upward of 220,000 Acres of rich land capable of giving support in profuse abundance to 50,000 of our Citizens; and that not one Acre in an hundred is cultivated or improved; the Importance of throwing open at least a portion of these extensive forests to the hand of Industry and enterprise, must be too obvious to require illustration.

19. Ibid. Ogden's complaints about the devaluation of Seneca lands through timber exploitation and sales and leasing activity was echoed in the New York State Assembly's report of March 4, 1819:

The facts pretty conclusively show that they [the Senecas] are incapable of protecting themselves in consequence of being surrounded by the whites and who have usurped nearly all their possessions, and from thence pilfer every stick and stone which can be converted into money, highly injurious to the interests of the State; who frequently pilfer the personal effects of those unfortunate beings; that they are overreached by the aid of ardent spirits & and after illegally obtaining the possession of those lands refuse to yield the possession; & when prosecuted delay the trial, until either the wants of the owner, or legislative provisions compel them to abandon justice & their rights, that most those invaders are of the most abandoned cast, by their conduct disarming.

Legislative Assembly Papers, 41:143–48, NYSA. Ogden commented on this report and lobbied further for Seneca concentration and removal in D. A. Ogden to J. C. Calhoun, March 16, 1819, David Ogden Papers, Clements Library, University of Michigan, Ann Arbor, in *DHSN*, reel 46. For an example of later, repeated complaints of trespassing and timber theft, see "Petition to the legislature of New York, proposing a law to govern trespassing, keeping of tavern or grocery, or selling spirituous liquors, etc., on lands of the Senecas in New York," January 18, 1836, Ely S. Parker Papers, PA 19, Huntington Library, San Marino, Calif.

20. This "talk" of a Christian party of chiefs is enclosed with documents related to a removal proposal to Green Bay, in Jasper Parrish to Thomas McKenney, November 30, 1826, LRNA M-234, roll 832; see also the Seneca chief Pollard's communication of July 10, 1819, a document enclosed with Morris I. Miller to Secretary of War John C. Calhoun, Utica, N.Y., July 25, 1819, LRNA M-271, roll 2. On Seneca leasing and its threatening quality, see Conable, "A Steady Enemy," 112–13 (quotation), 117.

21. Red Jacket's reply to Ogden's proposal, in council, July 9, 1819, document accompanying Miller to Calhoun, July 25, 1819, LRNA M-271, roll 2.

22. David Ogden to Thomas Stewardson, and the Indian Committee, April 7, 1819, I.C. Records, box 3; letter from Friends at Cattaraugus, October 2, 1818, I.C. Minutes, vol. 2; Fox to Fothergill, August 1, 1819, in Fothergill, "Account of Seven American Indians," 146. Fox's description accurately reflects the Seneca resistance, reported also in Miller to Calhoun, July 25, 1819, LRNA M-271, roll 2.

23. The commission's report inquiring into Seneca resistance to Ogden and removal, with numerous accompanying documents, is contained in Miller to Calhoun, July 25, 1819, LRNA M-271, roll 2. The federal commissioner Morris Miller represented himself as a neutral party and honest broker, but he clearly supported the emerging federal program of concentration and removal. Red Jacket caused some controversy when he accused the president of being "disordered in mind" for advocating Seneca concentration at Allegany or their more distant removal. To Ogden, Red Jacket expressed mock sympathy for his purchase of the preemption rights, which he suggested were worthless. And he berated Ogden: "You said you would not disturb us. And I told you then, as long as I lived, you must not come forward to explain that right. You have come, and I am living." "Let us

hear no more of," Red Jacket declared. The Christian chief Pollard, who represented an opposing Seneca faction, objected to Red Jacket's disrespect, but he agreed, "We all thought it was not right to part with the land."

24. Quaker reports, March 29, 1819, and April 15, 1819, in I.C. Records, box 3.

25. See generally Frank H. Severance, "Narratives of Early Mission Work," in *PBHS* 6 (1903): 165–380; Anthony F. C. Wallace, *The Death and Rebirth of the Seneca* (New York: Knopf, 1970), 322–23, summarizes increased intrusion of evangelical missionaries in this period.

26. Rev. Timothy Alden, *An Account of Sundry Missions, Performed among the Senecas and the Munsees; in a Series of Letters* (New York: J. Seymour, 1827), 44, 50, 58. Seneca factionalism is sometimes described in terms of a "Christian" and a "Pagan" party, but several scholars have pointed out the imprecision or inaccuracy of such a division. Ironically, those aligned with Quakers—and not with competing missionaries—were sometimes lumped with the pagans.

27. Joseph Elkinton to Indian Committee, December 3, 1820, I.C. Records, box 3. Note that Alden and other evangelical missionaries did not necessarily favor Seneca dispossession, even if they did not act as diligently as Quakers to prevent it. Still, men such as Red Jacket remained suspicious. As Augustus Fox reported in a letter, "the chief of Indians Red-jacket, & some others . . . are averse to every thing connected with the missionaries, as he thinks their only object is to possess themselves of their lands" (Fox to Fothergill, August 1, 1819, in Fothergill, "Account of Seven American Indians," 149).

28. Elkinton to Indian Committee, December 3, 1820, I.C. Records, box 3.

29. Ibid.; Wallace, *Death and Rebirth of the Seneca*, 331. Alternatively, Elkinton might have meant to quote another scripture, the Gospel of Matthew: "Then said the king to the servants, Bind him hand and foot, and take him away, and cast him into outer darkness, there shall be weeping and gnashing of teeth" (Matthew 22:13). Who, in this case, had been cast out—the missionary or the proselytes? Or perhaps Elkinton was citing 2 Peter 2:12–17, on the depravity of false teachers and their followers:

> But these, like natural brute beasts made to be caught and destroyed, speak evil of the things they do not understand, and will utterly perish in their own corruption, and will receive the wages of unrighteousness, as those who count it pleasure to carouse in the daytime. They are spots and blemishes, carousing in their own deceptions while they feast with you. . . . They have forsaken the right way and gone astray, following the way of Balaam the son of Beor, who loved the wages of unrighteousness; but he was rebuked for his iniquity: a dumb donkey speaking with a man's voice restrained the madness of the prophet. These are wells without water, clouds carried by a tempest, for whom is reserved the blackness of darkness forever.

If so, was Handsome Lake this mad prophet, and his followers the unrighteous carousers, to be relegated to the infinite "blackness of darkness"?

30. In 1821, the New York State Assembly, asserting its jurisdiction over Indian reservations—as it would in legislation following Tommy Jemmy's case—passed an act "for

the more effectual prevention of encroachment upon the lands of the Senecas." The assembly hardly intended that the law would be applied to Christian missionaries, whose influence they saw as benign, and their missions grew apace, in technical violation of the law. But Red Jacket, with the cooperation of some "white pagans" in Buffalo, was able to force compliance and have the Presbyterian missionary Thomas S. Harris removed from Buffalo Creek in 1824. Though Red Jacket gamely defended the law and pushed its enforcement, Harris and his mission were back by 1825, and the legislation was later repealed. Red Jacket made an exception for Friends. According to his nineteenth-century biographer William Leete Stone, "Red-Jacket was much better disposed" toward the Quakers; indeed, "He made a most urgent appeal to them, at about the same time, for assistance, or for the exertion of their influence in keeping the missionaries at a distance." They could not do so, but their presence over two decades had offered insulation critical to Seneca reconstruction and a renewed self-possession. See "Petition to Legislature to Keep Missionaries Off Indian Land," in Ganter, *Collected Speeches of Sagoyewatha, or Red Jacket*, 246–47; Stone, *The Life and Times of Red-Jacket, or Sa-Go-Ye-Wat-Ha; being the Sequel to the History of the Six Nations* (New York: Wiley and Putnam, 1841), 326–27, 329, quotation at 332.

31. For example, Jasper Parrish, the subagent at Canandaigua, wrote Secretary of War John C. Calhoun on December 14, 1823 that the Seneca chiefs requested further postponement of their consideration of the most recent offer of a new reservation in the West, near Green Bay; Parrish to Calhoun, December 14, 1823, LRNA M-234, roll 832. The next year, Parrish wrote that the Senecas "have come to no conclusion as to the project of removal to Green Bay," and that they were now, improbably, considering a proposal to relocate among the Cherokees; Parrish to Thomas McKenney, commissioner of Indian Affairs, January 5, 1825, ibid. Another letter followed to the new secretary of war, James Barbour, in September 1825, which reported that a delegation of Senecas had returned from a visit to the Cherokees and "reported unfavorably to the Emigration to the South West." Meanwhile, Parrish noted, Seneca leaders "have refused to confer with the [Ogden Land] Company or their Agent" regarding its efforts to purchase their land; Parrish to Barbour, September 21, 1825, ibid. But Barbour also received a letter from New York City, from representatives of the Ogden Land Company (now directed by David A. Ogden's brother, Thomas Ludlow Ogden), which suggested that the Senecas might finally be willing to sell some of their land and concentrate on that which they retained. This and follow-up correspondence lobbied the president to endorse their effort, inaugurate a new treaty proceeding, and appoint a commissioner to satisfy the letter of the law; Robert Troup, T. L. Ogden, and B. W. Rogers to James Barbour, secretary of war, July 23, 1825, ibid.; Troup et al. to Barbour, August 15, 1825, ibid. The president's endorsement was critical, as "the majority [of Senecas] are not yet prepared for so entire a change," Troup wrote in August 1826 (ibid.). See Jasper Parrish to Thomas McKenney, November 30, 1826, including a "talk" from chiefs of the Christian Party (quotation), LRNA M-234, roll 832; Seneca Chiefs and Warriors to James Barbour, December 28, 1827, ibid., roll 808. See Conable, "A Steady Enemy," 77–95. These speculators refused to take no for an answer.

As Conable notes, the Ogden Company prepared the way for the treaty with gifts and annuities to chiefs—considerations that Red Jacket and subsequent historians charged were bribes.

32. Parrish to McKenney, November 30, 1826, LRNA M-234, roll 832; Seneca Chiefs and Warriors to Barbour, December 28, 1827, ibid., roll 808. See Conable, "A Steady Enemy," 77–95; "land for peace" is Conable's telling phrase, from her chapter "Land for Peace, 1826"; as noted above, the Ogden Company's gifts and annuities to chiefs were considered bribes by Red Jacket and subsequent historians. See Hauptman, *Conspiracy of Interests*, 155–57. The 1826 proceedings generated tremendous controversy, which can be followed in the voluminous Office of Indian Affairs correspondence, as Red Jacket and others challenged the treaty's validity, and it produced a legal case resolved (unjustly) only in the late nineteenth century. President Adams ordered an investigation by the War Department, now headed by the Buffalonian Peter B. Porter, an original shareholder in the Ogden Company. That investigation was carried out by Richard Montgomery Livingston with concern and integrity, though it declared the Ogden Land Company's behavior "just and liberal." The treaty itself was not ratified by the Senate, but the Senate passed a resolution that nonetheless seemed to endorse the proceedings, arguing—in apparent violation of the Indian Trade and Intercourse Acts—that the federal government had no responsibility in the matter. Cf. Hauptman, *Conspiracy of Interests*, 158–60. For Livingston's report, see R. M. Livingston to Peter B. Porter, secretary of war, Buffalo, July 4, 1828, LRNA M-234, roll 832. Conable concludes, "The results of the 1826 council were serious but not catastrophic" ("A Steady Enemy," 95).

33. Declaration of Seneca Chiefs, in Council at Buffalo Creek, November 3, 1832, in the Maris B. Pierce Papers, box 2, folder 2, BECHS. A declaration the following year definitively rejected removal to Green Bay and deposed those chiefs who entertained the proposal, including the prominent Christian Seneca chiefs Pollard and Young King; Declaration of Seneca Chiefs, Buffalo Creek, July 3, 1833, Pierce Papers, box 2, folder 2, BECHS; this declaration was also signed by Tommy Jemmy.

34. The best treatment of the 1838 treaty and its aftermath, including the restoration of Seneca lands, is Conable, "A Steady Enemy," esp. 139–65, 249–82, 325–75; Hauptman, *Conspiracy of Interests*, 154–55, 176–77. For a thorough contemporary discussion of the debacle of the 1838 treaty and efforts to repair some of its damage, see Society of Friends, *The Case of the Seneca Indians in the State of New York. Illustrated by facts. Printed for the information of the Society of Friends, by direction of the Joint Committees on Indian Affairs, of the four Yearly Meetings of Friends of Genesee, New York, Philadelphia, and Baltimore* (Philadelphia: Merrihew and Thompson, 1840).

35. Countryman, "From Revolution to Statehood," 277; John Seelye, 'Rational Exultation': The Erie Canal Celebration, *Proceedings of the American Antiquarian Society* 94, part 2 (1985): 241–67.

36. A[uguste] Levasseur, *Lafayette in America in 1824 and 1825; or, Journal of a Voyage to the United States*, 2 vols. (Philadelphia: Carey and Lea, 1829), 2:186–87.

37. "The Indian Show of Storrs & Co.," appendix to Rev. Albert Bigelow, "The Early Firm of Juba Storrs & Co." *PBHS* 4 (1896): 415–16 (quotations); Carolyn Thomas

Foreman, *Indians Abroad, 1493–1938* (Norman: University of Oklahoma Press, 1943), 120–21.

38. "Indian Show of Storrs & Co.," 416. In fact, a contemporary account of the Indians' visit to England, written by Elizabeth Fothergill, a Quaker woman living at Fulford, near York, convincingly attributes the incident—related to her by Fox—to another member of the party, to Sta-cute (Steep Rock) rather than to Tommy Jemmy. See Fothergill, "Account of Seven American Indians," esp. 58–59. Fothergill's account is at odds with those of Bigelow and Foreman in several respects.

39. Foreman, *Indians Abroad*, 123; a list of New York Six Nations men who served in the War of 1812 is contained within a ledger, most likely compiled by Asher Wright, ca. 1835, updated and with notes by Nicholas Henry Parker, Ely S. Parker Papers, PA 1, Huntington Library, San Marino, Calif. At number 97 is "Tommy Jimmy."

40. Foreman, *Indians Abroad*, 123–24. Newspapers quoted in ibid.; Fothergill, "Account of Seven American Indians," notes that the Leeds Friends sought "to instruct and befriend the Indians," as one female Friend put it, "by any means in her power" (8). The Quakers did offer lessons in reading and writing; one Maria Nevins bought them oranges (9); another Friend, Ann Alexander, "remarked upon the Indians, alluding to their excellent behaviour, that 'we might be instructed by them'" (21); while in York, the Friends arranged to have the Seneca performers vaccinated (24).

41. Fothergill, "Account of Seven American Indians," 9–19, quotations at 10, 18.

42. Ibid., 10–19, quotations at 10, 18.

43. Ibid., 12, 16, 18, 25–28, 27–28.

44. Ibid., 12–13, 25–28; quotations at 27–28. Whitsuntide is the week beginning with Whitsunday (literally White Sunday), the seventh Sunday and fiftieth day of Eastertide; it is the Christian festival commemorating the descent of the Holy Spirit on the day of Pentecost (Acts 2:1–4).

45. "Relative to the Indians when in England" (December 9, 1819), a copy of the "talk" given by Quakers in Leeds, England, on April 20, 1818, to the seven Senecas traveling with the Storrs & Co. Indian Show, in I.C.Records, box 3.

46. "To the Friends in Philadelphia, from a deputation of Seneca chiefs from Buffalo, Allegany and Cattaraugus Villages met at our Residence, and made the following communication," December 12, 1819, I.C. Records, box 3.

47. Foreman, *Indians Abroad*, 124–25; the *Leeds Intelligencer*—rival newspaper of the *Leeds Mercury*, which promoted the Indian Show—lampooned the exhibition and its participants, calling "Signor 'Se-nung-gaze,' or 'Long Horns,'" an "Indian *cut-throat*" and the whole affair "as neat a humbug on John Bull as we remember" (*Leeds Intelligencer*, May 4, 1818, quoted in ibid., 124); "Indian Show of Storrs & Co.," 415. For more a detailed, firsthand account of the show's demise and the troupe's return to New York, see A. C. Fox to Elizabeth Fothergill, August 1, 1819, in Fothergill, "Account of Seven American Indians," 143–46. The impresario and agent Fox claimed not to have "realized a single shilling for my services," but he reported that the Indians did receive their wages, ironically through the proceeds of a land sale (presumably not of Indian land): "The Indians

had the good fortune to be secured in land, which has been sold for their benefit from which they realize enough to satisfy their monthly wages" (144).

48. Seelye, "Erie Canal Celebration," 256.

49. Society of Friends, *Case of the Seneca Indians in the State of New York*, 62.

50. The origins of the nickname are "shrouded in mystery," according to Milton M. Klein, who noted some references dating as early as the 1780s (Washington apparently called New York the "Seat of the Empire" in 1785 and, later in the 1790s, the "Pathway to Empire"). By the completion of the Erie Canal in 1825 (and perhaps as early as 1819), the name Empire State was universally acknowledged. See Klein, *The Empire State*, xix.

51. Hercules [Jesse Hawley], "Observation on Canals," *Genesee Messenger*, December 8, 1807, 3.

52. The best recent history of the Erie Canal is Carol Sheriff, *The Artificial River: The Erie Canal and the Paradox of Progress, 1817–1862* (New York: Hill and Wang, 1996).

53. See Hauptman, *Conspiracy of Interests: Iroquois Dispossession and the Rise of New York State* (Syracuse, N.Y.: Syracuse University Press, 1999), 60–63, quotation at 62; Barbara Graymont, "New York State Indian Policy after the Revolution," *New York History* 58 (October 1976): 438–74. New York State was encouraged in its imperial reach within its borders by the ambiguity expressed in the Articles of Confederation, ratified in 1781; Article IX gave Congress "the sole and exclusive right and power of . . . regulating the trade and managing all affairs with the Indians, not members of any of the States, provided that the legislative right of any State within its own limits not be infringed or violated." This qualification of the category "Indians" and the provision against national infringement seemed to inflate the state's and undermine the United States' authority.

54. Hauptman, *Conspiracy of Interests*, 62–81. New York's actions seemed to be at odds with stipulations of the new United States Constitution and federal law, but great ambiguity remained as contending parties—the states, Indian tribes and their advocates, the general government, the courts—worked out the logic of federalism.

55. Quoted in ibid., 65. In fact, as we have seen, loss of game, while troublesome, would not fundamentally undermine Native life, as the Senecas subsisted primarily through agriculture. Loss of resources (e.g., timber) and land itself could be devastating, however. On a national scale, President Thomas Jefferson outlined the approach in a letter to William Henry Harrison in 1803:

Our system is to live in perpetual peace with the Indians, to cultivate an affectionate attachment from them. . . . The decrease of game rendering their subsistence by hunting insufficient, we wish to draw them to agriculture, to spinning and weaving. . . . When they withdraw themselves to the cultivation of a small piece of land, they will perceive how useless to them are their extensive forests, and will be willing to pare them off from time to time. . . . To promote this disposition to exchange lands, . . . we shall push our trading houses, and be glad to see the good and influential individuals among them run in debt, because we observe that when these debts get beyond what the individual can pay, they become willing to lop them off by a cession of lands. . . . In this way our settlements will gradually circumscribe and approach the Indians, and they will in time either incorporate with us as citizens of the United States, or remove beyond the Mississippi.

See Jefferson to William Henry Harrison, February 27, 1803, in Francis Paul Prucha, ed., *Documents of United States Indian Policy*, 3d ed. (Lincoln: University of Nebraska Press, 2000), 22–23. The Senecas avoided debt bondage but faced many of these other dangers. See generally Richard White, *The Roots of Dependency: Subsistence, Environment, and Social Change among the Choctaws, Pawnees, and Navajos* (Lincoln: University of Nebraska Press, 1983).

56. New York began its assault on Indian and federal power in its attempt to impose the common law of murder in Indian cases—first cross-cultural murder, then homicides among Indians—in 1796; see Alan Taylor, *The Divided Ground: Indians, Settlers, and the Northern Borderland of the American Revolution* (New York: Knopf, 2006), 317–22.

57. "A Summary Abstract of Speeches made by the Seneca Chiefs to his Excellency the Governor, and the Commissioner on the part of the United States at the Treaty held at this City, for the Purchase of Land on the Niagara River," Albany, August 18, 1802, Colonial and Early Statehood Records: Petitions, Correspondence, and Reports Relating to Indians, 1783–1831, microfilm A1823, New York State Archives (NYSA), Albany, N.Y. Red Jacket's speeches were offered during discussion of the treaty to convey land along the Niagara River—clearly, the "disagreeable and melancholy" matter, an apparent distraction from these other issues, was vitally important to Red Jacket and the Senecas. Additional details of the case are revealed in the memorial of twenty-one grand jurors and others in Canandaigua, asking that Stiff-Armed George be pardoned, February 25, 1803, Petition to the Honorable the Legislature of the State of New York in Senate & Assembly Convened, Colonial and Early Statehood Records, microfilm A1823, NYSA. The events surrounding the case are narrated briefly in James W. Paxton, "Kinship, Communities, and Covenant Chains: Mohawks and Palatines in New York and Upper Canada, 1712–1830" (Ph.D. diss., Queen's University, 2006), 388; see also Christopher Densmore, *Red Jacket: Iroquois Diplomat and Orator* (Syracuse, N.Y.: Syracuse University Press, 1999), 61–63.

58. "Summary Abstract of Speeches," August 18, 1802. The controversy was reported in the *Albany Centinel*, August 20 and 24, and September 3, 1802 (quotation). At the end of the September 3, 1802 story, reprinted from the *Ontario Gazette* of August 12, the reporter added, "At these and subsequent meetings, they [Seneca and other Iroquois leaders] still continue to insist, in long speeches, upon their entire independence of the state of New-York"; Taylor, *Divided Ground*, 320–21. The national government did intervene after Stiff-Armed George's conviction, with a request for a pardon, forwarded to Governor Clinton by Secretary of War Henry Dearborn at the request of the president; see Dearborn to Clinton, February 14, 1803, in Colonial and Early Statehood Records, microfilm A1823, NYSA. Note that in the legal culture of this era pardons were considered somewhat less extraordinary—they were a regular part of judicial proceeding, even if they required spe-

cial intervention after conviction; for a discussion of the nature and place of pardons in judicial proceedings in Massachusetts during this period, see Irene Quenzler Brown and Richard D. Brown, *The Hanging of Ephraim Wheeler: A Story of Rape, Incest, and Justice in Early America* (Cambridge, Mass.: Harvard University Press, 2003), 90–91, 191–95.

59. "Summary Abstract of Speeches," August 18, 1802.

60. Memorial, February 25, 1803, and Dearborn to Clinton, February 14, 1803, in Colonial and Early Statehood Records, microfilm A1823, NYSA; Densmore, *Red Jacket*, 61–63; and see Taylor, *Divided Ground*, 319–20. Buffalo was a rough town, and some of its white residents felt trepidation in the wake of these violent incidents—they complained that they now "lay down every night in feir [fear] of the Natives"; that trepidation caused some to have second thoughts about settling in the vicinity and to petition the Holland Land Company for a refund of money paid for Buffalo lots; see W. Johnston, Vincent Grant, John Palmer et al. to Joseph Ellicott, August 5, 1802, Joseph Ellicott Papers, reel 3, book 4, p. 65, BECHS.

61. The Senecas claimed autonomy but not complete independence—they had acknowledged U.S. jurisdiction while denying the authority of New York. Of course, despite Dearborn's intervention, the Jefferson government did not seem interested in taking on New York State or challenging states' rights.

62. The "murder" was first reported in the *Niagara Journal* (Buffalo) on May 8, 1821, and soon reported in the *Spirit of the Times* (Batavia, N.Y.), May 11, 1821, the *Ontario Repository* (Canandaigua, N.Y.), May 15, 1821, and other papers; quotation "the death of various individuals . . . ," from the *Salem Gazette*, August 3, 1821 (reprinted from a Buffalo paper); Stone, *Life and Times of Red-Jacket*, 316–22. See also Robert W. Bingham, *The Cradle of the Queen City: A History of Buffalo to the Incorporation of the City* (Buffalo, N.Y.: Buffalo Historical Society, 1931), 386–88; William C. Bryant, "Orlando Allen: Glimpses of Life in the Village of Buffalo," *PBHS* 1 (1879): 335, 352; William C. Bryant, "The Brave's Rest; or, the Old Seneca Mission Cemetery," *PBHS* 1 (1879): 83; Ganter, *Collected Speeches of Sagoyewatha, or Red Jacket*, 231–22. Conable, "A Steady Enemy," 72–73, briefly discusses the Tommy Jemmy case in somewhat different terms. We have no additional information on the identity of the executioner or why he faltered, putting the knife in Tommy Jemmy's hand.

63. We can see how important the case remained to the Senecas—even after its memory had faded among the white public—in an article that appeared in *Scribner's*, July 1877, "The Last Indian Council on the Genesee," by David Gray, which reported the gleeful recollection of the trial and Red Jacket's famous lines in Tommy Jemmy's defense. The Seneca ethnologist Arthur C. Parker retained a clipping in his papers; Arthur C. Parker Papers, box 2, folder 54, New York State Library, Albany.

64. In the case of George Peter, Governor Clinton refused to pardon the convicted defendant; see his statement, January 30, 1802, Legislative Assembly Correspondence and Legislative Action Files, 1794–1827, New York State Assembly Papers, vols. 32–34, microfilm series A1818, reel 1, NYSA; Taylor, *Divided Ground*, 319. Note that in 1821, the white and Indian population of Buffalo was roughly equal and living in close proximity; see Conable, "A Steady Enemy," 77.

65. "Murder," *Niagara Journal*, May 8, 1821.

66. *Republican Chronicle*, July 25, 1821 (dateline, "Buffalo, July 17, 1821"); "Indian Justice," *Salem Gazette*, August 3, 1821; Bryant, "Orlando Allen," 352. The presiding judge, Joseph C. Yates, was another notable figure in these proceedings—he had been the mayor of Schenectady and a New York State senator before becoming a justice of the State Supreme Court; later he became the governor of New York, succeeding De Witt Clinton in 1823.

67. *Republican Chronicle*, July 25, 1821; Stone, *Life and Times of Red-Jacket*, 321; L. B. Proctor, *The Bench and the Bar of New York, Containing Biographical Sketches of Eminent Judges, and Lawyers of the New York Bar, Incidents of the Important Trials in Which They were Engaged* (New York: Diossy and Company, 1870), 304–53; see entry for John C. Spencer at *Biographical Directory of the United States Congress* at http://bioguide.congress .gov/. Heman B. Potter came to Buffalo in 1810 as a young lawyer, joined the first board of trustees of the newly incorporated village of Buffalo in 1816, founded one of its most prominent law firms, and served as the town's first district attorney; see H. Perry Smith, ed., *History of the City of Buffalo and Erie County*, 2 vols. (Syracuse: D. Mason, 1884), 1:677.

68. *Independent Chronicle and Boston Patriot*, August 22, 1821, reprinted from the *Albany Daily Advertiser*, August 16, 1821; Stone, *Life and Times of Red-Jacket*, 321–22. The wide reprinting of news of the case suggests its novelty and importance. On the complicated question of sovereignty, see Banner, *How the Indians Lost Their Land*, esp. 112–49. In the wake of the Revolution, Banner notes, the general government assumed that Indians had been conquered and proceeded accordingly, but it was forced to abandon such an approach in the face of the reality of Indian power. Indian sovereignty was a matter of debate, with some arguing that it had been relinquished to British authorities during the colonial period and others disputing this (historically problematic) claim. In practice, the U.S. government treated Native nations as sovereign and during the nineteenth century constructed that sovereignty as inferior to and dependent on the federal government—not individual states, despite their assertions. It's interesting that Spencer picked the date 1620—apparently elevating the Pilgrims over the Jamestown settlers as America's original founding fathers.

69. *Albany Daily Advertiser*, August 16, 1821; Stone, *Life and Times of Red-Jacket*, 321–22; *Biographical Directory of the United States Congress* at http://bioguide.congress.gov/, entry for Thomas J. Oakley.

70. *Independent Chronicle and Boston Patriot*, August 22, 1821; Stone, *Life and Times of Red-Jacket*, 321–22; Bingham, *Cradle of the Queen City*, 388; Densmore, *Red Jacket*, 96–97. On the ramifications of the case for Indian law, see Sidney L. Harring, *Crow Dog's Case: American Indian Sovereignty, Tribal Law, and United States Law in the Nineteenth Century* (Cambridge: Cambridge University Press, 1994), esp. 37–38.

71. *Norwich Courier* (Norwich, Conn.), November 7, 1821 (dateline "Buffalo, New York, October 23, 1821").

72. "An Act declaring the jurisdiction of the Courts of this State and pardoning

Soo-non-gize otherwise called Tommy Jemmy," *Laws of the State of New-York, Passed at the Forty-Fifth Session of the Legislature* (Albany: Cantine and Leake, 1822), 202. The legislative act was confirmed "At a meeting of the Council of Revisions at the Council Chamber in the Capitol the 12th day of April 1822," by Governor Clinton, Chancellor Kent, and Justice Yates, Minutes of the Council of Revisions, 1778–1824, 5 vols., 5:296, microfilm A0027, NYSA. Note that Justice Yates, riding circuit, had presided at Tommy Jemmy's original trial at a court of oyer and terminer. The 1822 act was included as part of the compilation of state laws related to Indian Affairs in a U.S. House of Representatives report in 1830; see U.S. House, 21st Cong., 1st sess., Committee Reports, Indian Affairs, No. 319: "Laws of the Colonial and State Governments, Relating to the Indian Inhabitants," March 19, 1830, 26–27.

73. In addition to the law itself, see Harring, *Crow Dog's Case*, 38. The 1822 legislation culminated a process, as we have seen, in which New York sought to assert its dominion over Indians within its borders. See, for example, the assembly's resolution of March 4, 1819 (I.C. Records, box 3), which declared, "the time has arrived when a change of policy toward them [Senecas and other Indians] should undergo an important change; that their independence as a nation ought to cease, that they ought to yield to public interest, and by a proper application of power they ought to be brought within the pale of civilization and law." The attached report advocated compulsion, arguing that "persuasion only can have no effect."

74. Harring, *Crow Dog's Case*, 38; "New-York Legislature," *Watch-Tower*, April 15, 1822; a manuscript copy of the New York State resolution, April 12, 1822, is among Quaker records, I.C. Records, box 3.

75. Ibid. The clemency portion of the manuscript document, later printed (with slight corrections) in *Laws of the State of New-York*, 202), read:

> whereas it has been represented that sonongis otherwise called Tommy Jimmy an Indian of Seneca tribe has been indicted for the murder of Cauquatua an in[dian] woman of same tribe which murder is alledged to have been committed within the Sen[eca] reservation in the county of Erie & whereas it is further represented that said murder was committed under the [Judgment] of authority derived from the Councils of the chief Sachems & warriors of the said tribe & under the then existing circumstances it is deemed by the legislature expedient to pardon him[.] Therefore Be it further enacted that the said Sonongise otherwise called Tommy Jimmy be & he is hereby fully & absolutely pardoned of & from the said felony.

76. See Harring, *Crow Dog's Case*, 26–34.

77. Ibid. This principle would be more definitively established in *Ex parte Crow Dog* (1883). Tribes' independence from state authority and jurisdiction would erode over time, culminating in 1952 in Public Law 280, which extended state criminal jurisdiction over reservations in certain states.

78. Harring, *Crow Dog's Case*, 32–33.

79. See Banner, *How the Indians Lost Their Land*, esp. 191–227. Though President

Jackson is conventionally charged with failing to execute the Court's decision, in fact the Court did not (and could not) order the federal government to intervene. Jackson would have been reluctant, but even if his attitude had been otherwise, as Banner writes, "there was simply no mechanism within the American legal system for the Cherokees to secure such an order" (222). The political atmosphere, the attitude of the Jackson administration, and structural limits placed on the courts all contributed to the Cherokees' failure to overcome injustice.

80. See ibid., 221–24; Francis Paul Prucha, "Andrew Jackson's Indian Policy: A Reassessment," *Journal of American History* 56 (December 1969): 527–39, though his interpretation of Jackson is, overall, unconvincingly apologetic; and see Joseph C. Burke, "The Cherokee Cases: A Study in Law, Politics, and Morality," *Stanford Law Review* 21 (1969), 500–531. The best recent treatment of Jackson is Andrew Burstein, *The Passions of Andrew Jackson* (New York: Knopf, 2003); the best recent treatment of Cherokee removal is Anthony F. C. Wallace, *The Long, Bitter Trail: Andrew Jackson and the Indians* (New York: Hill and Wang, 1993). New York would continue to exercise its claimed jurisdiction over Indians in criminal matters until challenged in 1914 in *Cusick v. Daly* (Harring, *Crow Dog's Case*, 38).

81. See the New York State Assembly (March 4, 1819) "Resolution on Indian Affairs," printed copy and accompanying report in I.C. Records, box 3. In the immediate aftermath of the Revolution, some American officials did articulate a right of conquest. Philip Schuyler, addressing the Iroquois in 1783, claimed "We are now Masters and can dispose of the lands as we think proper or most convenient to ourselves." "As we are the Conquerors, we claim the lands and property of all the white people as well as the Indians who have left and fought against us" (quoted in Banner, *How the Indians Lost Their Land*, 112). But the federal government soon abandoned such claims. And Americans generally chose not to invoke the rights of conquest over American Indians, even when militarily subdued. John C. Spencer's arguments before the New York Supreme Court in the Tommy Jemmy case—claiming the colonial conquest of Native people and denying Indian sovereignty— were exceptional in this regard. Usually white Americans preferred to imagine that they represented right rather than might, that their expropriation of land and assimilationist policies served a higher, more noble goal—"civilization," Christianity, and progress—which they sought to believe benefited Native people as much as white citizens. On the ongoing sovereignty battles between the Senecas and New York State, see especially Laurence M. Hauptman's masterful discussion *Historical Background to the Present Day Seneca Nation–Salamanca Lease Controversy: The First Hundred Years, 1851–1951* (Albany: Nelson A. Rockefeller Institute of Government, State University of New York, 1985); and Hauptman, *Formulating Indian Policy in New York State, 1970–1986* (Albany: State University of New York Press, 1988).

82. Harring, *Crow Dog's Case*, 34.

83. Seneca speeches, in Abler, *Chainbreaker*, 239.

84. Levasseur, *Lafayette in America*, 2:187.

85. Stone, *Life and Times of Red-Jacket*, 364; Ganter, *Collected Speeches of Sagoyewatha, or Red Jacket*, 225.

CONCLUSION

1. Frank H. Severance, ed., *Publications of the Buffalo Historical Society*, vol. 6 (Buffalo, N.Y., 1903); Paula Baker, "The Gilded Age (1860–1914)," part 5 in Milton M. Klein, ed., *The Empire State: A History of New York* (Ithaca, N.Y.: Cornell University Press, 2001), 479–82. And see Robert Rydell, *All the World's a Fair: Visions of Empire at American International Expositions, 1876–1916* (Chicago: University of Chicago Press, 1984). A number of writers have addressed this self-serving nostalgia for supposedly vanishing Indians. Laura Stevens, *The Poor Indians: British Missionaries, Native Americans, and Colonial Sensibility* (Philadelphia: University of Pennsylvania Press, 2004), is particularly illuminating; see also Renato Rosaldo, *Culture and Truth: The Remaking of Social Analysis* (Boston: Beacon Press, 1993), 69–70; Michelle Burnham, *Captivity and Sentiment: Cultural Exchange in American Literature, 1621–1861* (Hanover, N.H.: University Press of New England, 1997), 94; Lora Romero, "Vanishing Americans: Gender, Empire, and New Historicism," in Shirley Samuels, ed., *The Culture of Sentiment: Race, Gender, and Sentimentality in Nineteenth-Century America* (New York: Oxford University Press, 1992), 115. A recent rumination on the fate of Buffalo is Edward L. Glaeser, "Can Buffalo Ever Come Back?" *City Journal*, Autumn 2007.

2. Moses Shongo, "An Inscription," *PBHS* 6 (1903): v–vi.

3. Thomas S. Abler and Elisabeth Tooker, "Seneca," in William C. Sturtevant, gen. ed., *Handbook of North American Indians*, 20 vols. projected (Washington, D.C.: Smithsonian Institution, 1978–), vol. 15, *Northeast* (1978), ed. Bruce G. Trigger, 515. Note that contemporary Seneca economic and educational projects are funded in part by the $15 million settlement received in compensation for the inundation of one-third of their Allegany reservation by the Kinzua Dam in the 1950s. In a way congruent with their historical past, Senecas showed great resilience in the face of disaster and again benefited from Quaker aid in arranging the settlement. For the Seneca nation's Web site, see http:// www.senecanation.net/ and its various links.

4. As the *Richmond Enquirer* (Richmond, Va.) wrote, June 25, 1830, "The law of Georgia, extending the jurisdiction of that State over the Indians residing within its borders, is by no means either so unexampled, or of so oppressive a nature, as some of those prints which love to rail against the [Jackson] administration and against the south would have the public believe." A few paragraphs later, the piece quoted at length the precedent-making New York State legislation of 1822, "An act declaring the jurisdiction of the courts of this state, and pardoning Soo-non-gize, otherwise called Tommy Jemmy." And see the similar piece in the *Ithaca Journal and General Advertiser* (Ithaca, N.Y.), January 26, 1831, which gets some of the facts of the case wrong in the service of asserting states' rights. The piece asked, if the Supreme Court had interfered, as it did in Georgia's Corn Tassel case, "can there be a doubt that their pretensions would have been met by the government and people of the state of New-York in the same spirit that they are now met by those of Georgia?"

5. T. Hartley Crawford, commissioner of Indian affairs, to L. Osborne, subagent for

the Seneca Indians, Office of Indians Affairs, May 9, 1842, in Indian Collection, BOO-2, box 1, folder 3, Buffalo and Erie County Historical Society, Buffalo, New York (emphasis added). On the events leading up to the 1842 treaty, see Mary Conable, "A Steady Enemy: The Ogden Land Company and the Seneca Indians" (Ph.D. diss., University of Rochester, 1994), esp. 217–82. On Ambrose Spencer, see Laurence M. Hauptman, *Conspiracy of Interests: Iroquois Dispossession and the Rise of New York State* (Syracuse, N.Y.: Syracuse University Press, 1999), 199–208. Note that Spencer's advocacy, in concert with Hicksite Quakers, sought to end the prospect of removal in New York, address the worst grievances of the Senecas, support "civilization" programs, and extend New York State jurisdiction over the Senecas and other New York Indians (see ibid., 204–5); Spencer and others did not see these goals as mutually exclusive. Like his son, Ambrose Spencer advocated an end to Seneca sovereignty. As a New York Supreme Court justice, Spencer had argued in 1823, the Indians' "condition has been gradually changed, until they have lost every attribute of sovereignty, and become entirely dependent upon, and subject to our government. I know of no half-way doctrine on this subject" (quoted in ibid., 200). In 1823, Chancellor James Kent reversed Spencer, a reversal consistent with later rulings of the Marshall Court in the Cherokee cases.

INDEX

Abbot, Benjamin, 74
Abeal, Henry, 279 n.28
Adams, John, 95, 256 n.27
Adams, John Quincy, 188
Adriochten, 92
Aimwell School Association, 176
alcohol: and Iroquois witchcraft beliefs, 27;
    and Native land expropriation, 78, 248–49
    n.48; and Quaker civilization program, 48,
    141, 248 n.48, 251 n.7; and Seneca hybrid
    economy, 165, 280 n.34; and Seneca post-
    Revolutionary crisis, 47–48, 76; and Seneca
    women, 250 n.4. See also Handsome Lake's
    temperance movement
Alden, Timothy, 190, 289 n.27
Alexander, John, 58
Allen, Ebenezer, 42–45, 239 n.44, 240 n.50
allotment. See individual male land owner-
    ship; Native land expropriation
American Home Missionary Society, 57
American identity. See post-Revolutionary
    American identity
American Revolution. See Revolutionary War
angel visitation, 247 n.44. See also dreams
apocalypticism. See millenialism
Armstrong, John, 231–32 n.2
Articles of Confederation, 234 n.9, 293 n.53
Atotarho, 92, 93, 254–55 n.22

Banner, Stuart, 12, 23, 181, 232 n.2
Barclay, Henry, 25, 234 n.16
Beecher, Lyman, 57
Benjamin, Walter, 1
Big Kettle, 193
Big Tree (Seneca leader), 98
Big Tree, Treaty of (1797), 45, 46, 130
Black Robes. See Jesuit missionaries

Blacksnake, Governor, 37, 72, 118, 191, 192,
    193
Boyer, Paul, 11
Brant, Joseph (Thayendanegea), 36
Bressani, Francesco Gioseppe, 90
Brigham, Walter, 194–95, 200
Brock, Daniel J., 239 n.44, 240 n.50
Brooks, Charles E., 160
Brooks, Micah, 240 n.53
Buffalo, 182, 222, 295 nn. 60, 64
Burned-Over District, 54–55. See also Second
    Great Awakening
Burroughs, Stephen, 44–45
Burrowes, John, 34–35
Butler, John, 35

Calhoun, John C., 184
Canada, 31
Canandaigua, Treaty of (1794), 181, 185–86,
    204, 205, 285–87 nn. 14, 17
capitalist transformation. See commercial/
    industrial transformation
Caughnawaga, 30
Cawoncaucawheteda (Flying Crow), 35
Cayugas, and Revolutionary War, 36, 37
Cherokee Nation v. Georgia (1831), 12, 24, 215–
    16, 224, 233 n.9, 297–98 n.79, 299 n.4
Cherokees: Cherokee Nation v. Georgia, 12, 24,
    215–16, 224, 233 n.9, 297–98 n.79, 299 n.4;
    removal, 11, 224, 299 n.4; Worcester v. Geor-
    gia, 11, 24, 215
Christian missionaries. See non-Quaker
    Christian missionaries
Church of Jesus Christ of the Latter Day
    Saints (Mormons), 57
civilization concept, 120–21, 187, 278 n.19,
    287 n.18. See also Quaker civilization pro-
    gram

ACKNOWLEDGMENTS

So we beat on, boats against the current, borne back ceaselessly into
the past.
   —F. Scott Fitzgerald, *The Great Gatsby* (1925)

Fitzgerald was surely right that the past pulls on us, like the current we fight
as we push upstream. If only historical research and writing were as easy as
riding with the stream into the past. Instead, the historian's task is often to
row out against an incoming tide, and then in again after the tide has
shifted—the journey into the past through research is matched by the perils
of the return passage to deliver prose analysis to contemporary readers. Let
me therefore acknowledge those who have helped with the oars over this
arduous but ultimately satisfying voyage.

   I sincerely appreciate and acknowledge the assistance of numerous librar-
ies and archives and their helpful staffs, especially the American Philosophical
Society in Philadelphia, the University of Pennsylvania Library, the Friends
Historical Library at Swarthmore College, and the Library Company of Phil-
adelphia; the New-York Historical Society and the New York Public Library;
the New York State Archives and New York State Library; Cornell University
Library; the Buffalo and Erie County Historical Society and the Ontario
County Historical Society; the Beinecke Rare Book and Manuscript Library
and Yale University Library; the Princeton University Library; the Library of
Congress and the National Archives in Washington, D.C.; the American
Antiquarian Society in Worcester, Massachusetts; the Newberry Library in
Chicago; the Huntington Library in San Marino, California; and the Univer-
sity of Oregon Library, in Eugene, Oregon.
   My research was funded in part by the National Endowment for the
Humanities, the Beinecke Rare Book and Manuscript Library, the Center

for the Study of Women in Society at the University of Oregon, the Oregon Humanities Center, the University of Southern California–Huntington Library Early Modern Studies Institute, and of course the University of Oregon, my day job. I am most grateful for their beneficence.

I would like to thank various friends and colleagues for their diverse contributions to this project, including Steve Aron, Ray Birn, Andy Burstein, Richard Clark, Kathleen DuVal, Carla Gerona, Polly Good, Eric Hinderacker, Tom Humphrey, Nancy Isenberg, Paul Johnson, Richard Johnson, Bob Lockhart, Peter Mancall, Jane Merritt, George Miles, Ken Minkema, Michael Oberg, Paul Otto, Ann Plane, Lizzie Reis, Dan Richter, Nat Sheidley, John Smolenski, Ernie Stromberg, Kirk Swinehart, Alan Taylor, and Karim Tiro. I would also like to thank the staff at the University of Pennsylvania Press, especially Ashley J. Nelson, Jennifer Shenk, Senior History Editor Robert Lockhart, and Associate Managing Editor Erica Ginsburg. I am particularly indebted to Bob Lockhart and Dan Richter, for their readings, constructive criticisms, and support, and to Michael Oberg, who read the manuscript for the press and provided inestimable help in my revisions.

The contributions of some have been beyond description. Ray Birn read the manuscript twice and throughout provided critical suggestions and sustaining encouragement. Andy Burstein generously read and brilliantly critiqued a late version of the manuscript, when I needed his scholarly and editorial talents most. And Elizabeth Reis proved once again to be an incomparable partner in scholarship and, more important, in life. My children, Sam and Leah Reis-Dennis, know that my favorite book is *Moby-Dick*. With the completion of my scholarly journey in pursuit of *Seneca Possessed*, they can now be convinced that my alter ego is actually Starbuck or Ishmael, not the obsessive and ill-fated Ahab.

At the very end of *The Great Gatsby*, Fitzgerald considered the moment when colonialism commenced in what became New York, imagining the Dutch sailors' gaze upon "a fresh, green breast of the new world." "For a transitory enchanted moment," Fitzgerald wrote, "man must have held his breath in the presence of this continent, compelled into an aesthetic contemplation he neither understood nor desired, face to face for the last time in history with something commensurate to his capacity for wonder." In fact, we know, this new world was old to its indigenous inhabitants, who possessed their own aesthetics and gendered visions, their own hopes and dreams. History did not end with this colonialism, any more than colonialism itself ended. And we continue to face much that taxes our capacity to wonder—including the remarkable survival of America's Native people, among them the resourceful Senecas, with and despite the help of friends. I thank them.